In Praise of Being Called

"This fascinating book sheds much-needed light on what it means to find a calling in life—an experience that, although timeless and universal, has not been understood well in the human sciences. Through valuable insights from leaders in theology, philosophy, and contemporary psychology, the authors add greatly to our knowledge of this essential component of the examined life."

Dr. William Damon is professor of education at the Stanford
Graduate School of Education and author of
Good Work and the Path to Purpose

"*Being Called* is a groundbreaking work of scholarship on one of the most important issues that each and every person faces: How to find a transcendent meaning in life. This book, always engaging and often delightful to read, sheds light on that fundamental question with insights from psychology, neuroscience, and theology. Anyone who has ever wondered 'what should I do with my life?' will find nuggets of wisdom and inspiration in this important work."

Emily Esfahani Smith, writer, *The Atlantic*;
columnist, *The New Criterion*

"This is a fascinating book on what it means to be called, to have a calling, and to answer the call that comes from within. It is a rich tapestry of views on living an inspired life from a place that is deeper than mere pragmatics."

Roshi Dr. Joan Halifax PhD is a Zen priest, anthropologist, and author of
Being with Dying, who has served on the faculty of Columbia University,
the University of Miami School of Medicine, the New School for
Social Research, and Naropa University

"*Being Called* is an important, groundbreaking book. Until now the claim of 'being called' has fallen on deaf ears of both social scientists and vocational counselors."

Dr. George E. Vaillant, M.D. and
Dr. Diane M. Highum, M.D.

"As we try to assemble a genuinely global wisdom, it is good that this theme of 'calling' is being investigated from such diverse perspectives in a context which promises the possibility of a fruitful conversation."

The Rt Revd & Rt Hon Richard Chartres
KCVO DD FSA, Bishop of London

"*Being Called* skillfully weaves together a chorus of scientific, theological, and deeply personal voices—voices that reflect the diverse ways in which people experience a sense of calling in their lives. This is a refreshing, thought-provoking, timely book on an exciting topic, one that has too often been overlooked within scholarly circles."

Julie Exline, PhD, professor, department of Psychological
Sciences, Case Western Reserve University

BEING CALLED

Scientific, Secular, and Sacred Perspectives

David Bryce Yaden, Theo D. McCall, and J. Harold Ellens,
Editors

Introduction by Martin Seligman

Psychology, Religion, and Spirituality
J. Harold Ellens, Series Editor

 PRAEGER™

An Imprint of ABC-CLIO, LLC
Santa Barbara, California • Denver, Colorado

Library of Congress Cataloging-in-Publication Data

Being called : scientific, secular, and sacred perspectives / David Bryce
    Yaden, Theo D. McCall, and J. Harold Ellens, editors ; introduction by
    Martin Seligman.
        pages cm. — (Psychology, religion, and spirituality)
    Includes bibliographical references and index.
    ISBN 978-1-4408-3912-2 (alk. paper) — ISBN 978-1-4408-3913-9 (eISBN)
1. Psychology and religion.   2. Insight.   3. Spirituality.   I. Yaden,
David Bryce, editor.   II. McCall, Theo D., editor.   III. Ellens, J. Harold,
1932- editor.
    BF51.B45 2015
    155.2'5—dc23   2015014369

ISBN: 978-1-4408-3912-2
EISBN: 978-1-4408-3913-9

19 18 17 16 15   1 2 3 4 5

This book is also available on the World Wide Web as an eBook.
Visit www.abc-clio.com for details.

Praeger
An Imprint of ABC-CLIO, LLC

ABC-CLIO, LLC
130 Cremona Drive, P.O. Box 1911
Santa Barbara, California 93116-1911

This book is printed on acid-free paper ∞
Manufactured in the United States of America

To our families; and the families of all those called.

Contents

PART II
SACRED PERSPECTIVES

SERIES EDITOR'S FOREWORD

J. Harold Ellens

The Praeger series *Psychology, Religion, and Spirituality* has been publishing for 15 years and now includes more than 35 volumes. All of these are works dealing with the variety of topics suggested by the series title. The current volume and the three immediately previous volumes (*The Psychedelic Policy Quagmire: Health, Law, Freedom, and Society* and *Seeking the Sacred with Psychoactive Substances: Chemical Paths to Spirituality and to God,* two volumes) are groundbreaking works on the very frontier of scientific scholarly research in the fields of medicine, psycho-neurological, and psycho-spiritual experience.

The present volume deals with those life-changing events that many people experience and few people share with others. These are events of remarkable illumination that happen in life, opening us to new vistas of insight. They lead us to a sense of being called to a new vocation or way of life. The remarkable thing that current research is discovering is that most humans have such experiences and all of us wonder whether they come to us from some psychological source within us or from some congenial force outside us. In this volume we explore the intriguing aspects of that question.

Our society is at a new threshold of insight about the boundary-breaking work that heroic scientists are producing regarding the constructive perspective currently developing in this field. This book is unique in its exploration, the first in this new arena of truth seeking and truth telling. This is one of a kind.

PREFACE

J. Harold Ellens

Prospective Psychology is an intriguing concept. It might conceivably be defined in a number of ways. In this volume it refers to experiences that make us feel called into the future. Such moments are relatively common for most humans. They may be just a surprising aha!, moment of insight, or they may be life-changing illuminations. More often than we think they are momentous events of psycho-spiritual vision that show us our entire future. They may simply clarify some course of action we have been vaguely contemplating. Often they seem to be other worldly numinous events that give us the sense of being "called".

Prospective psychologists wonder whether such experiences are simply normal functions of the psyche or events in which the transcendent spirit calls us to our destiny. Such moments of life-changing insight open us to new views of the future that change our purposes, perspectives, and objectives. They tend to give one's life an unexpected but specific vision of one's future. In such a moment or process are we called by the future into our future? Is it a psychosocial process of awakening that happens to us? Or is it a transcendent calling of God to our enhanced destiny?

Perhaps it can be either, and perhaps, then, either can be just as warrantable as the other. Perhaps it is both, and we cannot sort out the difference. Or perhaps it is a psychospiritual event, in both cases. Does our psychological nature have within it the capacity to cause such insightful illuminating, or numinous and "divine" events? Does the human person have the capacity to receive such life-changing experiences that seem like visits from God-as-Spirit, with our spirits? Are psychology and spirituality two words for the same thing? They are derived from the same Greek word, after all. They both describe the function of the psyche. They come at the subject from different directions, with different universes of discourse, but they address the same subject: "the living human document." They both refer to and may be defined as the universal and irrepressible human hunger for meaning: transcendent or mundane, vertical or horizontal.

Such are the questions that prospective psychology sets before us and in this volume we intend to comment upon them from a practical point of view. This is an inviting opportunity that prospective psychology offers us. It is a new way of visioning how we find the meaning of our lives. It offers us new expectations about what can happen to us and often does happen to us.

This is a new and exciting way to quest for meaning and taking this perspective on understanding our relationship to our future can give us the potential of a new vision of reality. It encourages us to look beyond our boundaries, to view life as reaching out beyond our current construction about the way things are. It can give us the motivation to keep our eyes open for how the divine spirit will show up around the next corner, or the way in which our own creative mind has the surprising ability to see into and know the as yet "unknown."

To move beyond the predictable boundaries of our world and our concept of reality in this way we need to cultivate the special ability to *suspend our belief* in the traditional or historic forms of thought. This requires that we are able to envision a reality we do not know and have not seen as possible. Our worldview must be suspended; our belief systems held in abeyance; and our customary thought forms recognized as having limited application. We are invited to imagine a potential new reality and the science of a wide new arena beyond the boundaries to which we are accustomed. The constraints and definitions of our religious faith systems and their boundaries must be transcended by wider and more surprising possibilities. Can we hold ourselves open to such vast alternative realities?

On the other hand, to move into this potentially new and radically different world, see it for what it is, we need to *suspend disbelief*. This is something like going to a play. To get the thrust of the play you must get into the story on stage. The play is not reality. We all know that. We do not believe that real life is happening on the stage before us. It is only a suggestion of how reality can be. We disbelieve the play to be reality. To enjoy the play or profit from the play, however, we must suspend this disbelief and allow ourselves to enter into the play as though it is reality. So we laugh with those who laugh and we weep with those who weep, because we have allowed ourselves to be taken in by the new reality on the stage. When it is finished we feel like we have lived that new reality for a while. It may, in fact, have expanded the reality of our lives, to which we must then return.

To *suspend belief* in our traditional ways of seeing things simply requires that we cease believing, for the sake of our quest, that things must be and are the way we have always thought about them. We know that water boils at 212 degrees Fahrenheit at sea level, but we must suspend that belief if we want to discover if there is an altogether alternative way of "knowing" that reality in the world just beyond our boundaries. To put it a bit more believably, we know that cause and effect are predictable in the world we experience every day. We must suspend that belief for the sake of our quest, under the notion that there are possibilities in our future in which what we know about cause and effect may not apply or may be less limiting than what we can "know." Suspending all belief means being open to infinite alternative possibilities of experience and truth.

To *suspend disbelief* means to envision and to move into the future to which we are called as though its potentially new and strange experience has the genuine possibility of being reality. At present we disbelieve that anything different from what we already know very well, any alternative type of world than our world, is real. If we suspend that disbelief a great number of possible but alternate futures may manifest themselves. To suspend that disbelief opens to us an infinite potential for seeing things in a new way. Indeed, it empowers us for envisioning a new future and alternate future for ourselves.

That was the focus of the conclave at Canterbury Cathedral out of which this idea came. That is the creative vision this volume addresses.

Introduction

How Are We Called into the Future?

Martin Seligman

At my 50th college reunion in May 2014, I found myself on a panel of well-known Princeton alumni. "Career trajectory" was the topic.

"I wrote about cooking and it really felt good, so I wrote more funny stories about food."

"I picked up the banjo and the audience loved it, so I devoted myself to playing Blues."

The prevailing line was "I tried this . . . it felt good, so I did it more;" or "I tried that . . . people didn't like it, so I stopped" and so blown hither and thither by my proclivities, by prevailing winds and internal and external rewards and punishments, I arrived at my profession.

"Not me." I said. "I was called."

WHY TRADITIONAL PSYCHOLOGY SHUNS CALLINGS

The claim of *being called* falls on deaf ears to a modern audience and it is also a topic that psychological science has not dared to touch. Why this is so and why this should be changed is the core purpose of this volume.

Traditional psychology is dedicated to relieving misery and it is undergirded by the idea that human beings are driven by the past. Misery is often, but not always, in the past or in the present, and we have evolved to escape misery. Positive Psychology, the field I work in, is dedicated to building what makes life worth living and it is undergirded by the idea that human beings are drawn into the future. What we desire is often, but not always, in the future and we have evolved to approach what we desire. This asymmetry between approach and escape may be the deepest difference between psychology-as-usual and positive psychology, deeper even than the emphasis on misery versus well-being.

Traditional psychology is deterministic. Animals and people bring their rich past experience to every choice point and the choice is determined by some combination of the stimuli perceived in the present, the present drives, and the past experience. The details differ depending on the theory (behavioral, cognitive, or psychodynamic), but what all the theories share is the rock-bottom premise that past experience plus present stimuli drive the future. This is indeed what the words *stimuli* and *response* were carefully chosen to mean.

Positive psychology, at least in my hands, doubts the usefulness of "stimuli" and "response" and it also takes agnostic view of determinism. My skepticism has two sources, conceptual and empirical. First the conceptual reasons for skepticism:

Deterministic premises about apparently future-oriented human choices became so widely believed because of the promise of a completed, fully predictive science uniting micro- and macro-behavior, and the physical and human sciences, a science that relied only on past conditions. Pierre Simon Laplace (1749–1827) knew these attractions well when he gave this famous characterization of the Newtonian physics of his day:

> We may regard the present state of the universe as the effect of its past and the cause of its future. An intellect which at a certain moment would know all forces that set nature in motion, and all positions of all items of which nature is composed, if this intellect were also vast enough to submit these data to analysis, it would embrace in a single formula the movements of the greatest bodies of the universe and those of the tiniest atom; for such an intellect nothing would be uncertain and the future just like the past would be present before its eyes.
> —*Pierre Simon Laplace*, A Philosophical Essay on Probabilities (1814)

This view, however, describes no actual science or even the ambitions of any actual science. Not only are all empirical predictions in every science merely probabilistic, but contemporary microphysics is irreducibly, unashamedly probabilistic. Even before the quantum revolution, the problem of computing the precise trajectories of systems involving three or more interacting bodies—think of breaking a rack of pool balls—was known to be computationally intractable, and so subject only to statistical approximation or, more recently, computer simulation. The best that can be predicted at either the micro- or macro-level is only a distribution of possible outcomes, rather than one precise outcome. Keep in mind that even if the probability of the next event is extremely high (.99), a sequence of .99's multiplied together approaches zero distressingly soon.

My skepticism is also empirical. Laplace's spirit lives on in psychology in the thought that ultimately the best way to explain behavior is to push determinism as far as we can. But the psychological incarnations of determinism—behaviorism, psychoanalysis, and cognitive psychology—have not been crowned with success at predicting future actions. Psychologists are delighted if we can predict future choices at moderately better than chance and I cannot point to any program of work in which prediction is improving encouragingly.

If determinism by the past and the present has been banished from empirical science as a real possibility for precise *prediction*, and it has not paid off in actual psychological work, what next? How could anything but a vector sum of impinging present events and past habits explain human action? Is there any alternative to this picture?

WHY POSITIVE PSYCHOLOGY LIKES CALLINGS

Positive psychology proposes a figure-ground shift away from the way traditional psychology deals with the future. Traditional psychology claims that if we understand the past and present thoroughly then understanding and predicting the future will follow. Positive psychology suspends judgment about that and claims that the science should start by understanding the phenomenon of *prospection*—the ubiquitous imagination and evaluation of possible futures.

Do four brief mental exercises now:

1. The first is **navigation**: Imagine your residence and the nearest supermarket. Now mentally walk block by block from your front door to the supermarket. If you turned right out of your front door, do the exercise again starting with a left turn and taking therefore a different route to the supermarket (if you turned left start by turning right).

2. The second is **social**, about other minds: Imagine that you have been invited to have a chat with President Obama about whom he should choose as the "White House Person of the Year." Whom would you nominate? How would the president react to that nomination? Now imagine telling the president three reasons why he should choose your nominee. Imagine that he raises one objection; imagine the objection and what your response to that objection would be.

3. The third is **intellectual**: As you are reading this book, with its radical premise that callings should be taken seriously, what mental activity are you engaged in? If you are like most active readers, you are mentally

trying out various reactions to the material. You are making arguments against the idea, or thinking how you might improve, qualify, or defend it. You are imagining trying to explain the argument to a class, or a colleague, or how you might use it to advance your own arguments. You are asking if the idea is really so radical after all, or building toward a decision not to waste any more time on this book.

4. The fourth exercise is **memorial**: Recall a happening in your life that turned out badly because of something you said or did. What could you have said or done that might have made it turn out better? Run through that scenario.

What the first three exercises demonstrate is the process of running off conditional mental simulations of the future. What the fourth demonstrates is the process of running off counterfactual mental simulations. Each of these exercises demonstrates your enormous facility for generating, exploring, and evaluating alternatives to the present you now confront or the past you can't help but remember. In each case you "free" yourself from your actual condition and perceptions to take advantage of your powerful mind to "do," and perhaps learn from, something different. Ordinary mental life is chock-full of this activity. Daydreaming and fantasy are mundane examples; and navigation, appreciating other minds, intellectual processing, and counterfactual remembering are more sophisticated, but equally commonplace examples. We follow the usage of Gilbert (2006) and Buckner and Carroll (2007) in labeling these acts of thinking about the future, "prospections." Our guess is that a substantial proportion of mental life is filled with prospections.

The evolutionary importance of mental simulations is underscored by the discovery of parallel brain circuitry that underpins all four of these mental exercises (Buckner and Carroll, 2007) the knowledge of which begins with poor Phineas Gage. With massive damage to his frontal lobe by an errant tamping iron, Gage's deficits (centered on the absence of "planning and execution of personally and socially suitable behavior") are easily seen as deficits in prospection. Prefrontal lesions have since been commonly linked to a variety of deficits, such as lack of mental "time travel" and the inability to make predictions about one's own future, deficits which can be subsumed as deficits in the ability to shift perspective beyond the immediate present into the future: in other words, prospection deficits. Patients with amnesia, caused by damage to the hippocampus, have enormous trouble imagining new experiences. A few intriguing hints exist about where prospection occurs in brain, such as the activation of the paracingulate cortex when people are asked to imagine another person's perspective, a possibly shared "core" network with what is activated in episodic memory and in personal moral judgements.

While mapping out the underlying circuitry awaits future neuroscience, what is undeniable is that simulating and evaluating future events are ubiquitous mental processes, and it is this ability that draws human beings into the future. Positive psychology *in its conventional endeavors* endorses and sponsors research on the neuroscience, the cognitive science, the measurement, and the application of prospection.

This book is about an unconventional, even outlandish, approach to prospection: a science of being called into the future. *Feeling* or *believing* that one has been called by the future is not an uncommon human experience. Moses's Burning Bush is the paradigm case. But many of the rest of us have had such experiences. When Gallup (2003) asked respondents if they have had a "profound religious experience or awakening that changed the direction" of their life, 41 percent of Americans agreed that the statement "*completely* applies to them." Thirty to forty percent of people feel they have a calling (Duffy & Sedlacek, 2007; Wrzesniewski, McCauley, Rozin, & Schwartz, 1997).

I, it should be said, number myself among them. I was around 30, newly tenured at the University of Pennsylvania, and an animal experimental psychologist and a dyed-in-the-wool learning theorist. My mentor, Aaron Beck, warned me that if I continued on this path I would waste my life. But it took a numinous dream to shake the foundations.

> I find myself in the Guggenheim Museum slowly walking up the curving ramp. There are rooms off to the right every few paces and in the rooms people are playing with cards. I ask, "why is everyone playing with cards?" Whereupon the roof the museum opens and the godhead appears (yes: male, white-bearded with a booming bass voice). He says—unforgettably, "Seligman, at least you are starting to ask the right questions."

Even without such numinous experiences, many successful people across history have claimed that they were "Men of Destiny." Further, these experiences can be life changing and it is not uncommon for people to reorient their entire lives in the wake of one. (I changed my science to work on real people, not just in the laboratory, and using longitudinal methods in addition to experiments.)

This volume reviews this literature and it is a proper starting point for scientific investigation. But the science will never be able to evade the big question "What is the Ground of these experiences?" Are they illusions? Are they true? Can human beings really be visited by the future?

The *secular* approach is that numinous experiences are merely efflorescent products of a Darwinian brain. Evolutionary theorists see the hand of group selection at work here. Religious inspiration, undauntable high purpose, magnificent undertakings' bind, and unshakeable convictions tune and galvanize the group. Dreams, fantasy, and mental intrusions outside the control of consciousness may be some of the mechanisms that subserve call-ing. Hence their presence and the brain mechanisms that subserve them are selected for (e.g., Wilson, 2007). The ground of these experiences, however, is benign illusion. This view is well represented in this volume: Chapters by Amy Wrzesniewski and Ryan Duffy, Richard Douglass, and Kelsey Autin review how viewing one's work as a calling, as personally fulfilling and so-cially beneficial, boosts well-being at work and home. David Yaden and An-drew Newberg provide a new view of calling experiences by focusing on revelatory "road to Damascus moments." They suggest that the voices and visions during these calling experiences could be delivered to conscious-ness through a neurocognitive process similar to that of creative epiphanies. Bryan Dik and Michael Steger find a middle ground between callings as meaningful work and callings as revelatory experiences by framing callings as a "transcendent summons" that draw one toward a life path through viv-idly imagining and empathizing with one's possible future self.

The *supernatural* (or "Divine") approach is that they are *true*. Some of us really are visited by God and receive valid guidance and even instructions on how to proceed into the future. The ground of these experiences is reality. This view also is well represented in this volume: J. Harold Ellens, Thomas Singer, and Theo McCall relate personal testimony of their own calling ex-periences and attribute them to a higher cause beyond material explanations. Hugh Kempster calls for religions to return to honoring these experiences and bestowing them with the attention they deserve.

Of course there is a *compromise* approach between the first and the second, the "genetic fallacy"—explaining the origin of a belief satisfactorily does not tell us if the belief is false or true. Even if the brain mechanisms and selection benefits can be wholly explained by evolution, this does not deny that the experiences might actually be valid. I find this position, flying in the face of parsimony as it does, anesthetic and far-fetched.

I now propose a third approach not represented elsewhere in this volume. It *hypothesizes* that some of the experiences are *true and they are not benign illusions but they are not divine*. According to this view some human beings are actually visited and guided by the future, but that the *ground of these experi-ences is natural*. I assume that many readers will find this far-fetched—even shockingly so, but this hypothesis is a possibility and I would be a coward if I did not articulate it. It is not an obvious hypothesis and it requires some thinking about what *might* happen in the *very* long run of the universe.

HYPOTHESIS: WE ARE CALLED INTO THE FUTURE BY A NATURAL PROCESS

My thinking about very long issues, I am not ashamed to say, is strongly influenced by science fiction. Science fiction at its best speculates on very long issues and it is not constrained by the fashionable hegemonies of academia or the traditional religious hegemonies of theology. Two works by Isaac Asimov have shaped my thinking. Both have the same logic: there are possible naturalistic accounts of the very biggest of questions. The first argues for a naturalistic account of God. The other argues for an account of time travel in which (by extension) being called by the future results from a natural process.

Asimov (1956) opens in 2061 with the Earth cooling down. Scientists ask the giant computer, "can entropy be reversed?" and the computer answers "not enough data for a meaningful answer." In the next scene, earth's inhabitants have fled the white dwarf that used to be our sun for younger stars; and as the galaxy continues to cool, they ask the miniaturized supercomputer, which contains all of human knowledge, "can entropy be reversed?" It answers "not enough data." This continues through more scenes, with the computer even more powerful and the cosmos even colder. The answer, however, remains the same. Ultimately trillions of years pass, and all life and warmth in the universe have fled. All knowledge is compacted into a wisp of matter in the near-absolute zero of hyperspace. The wisp asks itself "can entropy be reversed?"

"Let there be light," it answers.

And there was light.

This story is a naturalistic account of a God, not present yet, who comes at the end. Robert Wright (*NonZero*, 2000) provides an evolutionary underpinning of such an account. He argues for an evolutionary design without a designer that favors complexity. This design is our destiny, pushed by the ineluctable, invisible hand of natural selection and of cultural selection, both of which favor more complexity and therefore more win-win. I think of this ever-increasing complexity as identical with greater power and greater knowledge. I also think of this increasing complexity as greater goodness, since goodness favors the group of virtues that all successful cultures have evolved. In any competition between less knowledge and less power and less goodness against greater knowledge and greater power and greater goodness, more will usually win. There are of course setbacks and reversals, but this produces a natural, if balky, progress of knowledge, power, and goodness.

Toward what, I want to ask you, *in the very long run*, is this process of growing power and knowledge and goodness headed?

God has four properties in the Judeo-Christian tradition: omnipotence, omniscience, goodness, and the creation of the universe. I think we must give up the last property, the supernatural Creator at the beginning of time. This is the most troublesome property anyway: it runs afoul of evil in the universe. If God is the preexisting designer, and also good, omniscient, and omnipotent, how come the world is so full of innocent children dying, of terrorism, and of sadism? The Creator property also contradicts human freewill. How can God have created a species endowed with free will if God is also omnipotent and omniscient? And who created the Creator anyway?

There are crafty, involuted theological answers to each of these conundrums and I discuss them elsewhere (Seligman, 2002, 2014). Instead I lean toward a different way out: it acknowledges that the Creator property is so contradictory to the other three properties as to require jettisoning the property of Creator. It is this property, essential to theism, that makes God so hard to swallow for the scientifically minded person. The Creator is supernatural, an intelligent and designing being who exists before time and who is not subject to natural laws. Let the unravelling of the facts of creation be consigned to the branch of physics called cosmology.

Does this non-Creator God—omniscient, omnipotent, righteous—now exist? Such a God cannot exist now because we would still be stuck with two of the same conundrums: how can there be evil in the world now if an existing God is omnipotent and righteous, and how can humans have free will if an existing God is omnipotent and omniscient? So there was no such God and there is no such God. But in the very longest run, where is the principle of increasing complexity ultimately headed? Toward a God who is not supernatural, who acquires omnipotence, omniscience, and goodness through a natural progress of complexification.

God comes at the end.

The thrust of the first Asimov story is the possibility of a Being who over the longest run of time becomes omnipotent, omniscient, and righteous as a result of the collective accumulation of vast knowledge and experience. Importantly this is a nonsupernatural account of God's existence.

The other Asimov story (1955) argues for a natural account of time travel, and hence for a nonsupernatural account of being called by the future. The plot: our descendants eventually discover time travel over the very long haul. In contrast to the first story they, bumblers like us, are very far from omniscient and omnipotent. They are merely very advanced scientifically. But they do want to go back in time to rectify the past (see also Card, 1996, in which our descendants try to prevent slavery in the first place, and attend as well to what the monoliths, programmed by the past not the future, do when they encounter primate dead ends in Clarke, 1968). In Asimov, Card and Clarke, our descendants reach back into the past by sending people from the future (ho-hum), but more interestingly by invading our dreams, our thinking, and our fantasies.

I certainly don't know if time travel will occur as a matter of fact or even if it is inherently impossible. Serious physicists and cosmologists debate this. See, for example, the literature on "quantum entanglement" (e.g., Shalm, Hamel, Yan, et al., 2012), and these debates are way beyond my competence. If time travel is impossible, we are left with only the supernatural and the secular approach to callings. But if time travel is possible and it does happen, what ought our present posture and our role toward callings be?

We should, I venture, reach out and build bridges to such a possible future. What might such bridges look like? What would our time travelling descendants want and expect from us?

In the very first place, they would want us to take seriously the possibility that callings can come from them. This is indeed my posture.

Lots of other questions thereupon present themselves:

- Can we distinguish between actual callings and delusions? Does the sense of the numinous matter? Fear and trembling?
- What is the typical grammar of a call? Auditory, visual? Beginning, ending?
- How can we increase our receptivity to callings—meditation, contemplation, drugs, prayer, brain stimulation technology?
- What is the epidemiology of calling? How frequent are they? Who tends to experience them? At what age? In what psychological state—dreaming, daydreaming, waking, inattentiveness?
- What properties make callings life-changing? Should we be encouraged to believe that they are real and to lead our lives around them?

So here is why we have created this book: we not only want science to test secular interpretations of the very common experience of being called, but we also want people to contemplate the possibility of divine and naturalistic explanations both of which contend that we are actually being messaged by the future.

These ideas are a version of Pascal's wager: if we are wrong, what we say here and what we do counts for little.

If we are right, it is momentous.

REFERENCES

Asimov, I. (1956). The last question. *Science Fiction Quarterly*, November 7–15.

Asimov, I. (1955). *The end of eternity*. New York: Tor Books.

Buckner, R., & Carroll, D. (2007). Self-projection and the brain. *Trends in Cognitive Science, 11*, 49–57.

Card, O. S. (1996). *Past watch: The redemption of Christopher Columbus*. Tor Science Fiction.

Clarke, A. (1968). *2001: A space odyssey*. New American Library.

Duffy, R., & Sedlacek, W. (2007). What is most important to student's long-term career choices: Analyzing 10-year trends and group differences. *Journal of Career Development, 34*, 149–163.

Gallup Organization (2003, January 14). Religious awakenings bolster Americans' faith. Available from http://www.gallup.com

Gilbert, D. (2006). *Stumbling on happiness.* New York: Knopf.

Laplace, P. -S. (1951). *A philosophical essay on probabilities* (F.W. Truscott & F.L. Emory, trans.) New York: Dover (originally published in 1814).

Seligman, M. (2002). *Authentic happiness.* New York: Simon and Schuster.

Seligman, M. (2014). God comes at the end. *Spirituality in Clinical Practice, 1,* 1–4.

Shalm, L.K., Hamel, D., Yan, Z., Simon, C., Resch, K., & Jennewein, T. (2012). Three-photon energy–time entanglement. *Nature Physics,* doi: 10.1038/nphys2492

Wilson, D.S. (2007). *Evolution for everyone: How Darwin's theory can change the way we think about our lives.* New York: Delacorte Press.

Wright, R. (2000). *Nonzero: The logic of human destiny.* New York: Pantheon.

Wrzesniewski, A., McCauley, C., Rozin, P., & Schwartz, B. (1997). Jobs, careers, and callings: People's relation to their work. *Journal of Research in Personality, 31,* 21–33.

PART I

SCIENTIFIC AND SECULAR PERSPECTIVES

CHAPTER 1

CALLINGS AND THE MEANING OF WORK

Amy Wrzesniewski

The notion of work as a calling has attracted urgent interest in recent years. Students strive to discover what their calling might be, adults wonder how to connect with a sense of calling in their work, and scholars of work study and write on the dynamics of having a calling. The emphasis in popular culture on finding a calling, discovering one's life purpose, or simply doing meaningful work is difficult to ignore. In this chapter, I consider why callings may have attracted such deep interest and what it means for our understanding of the meaning of work.

In secular research traditions, a calling is traditionally defined as a meaningful beckoning toward activities that are morally, socially, and personally significant (Baumeister, 1991; Bellah, Madsen, Sullivan, Swidler, & Tipton, 1985; Wrzesniewski, Dekas, & Rosso, 2009). While a calling can be understood to be the center of one's life, secular researchers have largely treated callings as expressed specifically through the domain of work. Interestingly, callings are simply one of many orientations or experiences individuals can have of their work; however, callings have stolen center stage in popular and scholarly interest. While other orientations toward work emphasize the pursuit of work in service of other ends (e.g., economic gain, career advancement), callings alone capture the most positive and deeply meaningful manifestation of the connection between people and their work (Wrzesniewski, 2010; Wrzesniewski, McCauley, Rozin, & Schwartz, 1997).

Scholars of work have traditionally studied callings from a secular perspective, in which the sense of calling is defined by the experience of the domain of work, rather than by a call from beyond the self. This is a departure from a sense of calling that is deeply rooted in Judeo-Christian tradition and theology, a departure that has generated debate among scholars of work (e.g., Bunderson & Thompson, 2009; Rosso, Dekas, & Wrzesniewski, 2010). In the Judeo-Christian tradition, individuals are "called" by God to their unique vocations and are expected to carry out their work in service of God and others (Calvin, 1574). John Calvin and Martin Luther, both Protestant theologians, have shaped modern understanding of religious callings in their influential writings on the service to God that one performs by engaging dutifully in whatever work one does on earth. Importantly, the perspective advanced by Calvin and Luther put God at the center of a calling, both as its source and its target. Callings were given and revealed by God to people, and people toiled in their callings in service and honor of their God.

The religious roots of the notion of a calling have left an important legacy for scholars of work. The idea that a calling is something every person is born with and can discover through processes of discernment has persisted, even when the source and target of callings have largely lost their religious connection. German sociologist Max Weber famously claimed that Calvin's idea of a calling is partly responsible for modern capitalism. In part, Weber claimed that callings helped to generate a "Protestant work ethic" that drove a movement of individual pursuit for success. Despite modern critiques of Weber's interpretation of Calvin, his perspective on the development of Western society greatly influenced scholarship on, and understanding of, the topic of callings.

As callings have increasingly lost their religious associations in modern times, they have gained associations with the self. Rather than understanding a calling as coming from God, to be pursued in service of God (or others), callings have taken on a self-referential cast. Individuals are more likely to attempt to discern a calling by reflecting on what they find most enjoyable, care most about, or have the deepest interest in, all while figuring out a way to pursue that as their work. Less apparent in modern times is the hand or voice of a religious source of these cues. Indeed, most definitions of calling are now focused in general on the individual experience of work as deeply meaningful and engaging, intrinsically motivating, and having a positive impact on the wider world (Dik & Duffy, 2012; Dobrow & Tosti-Kharas, 2011; Elangovan, Pinder, & McLean, 2010; Wrzesniewski et al., 1997). Meaningful work itself is overwhelmingly described in a range of research studies as a function of work that allows the self to feel authentic, fully expressed, or competent (Rosso et al., 2010). This renders a calling as a pursuit with overwhelmingly individual overtones. While Greek philosophers, including Aristotle (1912), argued that authentic fulfillment could be had through the pursuit of personally meaningful and intrinsically motivating activities, in the modern era, this focus potentially leaves individuals with few referents other than the self for understanding the meaning of their work.

The increased emphasis on individual, work-related meanings of a calling may simply be reflective of shifts in the role of work in society. As individuals spend more time working (Schor, 1992) and are more likely to define themselves and be defined by others through their work (Casey, 1995), the domain of work necessarily becomes more relevant to and referential of the self. If work is how we are defined by others, and how we define the self, then work that is somehow meaningful to the self takes on increased urgency.

While modern, secular callings are largely defined by work that is experienced as a meaningful end in itself, as defined by the self, the roots of service to something larger persist. For example, some scholars define callings as deeply fulfilling work that an individual believes makes the world a better place (Wrzesniewski et al., 1997). Others describe callings as being strongly prosocial combined with a strong sense of clarity of purpose (Elangovan et al., 2010). Still others contend that callings are an ultimate form of career success that transcends a particular job, while not emphasizing the service to some greater good (Dobrow & Tosti-Kharas, 2011; Hall & Chandler, 2005). Though the definitions vary, most scholars writing about callings in a secular sense emphasize the ways in which the work creates a sense of meaning by uniting the self with something larger. Bunderson and Thompson (2009), in their influential work on callings among zookeepers, have reunited callings with a sense that they come from a sense of destiny, thus hearkening back to the roots of religious callings that are given from beyond. Specifically, they note that a "sense of a calling is that place within the occupational division of labor in society that one feels destined to fill by virtue of particular gifts, talents, and/or idiosyncratic life opportunities" (p. 37). This neoclassical view of modern callings puts a sense of duty and moral responsibility to serving the greater good (or a higher power) at the center of what it means to be called.

Despite the ways in which the definitions of a calling differ, most modern conceptions of a calling share an assumption that it is the work itself that determines the deep level of meaning taken from it. However, researchers emphasize that callings are not the product of a particular kind of work. As Wrzesniewski and colleagues (1997) have suggested, many different kinds of work can be seen as one's calling, with similar effects. Rather, it is the view of the work as being a meaningful end in itself that somehow contributes to the world more broadly that imbues work with a sense that it is a calling. Of course, the same work can be experienced by others as "just a job" in which the focus is on working to make an income (a job orientation), or as a site for advancement and increased prestige and power (a career orientation; Bellah et al., 1985). While those with job or career orientations engage in work as a means to a financial or career achievement end, respectively, those with callings engage in work as an end in itself (Wrzesniewski et al., 1997). In both traditional and modern understandings of calling, there is an explicit assumption that callings can be enacted in any type of work and are not exclusively reserved for work defined by others as worthy. What differs is whether the self has defined the work as being a calling, or it has been defined by one's God.

WHY CALLINGS MATTER

Understanding the nature and dynamics of callings matters for individuals and organizations for several reasons. First and perhaps foremost is evidence suggesting that 20 percent of the variance in individual well-being is explained by the experience of work (Campbell, Converse, & Rodgers, 1976). The impact of work on well-being is likely greater now, when more pressure is put on the domain of work as a source of meaning and identity in life (Casey, 1995). If callings can be experienced in any line of work, then understanding the antecedents to this optimal experience of work matters for the promotion of positive impact of work in life. Of course, work represents a range of meanings beyond callings, and can just as easily be experienced as a source of alienation, pain, and dissatisfaction. More broadly, then, understanding the meaning of work across the full spectrum of human experience is an urgent research undertaking simply because of the depth of the impact of work on life. Second, more than any other activity, work consumes individuals' waking hours (Wrzesniewski et al., 1997). Given the centrality and focus work receives for most adults as a result, it becomes imperative to understand framings and experiences of work that seem to transform their experiences of a central domain of life.

From early research that associated a calling orientation toward work with greater job and life satisfaction, as well as more engagement with work in general (e.g., Dobrow, 2013; Wrzesniewski et al., 1997), callings have attracted attention due to their strong associations with thriving in work and life. Research has established a positive relationship between seeing work as a calling and finding work to be more meaningful, greater effort made at work, and stronger motivation to remain in a job, even if it no longer was paid (Bunderson & Thompson, 2009; Wrzesniewski et al., 1997). This body of research tends to investigate the outcomes of having a calling orientation toward one's specific job or occupation. In addition to positive effects for the self, this research shows that a sense of work as a calling drives identification with and attachment to the organizations of which those with callings are a part (Cardador, Dane, & Pratt, 2011). Indeed, those with callings report lower absenteeism from work and put in more hours—regardless of the type of occupation in which one works (Wrzesniewski et al., 1997).

The good news on callings for individuals and organizations extends to the increased effort and passion that those with callings bring to their work (Novak, 1996; Vallerand et al., 2003). While evidence on the performance implications of callings is still sparse, claims that callings are associated with better work performance have been made (Hall & Chandler, 2005).

Thus, callings appear to be ideal for both individuals and organizations. They augur satisfaction and engagement for the individual, and attachment, effort, and results for organizations. More recently, researchers have begun to consider the idea that callings might represent too much of a good thing, and can tip into an unhealthy or overly rigid attachment to work (Bunderson & Thompson, 2009) or biases that may deafen those with callings to the career advice of others (Dobrow & Tosti-Kharas, 2012). Further evidence suggests that among young musicians, the strength of one's calling orientation is associated with biased overestimation of one's own musical ability relative to ability as rated by outside experts (Dobrow, 2010). This bias may come at the cost of objective career success, as the pursuit of a music career in the face of data that one is not as talented as one thinks could end in frustration and failure. Alternatively, given that callings are associated with greater engagement and effort, perhaps musicians with callings grow into their positive view of their own talents through diligence, practice, and dedication in the development of their gifts (e.g., Dweck, 1986). Further, the positive impact of parents' calling orientations on their adult children's sense of work as a calling suggests that elements of investment, dedication, and passion are part of what gets passed between generations (Dekas & Baker, 2014).

Duffy and Dik (2013) further summarize research that notes the possibility that callings come with a dark side (see also Cardador & Caza, 2012). The risks they note seem to accrue mostly to those who have a calling orientation to a particular kind of work, but lack the opportunity to pursue that work in their actual jobs (e.g., Berg, Grant, & Johnson, 2010). For those lucky enough to find work in their calling, arguments and evidence have been offered to suggest that a sense of calling can contribute to unhealthy levels of focus on work that is out of balance with other life interests (see Duffy, Douglass, Autin, Chapter 2). However, others suggest that those with callings are less likely to suffer from stress, depression, and conflict between the work and nonwork spheres of their lives (Bunderson & Thompson, 2009; Oates, Hall, & Anderson, 2005; Treadgold, 1999). Further research is needed to better understand, using longitudinal designs, whether callings buffer individuals from negative experience in work and life, or whether the increased focus on work makes them more vulnerable to setbacks and frustrations in the expression of their callings.

WHERE NEXT? PROMISING DIRECTIONS FOR UNDERSTANDING CALLINGS

While the concept of a calling has been with us for centuries, social scientists are relatively new to the questions they pose for individuals and institutions. However, great promise abounds in the findings summarized above and the directions they suggest for further inquiry on how individuals come to have, experience, and live out their callings in modern contexts. It is a sign of the healthy development of research on callings that the topic has engendered so many different perspectives on their definition, expression, and source (Wrzesniewski, 2010). Below, I summarize the most important avenues for future research on the nature of callings.

First, productive engagement in academic dialogue among researchers is needed to begin to come to an understanding of what defines a calling. Debate persists on whether callings are defined by the enjoyment one has in pursuing work that is a calling, or by the (sometimes) grim sense of duty and service that accompanies a calling. Eudaimonic perspectives on human experience suggest that the prosocial element that accompanies many scholars' definitions of calling may be responsible for their positive effects in work and life. Understanding the unique contributions of the enjoyment, fulfillment, and service that callings represent will be important in reaching better definitional clarity. Otherwise, this developing field of inquiry runs the risk of remaining an attractive but ultimately disorganized and contradictory literature.

Second, this definitional clarity will help scholars of callings to converge around an agreed-upon way to measure the presence and strength of calling orientations. Currently, multiple measures of a calling exist and compete in a literature that reflects conflicting definitions of the construct (Bunderson & Thompson, 2009; Dobrow & Tosti-Kharas, 2011; Wrzesniewski et al., 1997). Chief among the contrasts among these measures is the question of whether a calling is the product of following one's career destiny, sensing a deep amount of meaning and contribution in the work, experiencing enjoyment and flow in the work, or some combination of these. Until the definitional debates on callings come to some resolution, the construct measurement issues will remain.

Third, while the accumulated findings on the experience of work as a calling are promising for individuals and organizations, much of this work has been correlational. Dobrow Riza and Heller's (in press) longitudinal research on callings among teenage musicians transitioning to adulthood is an exception; however, larger-scale long-term studies of a variety of occupations are necessary to discern how callings emerge and unfold over time. At this point, many of the studies most commonly cited regarding callings suffer from the possibility that it is the most satisfied, committed, and identified individuals who come to feel their work is a calling, rather than the reverse. A broader question is whether this reversal of causality would be a problem; if callings develop out a highly positive and satisfying experience of work that individuals find meaningful, as opposed to a sense of fate to do a type of work that has not yet been pursued, this would be a rather key development in the literature. To that end, longitudinal data suggest that when MBA graduates successfully pursue the work they most wanted to do, they are significantly more likely to experience that work as a calling years later (Wrzesniewski, Tosti-Kharas, Tschopp, & Landman, working paper).

Fourth, in both popular culture and in existing studies, a tension exists between whether callings are treated as defined entities that exist in the world for each individual, waiting to be discerned or discovered, or as orientations toward work that develop over time as individuals experience and make meaning of the jobs they hold. It is possible that cultural and religious narratives that suggest that callings are objective facts in hiding, to be found through deep reflection and analysis, shape the ways in which individuals come to experience their work. In contrast, a narrative that assumes no single "perfect" calling to a particular kind of work but rather advances the possibility that many kinds of work may bring deep meaning, fulfillment, and service of the greater good could shape different relationships to the experience of a calling. It is not hard to imagine the search and consecutive disappointments of individuals following the first model, who may expect that the "right" work for them will be meaningful, fulfilling, and joyful. It is perhaps more realistic to subscribe to a belief that there may be several possible "callings" that may be imperfect but still meaningful expressions of fulfillment and contribution. Just as there is a stark difference between individuals who expect that there is one perfect life mate in the world for them and those who believe that there are perhaps several possible good matches with whom a meaningful life could be built, individuals who subscribe to (or write about) callings along one or the other model may be talking, acting, and writing past each other.

Fifth, there is an opportunity to move beyond a treatment of callings as existing in relation to a particular job or occupation to instead consider the possibility that individuals could view the domain of work more broadly as a calling. Most research to date has assessed callings as they exist for the current jobs of research participants. It would shed helpful light to study the impact of seeing the life domain of work as a calling instead. Without this perspective, it becomes impossible to discern who among those who see their work as a job, a career, or something else are sensing a degree of mismatch between how they see their work and how they think of the domain of work in an ideal sense. Indeed, the mismatch is likely a source of dissatisfaction and disinvestment from work more generally.

Sixth, while scholars of positive psychology and positive organizational scholarship have sought to understand what it is that helps individuals, groups, and organizations to thrive, the dynamics and processes uncovered in both fields are best understood against a backdrop of the full range of human experience. Specifically, callings are but one orientation individuals can have toward their work. Early work canvassing a broad set of occupations suggests that they comprise only one-third of the experiences individuals have of their work, with job and career orientations representing the rest (Wrzesniewski et al., 1997). Future work should concentrate on the broad swaths of the population who labor in work in that they see in terms rather different than the positive and enthusiastic cast supplied by callings.

CONCLUSION

Areas of great promise abound in the future of callings research. Callings contain the seeds of what makes us fully human in our work, in our expression of self, of spiritual belief, of connection to humanity, or any combination of these. Building on the promising progress that has been made to better understand the antecedents and consequences of callings will be critical to this area of inquiry going forward in a productive way. The function of a calling in individual life, organizations, and society as a whole is only beginning to be understood. In this understanding lies great promise for helping to shape the relationship between individuals and their work so that those who yearn to experience a calling may know one.

REFERENCES

Aristotle (1912). *Politics*. London: J. M. Dent and Sons.

Baumeister, R. F. (1991). Work, work, work, work. In *Meanings of life* (pp. 116–144). New York: The Guilford Press.

Bellah, R. N., Madsen, R., Sullivan, W. M., Swidler, A., & Tipton, S. M. (1985). *Habits of the heart*. Berkeley: University of California Press.

Berg, J. M., Grant, A. M., & Johnson, V. (2010). When callings are calling: Crafting work and leisure in pursuit of unanswered occupational callings. *Organization Science, 21*(5), 973–994.

Bunderson, J. S., & Thompson, J. A. (2009). The call of the wild: Zookeepers, callings, and the dual edges of deeply meaningful work. *Administrative Science Quarterly, 54*, 32–57.

Calvin, J. (1574). *Sermons of M. John Calvin upon the Epistle of Saint Paul to the Galatians*. London: Lucas Harison and George Bishop.

Campbell, A., Converse, P. E., & Rodgers, W. L. (1976). *The quality of American life*. New York: Russell Sage Foundation.

Cardador, M. T., & Caza, B. B. (2012). Relational and identity perspectives on healthy versus unhealthy pursuit of callings. *Journal of Career Assessment, 20*, 338–353.

Cardador, M. T., Dane, E., & Pratt, M. G. (2011). Linking calling orientations to organizational attachment via organizational instrumentality. *Journal of Vocational Behavior, 79*, 367–378.

Casey, C. (1995). *Work, self, and society: After industrialism*. New York: Routledge.

Dekas, K. H., & Baker, W. E. (2014). Adolescent socialization and the development of adult work orientations. *Research in the Sociology of Work, 25*, 51–84.

Dik, B. J., & Duffy, R. D. (2012). *Make your job a calling: How the psychology of vocation can change your life at work*. West Conshohocken, PA: Templeton Press.

Dobrow, S. R. (2010). A siren song?: A longitudinal study of calling and ability (mis)perception in musicians' careers. Working paper.

Dobrow, S. R. (2013). Dynamics of calling: A longitudinal study of musicians. *Journal of Organizational Behavior, 34*(4), 431–452.

Dobrow, S. R., & Tosti-Kharas, J. (2011). Calling: The development of a scale measure. *Personnel Psychology, 64*, 1001–1049.

Dobrow, S. R., & Tosti-Kharas, J. (2012). Listen to your heart? Calling and receptivity to career advice. *Journal of Career Assessment, 20*, 264–280.

Dobrow Riza, S., & Heller, D. (in press). Follow your heart or your head? A longitudinal study of the facilitating role of calling and ability in the pursuit of a challenging career. *Journal of Applied Psychology*.

Duffy, R. D., & Dik, B. J. (2013). Research on calling: What have we learned and where are we going? *Journal of Vocational Behavior, 83*, 428–436.

Dweck, C. S. (1986). Motivational processes affecting learning. *American Psychologist, 41*, 1040–1048.

Elangovan, A. R., Pinder, C. C., & McLean, M. (2010). Callings and organizational behavior. *Journal of Vocational Behavior, 76*, 428–440.

Hall, D. T., & Chandler, D. E. (2005). Psychological success: When the career is a calling. *Journal of Organizational Behavior, 26*, 155–176.

Novak, M. (1996). *Business as a calling: Work and the examined life*. New York: The Free Press.

Oates, K. L. M., Hall, M. E. L., & Anderson, T. L. (2005). Calling and conflict: A qualitative exploration of interrole conflict and the sanctification of work in Christian mothers in academia. *Journal of Psychology and Theology, 33*, 210–223.

Rosso, B. D., Dekas, K. H., & Wrzesniewski, A. (2010). On the meaning of work: A theoretical integration and review. *Research in Organizational Behavior, 30*, 91–127.

Schor, J. (1992). *The overworked American: The unexpected decline in leisure*. New York: Basic Books.

Treadgold, R. (1999). Transcendent vocations: Their relationship to stress, depression, and clarity of self-concept. *Journal of Humanistic Psychology, 39*, 81–105.

Vallerand, R. J., Blanchard, C., Mageau, G. A., Koestner, R., Ratelle, C., Leonard, M., . . . Marsolais, J. (2003). Les passions de l'ame: On obsessive and harmonious passion. *Journal of Personality and Social Psychology, 85*, 756–767.

Wrzesniewski, A. (2010). Callings. In K. S. Cameron & G. Spreitzer (Eds.), *Handbook of positive organizational scholarship*. Cambridge: Oxford University Press.

Wrzesniewski, A., Dekas, K., & Rosso, B. (2009). Callings. In S. Lopez & A. Beauchamp (Eds.), *Encyclopedia of positive psychology*. Oxford, UK: Blackwell.

Wrzesniewski, A., McCauley, C., Rozin, P., & Schwartz, B. (1997). Jobs, careers, and callings: People's relations to their work. *Journal of Research in Personality, 31*, 21–33.

Wrzesniewski, A., Tosti-Kharas, J., Tschopp, C., & Landman, J. T. If I could turn back time: The lived experience of occupational regret. Yale University, Working paper.

CHAPTER 2

THE DARK SIDE OF A CALLING

Ryan D. Duffy, Richard P. Douglass, and Kelsey L. Autin

This present chapter highlights the dark side of a calling. Although the bulk of research to date has focused on positive outcomes of a calling, we discuss potential negative effects resulting from (a) having a calling, but not living it or (b) living out a calling in an unhealthy fashion. Specifically, a case is made that feeling a calling is only beneficial insomuch as an individual is able to live out that calling. Additionally, the unhealthy effects of living a calling that may exist from some individuals—burnout, organizational exploitation, and workaholism—are delineated. Practical suggestions are offered to help individuals turn felt callings into lived ones and also to help those living out a calling avoid negative consequences.

THE DARK SIDE OF A CALLING

Imagine for a moment someone in your life who is currently living out a career calling. Perhaps this is your spouse, parent, brother, sister, or friend. When you think about the type of job they have, what comes to mind? According to all available research, it is likely they are working in a job that is highly meaningful and is also used to help others in some fashion (Duffy & Dik, 2013). Now imagine how this person *feels* about their job and life in general. According to all available research, it is also likely they exude a sense of fulfillment with their work and, as a result, feel a very high sense of meaning and happiness in their lives. In fact, people in your life who are living a calling are likely to be some of the happiest people you know.

It shouldn't be surprising why these people love their jobs and are happy with their lives. Work represents the activity people spend more time doing than anything else but sleep (Ingraham, 2014); and meaning and prosocial behaviors are the key ingredients that make this time fulfilling (Grant & Berg, 2011; Rosso, Dekas, & Wrzesniewski, 2010). But are there times when having or living a calling is actually a *bad thing*? Drawing from recent theory-building efforts and a growing empirical literature (e.g., Bunderson & Thompson, 2009; Duffy & Dik, 2013; Duffy, Dik, & Steger, 2011), in this chapter we focus on the potentially counterintuitive notion that calling may have a dark side. Specifically, we focus on two areas where callings can go wrong: feeling a calling but being unable to live it and living a calling in an unhealthy fashion. We conclude this chapter by offering practical suggestions for avoiding calling's potential dark side.

FEELING IT, BUT NOT LIVING IT

What percent of people do you think have a calling? The answer might surprise you a bit. Over the past several years, our research team has asked this simple question to study participants: "People sometimes describe having a calling in life, often to a specific job or career. Do you have a calling?" Across thousands of participants from a variety of backgrounds according to age, social class, educational attainment, gender, race/ethnicity, and employment status, results are remarkably consistent—approximately 50 percent of all individuals feel they have a calling. We suspect this number may be surprising to you because it seems *surprisingly high*. This gap between how many people we perceive have a calling versus those who actually do may be due to the fact that many individuals who feel a calling don't have the opportunity to live it out. In fact, most studies show the correlation between these two variables to be around .50 (Duffy, Allan, Autin, & Bott, 2013; Duffy, Allan, Autin, & Douglass, 2014; Duffy, Bott, Allan, Torrey, & Dik, 2012).

The preponderance of initial studies on calling assessed the degree to which individuals perceived a calling and how this linked to work and well-being outcomes. Cumulatively, findings suggest that, for college students, feeling a calling is positively linked with aspects of career maturity (e.g., more established vocational identity, greater career self-efficacy, career adaptability) and academic satisfaction (Douglass & Duffy, 2015; Duffy, Allan, & Dik, 2011; Duffy & Dik, 2013). Students with a calling tend to have greater clarity concerning their vocational selves, are more adaptable in their career development, and are more satisfied with their academic pursuits. Similar positive findings exist with adults in the work domain. Employed adults with a calling tend to be more committed to their careers, find more meaning in their work, and experience greater job satisfaction (Duffy & Dik,

2013). Additionally—for both students and employed adults—feeling a calling has been linked with increased life meaning and life satisfaction (Duffy et al., 2013; Duffy, Allan, & Bott, 2012).

What these initial studies failed to acknowledge, however, was the critical distinction between having a calling and living a calling. Feeling a calling is a mental state analogous to a lifelong goal. It is something that an individual has—a noun—that can be described in a tangible fashion: "my calling is to be a doctor," "my calling is to be a teacher," "my calling is to enrich the lives of children." Having this type of goal is beneficial by providing an individual with a sense of meaning and purpose. But the real benefits of this goal likely arise when individuals have the opportunity to pursue it. To put it another way, having a calling is like owning a brand new car. Of course all of us would want a brand new car, but would we still want that car if we could never actually drive it? Might seeing that brand new car everyday just sitting there actually make us feel worse?

This paradox strikes at a potential dark side of a calling—feeling it but not living it. Several empirical studies have addressed this paradox. For example, Duffy, Dik, et al. (2011) examined how perceiving a calling related to work outcomes among a sample of university employees, finding career commitment to suppress the relation between perceiving a calling and withdrawal intentions. Specifically, individuals who felt a calling but were not committed to their careers—likely because they weren't actually working in the career that was their calling—were more likely to want to withdraw from their current employment. Other qualitative research by Berg, Grant, and Johnson (2010) highlighted individuals who had "unanswered callings," noting that this often led to regret for not pursuing them or stress attempting to pursue them but running into difficulties.

Other research has simultaneously assessed the degree to which individuals are perceiving and living a calling. Duffy, Bott, et al. (2012) surveyed a group of employed adults and examined how perceiving a calling is linked to job satisfaction. Specifically, it was hypothesized that the reasons individuals who felt a calling would be happier at work were because of increased career commitment and work meaning. Additionally, the authors examined how living a calling moderated these relations. Although career commitment and work meaning were found to mediate the relation between perceiving a calling and job satisfaction, this was only the case for individuals who felt they were living a calling. In other words, living a calling was required in order for participants to reap the work-related benefits of perceiving a calling.

In a follow-up study, Duffy et al. (2013) found that living a calling also fully explained the link between perceiving a calling and life satisfaction. Perceiving a calling was unrelated to life satisfaction if individuals weren't currently living that calling.

This handful of studies paints a clear picture: feeling a calling may be good only insomuch as someone is living it out, and in some cases "unanswered callings" may result in regret, stress, and greater intentions to withdraw form one's current employment. Understanding how a perceived calling translates into a lived one is important; and several studies have investigated how these two variables link together. Employed individuals are more likely to report living out their calling than unemployed individuals, even though each group demonstrates equal levels of perceiving a calling (Duffy, Bott, Allan, & Autin, 2014). When individuals are unemployed, perceiving a calling has been found to be unrelated to life satisfaction, whereas this relation is significant and positive for employed adults (Torrey & Duffy, 2012). Additionally, several studies have demonstrated that social status plays an important role—with employed adults who perceive a calling being more likely to live that calling when they report greater educational attainment, higher yearly incomes, and greater freedom of choice in selecting desired occupations (Duffy et al., 2013; Duffy & Autin, 2013).

These finding suggest that—not surprisingly—being employed is a prerequisite for living out a felt calling and that individuals who have higher social status will be more likely to fulfill the career to which they feel called. Higher social status likely allows greater access to finding and securing job opportunities that match an individual's calling. Considering these findings as a whole, it may be that under certain conditions feeling a calling leads to negative outcomes. These conditions include (a) being unemployed, (b) being employed in a job that is not one's calling, or (c) being unable to pursue a calling due to a lack of resources and/or privilege.

For some individuals who have a calling, that brand new car may be simply stuck in the driveway, only to serve as a symbol of what could have been or what could be, potentially leading to feelings of regret and discouragement. For others, they may be just driving a different car, longing for the opportunity to get behind the wheel of their pride and joy. What the accumulated research and each of these analogies showcase is the clear distinction between feeling and living a calling and the potential dark side of only having a calling.

UNHEALTHY LIVED CALLINGS

Although people who have a calling but are unable to live it may suffer negative effects, there are many people who are living out their calling that may also experience maladaptive consequences. Living out a calling is not always the pretty picture it is made out to be; some people who live out their callings don't experience the same degree of satisfaction and meaningfulness

that others experience, and even those who do may incur negative consequences that accompany these positive effects. In the following section
we focus on three variables—burnout, organizational exploitation, and
workaholism—that may either (a) minimize the degree to which living out
a calling is fulfilling or (b) add additional burdens for individuals living out
their calling.

Burnout

Burnout is often defined as a prolonged response to chronic emotional and
interpersonal stressors on the job (Maslach, Schaufeli, & Leiter, 2001). More
simply, the Mayo Clinic (2012) views burnout as "a state of physical, emotional, or mental exhaustion combined with doubts about your competence
and the value of your work." Not surprisingly, although living a calling may
lead to doing work that helps people and is meaningful in nature, it may also
draw people to work in highly emotional and stressful environments.

Picture nursing for a moment. Nurses who are living out their callings
may view their work as helpful to others and meaningful but still feel burnt
out from the highly emotional and stressful hospital environment. When
regarding the profession of nursing, Yancik (1984) talks about burnout as
"the social and psychological dysfunctioning of nurses who are repeatedly
exposed to suffering, death, and the demand for compassion and understanding." And nursing is indeed a profession associated with increased rates of
burnout (Sherman, 2004; Vinje & Mittelmark, 2007). Teachers are another
group that, despite engaging in meaningful and prosocial work, experience
elevated rates of leaving their profession during the first five years of service (Hartnett & Kline, 2005). In a qualitative study of teacher stressors, one
teacher reports "I arrive at school at 7:30 every morning to give myself some
extra time to prepare. [. . .] It's not enough. As a teacher I'm dealing with a
never ending barrage of things I must do. [. . .] Some of the kids need your
help desperately. [. . .] I'm so busy just trying to keep up with things, I can't
give the kids the attention they need" (Blase, 1986, p. 31). Another teacher
reported "I firmly believe that to do a good job of teaching, it takes all you've
got to give. [. . .] Teaching drains you. You lose your spirit" (p. 31). Clearly
some teachers—likely those living out their callings—want to give all they
can to help their students. The nature of this work, however, proves to be
stressful and draining and may result in burnout.

Building from the above findings, Cardador and Caza (2012) identified
burnout as a possible detrimental outcome associated with a calling. Cardador and Caza note that one reason why living a calling leads to burnout is
due to higher than normal expectations of one's performance and also others'

level of performance. The job is so central to one's identity that one feels required to put every ounce of energy into it. Taking all of this together, living out a calling—particularly in stressful and draining environments—has the potential to lead to burnout, perhaps due to increases in performance expectations of oneself and others.

Organizational Exploitation

"I would not tell them [how committed I am] because they can get a strong hold on you that way. If management knows you love your job, they'll try to do things to undercut your pay and stuff like that" (Bunderson & Thompson, 2009, p. 43). This was a common sentiment found in Bunderson and Thompson's in-depth study on the work lives of zookeepers. Another commented "They [managers] know that you're going to do [the work], so why free that money for this, or why go that extra mile" (p. 43). Bunderson and Thompson came to find that 21 of 23 zookeepers they interviewed were living out their calling and that living out these callings was associated with many consequences, one of which was organizational exploitation. In a further examination of their initial qualitative findings, Bunderson and Thompson conducted a quantitative study of 491 zookeepers and confirmed their initial findings: zookeepers with a sense of calling had an increased vulnerability to organizational exploitation. From a purely financial standpoint, results revealed calling was *negatively* associated with self-reported income after controlling for demographic variables.

Similarly, in another paper highlighting the potential pitfalls of having and living a calling, Berkelaar and Buzzanell (2014) suggested that organizations may exploit an employee's calling via dominance and control. They suggested that the outcomes of living a calling may be so beneficial to the organization that management will push workers to view their work as a calling. Ultimately, although workers living out their calling seem to be aware of the potential for organizational exploitation, the pull of the dark side may be too strong. As one zookeeper put it: "I don't know what they [management] could do that would make me leave. Even if I wasn't getting paid I would still be here" (Bunderson & Thompson, 2009, p. 43). Once again, the centrality a calling plays in one's sense of self may make an employee a target for scrupulous employers.

Workaholism

We all know what workaholics look like. These are the people who stay late at work while everyone else is at happy hour, the people who work through the weekend, and the ones who just never seem to shut it down.

Most simply, workaholism is an addiction to work. Ng, Sorensen, and Feldman (2007) noted that workaholics enjoy their work but, at the same time, they are obsessed with working and devote personal time and long hours to their work. Evidence has begun to emerge that supports many scholars' view that calling is linked to workaholism.

In the same zookeeper study previously mentioned, Bunderson and Thompson (2009) found that the zookeepers living out their callings reported elevated levels of investment in their work; these same zookeepers were also more likely to sacrifice their personal time for work. As one zookeeper put it: "When the nightwatch calls me up and says we've got a problem in your building, I'm out of bed and I'm in here" (p. 42). The idea of sacrificing personal time for work time was a large theme in Bunderson and Thompson's (2009) study, yet this is not a novel finding. Serow (1994), for example, suggested that the dedication one has to their calling often leads to personal sacrifices. Building from this assertion, Levoy (1997) contended that these sacrifices may come at the expense of other—nonwork—aspects of life.

As a result of these workaholic tendencies, work-life balance often suffers. According to one zookeeper: "Working here at the zoo has cost me a marriage" (Bunderson & Thompson, 2009, p. 42). In a review of the potential negative effects of calling, Berkelaar and Buzzanell (2014) note that workers with a calling will sacrifice their time and that the pursuit of a calling may increase family stress. Ultimately, pursuing a calling has the potential to interfere with one's personal relationships (Ng, Sorensen, & Feldman, 2007).

It is evident how living a calling can lead to workaholism. Callings are associated with work that is meaningful and prosocial—that is, callings are viewed as enhancing the greater good of society. When people are living out a calling, it may be easy for them to justify unhealthy levels of investment in their work as a necessity to accomplish the goals of helping society. Through this reasoning, these types of workers may be able to rationalize the sacrifice of personal time, even if it interferes with personal relationships. Thus, living out a calling can make people susceptible to workaholism and a lack of work-life balance.

Summary

After looking at the evidence, it seems that living out a calling may also have a dark side for some individuals. In particular, people living out a calling may have an increased risk of burnout, organizational exploitation, and workaholism. When considering that leaving a calling might be more difficult than leaving a job (Berkelaar & Buzzanell, 2014)—given that callings are viewed as being meaningful and helpful to the greater good—the dark side grows even darker. Imagine a person who is living out their calling, but begins to experience burnout, exploitation, or workaholism. Although the experience of these maladaptive outcomes is likely to have a negative impact on job satisfaction and performance, it may be that the calling is never abandoned and a vicious cycle ensues; the calling is lived, burnout, exploitation, or workaholism occurs, and satisfaction and/or performance declines. In such a case, the force of the dark side is evident.

PRACTICAL SUGGESTIONS

The bulk of research on work as a calling has focused on its positive effects. Accordingly, practical suggestions have often centered on helping people find a calling (Dik, Duffy, & Eldridge, 2009) with less attention paid to how to avoid the potential dark side of a calling. In this section we highlight practical strategies for (a) going from having a calling to living a calling and (b) living out a healthy calling.

Turning Having into Living

As previously mentioned, research shows that a surprising 50 percent of people report having a calling. However, as also indicated by research and likely your personal experience, only a small fraction of those people actually end up living that calling out. Unemployment and lack of access to resources are two major reasons that callings go unanswered. Given the systemic nature of these obstacles, it is important that policy-level changes are implemented to give more people better access to social and educational resources that lead to employment and more opportunities for work choice. But what might one do on an individual level turn a felt calling into a lived one? The most straightforward solution is addressing the third reason we attribute to unlived callings—poor fit between one's calling and one's current job.

If poor fit is the case, options for those who want to live out their callings might include changing jobs, changing the work environment, or psychological reframing of one's work. Typically, changing one's job or work environment involves overcoming difficult barriers. For various reasons, people often feel constrained in work. Although this is connected to privilege and access to resources (i.e., someone may feel constrained due to lack of educational attainment), even very privileged individuals can feel constrained at work. An attorney from a high social class background, for example, may feel constrained to a specific geographical region to accommodate a spouse's career. Or parents may feel unable to pursue a specific career due to child-rearing responsibilities. Life happens, and often it happens in such a way that makes it difficult to live out a dream job. Although changing jobs or one's work environment is possible for some, it is difficult for many and often not an option. Thus, experts on career calling often recommend *job crafting*—a process of extending job boundaries to extract a greater sense of purpose and fulfillment (Dik & Duffy, 2012; Wrzesniewski & Dutton, 2001).

Job crafting is based on the notion that individuals can find flexibility within their job requirements to create better person-environment fit (Wrzesniewski & Dutton, 2001). This can take the form of task crafting, relational crafting, or cognitive crafting. Task crafting involves altering how a task is done by approaching it in a novel way, directing more energy to certain parts of a task, adding to a task, or removing something from a task to make it better align with a person's skills and values (Berg, Wrzesniewski, & Dutton, 2010). Of course, the key to this is finding flexibility to alter tasks while fulfilling job requirements, a factor that largely depends on the job. Although certain aspects of a job may not be flexible, job crafting is often most effectively achieved through small, simple adjustments that can be made in almost any work setting. For example, if a cashier enjoys interacting with customers, she might direct more energy to that part of her job by setting a goal to spend more time talking to each customer (Dik & Duffy 2012).

Relational crafting draws upon the empirically demonstrated idea that humans have an innate need for relationships (Baumeister & Leary, 1995). The focus in relational crafting is that of creating more opportunity for building and deepening positive relationships as well as limiting unhelpful interactions in the workplace (Berg et al., 2010). This might mean adjusting the interpersonal climate among coworkers, customers, clients, or supervisors. For example, one way individuals can attempt to relationally craft is by establishing weekly lunches with a coworker, which can create a shared connection over a long period of time. Relational crafting provides social support in the workplace and provides a pathway to meaningful relationships with others.

A third type of job crafting is cognitive crafting. This type of crafting focuses on shifting one's perception of job tasks. In cognitive crafting, it is not the work itself that is altered, but the way in which the worker *thinks* about the work (Berg, et al., 2010). This may be especially useful for those who have little flexibility to engage in task or relational crafting (Dik & Duffy, 2012). Someone who uses cognitive crafting reframes the meaning of their work and significance of job tasks. This might require an individual to think more broadly about how her or his job impacts people or society. For example, when viewing the job description of a custodial worker at a hospital, one might find tasks such as sanitizing, changing bedsheets, and cleaning toilets. However, one who engages in effective cognitive crafting might recognize that they are keeping patients safe and comfortable, providing for the needs of sick people, and caring for individuals who may be experiencing major life crises. When one connects simple job tasks to their societal importance or benefit for others, it becomes more possible to finding meaningfulness and purpose in their work (Dik & Duffy, 2012).

Living in a Healthy Fashion

Once a person is living out their calling, what can they do to prevent the negative manifestations of calling? We recommend that burnout, workaholism, and worker exploitation are all best prevented by taking an active, approach-oriented stance. Instead of resolving to not get caught up in these traps of unhealthy calling orientations, it is best to take active steps to prevent them from happening (Dik & Duffy, 2012).

First, it is important to proactively set up a structure for work–life balance. Being open with friends and family about one's calling is helpful in setting up and maintaining a social support network (Dik & Duffy, 2012). In a qualitative study examining women with dual callings to both a career and motherhood, several of the women viewed their family members as active participants in living out their calling (Sellers, Thomas, Batts, & Ostman, 2005). This provided support for the mothers and helped to prevent family-work conflict by creating a collaborative role for family members. Inclusion of friends and family in one's calling not only provides support in times of stress, but also provides accountability for times the work role begins to encroach on other life roles (Dik & Duffy, 2012).

Additionally, it may be helpful to intentionally schedule time in the week specifically for nonwork activities. For example, parents with callings might schedule weekly or daily time to be enjoyed with their children. It is also beneficial to have hobbies and interests outside of work. Scheduling regular time for nonwork activities allows for boundaries that prevent burnout and overextension of oneself in the workplace. Dik and Duffy (2012) recommend scheduling the equivalent of one day per week of self-care activities.

Finally, for those who want to actively prevent burnout, workaholism, and workplace exploitation, we recommend regular "check-ins." This refers to regularly scheduled time to reflect upon how balanced one feels in work and nonwork activities. These might include both individual reflection as well as checking in with friends and family regarding work-life balance. Often, people are not aware that work may be encroaching upon other life roles until it is causing significant problems. Check-ins allow for greater awareness of any imbalances that may be occurring and thus, an opportunity to readjust early on.

Approaching work as a calling can help people experience a tremendous amount of fulfillment and meaningfulness. By incorporating the above recommendations, people who feel called might reap the benefits of this particular orientation to work while preventing unhealthy manifestations that may arise when the dark side of calling shows its face.

REFERENCES

Baumeister, R. F., & Leary, M. R. (1995). The need to belong: Desire for interpersonal attachments as a fundamental human motivation. *Psychological Bulletin, 117*(3), 497–529. doi:10.1037/0033-2909.117.3.497

Berg, J. M., Grant, A. M., & Johnson, V. (2010). When callings are calling: Crafting work and leisure in pursuit of unanswered occupational callings. *Organization Science, 21*, 973–994. doi: 10.1287/orsc.1090.0497

Berg, J. M., Wrzesniewski, A., & Dutton, J. E. (2010). Perceiving and responding to challenges in job crafting at different ranks: When proactivity requires adaptivity. *Journal of Organizational Behavior, 31*(2–3), 158–186. doi:10.1002/job.645

Berkelaar, B. L., & Buzzanell, P. M. (2014). Bait and switch or double-edged sword? The (sometimes) failed promises of calling. *Human Relations.* doi:10.1177/0018726714526265

Blase, J. J. (1986). A qualitative analysis of sources of teacher stress: Consequences for performance. *American Educational Research Journal, 23*(1), 13–40. doi:10.3102/00028312023001013

Bunderson, J. S., & Thompson, J. A. (2009). The call of the wild: Zookeepers, callings, and the double-edged sword of deeply meaningful work. *Administrative Science Quarterly, 54*(1), 32–57.

Cardador, M. T., & Caza, B. B. (2012). Relational and identity perspectives on healthy versus unhealthy pursuit of callings. *Journal of Career Assessment, 20*(3), 338–353. doi: 10.1177/1069072711436162

Dik, B. J., & Duffy, R. D. (2012). *Make your job a calling: How the psychology of vocation can change your life at work.* West Conshohocken, PA: Templeton Press.

Dik, B. J., Duffy, R. D., & Eldridge, B. M. (2009). Calling and vocation in career counseling: Recommendations for promoting meaningful work. *Professional Psychology: Research and Practice, 40*(6), 625–632. doi:10.1037/a0015547

Douglass, R. P., & Duffy, R. D. (2015). Calling and career adaptability among undergraduate students. *Journal of Vocational Behavior, 86*, 58–65. doi:10.1016/j.jvb.2014.11.003

Duffy, R. D., Allan, B. A., Autin, K. L., & Bott, E. M. (2013). Calling and life satisfaction: It's not about having it, it's about living it. *Journal of Counseling Psychology, 60*, 42–52. doi: 10.1037/a0030635

Duffy, R. D., Allan, B. A., Autin, K. L., & Douglass, R. P. (2014). Living a calling and work well-being: A longitudinal study. *Journal of Counseling Psychology, 61*(4), 605–615. doi:10.1037/cou0000042

Duffy, R. D., Allan, B. A., & Bott, E. M. (2012). Calling and life satisfaction among undergraduate students: Investigating mediators and moderators. *Journal of Happiness Studies, 13*(3), 469–479. doi:10.1007/s10902-011-9274-6

Duffy, R. D., Allan, B. A., & Dik, B. J. (2011). The presence of a calling and academic satisfaction: Examining potential mediators. *Journal of Vocational Behavior, 79*(1), 74–80. doi:10.1016/j.jvb.2010.11.001

Duffy, R. D., & Autin, K. L. (2013). Disentangling the link between perceiving a calling and living a calling. *Journal of Counseling Psychology, 60*, 219–227. doi: 10.1037/a0031934

Duffy, R. D., Bott, E. M., Allan, B. A., & Autin, K. L. (2014). Calling among the unemployed: Examining prevalence and links to coping with job loss. *Journal of Positive Psychology*. doi: 10.1080/17439760.2014.967798

Duffy, R. D., Bott, E. M., Allan, B. A., Torrey, C. L., & Dik, B. J. (2012). Perceiving a calling, living a calling, and job satisfaction: Testing a moderated, multiple mediator model. *Journal of Counseling Psychology, 59*(1), 50–59. doi:10.1037/a0026129

Duffy, R. D., & Dik, B. J. (2013). Research on calling: What have we learned and where are we going? *Journal of Vocational Behavior, 83*, 428–436. doi: 10.1016/j.jvb.2013.06.006

Duffy, R. D., Dik, B. J., & Steger, M. S. (2011). Calling and work related outcomes: Career commitment as a mediator. *Journal of Vocational Behavior, 78*, 210–218. doi: 10.1016/j.jvb.2010.09.013

Grant, A. M., & Berg, J. M. (2011). Prosocial motivation at work: When, why, and how making a difference makes a difference. In K. Cameron & G. Spreitzer (Eds.), *Oxford handbook of positive organizational scholarship* (pp. 28–44). New York: Oxford University Press.

Hartnett, S., & Kline, F. (2005). Preventing the fall from the call to teach. *The Journal of Christian Faith and Belief, 9*, 9–20.

Ingraham, C. (2014, June 20). 10 Maps that show how much time Americans spend grooming, eating, thinking and praying. Retrieved from: http://www.washingtonpost.com/blogs/wonkblog/wp/2014/06/20/ten-maps-that-show-how-much-time-americans-spend-grooming-eating-thinking-and-praying/

Levoy, G. (1997). *Callings: Finding and following an authentic life.* New York: Crown.

Maslach, C., Schaufeli, W. B., & Leiter, M. P. (2001). Job burnout. *Annual Review of Psychology, 52*, 397–422.

Mayo Clinic Staff. (2012, December 8). Job burnout: How to spot it and take action. *Adult health.* Retrieved from http://www.mayoclinic.org/healthy-living/adult-health/indepth/burnout/art-20046642

Ng, T.W.H., Sorensen, K. L., & Feldman, D. C. (2007). Dimensions, antecedents, and consequences of workaholism: A conceptual integration and extension. *Journal of Organizational Behavior, 28*(1), 111–136. doi: 10.1002/job.424

Rosso, B. D., Dekas, K. H., & Wrzesniewski, A. (2010). On the meaning of work: A theoretical integration and review. *Research in Organizational Behavior, 30*, 91–127. doi:10.1016/j.riob.2010.09.001

Sellers, T., Thomas, K., Batts, J., & Ostman, C. (2005). Women called: A qualitative study of Christian women dually called to motherhood and career. *Journal of Psychology and Theology, 33*(3), 198–209.

Serow, R. C. (1994). Called to teach: A study of highly motivated preservice teachers. *Journal of Research and Development in Education, 27*, 65–72.

Sherman, D. (2004). Nurses' stress and burnout: How to care for yourself when caring for patients and their families experiencing life-threatening illness. *American Journal of Nursing, 104*, 48–56.

Torrey, C. L., & Duffy, R. D. (2012). Calling and well-being among adults: Differential relations by employment status. *Journal of Career Assessment, 20*, 415–425. doi: 10.1177/1069072712448894

Vinje, H. F., & Mittelmark, M. B. (2007). Job engagement's paradoxical role in nurse burnout. *Nursing & Health Sciences, 9*(2), 107–111. doi:10.1111/j.1442-2018.2007.00310.x

Wrzesniewski, A., & Dutton, J. E. (2001). Crafting a job: Revisioning employees as active crafters of their work. *Academy of Management Review, 26*(2), 179–201. doi:10.5465/AMR.2001.4378011

Yancik, R. (1984). Coping with hospice work stress. *Journal of Psychosocial Oncology, 2*(2), 19–35. doi:10.1300/J077v02n02_02

CHAPTER 3

ROAD TO DAMASCUS MOMENTS: CALLING EXPERIENCES AS PROSPECTIVE EPIPHANIES

David Bryce Yaden and Andrew B. Newberg

Oft in these moments such a holy calm
Would overspread my soul, that bodily eyes
Were utterly forgotten, and what I saw
Appeared like something in myself, a dream:
A prospect in the mind

—Wordsworth

A "road to Damascus moment" is an expression currently used to describe intellectual realizations that mark important turning points. "The reversal of her position on climate change after the science briefing marked a *road to Damascus moment* in her presidency" could be a line lifted from the *New York Times*. But this contemporary use of the expression describes a more conscious, deliberate process than its source. Originally, the phrase referred to a sudden, life-changing transformation from an extraordinary experience.

In the biblical story of Saint Paul the Apostle (Acts 9, 1–9 New International Version), a man named Saul travels to the city of Damascus with the intention of arresting, questioning, and possibly executing members of a new religious movement called Christianity. He had already participated in stoning a Christian man to death, among similar acts of severe persecution. But as the story goes, his trip does not proceed according to plan. On the road to Damascus, Saul is blinded by "the light of heaven," falls to the ground, and a voice addresses him saying, "I am Jesus, whom you persecute, arise and go into the city." He does so, and after a few days of blindness, his health is restored. The psychological impact of the experience remains, however, and is so life-changing that he becomes a Christian—a convert to the very sect that he set out to persecute. "Saul" becomes known as "Paul" after his experience, and is eventually canonized as a saint by the Catholic Church for his prolific teaching and writing.

The road to Damascus moment that transformed Saul the persecutor into Paul the saint was a *calling* (Longenecker, 1997). "Calling," is a term with a similar history to the expression "road to Damascus moment." While a calling has come to refer to consciously viewing one's work as particularly meaningful, callings have a more experiential origin. Calling experiences, for our purposes, are *profoundly meaningful, temporary mental states that contain a revelation or directive that seems to come from beyond the self.* These experiences have occurred throughout history and remain prevalent in contemporary society. While they were once taken as an auspicious sign from heaven, modern psychological sciences have reflexively taken a reductive stance that casts such experiences as indicative of pathology.

In this chapter, we present relevant psychology and neuroscience research that provides an empirically grounded perspective of calling experiences that emphasizes their positive potential. Calling experiences contain aspects that bring them under the umbrella of religious, spiritual, and mystical experiences (RSMEs; Beauregard, 2011), but they also contain information content that can orient those who have them toward a particular life path. While the information content from calling experiences has often been taken as a sign of pathology in certain clinical contexts (e.g., "hearing voices"), we suggest that this information content is similar to that of epiphanies. Epiphany, an insight that enters into conscious awareness as a whole (Pawelski, 2012), provides a non-pathological perspective with which to frame calling experiences. While we cannot overstate the importance of subjecting epiphanies to rational and ethical analysis, such information can hold extraordinary value. Research on the creative process, for example, has uncovered many accounts in which an idea was delivered to an artist or scientist through an intuitive, nonconscious mental process (Ghiselin, 1952). Calling experiences may work through a means similar to that of epiphany, though in the case of callings, the content typically relates to one's own identity and future—a prospective epiphany.

BEING CALLED

The term "calling" can refer either to a conscious and deliberate process of viewing one's work as meaningful, or to an experience involving more intuitive psychological processes. Both senses of the term appear in definitions of calling in the psychological literature. While callings are conceptualized in different ways, there is some agreement that callings are closely related to intrinsically motivated, meaningful, and prosocially oriented work. Definitions differ, however, on whether a calling is the journey or the destination. That is, does a calling point one toward meaningful work or is the calling the meaningful work itself? The following section briefly reviews how callings are currently operationalized in the psychological literature and situates our own definition of experiential, "road to Damascus" callings.

Callings have been described as a conscious orientation toward work (Wrezesniewski, 2003). According to this *work orientation sense of callings*, a "job" is just a paycheck, a "career" is an opportunity for personal advancement, and a "calling" is work that is perceived as meaningful, intrinsically motivated, and prosocial (Bellah, Madsen, Sullivan, Swidler, & Tipton, 1985; Shwartz, 1986; Wrezesniewski, McCauley, Rozin, & Schwartz, 1997). This conceptualization is based, in part, on the idea that a sense of meaning can be *constructed* in a number of life domains (Baumeister, 1991). In this view, when one's work becomes meaningful, then it can be considered a calling (Baumeister & Vohs, 2002). Viewing one's work as a calling is associated with outcomes like higher job satisfaction, cooperation at work, productivity, zest, and life satisfaction (Hall & Chandler, 2005; Peterson, Park, Hall, & Seligman, 2009; Wrezesniewski, 2003). While individuals who lack the talents or opportunities to pursue what they perceive as their calling can experience profound frustration and regret (Gilovich & Medvec, 1995; Iyengar, Wells, & Schwartz, 2006), one can also work to construct meaning such that an initially disappointing occupation can become a calling (Berg, Grant, & Johnson, 2010). Saint Paul almost certainly had a work orientation that would be categorized as a calling, but his road to Damascus experience is outside the scope of this definition.

Another conceptualization of callings focuses on beliefs about one's own suitability for a particular kind of work. This sense usually includes the belief that one is hardwired for, or is destined to fill, a particular life role or career (Bunderson & Thompson, 2009). This is the *neoclassical sense of callings*. It is drawn from Protestant reformers like Martin Luther (1883), who extended the concept of callings beyond an exclusively religious sphere, such as the call to the monastic life or priesthood, to apply to any productive occupation that serves society (Weber, 1930). While the term has retained some of its sacred connotation, it is also used in secular contexts (Novak, 1996). For example, zookeepers often speak about their work in ways one might expect to find in the ministry, about how they were born to fill their role and that they are uniquely gifted to perform their work (Bunderson & Thompson, 2009). This view of callings is closely tied to a sense of moral duty and highlights how callings make for meaningful work but also require a degree of sacrifice for that benefit. Sacrifice can come in the form of working unpaid hours, expending additional effort, and the stress of caring deeply about one's work. Others have also cautioned that callings, as with most concepts in psychology, can be taken to an unhealthy extreme (Cardador & Caza, 2012; Grant & Schwartz, 2011). While Luther drew heavily on the writings of Saint Paul, and while Saint Paul likely also had this neoclassical sense of calling, his experience on the road to Damascus does not fit within this calling framework, either.

A definition of calling that better fits with Saint Paul's experience highlights the experiential "otherness" of calling experiences. The *transcendent sense of callings* comes as a "transcendent summons," experienced as originating beyond the self (Dik & Duffy, 2009; Duffy & Dik, 2009; 2013). This transcendent source of the call could involve God, destiny, society, or the world at large. Research has shown that feeling a transcendent sense of calling increases intrinsic work motivation, life satisfaction, prosocial motivation, and the sense of meaning in life (Dik, Duffy, & Steger, 2012; Steger & Dik, 2009; Steger, Pickering, Shin, & Dik, 2010). Saint Paul's experience does fall under the transcendent sense of calling, but this definition is so broad that it also admits many other callings that are felt on a much less experiential level. For example, the "transcendent summons" could come from one's life circumstances, interests, or abilities (Duffy & Dik, 2009). Something as mundane (but no less influential) as family pressure could fall under this definition, as this influence could be interpreted as coming from beyond the self. Thus, this definition includes Saint Paul's experience but is too broad to adequately capture it.

Our definition of callings fits under the transcendent sense of callings, but limits itself to intense, inner experiences. The *experiential sense of callings* is defined as: *profoundly meaningful temporary mental states that contain a revelation or directive that seems to come from beyond the self.* The experiential sense of calling therefore fits among the class of profound and visceral experiences described in James's (1902/1985) *The Varieties of Religious Experience.* James discusses a number of similarly extraordinary experiences. Most of this class of experiences contains an element of passivity, in that they seem to happen to an individual rather than being consciously commanded.

This sense of calling is related to Otto's (1958) numinous experiences, which contain awe, wonder, and fear for a presence that is perceived as "wholly other." Maslow (1964) also described "peak experiences" as possibly containing inner voices and revelations. Other intense inner experiences, such as mystical and self-transcendent experiences, which are characterized by a sense of unity beyond the self, have received interdisciplinary study (Baumeister & Exline, 2002; Haidt & Morris, 2009; Hood, 1975, 2005; Keltner & Haidt, 2003; Newberg et al., 2001; Newberg & d'Aquili, 2008; Yaden & Newberg, 2014). Calling experiences, however, have received less research attention than these related varieties of experiences.

While we use the experiential sense of callings and focus on events like Saint Paul's road to Damascus moment, these various senses of callings are generally complementary rather than contradictory. For example, a calling experience (experiential sense) is a form of calling (transcendent sense), which can lead to a belief about one's destined calling (neoclassical sense), that can then cause one to undertake work they view as a calling (work orientation sense). In other words, a calling can lead to a calling, resulting in a calling. In lived experience, these senses of calling undoubtedly overlap and interrelate with one another.

CONTEMPORARY CALLING EXPERIENCES

Callings remain prevalent in contemporary society. While figures differ depending on the definition, about 33–37 percent of people report a work orientation calling (Peterson et al., 2009; Wrzesniewski et al., 1997), which includes significant measurement overlap with the neoclassical sense of calling (Dobrow & Tosti-Kharas, 2011), and about 40 percent report a transcendent calling (Duffy & Sedlacek, 2007). For the prevalence of experiential callings we must draw from research measuring related varieties of experiences. When a 2002 Gallup poll asked if respondents have had *a profound religious experience or awakening that changed the direction of their life*, 41 percent of Americans indicated they have had a life-changing experience of this kind. We use this figure as a very rough approximation for the prevalence of calling experiences.

Scholarly research and statistcal factor analysis of the overlap between these various senses of callings has only just begun (Dobrow & Tosti-Kharas, 2011). Therefore, we illustrate the complex interplay of definitions of callings using the authors' stories, as both authors of this chapter feel called in ways that combine these various senses of calling.

Andrew Newberg: *My own personal calling cuts across two domains of my life. The first is my career as a physician and the second is related to the study of religious and spiritual phenomena via the field referred to as neurotheology. With regard to the first, since I can remember, I have always felt that I should be a doctor. I emphasize the word "should" since it felt like something I was supposed to be doing. The basis for this sense of "should" was always unclear to me. I did not have any specific influence from family members. No close relatives were doctors. It just felt to me as if that was my life's calling. In fact, when I was in kindergarten and was asked to write what I wanted to be, I clearly stated I wanted to be a doctor. While I have pondered the origin of this feeling, I cannot really identify any specific source. It did not seem to have a religious basis. And while I reasoned that being a doctor made sense since I liked science and liked the idea of helping people, there are certainly other professions that I could have considered. The closest I could come in my own mind to understanding this feeling is that "the world" was pulling me in that direction. Based on who I was and how I thought, it just seemed natural for me to pursue medicine as a career.*

The second aspect of my career has been my pursuit of studying various religious and spiritual phenomena, primarily from a neuroscientific perspective. This also originated from the time I was very young and was related to my constant questioning about the nature of things. I always wanted to know how things worked, why there were different religious and philosophical perspectives, and how our brain understood reality. But it was not a superficial level of questioning; I was always unsatisfied with the answers that people, both personal and historical, could provide to me. As I got older, my philosophical questioning became more of a philosophical meditation or contemplation. I came to realize that simply following a spiritual or philosophical approach, or a scientific approach, would never be complete in helping to answer these "big" questions about reality. Somehow, it made sense to me that I had to find an integrated approach. Again, it seemed as if "the world" itself was somehow pulling me to find the answers to these questions and providing me the methods and approaches that might help me to find them. This came in the form of my research, my mentors, family, friends, and colleagues who have all been part of that journey. It is a journey that I continue to feel pulled towards pursuing. In fact, part of the basis of my wanting to answer the questions is to find out exactly what it is that is pulling me.

David Yaden: *My calling came in the midst of a dark and directionless period in my life in the form of a dramatic, life-changing experience. While lying on my dorm room bed one night, I noticed a sensation of warmth in my chest that felt, at first, like heartburn. The warmth slowly spread out from the center of my chest to cover my entire body. At some point, I realized that the sensation felt a lot like love. In the instant of this recognition, I became unconscious of my body and was overcome by an experience of boundless unity. Time fell away and space opened up into an infinite horizon. Love saturated me absolutely and was reciprocated by a whole-hearted desire to put myself to use in the world. When I regained awareness of my body, I was laughing and crying with joy, filled with a sense of meaning and purpose—and wondering what it was that happened to me.*

In the weeks that followed, my dreams became so vivid that they seemed to extend into my waking consciousness, giving daily life a mythic quality, complete with archetypal roles and a clear sense of mission. At one point, I silently framed a question in my mind "what will I be?" To my surprise, an inner voice responded, "a scriptor." This word is Latin for author or scribe, but it is not a word I had ever used or that I was aware of knowing (I needed to look it up). Through this and similar inner experiences, I learned more about myself, my strengths, my interests, and what I wanted to do with my life over the course of a few weeks than I had in previous months and years.

Spirituality and religion made such intuitive sense to me after my experience that I became a seeker and a somewhat obsessive, amateur scholar of spiritual experiences. Even reading accounts of similar experiences, described by poets, sages, or other ordinary people would induce feelings similar to what I felt during my experience.

Philosophy courses combined with conversations with professors and religious lead-ers, however, led me to doubt my assumption of a spiritual basis to my experience. Neuroscience and cognitive science research (crucially including books by my coau-thor, Andrew Newberg) provided me with convincing alternative explanations. Ul-timately, I became agnostic about the source of my experience, but remain convinced of its value.

Psychology has allowed me to view experiences like mine from an agnostic perspec-tive while empirically investigating their outcomes. Previous research demonstrates that experiences like mine are relatively prevalent and often profoundly positive, but many questions remain. For example, what are the causes, effects, and population patterns of these experiences—their epidemiology? What changes to neurobiological and psychological processes make them possible—their neurocognitive grammar? Do they reliably lead to the long-term meaningful work of a calling? Answering these questions is my calling—and has been since the moment that I opened my eyes after my experience and began wondering what it was that happened to me.

SOURCE OF THE CALL

Callings beg the question of who, or what, is doing the calling—a calling implies a caller. This question is particularly salient in the transcendent and experiential sense of calling. For those who have experiences of calling that contain revelations and directives, the nature of the "caller" goes beyond mere speculation and becomes a pressing personal and existential concern. In our view, the source of the call can be broadly broken down into four common categories of interpretation. These are *not* meant to be logically exclusive or empirically exhaustive categories or a definitive classification, but rather a basic way of illustrating some of the most common interpretations of callings.

Supernatural/External

One can interpret their calling as *supernatural* in origin, coming from God or deities described in religious and spiritual traditions, which are *external* to one's mind. The possibility of a sudden revelation of a divine command, often experienced in a state of ecstasy, is important to a number of religious traditions. Saint Paul defended himself on these grounds to the Roman au-thorities, as Paul knew that even the Romans believed that heavenly mes-sages ought to be taken seriously. Accounts of calling experiences appear in the texts of every major religion: Abraham in Judaism; Saint Paul in Chris-tianity; Muhammad in Islam; Buddha in Buddhism; Arjuna in Hinduism—to name just a few examples. Importantly, each of these traditions also includes methods for questioning the call. For example, St Teresa of Avila wrestled with the source of her visions and ecstatic experiences, constantly wondering whether they came from God or the Devil. The following is an account typical of a supernatural interpretation of a calling experience:

> The very instant I heard my Father's cry calling unto me, my heart bounded in recognition. I ran, I stretched forth my arms, I cried aloud, "Here, here I am, my Father." Oh, happy child, what should I do? "Love me," answered my God . . . Had I not found my God and my Father? Did he not love me? Had he not called me? Was there not a Church into which I might enter? Since then I have had direct answers to prayer—so significant as to be almost like talking with God and hearing his answer. The idea of God's reality has never left me for one moment. (James, 1902/1985, p. 60)

Supernatural interpretations remain common, though they have been partially supplanted by other post-enlightenment perspectives.

Natural/External

Callings can also be interpreted as *natural* in origin but *external* to one's mind. Hypothetical mind control scenarios involving either malevolent or beneficent intentions fit into this interpretation. For example, movies like *The Manchurian Candidate* and *Upstream Color* provide examples of mind control using technological means. While such scenarios are not currently feasible, past ethical abuses of attempted mind control and recent technological advances make them a relevant bioethical concern (for a discussion, see Yaden, Anderson, Mattar, & Newberg, 2015). Some suggest that on a long enough timeline, other interesting science fiction-like scenarios present themselves, such as those sketched by Asimov (for a discussion see Seligman, this volume). The following is an interpretation of a calling experience that originates in the future and acts through more natural means.

> This is what drives the guru to make his statement, this is what kindles the messiah to his mission, this is what inspires the painter and the dreamer and the musician. There is an enormous source of affection and concern for humanity which is calling us toward it, across the plains of lower dimensional time and space, and the miracle is that through perturbing our neurochemistry in ways which shamans have always done we can turn to the last page, as it were, and can see there that the entire process was actually toward a good cause. (McKenna, June 15, 1992)

Such ideas cast callings as originating outside of one's mind, yet from a nonsupernatural source. These views typically derive from a teleological perspective of reality and human life. In essence, this view suggests a belief in human progress taken to its logical extreme.

Supernatural/Internal

Some people interpret callings as coming from an unconscious source *internal* to one's mind that is supernatural insofar as it is connected to "objective" aspects of reality. For example, Carl Jung (1938) articulated a quasi-spiritual aspect of the unconscious mind called "the objective psyche." According to this view, aspects of the unconscious mind are autonomous and capable of ascertaining facts about the future and perhaps other spiritual realities. Jung describes an experience of calling encountered by one of his patients or, perhaps, himself (Jung, 2012):

> The voice . . . always pronounces an authoritative declaration or command, either of astonishing common sense and truth, or of profound philosophic allusion. It is nearly always a definite statement, usually coming toward the end of a dream, and it is, as a rule, so clear and convincing that the dreamer finds no argument against it. It has, indeed, so much the character of indisputable truth that it often appears as the final and absolutely valid summing up of a long unconscious deliberation and weighing of arguments . . . I have to admit the fact that the unconscious mind is capable at times of assuming an intelligence and purposiveness which are superior to actual conscious insight. (Jung, 1938, p. 45)

This view can be interpreted in ways that extend beyond the admittedly overly simplistic labels of "supernatural" and "internal." But these categories illustrate a view of the psyche that posits a capacity to ascertain truths unknown to the conscious mind.

Natural/Internal

The default view of empirical science is to interpret callings as *natural* in origin and *internal* to one's mind. That is, callings can be explained through mental processes grounded in brain mechanisms. This view comes from the fact that most of the assumptions underlying the supernatural and external views of callings are untestable. Those aspects of callings that are not measureable by current scientific methods belong more to the realm of philosophy or theology than of science. However, it should be noted that even those experiences that are considered to have a supernatural origin by the experiencer, still have a natural/internal component that can potentially be evaluated from a scientific perspective. For example, an individual who experiences hearing God's voice and believes the origin to truly be God, still had to utilize her or his auditory and language areas of the brain as part of that experience. In any case, if science is to help explain callings at all, researchers must focus their efforts on the aspects of calling experiences that are measurable and thus subject to empirical research.

Two reflexes (which we informally call "Two Reflexes of Empiricism") are associated with empirical approaches to a broad range of psychological phenomenon outside of mainstream discourse, including calling experiences: the *reductive reflex* and the *pathological reflex*. Both reflexes spring from rules of thumb associated with the scientific method, but are not inherent to a scientific perspective. The reductive reflex is to seek explanations at lower levels of analysis, and the pathological reflex is to look for symptoms of pathology. Both reflexes consist of an important part of the scientific picture of any psychological phenomenon. However, they can both overreach. William James articulated an overreach of these reflexes by researchers in Paul's calling:

> Medical materialism finishes up Saint Paul by calling his vision on the road to Damascus a discharging lesion of the occipital cortex, he being an epileptic. (James, 1902/1985, p. 23)

Empirical approaches run the risk of trying to "explain away" calling experiences by reducing them to something better known, in this case seizures, rather than more fully admitting what cannot be scientifically tested. This is the reductive reflex. As James points out, medical materialism "finishes up" Saint Paul's experience as *nothing but* a seizure. The issue here is not whether Saint Paul was an epileptic, as evidence indicates that he was (Landsborough, 1987), it is whether one's interpretation of his experience stops there. While it is clear that there is a neurobiological basis for calling experiences, as there are for *all* experiences, this description alone does not explain the ultimate source, account for the content of the revelation, nor address the values and beliefs that surround calling experiences (Newberg & d'Aquili, 2008; Sacks, 2012).

The pathological reflex, on the other hand, has more to do with the sociology of science than tendencies inherent to a scientific worldview. The positive psychology movement has highlighted how fixated on pathology modern psychology has become (Gable & Haidt, 2005; Seligman & Csikszentmihalyi, 2000). When applied to experiences of calling, the pathological reflex has led to assumptions that calling experiences are indicative of mental illness.

Calling experiences do include a number of elements that can be interpreted as indicative of pathology, it is important to note. Hearing voices and seeing visions are symptoms that exist on a continuum between normality and pathological conditions like psychosis and schizophrenia (Stip & Letourneau, 2009). Furthermore, the ecstatic state that often accompanies experiences of calling can include feelings associated with dissociative states such as depersonalization and derealization, conditions that have also been linked to epilepsy (Saver & Rabin, 1997). Such reasoning can be somewhat tautological, however. If "hearing voices" necessarily defines one as a psychotic, then anyone hearing the voice of God would necessarily be considered to be psychotic. And if ecstatic states of self-transcendence are defined as disso-ciative, than many monks and nuns would be considered diagnosable with a psychiatric condition. Another problem with this pathologically biased rea-soning is that it does not take account of the many positive outcomes associ-ated with calling experiences.

The *DSM-IV* goes beyond the pathological reflex and makes explicit men-tion of how varieties of spiritual, religious, and mystical experiences—which includes experiences of calling—can be nonclinical and have positive poten-tial for individuals (Lukoff, Lu, & Turner, 1992). Of course, pathological and positive aspects of calling experiences can form a complicated relationship. For example, calling experiences can occur as a positive experience but can be integrated into one's life in an unhealthy way. Calling experiences can also occur amongst intense suffering, providing a healing experience that includes difficulty, but is eventually considered a positive experience. Em-pirical research shows that experiences similar to callings are among the most meaningful moments of peoples' lives and can increase well-being and prosocial behavior (Griffiths, Richards, McCann, & Jesse, 2006; Hood, Hill, & Spilka, 2009; Newberg & d'Aquili, 2008). These positive outcomes must be acknowledged.

A NEW VIEW OF CALLING EXPERIENCES

We elaborate on the psychologically beneficial outcomes of calling experi-ences by providing positive and nonreductive psychological and neurological explanations. As for the ultimate source of callings, we remain ultimately ag-nostic. But we believe that a positive perspective is possible within *any* meta-physical interpretation—including a natural/internal view of callings. Our view is nonreductive in that it does not rule out other possible mechanisms and interpretations. We acknowledge that any biological correlates of such experiences are correlates only and do not necessarily identify a definitive causal mechanism. Thus, we intend to identify psychological and neurobio-logical processes that may underlie such experiences, but we do not suggest that our theories explain calling experiences in full. We also acknowledge that such experiences can occur in the context of pathology and can have maladaptive outcomes, which has been discussed at length elsewhere (Lu-koff, Lu, & Turner, 1992). In short, our view is not an argument for a wholly positive perspective, but it rather aims to provide a framework for a more complete picture of calling experiences that includes their positive potential.

Psychological Perspectives

Psychological perspectives focus on the subjective content of calling expe-riences, the feelings, sensations, voices, visions, or intuitions that feel "other," and seem to originate beyond the self. This subjective content that falls under psychology's purview can be divided into two groups: the sensations felt and the content communicated. Here, we focus on the latter quality.

The first component includes the physical feelings and sensations that people report during calling experiences. During Saint Paul's experience, for example, he fell from his horse and reported seeing a vision of the light of heaven and hearing a voice. These embodied, sensory elements bring calling experiences under the umbrella of phenomena described by William James (1902/1985) in *The Varieties of Religious Experience*. They are akin to mystical experiences, temporary states of unity with all things, and numinous experiences, encounters with a sense of presence. These are now referred to under the broad construct of RSMEs (Beauregard, 2011), which include calling experiences. The increased well-being and prosocial motivation observed after RSMEs may help to explain why calling experiences often result in such positive psychological outcomes and dedication to prosocial work. These more subjective aspects have been discussed at length elsewhere (Griffiths et al., 2006; Hood et al., 2009; Newberg & d'Aquili, 2008; Yaden & Newberg, 2014).

The second component of calling experiences involves the information content, the revelations or directives communicated during the experience. Saint Paul describes receiving a specific sentence addressed to him that contained a command. Some interpretations of calling experiences seem to make this information easy to explain—it was the voice of God, for example. But even in the case of God communicating to an individual, the psychological means through which this message occurs must still be explained. Other interpretations, such as the natural/internal, which has borne the burden of the two reflexes of empiricism, have tended to dismiss these messages as delusions. But what if this information is valuable, and in some cases true—or at least useful—regardless of whether it comes from a supernatural or natural source?

Messages and mental processes that occur without conscious control have been of interest to psychology since the origin of the field. Automatisms, or involuntary verbal behavior, witnessed by Sigmund Freud in patients under hypnosis informed his theory of the unconscious. Carl Jung and William James also undertook studies of unbidden intrusions of information into consciousness awareness (Harrington, 2008). Freud, Jung, and James each arrived at different assessments of the value of such information (in general: Freud—negative, Jung—positive, James—it depends).

Later theories claim that inner voices and visions arose through natural selection and once served as a useful basis for behavior. Jayne's (1976) speculative theory of the "bicameral mind" suggests that inner voices and visions come from the nondominant brain hemisphere, which Nobel prize winning split-brain studies have shown can contain an intelligence distinct from conscious awareness (Sperry, 1964). According to this theory, early humans heard inner voices more frequently and often acted on their behalf. As conscious awareness became more dominant, however, these voices faded into the background of awareness. Now, as Jayne's theory goes, such voices arise only under certain circumstances, such as during experiences of calling.

In recent years, intuitive processes have come to be viewed with suspicion due, in part, to the dual process model of Kahneman and Tversky (2000). These researchers call intuitive processes "system 1" and more conscious, deliberate practices "system 2." Their research demonstrates a number of instances in which intuitive processes (system 1) provide incorrect answers to logic or math puzzles that can be solved by applying more rational deliberation (system 2). According to this framework, intuitive epiphanies are not to be trusted. Rather, conscious and deliberate thinking ought to be applied whenever possible. These researchers acknowledge that intuitive processes necessarily handle most of the multitude of decisions faced each day and that both systems are necessary. But in popular usage, the theory falls in line with others that view intuitive processes negatively. Philosopher David Hume, for example, took as part of his task to demonstrate "the natural infirmity and unsteadiness both of our imagination and senses" (as quoted in Atlas, 2012, p. SR4).

We take issue with this overly suspicious view of the imagination, and intuitive processes in general, on the grounds that it casts the creative process in an overly negative light. Alternately, the content of calling experiences may be viewed as similar to a creative epiphany, in which an idea is delivered from a source that seems to come from beyond one's conscious awareness (Pawelski, 2012). Creative epiphanies are usually preceded by conscious deliberation of a particular topic, followed by a period of "incubation," in which conscious attention is directed away from the subject (Ghiselin, 1952; Wallas, 1976). The epiphany then comes as an intrusion into conscious awareness—an "aha moment" (Jung-Beeman et al., 2004). While the content of epiphanies must be later analyzed by reason, they can deliver important insights. Philosopher Bertrand Russell (1959) articulates the value of this process, "Reason is a harmonising, controlling force rather than a creative one. Even in the most purely logical realm, it is insight that first arrives at what is new" (p. 10).

Prospection is another automatic, intuitive process that places epiphany in a more positive light. Prospection is the representation and evaluation of possible futures, a process that occurs almost continuously through daily life (Gilbert & Wilson, 2007; Seligman, Railton, Baumeister, & Sripada, 2013). This process was discovered through brain imaging research after scientists observed that a particular pattern of brain activity reliably occurs in subjects who are not given any task—when subjects are essentially daydreaming in the scanner. This pattern of brain activity, called the "default mode network," is also active when participants are asked to imagine themselves in different hypothetical scenarios, such as those in the future. Prospection has been formalized into a more general psychological orientation to the future (Seligman et al., 2013). An epiphany about one's future can thus be called a "prospective epiphany."

Therefore, calling experiences can be framed as prospective epiphanies. This view does not ignore the fact that the visions, voices, and intuitions during calling experiences can be wrong—they require critical examination like everything else. But this view does highlight the possibility that epiphanies can sometimes be right. Given this framing, calling experiences can provide insights into one's life-path similarly to how artists receive visions for new pieces, mathematicians receive solutions to problems, and scientists receive new hypotheses to test.

Neurological Perspectives

At present, there are few definitive studies that have explored the neurobiological correlates of calling experiences. However, a number of studies provide data suggesting possible neurophysiological models of such experiences. This research can inform how a model of calling experiences might be developed and tested in future studies.

To develop a neurocognitive model, we begin with the descriptive elements already considered in this chapter and others in this book. For a calling experience to occur, conscious, deliberate thought is likely momentarily suppressed. Several studies have evaluated the importance of the frontal lobes in the context of spiritual practices and experiences. Many spiritual practices, such as prayer or meditation, require purposeful attention. This attention to a particular prayer, phrase, or sacred object is frequently associated with increased activity in specific structures of the frontal lobes, most commonly the prefrontal cortex (Lazar et al., 2000; Newberg et al., 2001; Newberg & Iversen, 2003). But a separate set of spiritual practices also exist in which practitioners feel as if they have been "taken over" by God or some other, perhaps spiritual or otherwise mentally dissociated, entity. Studies of practices such as speaking in tongues or mediumship, in which the experience feels as if the process is coming into the brain from outside the body, have generally found reduced activity in frontal lobe structures (Newberg, Wintering, Morgan, & Waldman, 2006; Peres, Moreira-Almeida, Caixeta, Leao, & Newberg, 2012).

In addition to alterations in frontal lobe activity, other areas of the brain can be linked to specific elements of a calling experience (Newberg & Iversen, 2003). As we have mentioned, callings seem to come from beyond the self. Sensory regions of the brain in conjunction with temporal and parietal lobe activity help to establish a spatial orientation for the self and models bodily boundaries (Karnath, Ferber, & Himmelbach, 2001; Urgesi, Aglioti, Skrap, & Fabbro, 2010). A sense of calling that is perceived to come from an internal source may affect these orientation areas of the brain differently than an experience perceived to be originating from outside the body. Different neuronal responses may facilitate this type of spatial differentiation and enable an individual to experience a calling as coming from beyond the self.

A third element of many calling experiences relates to profound emotional states. Emotions associated with callings are often positive even though one's emotional state just prior to a calling experience can be very negative. During states of high distress associated with various life problems (i.e., near-death experiences), individual can experience profound spiritual states with a concomitant shift to a highly positive emotional state (Newberg and d'Aquili, 1994). It should be noted that the frontal lobes, along with the anterior cingulate cortex, tend to regulate emotional states that are associated with limbic system activity (i.e., the amygdala). Higher frontal lobe activity usually suppresses strong emotional responses (positive or negative) while low frontal lobe activity allows the limbic regions to become more active resulting in stronger emotions. If frontal lobe activity is low during calling experiences, it might allow for very powerful emotions arising from enhanced activity in the limbic regions, a finding that has been reported in certain meditative practices (Brewer et al., 2011; Xue, Tang, & Posner, 2011).

Strong emotions usually indicate the importance of stimuli in one's environment. In the case of calling experiences, powerful emotions may signal the importance of the calling experience, helping to account for their long-lasting outcomes. Once frontal lobe function is restored, since frontal lobe activity is associated with executive functions such as future planning, such activity can evaluate the content of the calling experience, the prospective epiphany, which may or may not guide future behavior.

It should be noted again that the initiation of these different brain processes could derive from several different sources. It is possible that a pathological condition, such as a seizure, might alter brain function in such a way as to reduce frontal lobe function enough in conjunction with other above-mentioned changes to result in a calling experience. Alternatively, these circuits may be activated by specific rituals, practices, life circumstances, or spontaneously. Finally, the religious individual would argue that God or some supernatural force activates this brain activity.

CONCLUSION

The study of road to Damascus moments inevitably leads to considering the road *from* Damascus (Longenecker, 1997). That is, in addition to psychological and neurological frameworks that help us understand the experiences themselves and what triggers them, we need to know more about the empirical outcomes of calling experiences: How often do they lead to long-term meaningful work? How frequently does the content of calling experiences, prospective epiphanies or otherwise, pass a rational assessment of their value? What advice can psychology offer those who have calling experiences and wish to integrate them into their lives? Answering these questions depends on bringing experiences of calling back into mainstream scientific conversations, taking epiphanies seriously, and investigating their long-term outcomes through longitudinal studies.

The emphasis on outcomes also relates to the broader study of RSMEs—and religious and spiritual phenomena in general—which focuses on *seeking* the sacred (Pargament, 2011). Calling experiences, however, emphasize one's *response* to the sacred. We suggest that the litmus test of calling experiences and other RSMEs ought to include not only how meaningful or positive experiences are at the time they occur, but also the long-term prosocial behavior that can result. After all, it is the very dailyness of the hard work that can follow from calling experiences that makes these experiences so interesting. It was not Paul's experience on the side of the road that made him a saint - such experiences can, and often do, rise and fade within the psyche like a spark in the night - rather, it was how he responded to the experience. Paul became a saint by allowing his calling experience to set his life on fire with continuing inspiration and a life-long commitment to his ministry.

Callings often offer us a glimpse of what could be, both for ourselves as well as for society. A better scientific understanding of calling experiences may help us understand the psychological dynamics that shape the everyday saints that surround us now—the firefighters, teachers, nurses, doctors, artists, engineers, and scientists (to name just a few classic cases)—who work day in and day out to make the world a better place.

REFERENCES

Atlas, J. (2012, May 13). The amygdala made me do it. *The New York Times*, p. SR4.

Baumeister, R. F. (1991). *Meanings of life*. New York: The Guilford Press.

Baumeister, R. F., & Exline, J. J. (2002). Mystical self loss: A challenge for psychological theory. *The International Journal for the Psychology of Religion, 12*(1), 1.

Baumeister, R. F., & Vohs, K. D. (2002). The pursuit of meaningfulness in life. In C. R. Snyder & S. J. Lopez (Eds.), *The handbook of positive psychology* (pp. 608–618). New York: Oxford University Press.

Beauregard, M. (2011). Neuroscience and spirituality–findings and consequences. In *Neuroscience, consciousness and spirituality* (pp. 57–73). New York: Springer.

Bellah, R. N., Madsen, R., Sullivan, W. M., Swidler, A., & Tipton, S. M. (1985). *Habits of the heart: Individualism and commitment in American life*. New York: Harper and Row.

Berg, J. M., Grant, A. M., & Johnson, V. (2010). When callings are calling: Crafting work and leisure in pursuit of unanswered occupational callings. *Organization Science, 21*(5), 973–994.

Brewer, J. A., Worhunsky, P. D., Gray, J. R., Tang, Y. Y., Weber, J., and Kober, H. (2011). Meditation experience is associated with differences in default mode network activity and connectivity. *Proceedings of the National Academy of Sciences, 108*(50), 20254–20259.

Bunderson, J. S., & Thompson, J. A. (2009). The call of the wild: Zookeepers, callings, and the double-edged sword of deeply meaningful work. *Administrative Science Quarterly, 54*(1), 32–57.

Cardador, M. T., & Caza, B. B. (2012). Relational and identity perspectives on healthy versus unhealthy pursuit of callings. *Journal of Career Assessment, 20*(3), 338–353.

Dik, B. J., & Duffy, R. D. (2009). Calling and vocation at work: Definitions and prospects for research and practice. *The Counseling Psychologist, 37*, 424–450. doi:10.1177/0011000008316430

Dik, B. J., Duffy, R. D., & Steger, M. F. (2012). Enhancing social justice by promoting prosocial values in career development interventions. *Counseling and Values, 57*, 31–37. doi: 10.1002/j.2161–007X.2012.00005.

Dobrow, S. R., & Tosti-Kharas, J. (2011). Calling: The development of a scale measure. *Personnel Psychology, 64*(4), 1001–1049.

Duffy, R. D., & Dik, B. J. (2009). Beyond the self: External influences in the career development process. *The career development quarterly, 58*(1), 29–43.

Duffy, R. D., & Dik, B. J. (2013). Research on calling: What have we learned and where are we going?. *Journal of Vocational Behavior, 83*(3), 428–436.

Duffy, R. D., & Sedlacek, W. E. (2007). The presence of and search for a calling: Connections to career development. *Journal of Vocational Behavior, 70*(3), 590–601.

Gable, S. L., & Haidt, J. (2005). What (and why) is positive psychology?. *Review of general psychology, 9*(2), 103.

Ghiselin, B. (Ed.). (1952). *The creative process: A symposium.* New York: Mentor.

Gilbert, D. T., & Wilson, T. D. (2007). Prospection: Experiencing the future. *Science, 317*(5843), 1351–1354.

Gilovich, T., & Medvec, V. H. (1995). The experience of regret: What, when, and why. *Psychological Review, 102*(2), 379–395.

Grant, A. M., & Schwartz, B. (2011). Too much of a good thing he challenge and opportunity of the inverted U. *Perspectives on Psychological Science, 6*(1), 61–76.

Griffiths, R. R., Richards, W. A., McCann, U., & Jesse, R. (2006). Psilocybin can occasion mystical-type experiences having substantial and sustained personal meaning and spiritual significance. *Psychopharmacology, 187*(3), 268–283.

Hall, D. T., D. E. Chandler. 2005. Psychological success: When the career is a calling. *Journal of Organizational Behavior, 26*(2), 155–176.

Haidt, J., & Morris, J. P. (2009). Finding the self in self-transcendent emotions. *Proceedings of the National Academy of Sciences, 106*(19), 7687–7688.

Harrington, A. (2008). *The cure within: A history of mind-body medicine.* New York: W. W. Norton & Company.

Hood Jr., R. W. (1975). The construction and preliminary validation of a measure of reported mystical experience. *Journal for the Scientific Study of Religion,* 29–41.

Hood, R.W. (2005). Mystical, spiritual, and religious experiences. *Handbook of the psychology of religion and spirituality*, 348–364. New York: Guilford Press.

Hood Jr., R.W., Hill, P.C., & Spilka, B. (2009). *The psychology of religion: An empirical approach*. New York: Guilford Press.

Iyengar, S.S., R.E. Wells, & B. Schwartz. (2006). Doing better but feeling worse: Looking for the "best" job undermines satisfaction. *Psychological Science, 17*(2), 143–150.

James, W. (1902/1985). *The varieties of religious experience*. Harvard University Press.

Jaynes, J. (1976). *The origin of consciousness in the breakdown of the bicameral mind*. New York: Mariner Books.

Jung, C.G. (1938/1966). *Psychology and religion*. Yale University Press: New Haven, CT.

Jung, C. G. (2012). *The red book: A reader's edition*. New York: W.W Norton & Company.

Jung-Beeman, M., Bowden, E.M., Haberman, J., Frymiare, J.L., Arambel-Liu, S., Greenblatt, R., Reber, P.J., & Kounios, J. (2004). Neural activity when people solve verbal problems with insight. *PLoS Biology, 2*(4), e97.

Kahneman, D., & Tversky, A. (Eds.). (2000). *Choices, values, and frames*. New York: Cambridge University Press.

Karnath, H.O., Ferber, S., & Himmelbach, M. (2001). Spatial awareness is a function of the temporal not the posterior parietal lobe. *Nature, 411*, 950–953.

Keltner, D., & Haidt, J. (2003). Approaching awe, a moral, spiritual, and aesthetic emotion. *Cognition & Emotion, 17*(2), 297–314.

Landsborough, D. (1987). St Paul and temporal lobe epilepsy. *Journal of Neurology, Neurosurgery & Psychiatry, 50*(6), 659–664.

Lazar, S.W., Bush, G., Gollub, R.L., Fricchione, G.L., Khalsa, G., & Benson, H. (2000). Functional brain mapping of the relaxation response and meditation. *Neuroreport, 11*(7), 1581–1585.

Longenecker, R. N. (Ed.). (1997). *The road from Damascus: The impact of Paul's conversion on his life, thought, and ministry*. Grand Rapids, MI: William B. Eerdmans Publishing.

Lukoff, D., Lu, F., & Turner, R. (1992). Toward a more culturally sensitive DSM-IV: Psychoreligious and psychospiritual problems. *Journal of Nervous and Mental Disease, 180*(11), 673–682.

Luther, M. (1883). Werke Kritische Gesamtausgabe. Weimar: Hermann Bohlaus.

Maslow, A.H. (1964). *Religions, values, and peak-experiences*. Columbus: Ohio State University Press.

McKenna, T. (1992, June 15). The Camden Centre Talk.

Newberg, A.B., Alavi, A., Baime, M., Pourdehnad, M., Santanna, J., & d'Aquili, E. (2001). The measurement of regional cerebral blood flow during the complex cognitive task of meditation: a preliminary SPECT study. *Psychiatry Research: Neuroimaging, 106*(2), 113–122.

Newberg, A.B., & d'Aquili, E.G. (1994). The near death experience as archetype: A model for "prepared" neurocognitive processes. *Anthropology of Consciousness, 5*, 1–15.

Newberg, A., & d'Aquili, E. G. (2008). *Why God won't go away: Brain science and the biology of belief.* New York: Random House LLC.

Newberg, A. B., & Iversen, J. (2003). The neural basis of the complex mental task of meditation: Neurotransmitter and neurochemical considerations. *Medical Hypothesis, 61*(2), 282–291.

Newberg, A. B., Pourdehnad, M., Alavi, A., & d'Aquili, E. (2003). Cerebral blood flow during meditative prayer: Preliminary findings and methodological issues. *Perceptual and Motor Skills, 97,* 625–630. Newberg, A., Wintering, N. A., Morgan, D., & Waldman, M. R. (2006). The measurement of regional cerebral blood flow during glossolalia: A preliminary SPECT study. *Psychiatric Research: Neuroimaging, 148*(1), 67–71.

Novak, M. (1996). *Business as a calling: Work and the examined life.* New York: Free Press.

Otto, R. (1958). *The idea of the holy* (Vol. 14). Oxford University Press.

Pargament, K. I. (2011). *Spiritually integrated psychotherapy: Understanding and addressing the sacred.* Guilford, CT: Guilford Press.

Pawelski, J. O. (2012). The dynamic individualism of William James. SUNY Press.

Peres, J., Moreira-Almeida, A., Caixeta, L., Leao, F., & Newberg, A. B. (2012). Neuroimaging during trance state: A contribution to the study of dissociation. *PLOS ONE 7*(11):e49360. doi: 10.1371/journal.pone.0049360

Peterson, C., Park, N., Hall, N., & Seligman, M. E. (2009). Zest and work. *Journal of Organizational Behavior, 30*(2), 161–172.

Russell, B. (1959). *Mysticism and logic.* London: Allen and Unwin.

Sacks, O. W. (2012). *Hallucinations.* New York: Pan Macmillan.

Saver, J. L., & Rabin, J. (1997). The neural substrates of religious experience. *The Journal of Neuropsychiatry and Clinical Neurosciences, 9*(3), 498.

Schwartz, B. (1986). *The battle for human nature: Science, morality, and modern life.* New York: Norton.

Seligman, M. E., & Csikszentmihalyi, M. (2000). *Positive psychology: An introduction* (Vol. 55, No. 1, p. 5). : New York: American Psychological Association.

Seligman, M. E., Railton, P., Baumeister, R. F., & Sripada, C. (2013). Navigating into the future or driven by the past. *Perspectives on Psychological Science, 8*(2), 119–141.

Sperry, R. (1964). The great cerebral commissure. *Scientific American, 210,* 42.

Steger, M. F., & Dik, B. J. (2009). If one is looking for meaning in life, does it help to find meaning in work?. *Applied Psychology: Health and Well-Being, 1*(3), 303–320.

Steger, M. F., Pickering, N., Shin, J. Y., & Dik, B. J. (2010). Calling in work: Secular or sacred? *Journal of Career Assessment, 18,* 82–96.

Stip, E., & Letourneau, G. (2009). Psychotic symptoms as a continuum between normality and pathology. *Canadian Journal of Psychiatry, 54*(3), 140–151.

Urgesi, C., Aglioti, S. M., Skrap, M., & Fabbro, F. (2010). The spiritual brain: selective cortical lesions modulate human self-transcendence. *Neuron, 65*(3), 309–319.

Wallas, G. (1976). Stages in the creative process. In A. Rothenberg & C. R. Hausman (Eds.), *The creativity question.* Durham, NC: Duke University Press.

Weber, M. (1930). *The Protestant ethic and the spirit of capitalism.* T. Parsons, trans. London: Routledge Classics.

Wrzesniewski, A. (2003). Finding positive meaning in work. *Positive Organizational Scholarship*, 296–308.

Wrzesniewski, A., McCauley, C., Rozin, P., & Schwartz, B. (1997). Jobs, careers, and callings: People's relations to their work. *Journal of Research in Personality, 31*(1), 21–33.

Xue, S., Tang, Y. Y., & Posner, M. I. (2011). Short-term meditation increases network efficiency of the anterior cingulate cortex. *NeuroReport, 22*(12), 570–574.

Yaden, D. B., Anderson, D. E., Mattar, M. G., & Newberg, A. B. (2015). Psychoactive stimulation & psychoactive substances: Conceptual and ethical considerations. In J. H. Ellens (Ed.) *The psychedelic policy quagmire: Health, law, freedom, and society.* New York: Praeger.

Yaden, D. B., & Newberg, A. B. (2014). A new means for perennial ends: Self-transcendent experiences and non-invasive brain stimulation. In J. H. Ellens (Ed.), *Seeking the sacred with psychoactive substances.* New York: Praeger.

CHAPTER 4

NEUROPSYCHOLOGICAL AND PERSONOLOGICAL ASPECTS OF SPIRITUALITY

Cristiano Crescentini, Cosimo Urgesi, and Franco Fabbro

INTRODUCTION: DEFINITION AND MEASUREMENT OF SPIRITUALITY AND BASIC NEUROPSYCHOLOGICAL CORRELATES

In recent decades, there has been a growing interest in the study of spirituality and religiousness in the context of cognitive neuroscience. Regardless of the diversity of cultural backgrounds and faith traditions, humans appear to be naturally driven to seek a religious or spiritual dimension in life. Most of the world's population hold religious or spiritual kinds beliefs, and report a subjective feeling of their presence (Zuckerman, 2005; Inzlicht et al., 2009). In line with this interest, recent studies in evolutionary psychology have tried to explain the presence of religious and spiritual beliefs and behaviors in many different cultures (Boyer, 2001; Wilson, 2002; Dennett, 2006).

In this chapter, we will discuss religiousness and spirituality (hereafter RS) as a single construct, although we are aware that the two concepts are at least partially independent (Fuller, 2001; Emmons and Paloutzian, 2003). While spirituality may be viewed as inherent to the concept of religion, and most people do describe themselves as both religious and spiritual, religiousness is often defined as more related to institutions and faith traditions and spirituality as more subjective and experience based, having more to do with one's personal relationships to transcendent realities (Wuthnow, 1998; Emmons and Paloutzian, 2003; Zinnbauer and Pargament, 2005; Piedmont et al., 2009).

We consider RS a multidimensional construct including complex and varied neuropsychological processes such as the thoughts, subjective feelings,

and behaviors that reflect the ultimate concerns of people in relation to unseen realities/supernatural agents and transcendent contexts (Emmons and
Paloutzian, 2003; Zinnbauer and Pargament, 2005; Kapuscinski and Masters, 2010). It has been argued that an important component of RS may be
associated with transcendental representations of the self. In particular, the
reduced awareness of self-other boundaries that often accompanies RS states
may lead to experiences of detachment of the self from the spatiotemporal
contingencies of the physical body together with increased feelings of connectedness with a larger reality and with religious or spiritual power (Paloutzian and Park, 2005; Fuller, 2008). Changes in complex self-awareness and
feelings of connection to something larger than the self also accompany experiences of calling that includes sudden spiritual epiphanies, visions, and
varieties of profound numinous experiences (Fabbro, 2010).

Although RS behaviors are ubiquitous phenomena in many people's lives,
individuals differ in their inherent predispositions to spiritual thinking and
feelings. Such differences shape aspects of character and personality, particularly a dimension of which seems indeed concerned with self-transcendence
(Cloninger et al., 1993, 1994; see next section for details). Interindividual differences in RS may consist of explicit representations of the self, such as attitudes that are available to our conscious thinking and intentional reasoning
and hence can be measured with self-report RS-related questionnaires. RS
also involves more automatic, possibly unconscious, intuitive evaluations and
feelings that shape implicit RS self-attitude and that can be assessed for instance by measuring automatic associations between the self and RS-related
concepts (e.g., Crescentini et al., 2014a; LaBouff et al., 2010; see next section).

In recent years, these phenomena have been considered amenable to scientific investigation. Some of this research was motivated by mounting evidence showing positive associations between practicing a spiritual/religious
life and mental health, in terms of better mood, psychological well-being,
perceived subjective happiness, life satisfaction, prosocial behaviors, and reduced levels of stress (e.g., Pichon et al., 2007; Borg et al., 2003; Cobb et al.,
2012). Researchers have also investigated the neurocognitive basis of RS beliefs, experiences, and practices by using in particular prayer and meditation
experiences and self-report questionnaires. Thus, a number of studies have
been conducted on people of different faiths as well as experts in different
forms of meditation or on people judging their RS beliefs through a number
of self-report questionnaires (Sudsuang et al., 1991; Lazar et al., 2000; Azari
et al., 2001; Newberg et al., 2001; Boyer, 2003; Newberg and Iversen, 2003;
Turner et al., 2003; Kaasinen et al., 2005; Beauregard and Paquette, 2006;
Cahn and Polich, 2006; Yamamoto et al., 2006; Brefczynski-Lewis et al.,
2007; Lutz et al., 2008; Fingelkurts and Fingelkurts, 2009; Harris et al.,
2009; Kapogiannis et al., 2009a, 2009b; Schjoedt et al., 2009). Globally, these

studies have also tried to correlate RS with more objective physiological parameters (e.g., heart rate, respiratory rate, blood pressure, oxygen metabolism, hormonal changes) and neurobiological changes measured through a
variety of techniques such as electroencephalography (EEG), magnetoen-
cephalography (MEG), functional (functional magnetic resonance imaging,
fMRI; positron emission tomography, PET; single photon emission computed
tomography, SPECT) and structural (e.g., voxel-based morphometry) imaging analyses (for an overall review of these methods applied to the study of
spirituality and meditation see Newberg, 2014; Fingelkurts and Fingelkurts,
2009; Cahn and Polich, 2006). Of particular importance, this last set of studies investigating the neurobiological correlates of RS has indicated that a
large cortical and subcortical brain network, including prefrontal, temporal
and parietal regions, is involved in RS.

Taken in sum, these studies suggest that RS beliefs and feelings involve a
complex network of neural systems and mental faculties such as, social exchange, moral intuitions, intentional agency and animacy, and understanding
of human misfortune (Boyer, 2003). On this view, increased frontal lobe activity may reflect the intense attentional processes required for meditation/
prayer (Newberg et al., 2001, 2003). Moreover, the often reported relationship between decreased parietal lobe activity and increased RS beliefs and experiences (e.g., Herzog et al., 1990; Newberg et al., 2001, 2003; Newberg and
Iversen, 2003; Brefczynski-Lewis et al., 2007; Tomasino et al., 2013) has been
interpreted as linking the altered or extended sense of awareness of the self
in space, which often accompanies RS experiences, with the basic involvement
of the posterior parietal cortex in self-awareness and in the representation of
bodily knowledge (e.g., Berlucchi and Aglioti, 2010; Previc, 2006).

Despite their value, these previous studies on RS using brain imaging measures cannot explain whether the structural and functional brain
changes during RS experiences, feelings, and beliefs causally determine individual prayer- and meditation-related states of consciousness (or changes in
RS questionnaires) or are epiphenomenal to them. Moreover, cross-sectional,
nonlongitudinal brain imaging studies cannot easily speak to the issue of
how fast personality traits related to RS can be shaped by practices, such as
meditation, are able to modify higher-order self-awareness. The next section
reviews the results of studies that provided crucial information on the causative link between specific neural structures and RS beliefs and feelings. To
this end, we will review evidence showing modifications of explicit RS attitudes (measured with self-reported RS-related questionnaires), and eventually implicit RS attitudes (measured with RS-related implicit association
tests), induced by "fast" brain plasticity phenomena occurring in frontal and
parietal brain regions from either brain lesion in patients or transcranial
magnetic brain stimulation (TMS).

NEUROPSYCHOLOGY OF SPIRITUALITY: EVIDENCE FROM BRAIN-DAMAGED PATIENTS AND BRAIN STIMULATION OF HEALTHY INDIVIDUALS

Evidence for changes in RS beliefs and behaviors has been reported in several populations of brain lesion patients with different pathologies, such as frontotemporal dementia (Miller et al., 2001), epilepsy (Devinsky and Lai, 2008; Tedrus et al., 2014), Parkinson's disease (McNamara et al., 2006; Butler et al., 2010, 2011a, 2011b; Giaquinto et al., 2011), and traumatic brain injury (TBI; Johnstone and Glass, 2008; Johnstone et al., 2012). Overall, the neuropsychological data confirm that RS is supported by extended brain networks, including prefrontal, temporal, and parietal regions. Nonetheless, research has identified regions that seem to play specific roles in critical aspects of RS beliefs, feelings, and behaviors. Research on epileptic patients and traumatic brain injury (TBI) patients has suggested that the temporal lobe and the limbic system are critical regions for the generation of emotionally intense RS experiences, including those accompanied by the perception of religious archetypes (symbols and figures) (e.g., Devinsky and Lai, 2008; Johnstone and Glass, 2008). Moreover, it has been argued that alterations in frontal lobe functions contribute to changing interests in RS values, convictions, and experiences (Miller et al., 2001; Devinsky and Lai, 2008). Thus, in a study with 20 TBI patients, Johnstone et al. (2012) found positive correlations between increased frontal lobe functioning (measured with the trail making test) and increased RS practices and experiences as measured by the brief multidimensional measure of RS (BMMRS). Similarly, in a series of studies on individuals with Parkinson's disease (e.g., Butler et al., 2010; see also McNamara et al., 2006), it was proposed that decreased striatal-prefrontal network functioning is associated with a reduced ability to activate "religious concepts."

With regard to the parietal lobe, the studies by Johnstone et al. (2012) and Johnstone and Glass (2008) using neuropsychological testing in TBI patients reported correlations between measures of decreased right parietal lobe functioning (judgment of line orientation test) and increased spiritual transcendence as measured by the index of core spiritual experiences (Inspirit) and BMMRS. In line with the findings from neuroimaging studies briefly reviewed above, these results were held to reflect increased transcendental experiences (e.g., an increased sense of unity over diversity or of a universal connectedness) as due to decreasing self-awareness after right parietal lobe dysfunction.

Although exceptionally interesting and valuable, these studies were conducted on small groups of patients, and, most critically, did not provide any direct information about the prelesional personality and/or RS profiles of the patients. Recently, Urgesi et al. (2010) combined advanced lesion-mapping procedures with the analysis of self-transcendence (ST) scores obtained before and after brain surgery in patients affected by brain tumors. In this study, we used the ST scale of the temperament and character inventory (TCI; Cloninger et al., 1993, 1994), a well-known psychobiological model of personality, to measure interindividual differences in spiritual thinking and feeling. ST reflects the supposedly stable predisposition to transcend contingent sensorimotor representations and to identify the self as an integral part of the universe as a whole. Different aspects of transcendental self-awareness are captured by three ST subscales which evaluate creative self-forgetfulness versus self-conscious experience, transpersonal identification versus personal identification, and spiritual acceptance versus rational materialism.

The approach used by Urgesi et al. (2010) thus allowed exploring the neural underpinnings of personality dimensions related to RS, namely ST. We expected that differences in this dimension could be measured in the same patients both before and soon after surgical ablation of tissue in specific brain regions. This design provided the opportunity to study the causative role of specific brain regions, such as frontal and temporoparietal structures, in changes to ST. In this study, Urgesi et al. (2010) assessed a large group of patients with brain tumors of varying severity: 24 patients with high-grade malignant glioma, 24 patients with low-grade malignant glioma, 20 patients with recurrent malignant glioma, and 20 patients with benign tumor (meningioma). Patients were chosen so that tumors were located in equal number in anterior or in posterior brain regions of the left and right hemispheres. Based on the notion that RS seems to be modulated by changes of neural activity in specific cortical regions (see above in this and in the previous section), it was hypothesized that selective damage to the frontal and temporoparietal areas could be associated respectively with a decrease and an increase of ST scores.

In line with these expectations, the results showed a significant increase of the ST scores (equally involving all the three subscales) only after removal of brain tumors in the left inferior parietal lobe or the right angular gyrus in the parietal lobe. In particular, while for the high-grade tumors the increase of ST in patients with tumors affecting the posterior brain areas was already evident before the intervention, in the low-grade tumors ST scores increased only after removal of the tumor. Contrary to predictions, there were no significant results concerning tumors affecting the frontal lobe regions. Moreover, no ST change was observed after removal of benign tumors that spare the nervous tissue (i.e., meningioma), thus indicating that the surgical procedure per se did not affect the level of self-transcendence; yet, the fast changes of ST induced by posterior cortical ablation appeared long lasting as posterior recurrent glioma patients showed increased ST scores both before and after the second operation, which could occur several months after the first one.

The brain structures associated with increased ST scores in Urgesi et al. (2010) were very close to a critical area for the representation of the body and the self, namely the temporoparietal junction (TPJ; Blanke et al., 2005). This structure has been previously associated with out-of-body experience (OBE) in patients with epilepsy (Blanke et al., 2002; Arzy et al., 2006). More generally, the reviewed neuropsychological studies suggest that some structures of the parietal lobe (inferior parietal lobule, angular gyrus, TPJ), in particular of the right hemisphere, are critically associated to RS experiences and with the mystical and ecstatic experiences described in patients with focal epilepsy (Devinsky and Lai, 2008; Fabbro, 2010).

The studies of the neural basis of RS performed so far in healthy subjects or in brain-damaged patients have a series of limitations. On the one hand, as already mentioned, the studies that have used brain imaging techniques (PET, fMRI, and SPECT) cannot easily distinguish whether changes of brain activity associated with RS beliefs and experiences are causally involved in such beliefs and experiences. On the other hand, many of these studies employed self-report questionnaires to measure RS attitudes, thus overlooking the fact that such explicit measures are clearly subjective in nature and susceptible to desirable responding (Schwarz, 1999; LaBouff et al., 2010). Third, with regards to studies on brain damage patients, it should be noted that RS changes may occur, as in Urgesi et al. (2010), after very invasive manipulations (brain surgery for tumor removal).

Recently, we have tried to solve these problems by conducting two studies in which we combined TMS with a more objective, implicit measure of RS, with the aim to assess the causal role of specific brain regions (right and left inferior parietal lobe, IPL, and dorsolateral prefrontal cortex, DLPFC) in producing fast changes (i.e., short-term plasticity) of RS self-representations (Crescentini et al., 2014a; Crescentini et al., under review). Indeed, TMS is a noninvasive procedure that allows one to interfere with neural activity in highly specific brain regions in order to establish the causal role of such regions in a given task (Walsh and Pascual-Leone, 2003). TMS also overcomes some of the problems of patient studies, such as the large extent of naturally occurring lesions or the potential differences in patients' premorbid status. Moreover, we employed an RS Implicit Association Test (IAT) to measure implicit RS (Greenwald et al., 1998; LaBouff et al., 2010). Generally speaking, through reaction time and accuracy performance in an IAT, individuals' implicit attitudes can be indirectly inferred. The IAT is one of the most commonly used implicit tests that, through a word categorization task, allow measuring the strength of automatic concept-attribute associations that could underlie specific aspects of implicit personality self-concepts such as RS (Schnabel et al., 2008; LaBouff et al., 2010; Crescentini et al., 2014a). Relative to self-report questionnaire used to measure explicit attitudes (e.g., the ST scale of the TCI), implicit tests do not require the intent to self-evaluate or self-reflection on the part of the respondent and thus are usually more difficult to fake or to control. In our studies, the RS-IAT allowed measuring the strength of automatic concept-attribute associations between two distinct groups of words that were or were not related to RS dimensions and words referring to the concept of self versus other. In other words, the RS-IAT allowed us to infer people's implicit attitudes toward RS. That is, the varying levels with which people automatically perceive the self as more religious/spiritual than nonreligious/nonspiritual.

In the first study (Crescentini et al., 2014a), we examined responses to the RS-IAT (and to a control IAT measuring participants' implicit self-esteem, SE-IAT) in 24 young healthy subjects while they received two pulses of TMS (paired-pulse TMS: a type of stimulation known to transiently disrupt the activity of the stimulated regions) in the right or left DLPFC and in the right or left IPL. In the second study (Crescentini et al., under review), 14 different young healthy participants performed the same IAT tasks right after having undergone, in three separate sessions, inhibitory, excitatory and sham theta burst stimulation (TBS) over the right IPL, a series of stimulation paradigms known to, respectively, inhibit, enhance, and leave unaltered the excitability level of the stimulated region (Huang et al., 2005). Strikingly, the overall results confirmed the previous data obtained in neuropsychological patients. Indeed, in the first study we found that TMS interfering with (disrupting) right or left IPL functioning increased subjects' implicit RS; in the second study we found a specific decrease of implicit RS induced by increasing right IPL excitability with excitatory TBS.

Overall, these results showed that neural activity in IPL regions is a central neurophysiological substrate of implicit RS. In particular, together with the patient studies, the data suggest that fast alteration in parietal lobe functions may lead individuals to experience an extended self-awareness in which the self is projected into dimensions that transcend sensorimotor contingencies of the body and more easily connected with things beyond the self.

EFFECTS OF MINDFULNESS MEDITATION ON EXPLICIT AND IMPLICIT INDEXES OF PERSONALITY AND SPIRITUALITY CHANGES

Despite the existence of multiple forms of religious/spiritual practices, each related to specific faith and cultural traditions, for the last two or three decades cognitive neuroscience and psychology studies have paid particular attention to the practice of meditation to investigate the neurocognitive mechanisms of self-transcendence and RS. Thus, it has been argued that meditation practice (and in particular mindfulness meditation, MM) favors the development of spiritual components such as interconnectedness, boundlessness, ultimacy, and self-transcendence (Falb and Pargament, 2012; see also Vago and Silbersweig, 2012; Berkovich-Ohana et al., 2013).

Many different forms of meditation, which are often used to cultivate physical and psychological well-being (Lutz et al., 2008), originated several centuries BCE in India, in the context of the Hinduism and Buddhism spiritual and healing traditions. Recent empirical evidence has confirmed the existence of a close link between meditation and spirituality. Most forms of meditation that have taken root in the West in the last 30 years have been generally applied in secular clinical and nonclinical contexts; despite this, it has been suggested that they may provide secular ways for people to realize greater spiritual growth and spiritual well-being, in particular the cultivation of a sense of peace and inner meaning (Carmody et al., 2008). One of the most common types of meditation practices is MM, a form of mental training that has been defined as a way of intentionally paying attention to present moment experience with a nonjudgmental attitude of openness and receptivity (Kabat-Zinn, 1990; Brown and Ryan, 2003; Lutz et al., 2008; for reviews on the health effects of MM see Baer, 2003; Didonna, 2009; Chiesa and Serretti, 2010; see also Fabbro and Crescentini, 2014). However, it should be noted that there has been less empirical research on the relationship between MM and spirituality compared to the many other areas whereby the effects of this practice have been documented (e.g., the effects of MM on attention and emotion regulation, Baer, 2010). It has recently been shown that participation in MM training can lead to increases in explicit measures of spirituality and to increased daily spiritual experiences and, more importantly, that spirituality is a crucial mechanism by which MM leads to improvements in medical and psychological symptoms (Carmody et al., 2008; Geary and Rosenthal, 2011; Greeson et al., 2011; Falb and Pargament, 2012).

More generally, in reference to personality dimensions, several recent empirical studies reinforce the idea that MM has great potential in personal development and in leading to positive changes in the way one experiences and faces life events (Kabat-Zinn, 1990). Some of these studies have used well-known self-report (explicit) personality inventories such as the big-five model (e.g., Costa and McCrae, 1992) and the TCI (Cloninger et al., 1994) to investigate the relationship between personality and MM practice or dispositional mindfulness skills (also assessed through self-report questionnaires such as the Five Facet Mindfulness Questionnaire, FFMQ, Baer et al., 2006, measuring the abilities to act with awareness, to describe, not to react, not to judge, and to observe one's own present moment internal experience; for review see Crescentini and Capurso, 2015). With regards to the relationship between the personality traits included in the big-five model (i.e., conscientiousness, agreeableness, extraversion, openness-to-experience, and neuroticism) and mindfulness skills, for example, a recent meta-analysis (Giluk, 2009) involving 29 studies showed that mindfulness skills positively correlate with conscientiousness (the tendency to be organized, efficient and to show high self-discipline) and positive affect but negatively with neuroticism (tendency toward worrying, moodiness, anxiety, and impulsiveness) and negative affect.

Other recent studies have focused on the impact exerted on personality by regular MM practice, rather than by mindfulness skills (Crescentini and Capurso, 2015). This was done both in cross-sectional studies in which individuals with different levels of meditation expertise underwent personality assessment (e.g., Haimerl and Valentine, 2001; van den Hurk et al., 2011) or in longitudinal studies in which personality was measured in the same subjects both before and after a MM training (Campanella et al., 2014; for a similar study see Crescentini et al., in press). For instance, Campanella et al. (2014) administered the TCI to three groups of meditation-naïve healthy individuals both before and after participation in an 8-week MM training; a control group not involved in meditation was also tested. Remarkably, we found increased scores in all three character scales of the TCI (self-directedness, cooperativeness, and self-transcendence) after MM training, specifically in those meditator groups whose participants practiced MM more regularly during the training (i.e., at least 4–5 days per week). In the TCI framework, the character scales refer to one's own self-evaluation and measure the maturity of the self respectively at the intrapersonal (linked to concepts such as self-esteem and self-efficacy), interpersonal (related to the capacity to be empathic, tolerant and compassionate), and transpersonal (linked to spirituality and creativeness) levels. Higher scores in the character scales are associated to a lower risk of personality disorder (Svrakic et al., 1993).

Overall, the reviewed studies on MM and personality suggest that this practice may lead to positive changes in individuals' self-concept and character. In particular, it has been proposed that such changes could be favored by a mindfulness-related increased ability to detach from a constant and unchanging sense of self, which instead starts to be experienced as a transitory entity (Hölzel et al., 2011; Campanella et al., 2014; Crescentini and Capurso, 2015). The process of disidentification from a static sense of self is a crucial aspect of mindful awareness that would give MM practitioners the possibility to better objectify and accept their own momentary internal experience, which, in turn, could help them to experience more authentic ways of being (Hölzel et al., 2011). Of importance, recent functional imaging studies have identified the putative neurofunctional signatures of the mindfulness-related increased ability to detach from a static sense of self. In particular, during MM states, this ability is associated with diminished self-referential and autobiographical processing paired with enhanced present-based, experiential processing of the self. In the brain, this may mean decreased activity in self-referential cortical midline structures, such as medial prefrontal cortex and posterior cingulate cortex/precuneus, and enhanced activity in lateral structures such as the insula and the somatosensory cortex associated more with a momentary analysis of exteroceptive (sensitivity to stimuli originating outside of the body) and interoceptive (sensitivity to stimuli originating inside of the body) sensory events (Farb et al., 2007; see also Hölzel et al., 2011 and Tomasino et al., 2013).

Most of the past research linking MM and personality/spirituality has made use of only explicit measures, thus overlooking the contribution of more objective, performance-based, implicit measures. However, a number of studies exist that investigated the impact of MM practice or mindfulness skills on implicit self-representations (Brown and Ryan, 2003; Levesque and Brown, 2007; Koole et al., 2009; Sauer et al., 2011). In particular, the psychological constructs of implicit self-esteem, motivation, and affective states have been considered in these studies (for a review of these and other relevant researches see Crescentini and Capurso, 2015 and Crescentini et al., 2014b).

Attempts to link the fields of mindfulness and implicit cognition are particularly important. MM is generally believed to promote self-insights and greater reliance and acceptance of one's own internal states including intuitive feelings and thus it is reasonable to predict an effect of this practice on implicit cognition (Brown and Ryan, 2003; Koole et al., 2009). With these studies it is possible to test whether MM contributes to promote a more coherent, integrated self-representation, in which explicit and implicit self-attitudes become better tuned with each other. This is reasonable, considering that when people's implicit and explicit sources of self-evaluative tendencies, namely evaluations based respectively on intuitive, possibly unconscious, feelings and on well-articulated rational beliefs and motivations, are largely incongruent, different forms of psychological suffering may be experienced (Gawronski and Bodenhausen, 2006; Jordan et al., 2007; Koole et al., 2009; Crescentini et al., 2014b).

Some of the studies investigating the relationship between dispositional mindfulness or MM practice and personality using implicit measures, also focused on the possible congruency between implicit and explicit self-representations (see Crescentini and Capurso, 2015). For instance, Brown and Ryan (2003) found that dispositional mindfulness (measured with the Mindful Attention Awareness Scale, MAAS) predicted concordance between explicit and implicit affect, where the latter was measured with an IAT for emotional well-being and the former with self-report measures. More specifically, a closer relation between implicit and explicit affective states was found in meditation-naïve individuals showing high versus low MAAS scores. Similarly, some years later, Koole et al. (2009) extended these findings to self-esteem and MM practice and reported greater congruence between implicit (name-letter preference task) and explicit (self-report measures) self-esteem in healthy young participants executing brief MM exercises before versus after being tested for the two types of self-esteem.

Finally, more recently we went a step further by showing that regular MM practice during an 8-week MM training may have an impact on both implicit (RS-IAT previously discussed in the TMS study by Crescentini et al., 2014a) and explicit (e.g., ST scale of the TCI) individuals' RS self-representations (Crescentini et al., 2014b). We also showed that implicit and explicit RS tended to change (i.e., increase) congruently after versus before the MM training. In particular, we interpreted these findings by suggesting that MM may lead to reduced identification with one's own static sense of self, an experience that could foster in the practitioner's intuitive feelings of an extended self, including feelings of connection with nature and other individuals at large or a sense of relationship with a transcendent power (Crescentini et al., 2014b; see Baer, 2010).

From a neuropsychological point of view, the effects on implicit and explicit RS and self-transcendence brought about by MM may relate to alterations in the activity in brain regions, such as the TPJ or the inferior parietal cortex, related to the sense of self and to perception of the regular bodily boundaries (Berkovich-Ohana et al., 2013; Dor-Ziderman et al., 2013).

More generally, the reviewed studies on MM and implicit self-attitudes indicate that mindfulness may promote changes in deeper, implicit feelings and self-concepts and may allow explicit and implicit self-representations to become better integrated with each other. This suggests that this practice fulfills significant self-regulatory functions and may critically shape individuals' personality, possibly contributing to a more coherent and authentic sense of self and identity. MM practice could thus help people following the pull toward particular life paths that align with their implicit and explicit personal strengths and authentic passions.

CONCLUSIONS

We discussed data obtained from neuroscience studies about the complex issue of religiousness/spirituality. Despite the heterogeneity of the tests, practices, and brain investigation methods, the results show that a wide network of fronto-temporo-parietal areas is involved in both RS states and traits. Within this complex brain network, many studies have shown that altered neural activity in parietal regions is a crucial neurophysiological substrate of RS. More specifically, a number of studies in brain-damaged patients (e.g., Johnstone and Glass, 2008; Urgesi et al., 2010) or in healthy individuals undergoing neurostimulation of parietal regions (Crescentini et al., 2014a; Crescentini et al., under review) have found that modifications of brain activity in these brain areas may lead to unusually fast modulations of supposedly stable personality traits related to RS and transcendental self-awareness. As we have discussed, this may be linked to the basic involvement of the parietal lobe structures in bodily self-representation (Berlucchi and Aglioti, 2010).

That some supposedly stable personality traits related to ST and RS are more malleable than previously believed, undergoing fast plastic changes, was supported by the studies reviewed here. We also reviewed evidence of a direct role of dispositional, everyday mindfulness or MM practice, in promoting changes in personality in general and in RS dimensions more in particular. Thus, despite the increasingly common trend followed in the West to secularize the practice of meditation by positioning it outside of specific religious/spiritual traditions, the reviewed studies highlight the existence of a close link between meditation and spirituality. This may promote further explorations of the spiritual growth and spiritual commitment components of meditation. This will help to foster our knowledge both of the positive effects on individuals' psychological health arising from MM practice and of the fundamental psychological mediators that underpin the therapeutic effects of mindfulness-based interventions.

We reported evidence pointing to a role of MM in influencing implicit, as well as explicit, self-referential representations and in promoting congruency between these two forms of self-evaluative tendencies. These results would carry out the fundamental implications that some forms of mental training, such as MM, may be crucial for developing a more authentic and healthy self-view in which implicit, deep motivations and feelings come to be better integrated into more conscious, explicit feelings, motivations, and goals. Crucially, this may suggest that forms of meditation such as MM could lead people to rely more on their feelings or beliefs about being called to a particular path or vocation in life.

Different forms of mental trainings or alterations of neural activity in different brain regions may impact different aspects of RS (for the relationship between meditation and different aspects of RS such as meaning and inner peace see Crescentini et al., 2014b; Carmody et al., 2008; Baer, 2010). In particular, we have focused on a RS dimension that emphasizes the transcendental representations of the self that may be experienced in case of temporary alterations of neural activity in parietal regions or during MM practice (Crescentini et al., 2014b). Nevertheless, it is recommended that further research both on the brain basis of personality dimensions related to RS and on the links between MM and spirituality will continue to benefit from both explicit and implicit measures. This research should try at the same time to devise and use more fine-grained separate measures of religiousness and spirituality that will allow tapping on different aspects of these multifaceted constructs (e.g., spiritual-acceptance vs. transpersonal identification).

We hope future investigations will continue to study individuals with different religious and cultural traditions or with expertise in different forms of spiritual practices. In fact, there is increasing evidence that religious and cultural backgrounds or different spiritual practices can importantly shape the neurocognitive bases of self-representation as well as the way one experiences self-transcendence (e.g., Chiao et al., 2010; Han et al., 2008, 2010; Tomasino et al., 2014; see also Crescentini et al., 2014a).

Studies on the neuropsychological bases of religion and spirituality remain neutral with respect to the possible purpose of their object of study. The target of their investigation concerns a cognitive dimension of human beings that is ubiquitously present in all human cultures. The importance of the religious and spiritual dimensions at the political, psychological, and clinical levels led us and many other researchers around the world to extend the neuroscientific and psychological research to a highly complex and disputed field, but also very interesting and useful to a better understanding of how the brain represents the self.

ACKNOWLEDGMENTS

This research was supported by grants from the Mind and Life Institute (Mind and Life Contemplative Fellowship 2012-04-001, to FF and CU). CC was supported by a post-doctoral research fellowship funded by the University of Udine.

REFERENCES

Arzy, S., Seeck, M., Ortigue, S., Spinelli, L., Blanke, O. (2006). Induction of an illusory shadow person. *Nature*, 443, 287.

Azari, N. P., Nickel, J., Wunderlich, G., Niedeggen, M., Hefter, H., Tellmann, L., et al. (2001). Neural correlates of religious experience. *European Journal of Neuroscience*, 13, 1649–1652.

Baer, R. A. (2003). Mindfulness training as a clinical intervention: A conceptual and empirical review. *Clinical Psychology: Science and Practice*, 10, 125–143.

Baer, R. A. (2010). *Assessing mindfulness and acceptance processes in clients: Illuminating the theory and practice of change*. Oakland, CA: New Harbinger Publications Inc.

Baer, R. A., Smith, G. T., Hopkins, J., Krietemeyer, J., Toney, L. (2006). Using self-report assessment methods to explore facets of mindfulness. *Assessment*, 13, 27–45.

Beauregard, M., Paquette, V. (2006). Neural correlates of a mystical experience in Carmelite nuns. *Neuroscience Letters*, 405, 186–190.

Berkovich-Ohana, A., Dor-Ziderman, Y., Glicksohn, J., Goldstein, A. (2013). Alterations in the sense of time, space, and body in the mindfulness-trained brain: a neurophenomenologically-guided MEG study. *Frontiers in Psychology*, 4, 912.

Berlucchi, G., Aglioti, S. (2010). The body in the brain revisited. *Experimental Brain Research*, 200, 25–35.

Blanke, O., Mohr, C., Michel, C.M., Pascual-Leone, A., Brugger, P., Seeck, M., et al. (2005). Linking out-of-body experience and self processing to mental own-body imagery at the temporoparietal junction. *Journal of Neuroscience*, 25, 550–557.

Blanke, O., Ortigue, S., Landis, T., Seeck, M. (2002). Stimulating illusory own-body perceptions. *Nature*, 419, 269–270.

Borg, J., Andree, B., Soderstrom, H., Farde, L. (2003). The serotonin system and spiritual experiences. *American Journal of Psychiatry*, 160, 1965–1969.

Boyer P. (2001). *Religion explained. The evolutionary origins of religious thought.* New York: Basic Books.

Boyer, P. (2003). Religious thought and behaviour as by-products of brain function. *Trends in Cognitive Sciences*, 7, 119–124.

Brefczynski-Lewis, J.A., Lutz, A., Schaefer, H.S., Levinson, D.B., Davidson, R.J. (2007). Neural correlates of attentional expertise in long-term meditation practitioners. *Proceedings of the National Academy of Sciences of the United States of America*, 104, 11483–11488.

Brown, K.W., Ryan, R.M. (2003). The benefits of being present: Mindfulness and its role in psychological well-being. *Journal of Personality and Social Psychology*, 84, 822–848.

Butler, P.M., McNamara, P., Durso, R. (2010). Deficits in the automatic activation of religious concepts in patients with Parkinson's disease. *Journal of the International Neuropsychological Society*, 16, 252–261.

Butler, P.M., McNamara, P., Durso, R. (2011a). Side of onset in Parkinson's disease and alterations in religiosity: Novel behavioral phenotypes. *Behavioural Neurology*, 24, 133–141.

Butler, P.M., McNamara, P., Ghofrani, J., Durso, R. (2011b). Disease-associated differences in religious cognition in patients with Parkinson's disease. *Journal of Clinical and Experimental Neuropsychology*, 33, 917–928.

Cahn, B.R., Polich, J. (2006). Meditation states and traits: EEG, ERP, and neuroimaging studies. *Psychological Bulletin*, 132, 180–211.

Campanella, F., Crescentini, C., Urgesi, C., Fabbro, F. (2014). Mindfulness-oriented meditation improves self-related character scales in healthy individuals. *Comprehensive Psychiatry*, 55, 1269–1278.

Carmody, J., Reed, G., Kristeller, J., Merriam, P. (2008). Mindfulness, spirituality, and health-related symptoms. *Journal of Psychosomatic Research*, 64, 393–403.

Chiao, J.Y., Harada, T., Komeda, H., Li, Z., Mano, Y., Saito, D., et al. (2010). Dynamic cultural influences on neural representations of the self. *Journal of Cognitive Neuroscience*, 22, 1–11.

Chiesa, A., Serretti, A. (2010). A systematic review of neurobiological and clinical features of mindfulness meditations. *Psychological Medicine*, 40, 1239–1252.

Cloninger, C. R., Przybeck, T. R., Svrakic, D. M., Wetzel, R. D. (1994). *The temperament and character inventory (TCI): A guide to its development and use.* St. Louis, MO: Center for Psychobiology of Personality, Washington University.

Cloninger, C. R., Svrakic, D. M., Przybeck, T. R. (1993). A psychobiological model of temperament and character. *Archives of General Psychiatry*, 50, 975–990.

Cobb, M., Puchalski, C. M., Rumbold, B. (2012). *Oxford textbook of spirituality in healthcare.* Oxford: Oxford University Press.

Costa, P. T., Jr., McCrae, R. R. (1992). *Revised NEO personality inventory (NEO PI-R) and NEO five-factor inventory (NEOFFI): Professional manual.* Odessa, FL: Psychological Assessment Resources.

Crescentini, C., Aglioti, S., Fabbro, F., Urgesi, C. (2014a). Virtual lesions of the inferior parietal cortex induce fast changes of implicit religiousness/spirituality. *Cortex*, 54, 1–15.

Crescentini, C., Capurso, V. (2015). Mindfulness meditation and explicit and implicit indicators of personality and self-concept changes. *Frontiers in Psychology*, 6, 44. doi:10.3389/fpsyg.2015.00044.

Crescentini, C., Di Bucchianico, Fabbro, F., Urgesi, C. (2015). Excitatory stimulation of the right inferior parietal cortex lessens implicit religiousness/spirituality. *Neuropsychologia*, 70, 71–79.

Crescentini, C., Matiz, A., Fabbro, F. (2015). Improving personality/character traits in individuals with alcohol dependence: the influence of mindfulness-oriented meditation. *Journal of Addictive Diseases*, 34, 75–87.

Crescentini, C., Urgesi, C., Campanella, F., Eleopra, R., Fabbro, F. (2014b). Effects of an 8-week meditation program on the implicit and explicit self-referential religious/spiritual representations. *Consciousness and Cognition*, 30, 266–280.

Dennett, D. C. (2006). *Breaking the spell.* New York: Viking.

Devinsky, O., Lai, G. (2008). Spirituality and religion in epilepsy. *Epilepsy & Behavior*, 12, 636–643.

Didonna, F. (Ed.). (2009). *Clinical handbook of mindfulness.* New York: Springer.

Dor-Ziderman, Y., Berkovich-Ohana, A., Glicksohn, J., Goldstein, A. (2013). Mindfulness-induced selflessness: A MEG neurophenomenological study. *Frontiers in Human Neuroscience*, 7, 582.

Emmons, R. A., Paloutzian, R. F. (2003). The psychology of religion. *Annual Review of Psychology*, 54, 377–402.

Fabbro, F. (2010). *Neuropsicologia dell'esperienza religiosa* (Neuropsychology of religious experience). Roma: Astrolabio.

Fabbro, F., Crescentini, C. (2014). Facing the experience of pain: A neuropsychological perspective. *Physics of Life Reviews*, 11, 540–552.

Falb, M. D., Pargament, K. I. (2012). Relational mindfulness, spirituality, and the therapeutic bond. *Asian Journal of Psychiatry*, 5, 351–354.

Farb, N.A.S., Segal, Z. V., Mayberg, H., Bean, J., McKeon, D., Fatima, Z., et al. (2007). Attending to the present: Mindfulness meditation reveals distinct neural modes of self-reference. *Social Cognitive and Affective Neuroscience*, 2, 313–322.

Fingelkurts, A. A., Fingelkurts, A. A. (2009). Is our brain hardwired to produce God, or is our brain hardwired to perceive God? A systematic review on the role of the brain in mediating religious experience. *Cognitive Processes*, 10, 293–326.

Fuller, R. C. (2001). *Spiritual but not religious: Understanding unchurched America*. New York: Oxford University Press.

Fuller, R. C. (2008). *Spirituality in the flesh: Bodily sources of religious experiences*. New York: Oxford University Press.

Gawronski, B., Bodenhausen, G. V. (2006). Associative and propositional processes in evaluation: An integrative review of implicit and explicit attitude change. *Psychological Bulletin*, 132, 692–731.

Geary, C., Rosenthal, S. L. (2011). Sustained impact of MBSR on stress, well-being, and daily spiritual experiences for 1 year in academic health care employees. *Journal of Alternative and Complementary Medicine*, 17, 939–944.

Giaquinto, S., Bruti, L., Dall'Armi, V., Palma, E., Spiridigliozzi, C. (2011). Religious and spiritual beliefs in outpatients suffering from Parkinson disease. *International Journal of Geriatric Psychiatry*, 26, 916–922.

Giluk, T. L. (2009). Mindfulness, big five personality, and affect: A meta-analysis. *Personality and Individual Differences*, 47, 805–811.

Greenwald, A. G., McGhee, D. E., Schwanz, J.L.K. (1998). Measuring individual differences in implicit cognition: The implicit association test. *Journal of Personality and Social Psychology*, 74, 1464–1480.

Greeson, J. M., Webber, D. M., Smoski, M. J., Brantley, J. G., Ekblad, A. G., Suarex, E. C., et al. (2011). Changes in spirituality partly explain health-related quality of life outcomes after mindfulness-based stress reduction. *Journal of Behavioral Medicine*, 34, 508–518.

Haimerl, C. J., Valentine, E. R. (2001). The effect of contemplative practice on intrapersonal, interpersonal, and transpersonal dimensions of the self-concept. *Journal of Transpersonal Psychology*, 33, 37–52.

Han, S., Gu, X., Mao, L., Ge, J., Wang, G., Ma, Y. (2010). Neural substrates of self-referential processing in Chinese Buddhists. *Social and Cognitive Affective Neuroscience*, 5, 332–339.

Han, S., Mao, L., Gu, X., Zhu, Y., Ge, J., Ma, Y. (2008). Neural consequences of religious belief on self-referential processing. *Social Neuroscience*, 3, 1–15.

Harris, S., Kaplan, J. T., Curiel, A., Bookheimer, S. Y., Iacoboni, M., Cohen, M. S. (2009). The neural correlates of religious and nonreligious belief. *PLoS One*, 4, e7272.

Herzog, H., Lele, V. R., Kuwert, T., Langen, K. J., Kops, E. R., Feinendegen, L. E. (1990). Changed pattern of regional glucose metabolism during Yoga meditative relaxation. *Neuropsychobiology*, 23, 182–187.

Hölzel, B. K., Lazar, S. W., Gard, T., Schuman-Olivier, Z., Vago, D. R., Ott, U. (2011). How does mindfulness meditation work? Proposing mechanisms of action from a conceptual and neural perspective. *Perspectives on Psychological Science*, 6, 537–559.

Huang, Y. Z., Edwards, M. J., Rounis, E., Bhatia, K. P., Rothwell, J.C. (2005). Theta burst stimulation of the human motor cortex. *Neuron*, 45, 201–206.

Inzlicht, M., McGregor, I., Hirsh, J.B., Nash, K. (2009). Neural markers of religious conviction. *Psychological Science*, 20, 385–392.

James, W. (1958). *Varieties of religious experience*. New York: Mentor (original work published 1902).

Johnstone, B., Bodling, A., Cohen, D., Christ, S.E., Wegrzyn, A. (2012). Right parietal lobe-related "selflessness" as the neuropsychological basis of spiritual transcendence. *International Journal for the Psychology of Religion*, 22, 267–284.

Johnstone, B., Glass, B.A. (2008). Evaluation of a neuropsychological model of spirituality in persons with traumatic brain injury. *Zygon*, 43, 861–874.

Jordan, C.H., Whitfield, M., Zeigler-Hill, V. (2007). Intuition and the correspondence between implicit and explicit self-esteem. *Journal of Personality and Social Psychology*, 93, 1067–1079.

Kaasinen, V., Maguire, R.P., Kurki, T., Bruck, A., Rinne, J.O. (2005). Mapping brain structure and personality in late adulthood. *NeuroImage*, 24, 315–322.

Kabat-Zinn, J. (1990). *Full catastrophe living: Using the wisdom of your body and mind to face stress, pain, and illness*. New York: Delacorte.

Kapogiannis, D., Barbey, A.K., Su, M., Krueger, F., Grafman, J. (2009a). Neuroanatomical variability of religiosity. *PLoS One*, 4, e7180.

Kapogiannis, D., Barbey, A.K., Su, M., Zamboni, G., Krueger, F., Grafman, J. (2009b). Cognitive and neural foundations of religious belief. *Proceedings of the National Academy of Sciences of the United States of America*, 106, 4876–4881.

Kapuscinski, A.N., Masters, K.S. (2010). The current status of measures of spirituality: A critical review of scale development. *Psychology of Religion and Spirituality*, 2, 191–205.

Koole, S.L., Govorun, O., Cheng, C.M., Gallucci, M. (2009). Pulling yourself together: Meditation promotes the congruence between implicit and explicit self-esteem. *Journal of Experimental and Social Psychology*, 45, 1220–1226.

LaBouff, J.P., Rowatt, W.C., Johnson, M.K., Thedford, M., Tsang, J.A. (2010). Development and initial validation of an implicit measure of religiousness/spirituality. *Journal for the Scientific Study of Religion*, 49, 439–455.

Lazar, S.W., Bush, G., Gollub, R.L., Fricchione, G.L., Khalsa, G., Benson, H. (2000). Functional brain mapping of the relaxation response and meditation. *NeuroReport*, 11, 1581–1585.

Levesque, C., Brown, K.V. (2007). Mindfulness as a moderator of the effect of implicit motivational self-concept on day-to-day behavioral motivation. *Motivation and Emotion*, 31, 284–299.

Lutz, A., Slagter, H.A., Dunne, J.D., Davidson, R.J. (2008). Attention regulation and monitoring in meditation. *Trends in Cognitive Sciences*, 12, 163–169.

McNamara, P., Durso, R., Brown, A. (2006). Religiosity in patients with Parkinson's disease. *Neuropsychiatric Disease and Treatment*, 2, 341–348.

Miller, B.L., Seeley, W.W., Mychack, P., Rosen, H.J., Mena, I., Boone, K. (2001). Neuroanatomy of the self: evidence from patients with frontotemporal dementia. *Neurology*, 57, 817–821.

Newberg, A.B. (2014). The neuroscientific study of spiritual practices. *Frontiers in Psychology*, 5, 215.

Newberg, A., Alavi, A., Baime, M., Pourdehnad, M., Santanna, J., d'Aquili, E. (2001). The measurement of regional cerebral blood flow during the complex cognitive task of meditation: a preliminary SPECT study. *Psychiatry Research,* 106, 113–122.

Newberg, A. B., Iversen, J. (2003). The neural basis of the complex mental task of meditation: neurotransmitter and neurochemical considerations. *Medical Hypotheses,* 61, 282–291.

Newberg, A., Pourdehnad, M. Alava, A., d'Aquili, E. G. (2003). Cerebral blood flow during meditative prayer: Preliminary findings and methodological issues. *Perceptual and Motor Skills,* 97, 625–630.

Paloutzian, R., Park, C. (2005). *Handbook of the psychology of religion and spirituality.* New York: The Guilford Press.

Pichon, I., Boccato, G., Saroglou, V. (2007). Nonconscious influences of religion on prosociality: A priming study. *European Journal of Social Psychology,* 37, 1032–1045.

Piedmont, R. L., Ciarrochi, J. W., Dy-Liacco, G. S., Williams, J. E. G. (2009). The empirical and conceptual value of the spiritual transcendence and religious involvement scales for personality research. *Psychology of Religion and Spirituality,* 1, 162–179.

Previc, F. H. (2006). The role of the extrapersonal brain systems in religious activity. *Consciousness and Cognition,* 15, 500–539.

Sauer, S., Walach, H., Schmidt, S., Hinterberger, T., Horan, M., Kohls, N. (2011). Implicit and explicit emotional behavior and mindfulness. *Consciousness and Cognition,* 20, 1558–1569.

Schjoedt, U., Stødkilde-Jørgensen, H., Geertz, A. W., Roepstorff, A. (2009). Highly religious participants recruit areas of social cognition in personal prayer. *Social Cognitive Affective Neuroscience,* 4, 199–207.

Schnabel, K., Asendorpf, J. B., Greenwald, A. G. (2008). Using implicit association tests for the assessment of implicit personality self-concept. In J. B. Boyle, G. Matthews, & D. H. Saklofske (Eds.), *Handbook of personality theory and assessment: Personality measurement and testing* (pp. 508–528). London: SAGE Publications.

Schwarz, N. (1999). Self-reports: how the questions shape the answers. *The American Psychologist,* 54, 93–105.

Sudsuang, R., Chentanez, V., Veluvan, K. (1991). Effects of Buddhist meditation on serum cortisol and total protein levels, blood pressure, pulse rate, lung volume and reaction time. *Physiology & Behavior,* 50, 543–548.

Svrakic, D. M., Whitehead, C., Przybeck, T. R., Cloninger, C. R. (1993). Differential diagnosis of personality disorders by the seven-factor temperament and character inventory. *Archives of General Psychiatry,* 50, 991–999.

Tedrus, G. M., Fonseca, L. C., Höehr, G. C. (2014). Spirituality aspects in patients with epilepsy. *Seizure,* 23, 25–28.

Tomasino, B., Chiesa, A., Fabbro, F. (2014). Disentangling the neural mechanisms involved in Hinduism-and Buddhism related meditation. *Brain and Cognition,* 90, 32–40.

Tomasino, B., Fregona, S., Skrap, M., Fabbro, F. (2013). Meditation-related activations are modulated by the practices needed to obtain it and by the expertise: An ALE meta-analysis study. *Frontiers in Human Neuroscience,* 6, 346.

Turner, R. M., Hudson, I. L., Butler, P. H., Joyce, P. R. (2003). Brain function and personality in normal males: A SPECT study using statistical parametric mapping. *NeuroImage*, 19, 1145–1162.

Urgesi, C., Aglioti, S. M., Skrap, M., Fabbro, F. (2010). The spiritual brain: selective cortical lesions modulate human self-transcendence. *Neuron*, 65, 309–319.

Vago, D. R., Silbersweig, D. A. (2012). Self-awareness, self-regulation, and self-transcendence (S-ART): A framework for understanding the neurobiological mechanisms of mindfulness. *Frontiers in Human Neuroscience*, 6, 296.

van den Hurk, P.A.M., Wingens, T., Giommi, F., Barendregt, H.P., Speckens, A.E.M., Van Schie, H. T. (2011). On the relationship between the practice of mindfulness meditation and personality: An exploratory analysis of the mediating role of mindfulness skills. *Mindfulness*, 2, 194–200.

Walsh, V., Pascual-Leone, A. (2003). *Transcranial magnetic stimulation: A neurochronometrics of mind.* Cambridge, MA: MIT Press.

Wilson, D. S. (2002). *Darwin's Cathedral: Evolution, religion, and the nature of society.* Chicago, IL: Chicago University Press.

Wuthnow, R. (1998). *After heaven. Spirituality in America since the 1950s.* Berkeley: University of California Press.

Yamamoto, S., Kitamura, Y., Yamada, N., Nakashima, Y., Kuroda, S. (2006). Medial profrontal cortex and anterior cingulate cortex in the generation of alpha activity induced by transcendental meditation: A magnetoencephalographic study. *Acta Medica Okayama*, 60, 51–58.

Zinnbauer, B.J., Pargament, K.I. (2005). Religiousness and spirituality. In R.F. Paloutzian, & C.L. Park (Eds.), *The handbook of the psychology of religion and spirituality* (pp. 21–42). New York: Guilford Press.

Zuckerman P. (2005). Atheism: Contemporary rates and patterns. In M. Martin (Ed.), *The Cambridge companion to atheism* (pp. 47–67). Cambridge, England: Cambridge University Press.

CHAPTER 5

CALLED TO NONDUALITY

Zoran Josipovic and Judith Blackstone

Introducing emptiness to be awareness, the nature of awareness itself becomes indivisible with space.

Jigme Lingpa (1729–1798)

Rabbi Zusya, when he was an old man, said, "In the coming world, they will not ask me: 'Why were you not Moses?' Rather, they will ask me: 'Why were you not Zusya?' "

Martin Buber (1878–1965)

INTRODUCTION

In this chapter we will discuss how nonduality and calling are understood in the Asian nondual traditions. We will also present the stories of how we were called to nonduality and the work that emerged from it: Zoran to the scientific research of nonduality and Judith to teaching a method for its embodied realization. While our chapter is in the "scientific" section of this volume, and discusses some of the neuroscience findings on nonduality, our approach is scientific, secular, and sacred.

From time immemorial, human beings have found ways to ameliorate the stress, disharmony, and alienation of environmental and social pressures, by returning to a state of oneness or, nonduality, and to the well-being that results from it. The records of these experiences can be found among some of the most inspired sayings of the major religious traditions of the world (Huxley, 2004). They point to a way of being that is authentic and free, in which we are not fragmented into acceptable and unacceptable parts of ourselves, limited by our personal and cultural conditioning. Arguably, the most detailed descriptions of these experiences and the most systematic methods for realizing them can be found within the Asian nondual contemplative traditions, those of Dzogchen and Mahamudra in Tibetan Buddhism, Advaita Vedanta and Kashmiri Shaivism in Hinduism, and Chan or Zen Buddhism in China and Japan.

These contemplative traditions describe ordinary human experience as structured along a rigidified subject–object boundary, resulting in the fragmenting of the field of experience into antagonistic poles, such as good versus bad, self versus other, in-group versus out-group, and mind versus matter (Dreyfus and Thompson, 2007; Loy, 1998; Radhakrishnan, 1995). In this fragmented state, phenomena are experienced as somehow essentially different from the experiencing subject, leading to a loss of contact with one's authentic being, and to a subtle state of alienation from others, from the environment, and from life as lived in one's body.

However, such fragmentation, though a universal condition of human life, is regarded by these traditions as secondary to a more unified reality. Discovering this unified dimension is possible because of the presence of an aspect of our consciousness that does not rely on dualistic conceptual constructs and symbolic representations in order to cognize, but that is "primordially present," though ordinarily unrecognized, in the background of all conscious experiencing (Trangu, 2001). It has been named differently in different traditions, as clear light, pure consciousness, intrinsic awareness, or Self, but can be termed, according to its unifying characteristic, as "nondual awareness." This background awareness is a nonconceptual unitary cognizance, itself empty of content, yet clearly aware and blissful (Lama XIV, 2004). It is self-knowing or reflexive, in that it knows itself to be aware, directly, without relying on concepts, words, or images, and subsequent cognitions (Williams, 2000). As such it has been regarded as the conscious noumenon (Mipam and Hopkins, 2006).

The failure of nondual awareness to "recognize" itself, either due to mistaken cognitions or due to being obscured by an unconscious substrate, is seen by some nondual traditions as the root cause of dualistic cognition and fragmented experience (Norbu and Lipman, 1987). Though itself empty of phenomenal content, phenomena such as various sensory, affective, and cognitive contents, and the states of arousal, appear to it like images in a mirror-, a well-known metaphor for these states. When realized, nondual awareness confers the wisdom that all phenomena are part of one unified reality, and are of the same essential nature as nondual awareness itself. This realization reveals a fundamental freedom of being: freedom to be authentic irrespective of experiences we are having. It also reveals the spontaneous presence of the essential qualities of being, such as pleasure, strength, happiness, love, and compassion (Blackstone, 2007). Admittedly, it is difficult for a western scientific mind raised on postmodernist constructivism to conceive of the possibility this background awareness, let alone that the positive qualities we are so accustomed to thinking of as requiring effort and cultivation could somehow be spontaneously present within us. Yet such realization has been known experientially throughout history, by countless people of all faiths and walks of life.

JUDITH

One of the main figures in the Buddhist pantheon is the bodhisattva Avalokitesvara. He (or sometimes she in the guise of Kuan Yin) is described as the one who "hears the cries of the world" (Loori, n.d.). If our future is to serve, to hear the cries of the world and respond to them, then we are called by our own discernment of the audible, visible suffering of the human beings we encounter.

I was called to nondual spiritual awakening in much the same way. I felt compelled to draw closer to a unitary spiritual aspect of life, because, from early in my life, I could detect its presence shining through the materiality of the world around me.

Since my childhood, I have been attracted to a particular type of information about life. When I try to analyze it, this guidance seems to rest on my characteristic mode of attunement to the people around me. Like picking out a single melodic line in a complex symphony, my senses have picked out one distinct strain of distress in myself and others, along with clues to a specific type of remedy.

It began in my childhood as a vague impression. I remember having a general feeling of suppression surrounding the adults in my life like a thin layer of bubble wrap. There seemed to be something important going on beneath the surface that was not expressed and some sort of yearning or incompleteness that went unsatisfied. Over the years, my recognition of both ailment and cure has gradually become more defined. I now understand that what seems most painful to me is a lack of genuine contact, both with oneself and in relationships. I think that I was called to nonduality because I sensed its potential to fulfill the need for authenticity and contact. This calling determined the type of nondual teachings that attracted me. It also engendered some of the less typical components of the nondual teachings that I now bring to my students.

When I was in my early twenties, a back injury forcefully awakened me to my need to deepen contact with myself. As a child and young adult, I was a professional dancer. I began performing when I was nine and devoted myself to the rigorous training and one-pointed focus that this art form demands. When I was 25 I injured my back so severely that I required surgery. I had known for many years that I had a "well-compensated" spine curvature, in which my head was centered over the base of my torso. But the surgery fused me in the off-center position that had occurred during the injury and produced areas of rigidity throughout the whole internal space of my body. It was a sudden loss of my career and the physical agility that I had possessed as a young adult.

I entered a period of despair in which I felt that my life was over. But during that time I had two dreams that turned out to be harbingers of my life ahead. First, I dreamt that I was entering a dark stage in a dark theatre. My body was made of light. All of the shapes that I made as I slowly danced across the stage were shapes of light. A few weeks later, I dreamt that I was looking at a blank screen. At the bottom of the screen, like the subtitle of a movie, were the words, "God is consciousness."

As far as I knew, I had never heard of this idea before. And yet it was a principle that would become vitally important to me as the vehicle of my healing, my spiritual awakening, and my function in the world. The discomfort in my body brought me to a wide variety of bodyworkers and healers. When they were unable to help me, it became imperative for me to heal myself. To do this, I began to focus inward, to contact myself as deeply and subtly as I could. It became clear to me in this process that my healing would not just be physical. I had to penetrate through the physical to the psychological and the spiritual aspects of myself.

At the same time, I had people coming to my loft for dance classes, for that was how I made my living. Unable to dance, I began to engage them in the exploration of the psychological and spiritual dimensions of the body. I noticed that there were places in their bodies that seemed transparent, where I could look into them, and other places where they seemed dense and opaque. I had another pivotal dream in which people appeared to be like Christmas trees, with lights strung at different places and depths within their bodies.

One day, lying on the floor of my dance studio, I noticed what felt like currents of energy rising from the ground and moving through my body. Without any effort on my part, these currents pulled the internal space of my body toward balance. There seemed to be some natural balancing function related to gravity. I also noticed that if I found a place to the right and the left of my head at the same time, my spine moved spontaneously from its imbalanced position toward center. I shared each new discovery with my dance students, modifying the practices that I was developing for my own healing to fit their needs.

Although I earned advanced degrees in psychotherapy, the most important aspects of my education have been self-taught. Since that first wake-up call of my back injury, I have been attracted to any knowledge that shed light on the relationship between the body, psychological healing and maturity, and spiritual awakening.

ZORAN

I seem to have been interested in the big questions and in consciousness, in one way or another, ever since I was a teenager, perhaps driven by my own sense of alienation and the perceived lack of authenticity in my surroundings, perhaps due to a persistent idea I had then, that there had to be something more fundamental and real behind the life's constantly changing drama of existential meaninglessness.

I came in contact with nonduality quite unexpectedly when I was about 18 years old. I was attempting to cross a rather tricky intersection, where several streets of slow-moving traffic encountered a steep off-ramp, onto which all sorts of vehicles descended at maniacal speeds from a nearby bridge. I was about to put my foot in the gutter, when all of a sudden I had a sensation, as if the top of my skull had been blown off, and I had eyes on all sides of my head. I was seeing in all directions at the same time! The bizarreness of it made me nauseated, but in the next instant, a strange kind of peace engulfed me: I was not watching the intersection anymore; instead, I felt I was somehow witnessing the primordial Being itself, that which is eternal and always here, silently existing in the background of our world. It was so immense and so real, that my own angst, which had until then completely consumed me, seemed no more than silly, self-imposed mind chatter.

After this experience, I became interested in Asian philosophy and started experimenting with meditation. When I discovered practices that concerned themselves with realizing nondual awareness—sometimes aptly termed "true self" or "innermost essence"—this seemed to me just what I was searching for. Realizing it seemed to resolve both the issue of fundamental self-identity, and an authentic way of relating to others. Over the years I encountered different views on nonduality and practiced different meditation styles before I eventually settled on a Dzogchen-style practice. This approach resonated with me because of its emphasis on the freedom inherent in nondual awareness. According to the Dzogchen view, to the extent that one realizes the innermost essence of nondual awareness, one also recovers the spontaneous presence of positive qualities.

I had a dream around that time in which I found myself attending a large party, wondering what type of work I was called to. Suddenly I experienced a clear, blissful light of nondual awareness radiating from my heart-center, and a voice saying, with just a touch of humor: "This is all you've got." While over the years my professional life shifted from working as a body-worker, then a psychotherapist, and finally a scientist, the main theme remained my interest in nondual awareness.

JUDITH

Within Asian nondual traditions, the questions of whether there is an ongoing, unified ground of awareness, and also whether positive qualities are spontaneously present in this ground or require cultivation have long been debated. Within the Tibetan Buddhist tradition, these two main viewpoints are clearly described (Hookham, 1991). One, called "empty of itself" (Tib. *Rangtong*) claims that there is no ground of unitary awareness. It teaches that even our basic nature is empty of intrinsic reality.

The other view, called "empty of other" (Tib. *Shentong*), asserts that there is a basic, primordial awareness, along with inherent qualities, spontaneously present and accessible in every human being. This has been called "wisdom mind," "buddha-nature" and "natural mind," among other names. "Empty of other" refers to the mental ideation and negative emotions that obscure the wisdom mind and that must be emptied in order for it to shine through. Although they are careful not to reify this inherent nature into an object, they say that it is "self-recognizing" (Rabjam, 2001), that it realizes itself. This view is similar (the differences are beyond the scope of this chapter) to the Hindu Advaita Vedanta teaching of an unchanging, unified ground of being, also called by various names including "pure consciousness" and "Self." Both Zoran and I experienced the unitary ground of consciousness early in our spiritual paths and so we have both felt more aligned with the "empty of other" view. We both sensed an essence of existence beyond the "bubble wrap" that dulls us to ourselves and each other.

Teachings about this essence can also be found in Zen Buddhism. The ninth-century Chinese Zen Buddhist master, Lin Chi (Japanese: *Rinzai*) said: "Followers of the way: the Dharma of the heart has no form and pervades the ten directions. In the eye, it is called seeing; in the ear, hearing; in the nose, smelling; in the mouth, talking; in the hands, grasping; in the feet, walking. Fundamentally, it is one light; differentiated, it becomes the six senses" (Schloegl, 1975, p. 22).

In contrast, here is a description that represents the "empty of itself" view:

> Paradoxically, the only way that we can know ourselves is in learning to be mindfully aware of the moment-to-moment goings-on of our body and mind as they exist through various situations occurring in time. We have no experience of anything that is permanent and independent of this. Thus there is no ego or self, just a counterfeit construction. (Levine, 2010, p. 287)

The traditional argument against this assertion is that in order to know that experience is constantly changing, there needs to be an aspect of consciousness that is constant and can witness the changes. Who or what is witnessing this constantly changing display? Lin Chi says in a lecture to his students,

> Who then can understand the Dharma and can listen to it? The one here before your very eyes, brilliantly clear and shining without any form—there

he is who can understand the Dharma you are listening to. If you can really grasp this, you are not different from the Buddhas and patriarchs. Ceaselessly he is right here, conspicuously present. (Watson, n.d.)

The contemporary Tibetan Buddhist teacher, Tsultrim Gyamtso Rinpoche (2001), offers a similar perspective. He writes,

The perfectly existent nature is the ultimate absolute emptiness. It is the non-conceptual Wisdom Mind, non-arising, non-abiding, and non-perishing. It is primordially existent and endowed with qualities. It is empty in the sense that it is free from all the obscurations created by the conceptual mind. Therefore when the conceptual mind tries to grasp it, it finds nothing and so it experiences it as emptiness. Thus it is empty to the conceptual mind, but from its own point of view it is the Clear Light Nature of Mind together with all its qualities. (p. 75)

This self-existent, spontaneously arising dimension of ourselves is not constructed, and therefore it is not subject to deconstruction or impermanence. And it cannot be grasped conceptually. For me, this is the key difference between the "empty of itself" and "empty of other" perspectives. We not only understand that there is a fundamental dimension beyond the constantly changing display of phenomena, we also realize that we are that dimension, we lay it bare, we discover ourselves as that.

ZORAN

The Mahayana Buddhist tradition regards the altruistic compassion to relieve others' suffering (Sansk. *Boddhicitta*, the mind of enlightenment) as the chief motivating force in one's life and in one's spiritual endeavor (Rabjam, 2007). Such compassion is based on an understanding derived from empathic resonance that all beings are basically alike to oneself in that they too experience suffering, and want to be happy and free of suffering. The aim of such practices is to develop compassion that is universal and nonreferential, so that instead of being experienced only for someone that one cares for, it becomes unbiased compassion for all, including one's enemies. *Rangtong* followers hold that such compassion cannot arise spontaneously, but must be cultivated through creative visualization and analysis of one's experience (Lama XIV, 1985). In contrast, the followers of *Shentong* hold that nonreferential compassion is an inherent quality of one's authentic presence, and that constructed practices involving analysis of experience and cultivation of it through creative imagination are only there to help one reconnect with it. Interestingly, Dzogchen tradition redefines compassion as the creative energy of nondual awareness, whose primary objective is to know itself. This impulse to know is seen as the motivating force that ultimately propels the unfolding of one's life experiences, both positive holistic ones, and negative neurotic ones (Padmasambhava, 2010).

JUDITH

As I progressed in my self-healing, I found that in order to heal, I had to enter into and live within the internal space of my body. I experienced this as an integration, or unification, of my body and mind. It felt as if I were present, and conscious, throughout my whole body. Living within the internal space of my body, I was able to know myself as made of light, as I had dreamt at the beginning of my path.

Contemporary Zen philosopher Yuasa (1987) writes "The 'mind' here is not surface consciousness, but is the 'mind' that penetrates into the body and deeply subjectivizes it" (p. 105). The sense of oneself as "made of" consciousness is an experience of both wholeness and permeability. It means that we can function in a more unified manner, for example, thinking and feeling at the same time. It also means that we are open to the environment. We experience the same dimension of unified consciousness pervading our body and our environment at the same time. This dimension of ourselves is experienced as both immanent and transcendent. Yuasa writes, "Every being is changed to a perfectly coherent radiance, made transparent through the illumination of the transcendent" (p. 156). This is an experience of the mutual permeability or mutual transparency of self and other. We are both whole within our own body and one with our environment, at the same time.

While living at a Zen monastery in the early eighties, I had my first experience of this mutual transparency. It was a realization that has never left me. There was a stream near the monastery where I loved to spend the daily break in the monastic schedule. One day, sitting on my favorite flat stone, I suddenly realized that everything around me seemed weightless. Even the rocks were both substantial and permeable at the same time, as if they were made of space. Instead of separate objects there was a vast oneness, a single luminous space. The space both revealed the separate forms and unified them.

Since I was called to nonduality as a quest for deepening contact with myself and other people, the psychological and embodiment aspects of nondual teachings have been central to my own work as a nonduality teacher. Over the past three decades I developed a series of meditative practices called the Realization Process that includes the embodiment, psychological and relational aspects of nondual realization.

In the Realization Process, we uncover the dimension of unified consciousness by contacting, and living in the internal depths of the whole body. In this way, we let go of ourselves from deep within our whole form. We open to unified consciousness everywhere in our being. It feels as if we have un-covered our basic nature, our true identity.

The realization of unified consciousness pervading our whole body pro-duces a shift in how it feels to be an individual. Rather than knowing our-selves as a conglomerate of abstract ideas (e.g., "I am a teacher") it provides a felt experience ourselves as a cohesive, sentient ground of being. This does not eradicate our sense of being an individual. Rather, it deepens our contact with ourselves as individuals. As this unified ground of being, the changing array of our personal experience, our thoughts, emotions, and sensations is clearly revealed. The philosopher, Keiji Nishitani (1983) writes, "It is the field in which each and every thing—as an absolute center, possessed of an absolutely unique individuality—becomes manifest as it is in itself" (p. 164). When we know ourselves as this pervasive consciousness, we are privy to the original flow of our own thoughts; we are able to truly see with our own eyes, to truly touch with our own hands.

Most of the Realization Process practices are ways to open to unified con-sciousness pervading our body and environment at the same time. But there is also a component of the work that focuses on psychological healing. My clinical observation has been that to fully inhabit our body, we need to recog-nize and release psychological constrictions (Blackstone, 2012).

In *The Empathic Ground* (Blackstone, 2007), I write,

> We are born with the ability to adjust to our environment, and to pro-tect ourselves from our environment, by diminishing both the impact of our own being on others and the impact of our environment on ourselves. Through the interface of the mind, brain, energy system and connective tissue (fascia) of the body, we are able to bind and diminish any aspect of our being, including our capacities for perception, cognition, emotion, physical sensation, verbal expression and physical movement. This con-striction is our unconscious response to painful or confusing events in our childhood relationships. (p. 71)

As a psychotherapist and nonduality teacher, I have observed that these constrictions and fragmentations limit one's contact with oneself and with others.

The Realization Process also includes a relationship component (Black-stone, 2007). Since most psychological constrictions were created in relation to significant others, we may experience unified consciousness while sitting alone in meditation, but revert to our habitual fragmentation of self and other as soon as we encounter another human being. For this reason, the Realiza-tion Process includes specific practices for attuning to unified consciousness with another person. In these practices, two people can experience that they are "made of" the same single transparency. However, they retain their inward contact with themselves as they experience oneness with each other, so that they are both individual and unified at the same time.

As we realize ourselves as unified consciousness pervading everywhere, we experience in-depth contact with ourselves, with other human beings and with our whole environment. It has been a great pleasure, and also a relief, for me to facilitate this deepened contact and authenticity in my role as a nonduality teacher. I feel that I am doing exactly what I have been called to do.

ZORAN

Over the past 20 years, studies of the neural correlates of meditation and other contemplative techniques have emerged into the mainstream as a new, rapidly growing field of contemplative neuroscience. However, efforts to study unitary spiritual states, and nondual awareness in particular, have been slow to gain traction, despite studies that have gained considerable notice (Lutz et al., 2004; Newberg et al., 2001). Some of the obvious challenges are that such states can be difficult to reproduce reliably in an experimental setting, or assess independently from subjective reports, and different meditation techniques can have different neural signatures even when they appear to aim at a similar level of consciousness (Lutz et al., 2008; Nash and Newberg, 2013; Travis and Shear, 2010). Perhaps the main stumbling block is difficulty in defining this topic of research in a nonreductionist way that can be understood by the rest of the scientific community (Josipovic, 2010; Lutz et al., 2008; Nash and Newberg, 2013). The diversity of views on nonduality among researchers, and, perhaps more importantly, among the participants, contributes to the diversity of results, making it difficult for those outside of the field to assess the meaning of the findings. For example, a preexisting commitment to a view about the presence or absence of self, or thoughts in general, in nondual awareness can bias both the ways in which researchers set up experiments, and the ways in which practitioners abide in nondual awareness during the experiment (Garrison et al., 2013).

Understanding the overall taxonomy of consciousness according to nondual contemplative traditions can help clarify some of these research-related issues. Table 5.1 presents a summary of the taxonomies found in Tibetan Buddhism, and in Dzogchen in particular, with the overall division into the relative aspect (termed "mind"), and the absolute aspect (termed "the nature of mind") (Lama XIV, 2004; Trangu, 2001). It includes some relabeling from contemporary cognitive sciences. In this table, nondual awareness, being unitary and all-encompassing, is treated as one category, although traditions often assign different labels to its different aspects, or to the stages of its realization.

Table 5.1   A taxonomy of consciousness from a nondual perspective

Relative: *the mind*
- Contents (qualia)
- Functions (sensory, affective and cognitive)
- States of arousal (waking, dreaming, deep sleep, orgasm, death, meditative absorption states, misc. altered states)
- Conscious/unconscious substrate—reduced or absent phenomenal content, but without self-recognition of nondual awareness; akin to deep sleep but not completely unconscious.

Absolute: *the nature of mind*
- Nondual awareness—self-knowing cognizance devoid of content; empty, luminous, blissful, and unified.

Various meditation techniques for realizing nondual awareness fall into two main categories, those that isolate nondual awareness from phenomenal content through meditative absorption and those that facilitate self-recognition of nondual awareness within ordinary experience (Lama XIV, 2004). This is often described as the coemergence of the absolute and relative. Bearing this in mind, we can now see how the table assists in understanding the results of different studies:

1. Meditations that, during experiments, primarily exercise attention, whether endogenous or exogenous, usually result in increases of activity in the brain areas involved in dorsal and/or ventral attentional systems, and in the perceptual areas representing attended contents (Brefczynski-Lewis et al., 2007; Jha et al., 2007; Slagter et al., 2007; Tang et al., 2007).

2. Meditative absorption practices that primarily create reduced states of arousal, usually through sustained focused attention with progressively decreased effort, are accompanied by the subjective experience of mental quiescence, and result in an overall decrease in cortical activity and functional connectivity (Berkovich-Ohana et al., in press; Hinterberger et al., 2014; Lehmann et al., 2012).

3. When meditation involves the monitoring of experience without suppressing the perceptual content, decreases in cortical activity and functional connectivity affect predominantly the midline cortical structures that are part of the intrinsic default network (Brewer et al., 2011; Farb et al., 2007; Vago and Silbersweig, 2012). Participants report a decrease in self-related mentation, or even an absence of the narrative or autobiographical self (Austin, 2009; Dor-Ziderman et al., 2013).

4. When meditative absorptions are deep and reach the unconscious substrate, subjects report feelings of "oceanic" expansion and reduced or absent phenomenal content, accompanied to a different degree by a loss

of sense of time, spatial distance and orientation, inside/outside boundary, agentic self, or observing consciousness (Austin, 1998; Berkovich-Ohana et al., 2013; Hagerty et al., 2013; Lehmann et al., 2012; Newberg et al., 2001). Often such absorptions are referred to by the Sanskrit term *samadhi*, and can be akin to a deep sleep and known only retroactively. However, different Hindu and Buddhist sects use this term differently, and the discussion of its many meanings is beyond the scope of this chapter.

While the above meditations can result in various unitary states of consciousness, such states are technically not yet nonduality, since nondual awareness, the basic nature of mind, has not yet been realized (Lama XIV, 2004). Nondual awareness differs distinctly from focused or monitoring attention, and from mere vigilance/arousal in the brain, so it stands to reason that its neural correlates would be different as well (Josipovic, 2010, 2014).

5. When nondual awareness is clearly revealed, but the phenomenal content is still reduced or absent, neural signatures can resemble aspects of deep sleep with added lucidity (Mason et al., 1997). To the extent that this occurs during the Transcendental Meditation technique, increases in the default network activity, the prefrontal alpha coherence, and in the anterior–posterior alpha synchronization have been observed (Travis et al., 2010; Travis and Shear, 2010). When the self-knowing dimension of nondual awareness is vividly present, the functional connectivity between the precuneus and dorsolateral prefrontal cortex is increased (Josipovic, 2014). If the empty, nonreferential dimension predominates, increased activity is mainly in the posterior, parietal areas of the brain, the precuneus and the temporo-parietal junction (Josipovic, unpublished data).

6. Finally, when nondual awareness is stabilized and integrated with experience, an increase in functional connectivity between intrinsic, self-referential, and extrinsic, task-positive networks in the brain can be observed (Josipovic et al., 2012). Unlike the increases of functional connectivity between the nodes of these two networks that have been observed in mental illness, or under the influence of hallucinogens, and are accompanied with internal disorganization of the default network (Carhart-Harris et al., 2013), in nondual awareness the default network retains its internal coherence (Josipovic et al., 2012). Suppression of activity in the brain areas involved in either self-related or other related aspects of experience, or significant increases in areas mediating attention systems, may indicate that participants are still relying on some form of attention, rather than abiding in nondual awareness (for a detailed discussion see Josipovic 2014).

Is the brain innately wired for nonduality? When realized, nondual awareness feels like it has always been there, "underneath" of all our experiences, we have just failed to recognize it. If such "high order" unity consciousness is present in all of us even when unrecognized, this may imply that the neuronal processes mediating it are present in the brain as a potential, even when not fully expressed. My future research will explore genetic and neuronal processes that may account for the latent presence of nondual awareness in the brain, and how and why they become expressed under certain conditions.

REFERENCES

Austin, J. (1998). *Zen and the brain.* Cambridge, MA: MIT Press

Austin, J. H. (2009). *Selfless insight.* Cambridge, MA: MIT Press.

Berkovich-Ohana, A., Wilf, M., Kahana, R., Arieli, A., & Malach, R. Repetitive speech elicits widespread deactivation in the human cortex: The "Mantra" effect? *Brain and Behavior,* in press.

Berkovich-Ohana, A., Dor-Ziderman, Y., Glicksohn, J., & Goldstein, R. (2013). Alterations in the sense of time, space and body in the Mindfulness-trained brain: A neurophenomenologically-guided MEG study. *Frontiers in Psychology 4,* DOI=10.3389/fpsyg.2013.00912

Blackstone, J. (2007). *The empathic ground.* Albany, NY: State University of New York Press, p. 71.

Blackstone, J. (2012). *Belonging here.* Boulder, CO: Sounds True.

Brefczynski-Lewis, J. A., Lutz, A., Schaefer, H. S., Levinson, D. B., & Davidson, R. J. (2007). Neural correlates of attentional expertise in long-term meditation practitioners. *Proceedings of the National Academy of Sciences 104,* 11483–11488.

Brewer, J. A., Worhunsky, P. D., Gray, J. R., et al. (2011). Meditation experience is associated with default mode network activity and connectivity. *Proceedings of the National Academy of Sciences 108,* 20254–20259.

Buber, M. (1991). *Tales of Hassidim.* Tel Aviv: Schocken.

Carhart-Harris, R. L., Leech, R., Erritzoe, D., Williams, T. M., Stone, J. M., Evans, J., . . . Nutt, D. J. (2013). Functional connectivity measures after psilocybin inform a novel hypothesis of early psychosis. *Schizophrenia Bulletin, 39*(6), 1343–1351.

Dor-Ziderman, Y., Berkovich-Ohana, A., Glicksohn, J., & Goldstein, A. (2013). Mindfulness-induced selflessness: A MEG neurophenomenological study. *Frontiers of Human Neuroscience 7,* 582. doi: 10.3389/fnhum.2013.00582.

Dreyfus, G., & Thompson, E. (2007). "Asian perspectives: Indian theories of mind." In *The Cambridge handbook of consciousness.* P. D. Zelazo, M. Moscovitch, & E. Thompson (Eds.), pp. 89–114. Cambridge: Cambridge University Press.

Farb, N. A. S., Segal, Z. V., Mayberg, H., et al. (2007). Attending to the present: Mindfulness meditation reveals distinct neural modes of self-reference. *Social Cognitive and Affective Neuroscience 2,* 313–322.

Garrison, K. A., Santoyo, J. F., Davis, J. H., Thornhill, T. A., Kerr, C. E., & Brewer, J. A. (2013). Effortless awareness: Using real time neurofeedback to investigate correlates of posterior cingulate cortex activity in meditators' self-report. *Frontiers in Human Neuroscience, 7,* 440. doi: 10.3389/fnhum.2013.00440.

Hagerty, M. R., Isaacs, J., Brasington, L., Shupe, L., Fetz, E. E., & Cramer, S. C. (2013). Case study of ecstatic meditation: fMRI and EEG evidence of self-stimulating a reward system. *Neural Plasticity 2013,* 653572. doi: 10.1155/2013/653572.

Hinterberger, T., Schmidt, S., Kamei, T., & Walach, H. (2014). Decreased electro-physiological activity represents the conscious state of emptiness in meditation. *Frontiers in Psychology 5*, 99. doi: 10.3389/fpsyg.2014.00099.

Hookham, S. K. (1991). *The Buddha within*. Albany, NY: State University of New York Press.

Huxley, A. (2004). *Perennial philosophy*. New York: HarperCollins.

Jha, A., Klein, R., Krompinger, J., & Baime, M. (2007). Mindfulness training modifies subsystems of attention. *Cognitive, Affective, and Behavioral Neuroscience, 7*, 109–119.

Josipovic, Z. (2010). Duality and nonduality in meditation research. *Consciousness and Cognition* 19, 1119–1121.

Josipovic, Z., Dinstein, I., Weber, J., & Heeger, D. J. (2012). Influence of meditation on anti-correlated networks in the brain. *Frontiers in Human Neuroscience, 5*, 183. doi: 10.3389/fnhum.2011.00183.

Josipovic, Z. (2014). Neural correlates of nondual awareness in meditation. *Annals of New York Academy of Science, 1307*(1), 9–18.

Lehmann, D., Faber, P. L., Tei, S., Pascual-Marqui, R. D., Milz, P., & Kochi, K. (2012). Reduced functional connectivity between cortical sources in five meditation traditions detected with lagged coherence using EEG tomography. *NeuroImage 60*, 1574–1586.

Lama, D., XIV. (1985). *Kindness, clarity and insight*. Ithaca, NY: Snow Lion.

Lama, D., XIV. (2004). *Dzogchen*. Ithaca, NY: Snow Lion.

Levine, P. A. (2010). *In an unspoken voice*. Berkeley, CA: North Atlantic Books, p. 287.

Loori, J. (n.d.). in Avalokiteshvara Bodhisattva by Barbara O'Brien, Retrieved from buddhism.about.com/od/thetriyaka/a/avalokeshvara.htm

Loy, D. (1998). *Nonduality: A study in comparative philosophy*. Amherst, NY: Humanity Books.

Lutz, A., Greischar, L. L., Rawlings, N. B., Ricard, M., & Davidson, R. J. (2004). Long-term meditators self-induce high-amplitude gamma synchrony during mental practice. *Proceedings of the National Academy of Sciences 101*, 16369–16373.

Lutz, A., Slagter, H. A., Dunne, J. D., & Davidson, R. J. (2008). Attention regulation and monitoring in meditation. *Trends in Cognitive Sciences, 12*, 163–169.

Mason, L. I., Alexander, C. N., Travis, F., Marsh, G., Orme-Johnson, D., Gackenbach, et al. (1997). Electrophysiological correlates of higher states of consciousness during sleep in long term practitioners of the transcendental meditation program. *Sleep, 20*, 102–110.

Mipam, G., & Hopkins, J. (2006). *Fundamental mind*. Ithaca, NY: Snow Lion.

Nash, J. D., & Newberg, A. (2013). Toward a unifying taxonomy and definition for meditation. *Frontiers in Psychology, 20*. doi: 10.3389/fpsyg.2013.00806.

Newberg, A., Alavi, A., Baime, M., Pourdehnad, M., Santanna, J., & d'Aquili, E. (2001). The measurement of regional cerebral blood flow during the complex cognitive task of meditation: A preliminary SPECT study. *Psychiatry Research, 106*(2), 113–122.

Nishitani, K. (1983). *Religion and nothingness*. Berkeley: University of California Press, p. 164.

Norbu, N., & Lipman, K. (1987). *Primordial experience*. Boston, MA: Shambala.

Padmasambhava. (2010). *Essential instructions on mastering the energies of life* (K. Lipman, Trans.). Boston, MA: Shambala.

Rabjam, L. (2001). *The precious treasury of the basic space of phenomena* (R. Barron, Trans.). Junction City, CA: Padma Publishing.

Rabjam, L. (2007). *The precious treasury of philosophical systems* (R. Barron, Trans.). Junction City, CA: Padma Publishing.

Radhakrishnan, S. (1995). *The principal upanishads*. New Delhi: HarperCollins.

Schloegl, I. (1975). The Zen teaching of Rinzai. Berkeley, CA: Shambhala Publications, p. 22.

Slagter, H. A., Lutz, A., Greischar, L. L., Francis A. D., Nieuwenhuis, S., et al. (2007). Mental training affects distribution of limited brain resources. *PLOS Biology 5*, e138.

Tang, Y.-Y., Ma, Y., Wang, J., et al. (2007). Short-term meditation training improves attention and self-regulation. *Proceedings of the National Academy of Sciences 104*, 17152–17156.

Trangu, K. (2001). *Five Buddha families and eight consciousnesses*. Auckland, New Zealand: Zhyisil Chokyi Ghatsal Publications.

Travis, F., Haaga, D., Hagelin, J., Arenander, A., Tanner, M., & Schneider, R. (2010). Self-referential awareness: Coherence, power, and eLORETA patterns during eyes-closed rest, transcendental meditation and TM-Sidhi practice. *Cognitive Processing 11*, 21–30.

Travis, F., & Shear, J. (2010). Focused attention, open monitoring and automatic self-transcending: Categories to organize meditations from Vedic, Buddhist and Chinese traditions. *Consciousness and Cognition 19*, 1110–1118.

Tsultrim, G. (2001). Progressive stages of meditation on emptiness. (S. Hookham, Trans.). Auckland, New Zealand: Zhyisil Chokyi Ghatsal Publications, p. 75.

Vago, D. R., & Silbersweig, D. A. (2012). Self-awareness, self- regulation, and self-transcendence (S-ART): A framework for understanding the neurobiological mechanisms of mindfulness. *Frontiers in Human Neuroscience, 6*, 296. doi: 10.3389/fn- hum.2012.00296.

Watson, B. (n.d.). The Zen teaching of Master Lin Chi. Retrieved from http://allspirit.co.uk/rinzai.html

Williams, P. (2000). *The reflexive nature of awareness*. New Delhi: Motilal Banarsidass.

Yuasa, Y. (1987). The body: Toward an Eastern mind-body theory (N. Shigenori & T. P. Kasulis, Trans.). Albany: State University of New York Press, p. 105, 156.

CHAPTER 6

FOLK THEORIES OF CALLING IN CHINESE CULTURAL CONTEXTS

Kaiping Peng and Yukun Zhao

Contemporary research in psychology has found that people hold a constellation of folk theories in various domains, including agency, causality, freewill, human nature, to name a few, and the content of these theories varies across cultures. What is missing in this line of research is a cultural–psychological approach to calling—an investigation of people's folk theories of calling across cultures, as it is an important piece of this epistemic puzzle. We know that people act as intuitive scientists, collecting data, generating hypotheses, and making predictions, when faced with understanding epistemological matters (see Gopnik & Wellman, 1994 for an overview). People also act as intuitive economists, aiming to maximize utility (Edwards, 1962); pragmatic politicians, coping with accountability demands from others; principled theologians, protecting sacred values; and prudent prosecutors, enforcing social norms (Tetlock, 2002). Continuing this domain-specific theory approach, the research presented here will propose both a theory-based and culture-based approach to understanding callings.

THE FOLK THEORY APPROACH

What Is a Folk Theory?

A folk theory is an interpretive framework or mental model (Levy, Plaks, & Dweck, 1999) that ascribes meaning to a person's everyday interactions and relationships by assisting him or her to explain, predict, and control his or her social world. For decades, psychology has recognized that people give meaning to their experiences and to their interactions with the world around them. Moreover, the notion that people structure and relate to the world differently as a function of the meaning that they assign to events in their social and physical environments has significant roots in the social sciences (see, e.g., Molden & Dweck, 2006). Within psychology, social cognitive approaches have analyzed the techniques that people use to interpret, explain, and predict behavior, and cultural psychological approaches in tandem have concentrated on how these techniques vary across cultures—how members of different cultures assign meaning to their experiences.

A wealth of research suggests that people form naïve "folk" theories, fundamental assumptions about the nature of the self and the social world (Molden & Dweck, 2006; Morris, Ames & Knowles, 2001). Thus, a folk theory analysis identifies particular domain-specific folk theories and explores their influence upon psychological functioning. Dweck (2006) has focused on how meaning systems that emerge from folk theories can alter general cognitive structures and processes through which a person perceives the world. For instance, research indicates that a particular folk theory can radically influence one's self-regulatory abilities and social perception (see, e.g., Levy, Plaks, Hong, Chiu, & Dweck, 2001). Folk theories are domain specific (Gopnik & Wellman, 1994; Dweck, 1999), involve individual differences (Levy et al., 2001), and may be unconscious (Wegener & Petty, 1998).

Folk Theories Vary Across Cultures

Cultural psychologists have focused on various folk theories shared by a culture's members as a platform for analyzing similarities and differences across cultures. Within this discipline, the theory tradition has emerged as a method of assessing cultures in terms of their widely shared implicit folk theories (Peng, Ames, & Knowles, 2001). Research within the theory tradition focuses on widespread belief systems that have been described as cultural models (Holland & Quinn, 1987); cosmologies (Douglas, 1982); cultural representations (Boyer, 1993; Sperber, 1990); naïve ontologies and epistemologies (Peng & Nisbett, 1999); and folk psychologies, biologies, sociologies, and physics (e.g., Ames, 1999; Atran, 1990; Fiske, 1992; Lillard, 1998; Peng & Knowles, 2003; Vosniadou, 1994) (for a more extensive review, see Peng et al., 2001).

Researchers have examined a wide variety of folk theories about the world. For example, Chiu, Hong, and Dweck (1997) investigated folk theories about personality change, finding that Americans tend to assume stability in personality, while Hong Kong Chinese often expect malleability. Peng, Ames, and Knowles (2001) demonstrated that Chinese are guided by more holistic theories of impressions when getting to know a target person, compared to

Americans. In addition, Menon, Morris, Chiu, and Hong (1999) showed that Chinese were more willing to make attributions of causality and responsibility at the group level, while Americans were less willing to make such attributions.

In the theory of mind domain, controversy exists regarding the cross-cultural aspect of theory of mind development. Henry Wellman, Cross, and Watson (2001) presented a meta-analysis that suggested that children's theories of mind follow a consistent developmental pattern across cultures. Other research exists, however, to indicate that theory of mind development does indeed vary across cultures. For instance, Angeline Lillard (1997, 1998, 1999) has extensively offered evidence that an individual's every day, basic understanding of other's mental states and behaviors may be influenced by her culture. Lillard (1997) provides specific examples of cultures that have radically different theory of mind developmental trajectories. The Illongot people of the Philippines, for example, do not have a concept analogous to "mind," and the Azande of Central Africa attribute any sort of unfortunate event or behavior to witchcraft. Lillard argues that cultural variation is an essential component to understanding how one's folk theory of mind develops and functions. In sum, a significant amount of evidence suggests that people's theories of mind vary across cultures.

Folk Theories Are Domain Specific

The structure and content of an individual's folk theories vary across domains; and researchers study folk theories in domain-specific areas. As discussed earlier, rich theoretical and empirical research programs exist in the theory of mind, economic theory, and causality theory domains, to name but a few.

Thus, a folk theory is a culture specific, domain specific, malleable, interpretive framework with which to view the world. One's personal experiences, as well as a set of culture-specific values and beliefs, form an individual's folk theory. At the representational level, folk theories provide a lens for examining individual and group attitudes, inferences, and behaviors. The research program presented here uses the folk theory analysis to analyze a sample of Chinese theories of human nature.

CALLING IN CHINESE CONTEXTS

Throughout history, people have been forming opinions on the fundamental questions of meaning of life. The basic question, "What is meaning of life?" has captivated and eluded the masses. An inquiring mind will find a different answer to this question depending on whom he or she asks. Indeed, a philosopher, a biologist, an economist, a politician, a religious leader, a lawyer, and a tax collector are likely to provide wildly divergent responses to his or her inquiry.

The present analysis focuses on people's everyday understandings of meaning of life, in particular, people's understanding of the sense of calling. Basic questions in this regard include, "When and in what way people sense the calling? Who is making the calling? How do they response to the calling? Do people from different cultures hold divergent folk theories about the calling?"

Cultural psychologists have found systematic differences in values such as individualism-collectivism (Triandis, 1995) being the most thoroughly researched dimension. Cultures defined the ways of "being a self," and, in particular, how self-conceptions may be at the core of a culture's composition, with independent and interdependent self-construals (Markus & Kitayama, 1991) being the most widespread research. Cultural psychologists argue that culture-specific folk theories guide how members of a given culture collect and interpret evidence and support inferences and judgments that go beyond the immediate data, while values and concepts of self shape the folk theories and the contexts in which the inferences are turned into action (see, e.g., Peng et al., 2001). In almost all the areas the cross-cultural research that has been conducted thus far, the Chinese samples seem to be the most different from the Western perspectives (Bond, 1996), which is also the case in the domain of calling.

Philosophers and scientists in China have been devising theories of calling for thousands of years. The *early Chinese* believed the heaven created humans to occupy a special position in the universe, to have dominion over the rest of creation. The human race is unique in that it possesses self-consciousness. The human race is continuous with the rest of creation, made of the dust from the ground. The attainment of the true purpose of human life—to respect the heaven and living a life according to the Tao of nature—is available to all, and there is a destination for every one of us in the society we should all follow.

However, *Confucius* believes everything about people is determined by the positions people hold in their lives. The real nature of humanity is the totality of social relations, our essential responsibility for everyone in the relational circle and hierarchy. An individual's actions are inherent social acts that presume the existence of a relationship with other people. People are active, productive beings, distinguished from other animals by the fact that they produce their means of subsistence. The way in which we eat, sleep, copulate, and defecate are learned and socialized. The kind of person one is and one's actions are determined by the kind of society in which one lives; the calling is the responsibility for other people.

Our Approach

We are adopting a bottom-up approach to this investigation of people's conceptions of calling. In short, based on the research that we conducted (discussed below), we are proposing that people have implicit, working theories of calling that link into their larger theories of meaning of life and that these folk theories may vary across cultures.

We propose that an individual's conceptions of calling can be best described as a *folk theory* and we take a theory-based approach to studying this phenomenon (Gopnik & Wellman, 1994; Kuhn, 1989; Nisbett & Ross, 1980). A folk theory of calling consists of an individual's working system of social knowledge acquired through instruction and experience. The system is theory-like because it can predict, explain, and interpret and is coherent and subject to revision (Lillard, 1997).

The content of this theory is formed from social and cultural information acquired through instruction and experience. At the instructional level, one's parents, teachers, siblings, peers, and community members convey information to the individual through their attitudes, actions, and direct instructions regarding the world and how people are likely to act in it. Indirectly, one's culture provides an overarching source of information to the individual through, for instance, the mass media, institutional practices, and social norms. At the experiential level, an individual's positive and negative experiences with others will add input to the theory, either strengthening the theory or providing counterevidence to the theory.

The exact way in which callings are understood, realized, and used in Chinese cultural contexts is difficult to predict, given the dearth of cultural psychological research in this area. Based on conventional cultural psychology research, however, one could predict that Chinese participants would take a more relational, collective, and duty-bound view of callings.

Hypotheses

With historical and cross-cultural research in mind, a set of studies were drafted with the following overarching research questions: Do people have stable and measurable beliefs about calling in general? Is there variety in these beliefs among individuals and across cultures?

Based on the above research questions, we proposed the following hypotheses:

Hypothesis I: People have stable and measurable beliefs about calling in general. These lay theories can be measured.
Hypothesis II: There is variety in these beliefs across cultures.

Hypothesis III: The Chinese folk theories of calling should be more relational, hence duty-bounded and collective.

We conducted a study (described below) to test Hypothesis III.

Method

A survey was run to investigate the calling of contemporary Chinese. Most
of the existing calling questionnaires focus in vocation and work-related domains (e.g., Dik, Eldridge, Steger, & Duffy, 2012; Dobrow & Tosti-Kharas,
2011; Dreher, Holloway, & Shoenfelder, 2009). Since we needed to investigate
the sense of being called of the participants in all of their life domains, we developed an inventory for this purpose. It consists of four questions. The first
one is the frequency of calling question, "How often do you have the sense
of calling?" The participants needed to choose from a seven-point Likert
scale, from 1—Never to 7—Always. The second one is the strength question, "How strong do you feel the sense of calling?" The participants needed
to choose from a seven-point Likert scale, from 1—Very weak to 7—Very
strong. The sense of being called is calculated as the square root of product
of the grades of these two questions.[1] The other two questions are open
questions inquiring participants' experience of calling: "What makes you feel
called (e.g., a situation, an event, a thing, a vocation, or people)?" "What was
it like when you felt being called?"

The participants were the students of the first author's Massive Open
Online Course (MOOC) *Introduction to Psychology*,[2] offered by Tsinghua
University. The course is open to public, but to receive a credit from the
MOOC, a student has to complete all the assignments. This survey was one
of the required assignments, along with other surveys that measured the
students' subjective well-being, personality, prosocial tendency, meaning in
life, and so on. A total of 188 students completed all the surveys with valid
answers, among whom 81 were males, 107 were females. The average age
was 25.9 years (SD = 7.3); 167 of them (89%) don't belong to any religion;
89 (47%) were full-time students, 18 (10%) were professionals, 18 (10%) were
office workers, 15 (8%) were teachers, 15 (8%) were managers, the rest were
from other professions like technicians, treasurers, and so on. Excluding
those with no income like students, the average monthly income was 5670
RMB (SD = 2610), which was about 913 USD.

Subjective well-being was measured in three dimensions: positive affect,
negative affect, and life satisfaction. Positive affect and negative affect were
measured by the 20-item positive and negative affect schedule (PANAS; Watson, Clark, & Tellegen, 1988). Life satisfaction was measured by the five-item
satisfaction with life scale (SWLS; Diener, Emons, Larsen, & Griffin, 1985).

Subjective well-being was then calculated as the sum of the life satisfaction and the affective balance, which was positive affect minus negative affect. Personality was measured by the 44-item Big Five Inventory (BFI) questionnaire (John & Srivastava, 1999). The prosocial behaviors were measured by the 23-item questionnaire developed by Carlo and Randall (2002). Meaning in life was measured by the 10-item meaning in life questionnaire (Steger, Frazier, Oishi, & Kaler, 2006), with five items for the "Presence" subscale that measures how much one currently has meaning in life, and five items for the "Search" subscale that measures how much one is looking for meaning in life.

Results

As Table 6.1 shows, the sense of being called is significantly correlated to a person's positive affect, but only mildly negatively to not correlated to negative affect, and it is not correlated to life satisfaction. The correlation between one's calling and overall subjective well-being is mild. In general, these results mean that contemporary Chinese with a sense of calling are happier. They enjoy more positive emotions, and suffer a little less negative emotions. Furthermore, calling is significantly correlated to prosocial behaviors, which implies that those who help often have more sense of calling, and vice versa.

Not surprisingly, calling is significantly correlated to one's sense of having meaning in life. When one feels called, he or she has a clear purpose of life and understands his or her life's meaning. These made him or her score

Table 6.1   Intercorrelations between calling and well-being measures

	PA	NA	LS	SWB	Prosocial	Meaning_ Presence	Meaning_ Search	Calling
PA	1	−.224**	.418**	.663**	.218**	.269**	−.019	.311**
NA	−.224**	1	−.320**	−.610**	.080	−.258**	.258**	−.127
LS	.418**	−.320**	1	.897**	.070	.257**	−.202**	.014
SWB	.663**	−.610**	.897**	1	.088	.339**	−.224**	.148*
Prosocial	.218**	.080	.070	.088	1	.164*	.112	.300**
Meaning_ Presence	.269**	−.258**	.257**	.339**	.164*	1	−.139	.341**
Meaning_ Search	−.019	.258**	−.202**	−.224**	.112	−.139	1	.065
Calling	.311**	−.127	.014	.148*	.300**	.341**	.065	1

** $p < 0.01$.
* $p < 0.05$.

Table 6.2 Intercorrelations between calling and personality

	Extraversion	Agreeableness	Conscientiousness	Neuroticism	Openness	Calling
Extraversion	1	.316**	.325**	−.492**	.364**	.323**
Agreeableness	.316**	1	.262**	−.389**	.195**	.106
Conscientiousness	.325**	.262**	1	−.446**	.322**	.274**
Neuroticism	−.492**	−.389**	−.446**	1	−.074	−.172*
Openness	.364**	.195**	.322**	−.074	1	.400**
Calling	.323**	.106	.274**	−.172*	.400**	1

** $p < 0.01$.
* $p < 0.05$.

high in the Presence subscale of meaning. However, calling is not correlated to the Search subscale of meaning. This is probably because one can't feel called when he or she is still looking for the meaning of life. On the other side, if one feels called, he or she should've probably finished the search for meaning.

We also calculated the correlations between calling and personality. Our results showed that, as demonstrated in Table 6.2, the sense of being called is significantly correlated to extraversion, conscientiousness, and openness, mildly negatively correlated to neuroticism, and slightly correlated to agreeableness. This means an open, conscientious, emotionally stable extravert is more likely to feel called.

The answers to the qualitative questions showed a consistent pattern with the previous theoretical analysis. To the question "What makes you feel called (e.g., a situation, an event, a thing, a vocation, or people)?," 84 themes were identified from the 188 entries. We further grouped these themes into six categories: *others, work, responsibility, society, individual goals*, and *transcendence*. The occurrences and examples of each category are shown in Table 6.3.

Clearly, contemporary Chinese are typically called by secular and mundane objects. They feel called when other people need them, when they are required to do something in the work, or expected to take care of others. The most frequently mentioned group in the "others" category is *family* (38, or 42%), which means not only love and relationship, but also responsibility in Chinese culture. Similarly, the category of "*work*" implies responsibility for Chinese people. Therefore, we can find a strong characteristic of responsibility in what makes Chinese feel called. In contrast, Chinese people are less called to *individual goals. Transcendent objects*, no matter whether they are spiritual like religion, or nonspiritual like arts and sciences, are least likely to make contemporary Chinese feel called.

Similarly, 86 emotions were identified from the answers to the question "What was it like when you felt being called?" We grouped them into 24

Table 6.3   Occurrences of objects that make people feel called

Category	Occurrences	Examples
Others	91	Family, friends, students
Work	56	Jobs, education, police, soldier
Responsibility	51	When others need me, when only I can do it
Society	40	Country, social justice, environment
Individual goals	31	Skills, study, success, life, exams
Transcendence	22	Art, science, culture, philosophy, religion

Table 6.4   Emotions aroused by calling

Motivated	58	Happy	8	Satisfied	5
Excited	38	Meaningful	6	Engaged	4
Stressed	23	Reflecting	6	Existential	4
Valued	17	Resilient	6	Purposeful	4
Responsible	12	Confident	5	Dedicated	3
Striving	11	Passionate	5	Elevated	3
Achieved	10	Prospecting	5	Prudent	2
Proud	10	Purposeless	5	Optimistic	1

categories. Table 6.4 shows the occurrences of these emotions in the participants' answers. As expected, *motivated* and *excited* are the top two emotions aroused by calling. But *stressed* and *responsible* made into the top five list too. Since people most likely feel stressed because of the responsibility, the combination of these two emotions would surpass *excited*, and is almost as common as *motivated*. This, again, shows that Chinese people's calling is closely related to responsibility.

We can further categorize these emotions into positive emotions and negative emotions. Most of the emotions are easy to categorize, for example, *excited*, *valued*, and *proud* are positive emotions, *stressed* and *purposeless* are negative emotions. The feeling of being *responsible* is, however, difficult to be categorized as simply positive or negative. Peng and Nisbett (1999) found that Chinese people experience dialectical emotion more often than Westerners, which means they often feel positive and negative at the same time. Therefore the number of occurrences of *responsible* was divided evenly between the category of positive emotion and negative emotion. Then positive emotions consist of 87 percent of the occurrences, while negative emotions only consist of 13 percent. This is consistent with our quantitative results from the correlation analysis that the sense of being called is significantly correlated to positive affect, and its correlation to negative affect is minimal.

Discussion

The survey results are consistent with our theoretical analysis that Chinese people's sense of being called is heavily influenced by the collectivistic, holistic, dialectic, and practical characteristics of Chinese culture. According to our survey results, callings of contemporary Chinese are typically secular, driven by responsibility rather than called by transcendent causes or personal strengths. The survey confirmed our Hypothesis III that the

Chinese folk theories of calling to be more relational, hence duty bounded and collective.

This study also has its limitations. First, as in many cross-cultural studies, the accuracy of the translation of the terms could jeopardize the credibility of the study. There's no Chinese word that exactly correspond to the word "calling." We had to use two words to describe it, *zhaohuan* which means "summoning," and *shiminggan* which means sense of mission. This may have led to misunderstanding of some participants which made them fail to answer the questions in the way we hoped. Second, due to the time constraint, we didn't run a similar survey in other cultural context, especially in the Western culture, to compare the results. Our study found some influences of Chinese culture to calling, for example, the driving force of responsibility, the collectivistic thinking style. But we also found some psychological features of the sense of being called that seem to be generic across cultures, for example, calling is significantly correlated to presence of meaning but not to search of meaning, the most common emotions people have when feel called are motivated and excited. Further research is expected to complement this study for a better comparison between callings of Chinese and those of other cultures.

GENERAL DISCUSSION

Increasingly, psychologists are discovering that people's existing patterns of social beliefs affect the way in which they process social information. For example, children hold systematic beliefs about the relationship between gender and aggression, and these beliefs affect the way children reason about aggression (Giles & Heyman, 2005). We posit that an individual's existing pattern of social beliefs about calling will affect his or her process of making judgments about the meaning of life.

Conceptually, a folk theory of calling can fit into a larger theory of meaning of life. The folk theory can color (or perhaps paint) the way in which an individual judges the purpose and meaning of his or her lives. In terms of the mechanics of finding the meaning of life, the folk theory of calling can be incorporated into the current, dominant approaches to meaning of life in positive psychology.

IMPLICATIONS FOR CULTURE

Another facet of this research inquires as to whether Westerners make different assumptions about calling compared to Easterners. Do the contents of a Western adult's folk theories differ from those of an East Asian adult? Research has indicated that East Asians adopt a holistic cognition, attending to the entire field and assigning causality to it, making relatively little use of categories and formal logic, and relying on dialectical reasoning (Nisbett, Peng, Choi, & Norenzayan, 2001). Westerners are more analytic, following an essentialist orientation, paying attention primarily to the object and the categories to which it belongs and using rules, including formal logic, to understand its behavior. These cultural differences may influence the content and structure of individuals' folk theories. The theories of Westerners may be more essentialistic, category based, dispositionalistic, and rationalistic, whereas East Asian theories may be more dialectical and focus more on social context, background setting, and variability among humans.

This research project was intended to be a starting point for future investigations on the topic of folk theories of meaning of life and calling, and how these theories relate to, and interact with, other core theories in a social cognitive system. Further research can continue to explore the dynamics of such folk theories, the diversity of theories across cultures, and the intricacies of the theories' operations with other social cognitive components.

ACKNOWLEDGMENT

With thanks to Min Zhou for assisting to run the survey.

NOTES

1. We also tried two other ways to calculate the total sense of calling: sum of frequency and strength, and the square root of the sum of the square of frequency and strength. The quantitative results were very similar.

2. The details of the course can be found at http://www.xuetangx.com/courses/TsinghuaX/30700313_2014X/2014_T2/info (in Chinese).

REFERENCES

Ames, D. (1999). Folk psychology and social inference: Everyday solutions to the problem of other minds. Unpublished doctoral dissertation, University of California, Berkeley.

Atran, S. (1990). *Cognitive foundations of natural history: Towards an anthropology of science.* New York: Cambridge University Press.

Bond, M. H. E. (1996). *The handbook of Chinese psychology.* Oxford University Press.

Boyer, P. (1993). *The naturalness of religious ideas.* Berkeley: University of California Press.

Carlo, G., & Randall, B. A. (2002). The development of a measure of prosocial behaviors for late adolescents. *Journal of Youth and Adolescence, 31*(1), 31–44.

Chiu, C. Y., Hong, Y. Y., & Dweck, C. S. (1997). Lay dispositionism and implicit theories of personality. *Journal of Personality and Social Psychology, 73*(1), 19.

Diener, E., Emmons, R. A., Larsen, R. J., & Griffin, S. (1985). The satisfaction with life scale. *Journal of Personality Assessment, 49,* 71–75.

Dik, B. J., Eldridge, B. M., Steger, M. F., & Duffy, R. D. (2012). Development and validation of the calling and vocation questionnaire (CVQ) and brief calling scale (BCS). *Journal of Career Assessment*, 1069072711434410.

Dobrow, S. R., & Tosti-Kharas, J. (2011). Calling: The development of a scale measure. *Personnel Psychology*, *64*, 1001–1049.

Douglas, M. (1982). *In the active voice*. London: Routledge & Kegan Paul.

Dreher, D. E., Holloway, K. A., & Schoenfelder, E. (2007). The vocation identity questionnaire: Measuring the sense of calling. *Research in the Social Scientific Study of Religion*, *18*, 99–120.

Dweck, C. (1999). *Self-theories: Their role in motivation, personality, and development*. Philadelphia, PA: Psychology Press.

Dweck, C. (2006). *Mindset*. New York: Random House.

Edwards, W. (1962). Subjective probabilities inferred from decisions. *Psychological Review*, *69*, 109–135.

Fiske, A. (1992). The four elementary forms of sociality: Framework for a unified theory of sociality. *Psychological Review*, *99*, 689–723.

Giles, J. W., & Heyman, G. D. (2005). Young children's beliefs about the relationship between gender and aggressive behavior. *Child Development*, *76*, 107–121.

Gopnik, A., & Wellman, H. (1994). The "theory theory". In L. Hirschfeld and S. Gelman (Eds.), *Domain specificity in culture and cognition*. New York: Cambridge University Press.

Holland, D., & Quinn, N. (1987). *Cultural models in language and thought*. Cambridge: Cambridge University Press.

John, O. P., & Srivastava, S. (1999). The big five trait taxonomy: History, measurement, and theoretical perspectives. In Pervin, L. A., & John, O. P. (Eds.). *Handbook of personality: Theory and research* (Vol. 2, pp. 102–138). Amsterdam: Elsevier.

Kuhn, D. (1989). Children and adults as intuitive scientists. *Psychological Review*, *96*, 674–689.

Levy, S., Plaks, J., Hong, Y., Chiu, C., & Dweck, C. (2001). Static versus dynamic theories and the perception of groups: Different routes to different destinations. *Personality and Social Psychology Review*, *5*, 156–168.

Levy, S., Plaks, J., & Dweck, C. (1999). Modes of social thought: Implicit theories and social understanding. In S. Chaiken & Y. Trope (Eds.), *Dual process theories in social psychology* (pp. 179–202). New York: Guilford.

Lillard, A. S. (1997). Other folks' theories of mind and behavior. *Psychological Science*, *8*, 268–274.

Lillard, A. S. (1998). Ethnopsychologies: Cultural variations in theory of mind. *Psychological Bulletin*, *123*, 3–30.

Lillard, A. S. (1999). Developing a cultural theory of mind: The CIAO approach. *Current Directions in Psychological Science*, *8*, 57–61.

Markus, H., & Kitayama, S. (1991). Culture and self: Implications for cognition, emotion and motivation. *Psychological Review*, *98*, 224–253.

Mauter, Thomas. (Ed.) (1998). *The Penguin dictionary of philosophy*. New York: Penguin Books.

Menon, T., Morris, M., Chiu, C., & Hong, Y. (1999). Culture and the construal of agency: Attribution to individual versus group dispositions. *Journal of Personality and Social Psychology*, *76*, 701–727.

Molden, D., & Dweck, C. (2006). Finding "meaning" in psychology: A lay theories approach to self-regulation, social perception, and social development. *American Psychologist, 61*, 192–203.

Morris, M. W., Ames, D., & Knowles, E. (2001). What we theorize when we theorize that we theorize: Examining the "implicit theory" construct from a cross-disciplinary perspective. In G. D. Moscowitz (Ed.), *Cognitive social psychology: The Princeton symposium in the legacy and future of social cognition* (pp. 245–264). Mahwah, NJ: Erlbaum.

Nisbett, R., Peng, K., Choi, I., & Norenzayan, A. (2001). Culture and system of thought: Holistic versus analytic cognition. *Psychological Review, 108*, 1–20.

Nisbett, R., & Ross, L. (1980). *Human inference: Strategies and shortcomings of social judgment.* Englewood Cliffs, NJ: Prentice-Hall.

Peng, K., Ames D., & Knowles, E. (2001). Culture and human inference: Perspectives from three traditions. In D. Matsumoto (Ed.), *Handbook of culture and psychology.* New York: Oxford University Press.

Peng, K., & Knowles, E. (2003). Culture, ethnicity and attribution of physical causality. *Personality and Social Psychology Bulletin, 29*, 1272–1284.

Peng, K., & Nisbett, R. (1999). Culture, dialectics, and reasoning about contradiction. *American Psychologist, 51*, 252–264.

Sperber, D. (1990). The epidemiology of beliefs. In C. Fraser & G. Gaskell (Eds.), *The social psychological study of widespread beliefs* (pp. 24–44). Oxford, England: Clarendon Press.

Steger, M. F., Frazier, P., Oishi, S., & Kaler, M. (2006). The meaning in life questionnaire: Assessing the presence of and search for meaning in life. *Journal of counseling psychology, 53*(1), 80.

Tetlock, P. (2002). Social functionalist frameworks for judgment and choice: intuitive politicians, theologians, and prosecutors. *Psychological Review, 109*, 451–471.

Triandis, H. (1995). *Individualism and collectivism.* Boulder, CO: Westview Press.

Vosniadou, S. (1994). Universal and culture-specific properties of children's mental models of the earth. In L. Hirschfeld & S. Gelman (Eds.), *Mapping the mind: Domain specificity in cognition and culture.* New York: Cambridge University Press.

Watson, D., Clark, L. A., & Tellegen, A. (1988). Development and validation of brief measures of positive and negative affect: The PANAS scales. *Journal of Personality and Social Psychology, 54*, 1063–1070.

Wegener, D., & Petty, R. (1998). The naïve scientist revisited: Naïve theories and social judgment. *Social Cognition, 16*, 1–7.

Wellman, H., Cross, D., & Watson, J. (2001). Meta-analysis of theory-of-mind development: The truth about false belief. *Child Development, 72*, 685–707.

CHAPTER 7

CALLING COUNSELORS: A NOVEL CALLING INTERVENTION FOR CAREER DEVELOPMENT AND WELL-BEING

Susanna Wu-Pong

"The Hero's Journey," the personal quest to fulfill one's life's purpose, has been described in myths, legends, and religions across the world (Campbell, 2008). Typically, a call to adventure initiates the journey. The way is difficult, battles are fought, but the rewards are great. One who completes the hero's journey can expect a sense of personal triumph and wisdom to bring back to the community at large. In contrast, failing to heed the call changes the hero's life into a wasteland. This nearly universal story, or "monomyth" can be interpreted metaphorically as the psychological journey to find an authentic role worthy of one's hard work and devotion—in other words, to find meaning and purpose in life through a calling. Career counselors, individuals who are institutionally charged to help students find their way into a fulfilling and meaningful future career, are uniquely positioned to help students on the journey to find their calling.

Callings describe work that serves a cause greater than oneself and provides meaning and purpose in life (for reviews, see Dik & Duffy, 2012; Yaden & Newberg, this volume). According to one definition, *callings* are contrasted with *jobs*, which are seen as just means to a paycheck, and *careers*, which are seen primarily as an opportunity for personal and professional advancement. Work perceived as a calling has been linked with a number of positive outcomes including well-being, intrinsic motivation, as well as life and work satisfaction (Wrzesniewski, McCauley, Rozin, & Schwartz, 1997).

Helping students to find their calling is among the highest aims of career counselors. This inspiration is often lost amidst the practicalities of contemporary student advising, but a return to an emphasis on calling may help to reinvigorate both counselor and student. In the same way that a *calling* has certain benefits over a *career*, given the framework described above, we suggest (also described by Elangovan, Pinder, & McLean, 2010) that construing "career counselors" as "*calling* counselors" may likewise emphasize the latent potential for counselors to help students to find more meaningful work.

In this chapter, I describe a career and professional development class at a major university designed to help professional, graduate, and postdoctoral students, predominantly in biomedical disciplines, find their callings. The class incorporates classic career counseling concepts alongside a calling intervention, which includes self-awareness, authentic purpose, and strengths. This chapter provides an overview of the course with an emphasis on the elements that relate to callings, as well as a description of the callings exercise. I suggest that helping students to uncover their calling can enrich existing career development programs and their personal career journeys.

CALLING

No single definition of callings enjoys consensus among scientists in the field (for reviews, see Dik & Duffy, 2012; Yaden & Newberg, this volume). Many definitions exist, each of which encompasses a range of criteria with some points of agreement. In general, callings may include some combination of authenticity or specificity to the individual, prosocial or altruistic orientation where the focus is on serving others, creation of meaning in one's life, and a transcendent summons from beyond the self. For the purposes of this chapter, Elangovan et al.'s (2010) definition of callings will be used: "course of action in pursuit of prosocial intentions embodying the convergence of an individual's sense of what he or she would like to do, should do, and actually does."

While estimates vary according to the definition used, callings (as opposed to jobs or careers) are reported by about 30–40 percent of people (Duffy & Sedlacek, 2007; Wrzesniewski et al., 1997). College students who sense a calling report improved career decidedness, comfort and clarity in their career path (Duffy & Sedlacek, 2007). Callings also positively impact career engagement, career decision self-efficacy, and intrinsic work motivation (Hirschi, 2011; Duffy, Bott, Allan, Torrey, & Dik, 2012). In contrast, approximately half of those without a calling either are searching for their calling or struggling to find their vocational identity that will lead them to their calling (Dik, Duffy, & Eldridge, 2009; Duffy, Dik, & Steger, 2011; Duffy & Sedlacek, 2007; Wrzesniewski et al., 1997).

The 60–70 percent that lack a calling and who feel that their work is either a job or a career provide a potential population for callings interventions. Whereas a calling benefits others and serves as an end to itself, a career involves obtaining promotions, is moderately fulfilling, and focuses on personal investment and professional advancement. In contrast, a job is a way to make money and primarily provides material benefit (Dik & Duffy, 2009; Wrzesniewski et al., 1997). Though the binary (present vs. absent) or ternary (calling, career, job) calling construct (Dik et al., 2009; Duffy & Sedlacek, 2007; Wrzesniewski et al., 1997) provides a useful framework for assessing callings, newer calling assessments are based on the assumption that callings occur on a spectrum (Dik, Eldridge, Steger, & Duffy, 2012; Hagemeir & Abele, 2012).

Callings promote a number of psychological benefits. Having a calling is associated with life satisfaction and well-being (Duffy, Allan, Autin, & Bott, 2013; Duffy et al., 2012; Hunter, Dik, & Banning, 2010; Steger, Pickering, Shin, & Dik, 2010; Wrzesniewski et al., 1997). Wrzesniewski et al. (1997) found that when surveying individuals among a wide range of professions, those who viewed their job as a calling had better life, health, and job satisfaction, regardless of the job level. Certain downsides are also associated with callings, however. Employers can take advantage of employees with a sense of calling, as they are more likely to work more unpaid hours (Bunderson & Thompson, 2009). Also, failing to achieve one's calling can create ongoing frustration and disappointment (Berg, Grant, & Johnson, 2010).

In addition to the known benefits and downsides of callings, several obstacles to finding and living out one's calling have been identified. Life barriers and constraints such as socioeconomics, family demands, negative thinking, unemployment, poor self-confidence, and dysfunctional career thoughts can infringe on effective career problem solving, decision-making, and the pursuit of preferred career decisions. For instance, as reviewed by Duffy et al. (2012), racial or gender identity minorities also often have difficulty obtaining or maintaining employment in their chosen field suggesting that discrimination and minority status may also play a role. For example, discrimination in promotion procedures may prevent a female or person of color from rising to the role that she finds satisfying or believes to be her calling. Some solutions have been suggested, such as maintaining independence from cultural influence, emotional intelligence (EQ), authenticity, and improving career decision-making (reviewed by Erford & Crockett, 2012). In this chapter, I focus on the ability to first identify one's calling.

CAREER AND CALLING COUNSELING

The modern search for meaning through work provides an enticing opportunity to enrich current career counseling strategies using innovative calling interventions. According to the National Employment Counseling Association (employmentcounseling.org), formerly the National Vocational

Guidance Association, vocational, employment, or career counselors help individuals with career development and job placement. Career counselors assist individuals with vocational choice, that is, in making wise career choices, which are understood to then positively impact the rest of one's life. However, this discipline focuses on identifying a suitable career or job that fits one's needs, interests, and values instead of helping one to identify a deeper passion manifested by their calling. Thus, a successful career counseling intervention would be a useful tool for vocational counselors to help individuals foster achievement, meaning, and purpose at work, and to create a satisfying and flourishing life through finding and living one's calling.

Traditional career counseling focuses on helping people, usually high school and college students, to select a career based on their personal qualities and their "vocational personality type." The process relies predominantly on Holland's (1997) vocational theory, which matches individuals to occupations that fit their vocational personality. The theory assumes six vocational personalities summarized by the acronym RIASEC (realistic, investigative, artistic, enterprising, social, conventional) and is assessed using instruments like the Strong Interest Inventory or the Vocational Preference Inventory. The theory is the most widely used model for career assessment (Gottfredson & Holland, 1996).

Career counselors also help individuals overcome obstacles in career decision-making. Obstacles include narrowing the number of choices, considering job factors such as required training and salaries, matching personal qualities with the job, helping to mitigate perceived social barriers and improving student self-efficacy in the decision process. Other assessments (e.g., Career Decision-Making Difficulties Questionnaire) may be used to help with the counseling process. Newer assessments in career decision-making, maturity, and self-efficacy are also being empirically tested. For example, the Career Development Inventory is used to measure the age appropriateness of career-related tasks to help address career development deficiencies (summarized by Erford & Crockett, 2012; Gati & Levin, 2012; Gelso, Williams, & Fretz, 2014, Chapter 15).

Modern enhancements in theory (for review, see Gelso et al., 2014, Chapter 5) and practice to traditional career counseling seek to more effectively incorporate individual characteristics into the career development process. For example, the career constructivism theory builds upon RIASEC by using personal narratives to assess and integrate personal identity into the career development and design process (reviewed by Dik et al., 2013, Chapter 6 and Erford & Crockett, 2012). Career counselors help to guide the process based on the students' aptitude, interests, and track record. However, because of the challenges in the changing economy and workplace, some contend that the field must evolve to accommodate the modern graduates' need for greater resilience, creativity, and entrepreneurship (Brown & Lent, 2013, p. 21–25; Hartung & Tabor, 2013).

More recently, some have proposed that callings should be included in the career development process (Dik & Duffy, 2012; Elangovan et al., 2010; Hirschi, 2011) in part because of the work and life satisfaction provided by callings. Accordingly, Elangovan and colleagues (2010) suggest that the field move toward a "calling counselors" approach. In other words, in addition to focusing on aligning student interests with available jobs, the role of the counselor can be extended into helping others align and integrate their authentic passions, interests, and desires with their career development. In short, career counselors can evolve to help students find their calling.

CALLING INTERVENTIONS

Empirically tested interventions designed to help one create or find a calling are absent in the literature, perhaps in part because of the lack of agreement on definitions. However, empirically tested interventions have been shown to improve certain subcomponents of a calling. For example, meaning in the workplace can be enhanced through "job crafting" (Rosso, Dekas, & Wrzesniewski, 2010; Wrzesniewski, Berg, & Dutton, 2010). Job crafting operates within the context of one's current job regardless of whether it is considered a calling. A useful illustration is provided in the classic study by Bunderson and Thompson (2009), who showed that the majority of zoo animal caretakers, whose tasks mostly comprise of cleaning cages and feeding animals, indicated that their work as animal caretakers was a deeply meaningful calling. As such, workers can be encouraged to reframe the importance of their work tasks in a way that increases meaning. Furthermore, empirical studies show that job crafting increases skill, task complexity, efficiency, quality, job satisfaction, and commitment (Rosso et al., 2010; Wrzesniewski et al., 2010).

However, job crafting is not designed to prospectively identify a career consistent with one's calling. Therefore, calling interventions are needed that can help students and workers prospectively select a career that can provide a deep sense of meaning and purpose. Such interventions have been proposed, but none have been tested empirically. For example, to identify a unique sense of calling, Hirschi (2011) recommends that one uses self-reflection and self-exploration to discover authentic personal interests, values (i.e., what is important to individuals), and work preferences. In contrast, Dik et al.'s (2009) calling intervention suggests that one intentionally craft a meaningful and purposeful future by either assessing the importance of one's sense of summons or focusing on meaning making.

The Dik et al.'s (2009) approach is consistent with job crafting where workers are encouraged to shift to tasks that enable the use of their interests, strengths, and passions or to find meaning in their current roles. Meaning at work can also be acquired through authenticity, self-efficacy, self-esteem, purpose, a sense of belonging, transcendence, and finding meaning in cultural and interpersonal contexts (Rosso et al., 2010), but specific or empirically tested methods are not available. Thus, though conceptually useful, current approaches fail to clearly demonstrate how to create a sense of calling that can help one select a life and career path infused with a sense of deep meaning and purpose.

In order to prospectively identify callings, career counselors may need to evolve to play the part of a "calling counselor." I believe that a successful calling intervention will improve efforts to put a graduate on a path toward a personally successful career and will increase her or his sense of meaning in life and general well-being. Therefore, I piloted a program that combines traditional career counseling with a novel calling intervention to help students identify and pursue an authentic career filled with meaning and purpose.

METHODS

Course and Program Overview

A novel calling intervention was developed in a new, graduate-level course called Professional and Personal Development (PPD) offered at a large, research-intensive university located in the mid-Atlantic region. The course was designed as a student professional and personal development program for professional, graduate (MS and PhD) and postdoctoral students in biomedical disciplines, but students from every discipline across campus were invited. The PPD course has four related learning objectives: self-awareness, personal brand, managing relationships, and motivating yourself and others (Table 7.1).

Table 7.1   Components of calling developed in the PPD course and the Career Program

Calling and vocational components	PPD course	Three-semester Career Program
Prosocial and work/life orientation	Personal Mission Statement coaching	
Meaning and purpose	Personal Mission Statement	
Action orientation	Individual Development Plan	

Calling and vocational components	PPD course	Three-semester Career Program
Values	LuckStone Igniter (valuesbasedleader.com)	
Strengths	Flow journal assignment Clifton StrengthsFinder assessment and training VIA strengths assessment Peak experiences Moments of excellence exercise Strengths spotting	
Authenticity	Excavation exercise (based on Ban Breathnach, 1998) Best Reflected Self* Best Possible Self* Personal Mission Statement	
Career options		Seminar course Career mentor Shadowing Vocational counseling
Career and vocational counseling	Begin assessments	Longitudinally throughout the Career Program
Interest and personality assessments	Strong Interest Inventory Five Factor Model (Costa & McCrae, 1992) Emotional Intelligence (EQ)	
Job crafting	(Optional exercise)	Career skill development Interdisciplinary project courses
Self-reflection	Journaling and blog assignments Group discussions Elevator speech Final essay Personal Mission Statement, starting with Covey (http://www.franklincovey.com/msb/) Individual Development Plan Passions Glimpses of excellence	Longitudinally throughout Career Program

*Seligman, Steen, Park, and Peterson (2005).

The PPD course is part of a larger, elective three-semester professional and career development program for graduate, professional, and postdoctoral students. This larger Career Program offers a range of self-assessment, experiential and didactic components, and traditional career counseling interventions beginning in the PPD course for the purposes of identifying an authentic, meaningful, and successful career path (Table 7.1). Students had access to faculty mentors, trained strengths and executive coaches and vocational counselors throughout the Career Program.

During 2014–2015, PPD enrolled a total of 27 students comprised mostly of graduate students, but also included postdoctoral fellows, a clinical fellow, and faculty. An additional 39 students have enrolled in other elements of the Career Program. The two PPD cohorts was comprised predominantly of female (74%) and domestic (85%) students who were recruited via flyers and e-mail announcements to all graduate students and graduate faculty.

Calling Intervention

I believe that a successful calling intervention could be used in career counseling and development programs to help students identify and create a deeply satisfying career. Therefore, a calling intervention was created for use in the PPD course in an attempt to use callings to enhance student career development. The PPD course included interventions (Table 7.1) that fostered several calling components including meaning and purpose, values, authenticity, prosocial orientation and personal reflection to create an environment conducive to finding one's calling. Two tools, the personal mission statement and individual development plan, comprised the intervention itself.

First, the students created their personal mission statement, which was designed to reflect the student's authentic purpose or call. Prior to the exercise, students were given assignments aimed at helping them to rediscover their early interests and desires (Excavation Exercise), learn what others view as their best attributes (Reflected Best Self Exercise), and envision their ideal future self (Best Possible Self) (Table 7.1). The students were then instructed to begin broadly drafting their personal mission statement using additional self-reflection and envisioning exercises. The personal mission statement was later narrowed through coaching by a trained coach, consistent with the Elangovan and colleagues' (2010) callings counselor concept.

Students were also asked, verbally and through coaching, to make their personal mission statements concise and memorable (one sentence or less), global (applicable to both professional and personal life), actionable, and to consider whether a prosocial orientation was present. For example, my mission statement is to "help others (individuals and organizations) become the best possible versions of themselves." My mission is global, memorable, and resonant because it is applicable throughout my life. It's also highly specific because any changes in the wording will feel "wrong" to me: Changing "best possible versions" to "excellent" just doesn't feel right. I can also act on and find ways to develop my ability to execute my mission successfully throughout my life, such as acquiring coaching skills and credentials.

After the first semester of the course, the personal mission statement exercise was used in two additional ways. First, the exercise has been used to coach individuals outside the class setting and so lacked the class's envisioning and authenticity pre-work. Second, the exercise was used in a peer coaching model during the second year of the course. Peer coaching allows for scaling the exercise for larger groups. In this approach, students and participants are given a worksheet reiterating coaching and mission statement fundamentals, and a template for crafting the mission statement (Table 7.2). The facilitator explains the exercise including basic coaching techniques, then models the coaching (question asking) part of the exercise. After peer coaching in small groups, students are brought back together to review their revised statements for group feedback.

The personal mission statement by itself is insufficient as a career guide since it reflects a life philosophy and is accordingly global and broad. Thus, the individual development plan was next used to help to focus, direct, and plan the use of the student's energy toward his or her authentic life purpose, consistent with the Elangovan and colleagues' (2010) action-oriented calling construct. Students were encouraged to create a plan that considers their life as a whole, not solely in the context of a single domain such as work.

Students were asked to start with their personal mission statement and then follow the clues, or what I call "breadcrumbs," to their calling in order to create their individual development plan and authentic purpose statement (Table 7.3). These breadcrumbs are energizing activities or traits that include (a) their strengths (Clifton StrengthsFinder and VIA strengths; Rath & Conchie, 2009; authentichappiness.com; Peterson & Seligman, 2004), (b) peak and flow experiences, where flow refers to the experience where an individual is fully engaged and absorbed in the activity (Csikszentmihalyi & LeFavre, 1989), (c) values and passions, and (d) glimpses of excellence. The guidance provided by breadcrumbs helps the students focus their individual development plan on following their personal mission through development of their skills, exploring their interests, and identifying opportunities that enable use of their talents and passions.

In summary, the calling intervention was designed to help the students identify their calling and their plan to follow their calling through their personal mission statement and individual development plan, respectively. The plan involved identification of broad goals that enable realization of their authentic purpose as well as specific strategies using breadcrumbs (Table 7.3)

Table 7.2 Personal Mission Statement Exercise Template

	Verb	+/– subject (optional)	Consequence	+/– tool (optional)
Qualities	– Actionable (starts with a verb) – Positive (generative)	– Generic or specific other	– Overall impact – Reflects an innermost longing	
Your words	**To (verb)**	**(whom/what)**	**to (consequence)**	**using (tool).**
Examples	– To guide – To help – To enable – To facilitate – To build – To foster	– Others – Students – The helpless – Community – Minorities – Organizations	– Achieve balance – Foster excellence – Grow achievement – Create harmony – Create success – Improve health – Create well–being – Improve understanding – Reduce suffering – Empower others	– Using humor – Through leadership – Using active love – Through education – Through training – Through fundraising – Through problem–solving – By providing resources – Using empathy

Sample Coaching prompts	**Subject** – What group do you most want to impact? Everyone? Kids? The helpless? The sick?
	
	– Too narrow – You might say you want to help kids with cancer. That works in terms of perhaps one domain of your life (work or your volunteer activity). What about your friends and family? How does the impact you want to have on your family relate to kids with cancer?
	– Too broad – You might say you want to help everyone. That may be true, but you may want to narrow it. Who tugs at your heartstrings and why? It's OK to leave it open–ended.
			Consequence – What impact do you long to have on the world?
			
			– Too narrow – If you were to die tomorrow, would that impact be good enough for you?
			  ○ For example, you might say you want to live a good life. If you died having lived a good life but had no impact on anyone else, would that be enough for you?
			– Too diffuse – What is the common theme for those things you want to accomplish?
			  ○ For example, you might say you want to take care of your family but also do a good job at work. Describe what it means to take care of your family or to do a good job? Is there a common theme?	

Table 7.3 Pointing Your Personal Mission Statement—creating your authentic purpose statement using breadcrumbs

Aspect of me:	Where I can find this:	Specifically . . . .
What I'm here for:	PMS	(Enter your personal mission statement here)
What's important to me:	Values (Luck Stone Igniter)	(Circle the ones that resonate the most with me)
Things I love to do:	• Flow • Yearning • Energizing activities	(Circle the ones that resonate the most with me)
Things I'm really good at doing:	• Peak experiences • Things people say I should do for a living	(Circle the ones that resonate the most with me)
Setbacks disguised as breadcrumbs	• Obstacles surmounted • New pathways discovered	
What I'm good at/ How I approach relationships:	VIA strengths	
How I'm successful:	Clifton StrengthsFinders	
My Authentic Purpose - I am going to _____*(PMS)*_____ by___ *(things I love to do/am good at doing)*_____ and living by my values of _____*(values)*_____.		

to implement their goals (following their energy; using their strengths to find flow, peak experiences, and excellence). I anticipate that combining their authentic purpose with strengths/energy will increase motivation, self-efficacy, high performance, well-being, while helping to lead students toward the meaningful and purposeful work of a calling.

RESULTS

The calling intervention relied primarily on the personal mission statement and individual development plan. Students as well as coaching clients were provided with coaching to facilitate the creation of their personal mission statements. Coaching continued until they indicated that that they achieved just the right wording (or really close) and that the mission was applicable to their entire life. I took this as significant: a sign that these mission statements were meaningful and highly personal to the individual. This model also worked well in the peer coaching models in terms of participants being able to identify a highly resonant guiding statement for their careers and lives.

Feedback regarding intervention effectiveness was derived from the final essays, course evaluation and/or immediate feedback from participants. Based on course comments, the course appeared to have broad impact on many students in terms of an increase in self-efficacy, self-awareness, authenticity, empowerment, growth and change. Additional details about the course and student work can be found on the course website: rampages.us/vcubest/.

DISCUSSION

The current course represents an initial effort to develop a calling intervention in combination with traditional career counseling to better prepare professional, graduate, and postdoctoral students for a future of successful and fulfilling work (Table 7.1). The calling intervention was based on Elangovan et al.'s (2010) calling construction and was designed to enhance motivation, meaning, purpose, engagement, and achievement. To this end, the intervention consisted of two main tools: the personal mission statement and individual development plan, that is, identification of the student's global authentic purpose and the subsequent action plan, respectively. I started with a traditional personal mission statement exercise that used self-reflection, interests, values and passions that may contribute to an internal calling (reviewed by Duffy & Dik, 2013). Next, individual or peer coaching ensured the personal mission statement was consistent with their innermost desire for impact on the world, was as concise as possible, felt deeply authentic to the student, and applied globally to their life (Table 7.2).

Authenticity, or "true self-knowledge," predicts life meaning (Schlegel, Hirsch, & Smith, 2013). Thus a deeply authentic personal mission statement or calling could infuse a life and work with meaning and purpose. The individual development plan was used to plan the integration of the personal mission statement into the student's life. Energy, strengths, yearnings and flow were central components of the plan designed to explore and plan students' career trajectory (Table 7.3). This preliminary effort suggests that the calling intervention may be helpful in providing global direction and focus to students' lives and career planning.

The current effort suggests that developing calling through identification of authentic purpose and an implementation action plan may provide a useful starting point for students' journey into the world of work. However, though results appear favorable, the degree of efficacy of this intervention is unknown. Future studies in the areas of resulting student achievement, long-term outcomes, and optimum age/career stage for intervention are needed. Also, since this intervention took place in the context of a larger course that had several positive interventions, the calling intervention should be tested in isolation from other positive interventions to determine the minimum ingredients for efficacy.

Practical implications of a successful calling intervention include enhancing career counseling and career development programs by helping individuals find and live their calling. In the meantime, career counselors can begin their own transition to calling counselors. Calling counseling can employ the tools, concepts, and assessments mentioned in this study. For example, questions that are directed at helping young people to identify the impact they are yearning to make on the world, followed by working to identify the unique strengths, talents, interests, and values that can help them to achieve that goal. A combination of traditional career counseling methods and contemporary calling interventions could provide a potent approach to help students achieve meaning and satisfaction in their personal and professional lives.

CONCLUSION

Emerging research on callings can productively complement traditional career counseling approaches. I encourage career counselors to expand their roles to include that of a calling counselor, whose goal is to enable individuals to identify authentic pathways to deeply meaningful careers and lives. This pilot study and course represent first steps toward empirically demonstrating the feasibility of this approach given the number of students who discuss the newfound sense of direction in their careers.

Beyond the professional and personal benefits callings bring to individuals, by helping more individuals find their calling, calling counselors may benefit society as a whole. After all, callings involve a devotion to prosocial behavior. As evidenced by myths and legends from around the world, the boons of meaning and purpose that the hero discovers at the end of the journey can be brought back to enrich the entire community. Campbell writes:

> The modern hero, the modern individual who dares to heed the call and seek the mansion of that presence with whom it is our whole destiny to be atoned, cannot, indeed must not, wait for his community to cast off its slough of pride, fear, rationalized avarice, and sanctified misunderstanding. "Live," Nietzsche says, "as though the day were here." It is not society that is to guide and save the creative hero, but precisely the reverse. (Campbell, 2008, p. 391)

Due to the social and personal values that often result from people living their calling, we support the use of evidence-based recommendations to help guide individuals to a meaningful and authentic professional journey. Career counseling and development programs represent ideal structures to administer interventions designed to foster callings. Career counselors, reimagined as calling counselors, are especially positioned to carry out this service to students and society. I hope calling interventions will help more "heroes" on their journeys to live out their highest calling through personally meaning-ful and socially constructive work.

REFERENCES

Ban Breathnach, S. (1998). *Something more: Excavating your authentic self.* New York: Warner Books.

Berg, J. M., Grant, A. M., & Johnson, V. (2010). When callings are calling: Crafting work and leisure in pursuit of unanswered occupational callings. *Organization Science, 21*(5), 973–994. doi:10.1287/orsc.1090.0497

Brown, S. D., & Lent, R. W. (2013). *Career development and counseling: Putting theory and research to work* (2nd ed.). Hoboken, NJ: John Wiley & Sons, Inc.

Bunderson, J., & Thompson, J. A. (2009). The call of the wild: Zookeepers, callings, and the double-edged sword of deeply meaningful work. *Administrative Science Quarterly, 54*(1), 32–57. doi:10.2189/asqu.2009.54.1.32

Campbell, J. (2008). *The hero with a thousand faces* (3rd ed.). San Anselmo, CA: Joseph Campbell Foundation.

Costa, Jr., P. T., & McCrae, R. R. (1992). *Revised personality inventory (NEO-PI-R) professional manual.* Odessa, FL: Psychological Assessment Resources.

Csikszentmihalyi, M., & LeFevre, J. (1989). Optimal experience in work and leisure. *Journal of Personality and Social Psychology, 56*(5), 815–822. doi:10.1080/0261436 0310001594122

Dik, B. J., & Duffy, R. D. (2009). Calling and vocation at work: Definitions and prospects for research and practice. *The Counseling Psychologist, 37,* 424–450. doi:10.1177/0011000008316430

Dik, B. J., & Duffy, R. D. (2012). *Make your job a calling: How the psychology of vocation can change your life at work.* Conshohocken, PA: Templeton Press.

Dik, B. J., Duffy, R. D., & Eldridge, B. M. (2009). Calling and vocation in career counseling: Recommendations for promoting meaningful work. *Professional Psychology: Research and Practice, 40*(6), 625–632. doi:10.1037/a0015547

Dik, B. J., Eldridge, B. M., Steger, M. F., & Duffy, R. D. (2012). Development and validation of the calling and vocation questionnaire (CVQ) and brief calling scale (BCS). *Journal of Career Assessment, 20*(3), 242–263. doi:10.1177/1069072711434410

Duffy, R. D., Allan, B. A., Autin, K. L., & Bott, E. M. (2013). Calling and life satisfaction: It's not about having it, it's about living it. *Journal of Counseling Psychology, 60*(1), 42–52. doi:10.1037/a0031934

Duffy, R. D., Bott, E. M., Allan, B. A., Torrey, C. L., & Dik, B. J. (2012). Perceiving a calling, living a calling, and job satisfaction: Testing a moderated, multiple mediator model. *Journal of Counseling Psychology, 59*(1), 50–59. doi:10.1037/a0026129

Duffy, R. D., & Dik, B. J. (2013). Research on calling: What have we learned and where are we going? *Journal of Vocational Behavior, 83,* 428–436.

Duffy, R. D., Dik, B. J., & Steger, M. F. (2011). Calling and work-related outcomes: Career commitment as a mediator. *Journal of Vocational Behavior, 78*(2), 210–218. doi:10.1016/j.jvb.2010.09.013

Duffy, R. D., & Sedlacek, W. E. (2007). The presence of and search for a calling: Connections to career development. *Journal of Vocational Behavior, 70*(3), 590–601. doi:10.1016/j.jvb.2007.03.007

Elangovan, A.R., Pinder, C.C., & McLean, M. (2010). Callings and organizational behavior. *Journal of Vocational Behavior, 76*(3), 428–440. doi:10.1016/j.
jvb.2009.10.009

Erford, B.T., & Crockett, S.A. (2012). Practice and research in career counseling and development—2011. *Career Development Quarterly, 60,* 290–332.
doi:10.1002/j.2161–0045.2012.00024.x

Gati, I., & Levin, N. (2012). Counseling for career decision-making difficulties: measures and methods. *Career Development Quarterly, 62,* 98–113.
doi:10.1002/j.2161–0045.2014.00073.x

Gelso, C.J., Williams, E.N., & Fretz, B.R. (2014). *Counseling psychology. Third edition.*
Washington, DC: American Psychological Association.

Gottfredson, G.D., & Holland, J.L. (1996). Dictionary of Holland occupational codes
(3rd ed.). Odessa, FL: Psychological Assessment Resources.

Hagmaier, T., & Abele, A.E. (2012). The multidimensionality of calling: Conceptualization, measurement and a bicultural perspective. *Journal of Vocational Behavior,
81*(1), 39–51. doi:10.1016/j.jvb.2012.04.001

Hartung, P.J., & Tabor, B.J. (2013). Career construction: Heeding the call of the heart.
In B.J. Dik, Z.S. Byrne, & M.F. Steger (Eds.), *Purpose and meaning in the workplace.*
Washington, DC: American Psychological Association. doi:10.1037/14183-001

Hirshi, A. (2011). Callings in career: A typological approach to essential and op-
tional components. *Journal of Vocational Behavior, 79,* 60–73. doi:10.1016/j.
jvb.2010.11.002

Holland, J.L. (1997). *Making vocational choices: A theory of vocational personalities and
work environments* (3rd ed.). Odessa, FL: Psychological Assessment Resources.

Hunter, I., Dik, B.J., & Banning, J.H. (2010). College students' perceptions of calling in work and life: A qualitative analysis. *Journal of Vocational Behavior, 76*(2),
178–186. doi:10.1016/j.jvb.2009.10.008

Peterson, C., & Seligman, M. (2004). *Character strengths and virtues.* New York: American Psychological Association Press.

Rath, T., & Conchie, B. (2009). *Strengths-based leadership.* New York: Gallup Press.

Rosso, B.D., Dekas, K.H., & Wrzesniewski, A. (2010). On the meaning of work:
A theoretical integration and review. *Research in Organizational Behavior, 30*(0),
91–127. doi:dx.doi.org.proxy.library.vcu.edu/10.1016/j.riob.2010.09.001

Schlegel, R.J., Hirsch, K.A., & Smith, C.M. (2013). The importance of who you really are: The role of the true self in eudaimonia. In A.S. Waterman (Ed.), *The best
within us: Positive psychology perspectives on eudaimonia* (pp. 207–225). Washington,
DC: American Psychological Association. doi:10.1037/14092-011

Seligman, M.E.P., Steen, T.A., Park, N., & Peterson, C. (2005). Positive psychology progress: Empirical validation of interventions. *American Psychologist, 60*(5),
410–421. doi:10.1037/0003–066X.60.5.410

Steger, M.F., Pickering, N.K., Shin, J.Y., & Dik, B.J. (2010). Calling in work: Secular or
sacred? *Journal of Career Assessment, 18*(1), 82–96. doi:10.1177/1069072709350905

Wrzesniewski, A., Berg, J.M., & Dutton, J.E. (2010). Turn the job you have into the
job you want. *Harvard Business Review, June,* 114–117.

Wrzesniewski, A., McCauley, C., Rozin, P., & Schwartz, B. (1997). Jobs, careers, and
callings: People's relations to their work. *Journal of Research in Personality, 31*(1),
21–33. doi:10.1006/jrpe.1997.2162

CHAPTER 8

On Call: Physician Perspectives on Callings in Medicine and Medical Education

Mary "Bit" Smith and Susan Rosenthal

The practice of medicine is an art, not a trade; a calling, not a business; a calling in which your heart will be exercised equally with your head.

—William Osler

In a discipline where the revelations of science are held above the revelations of God, what or who calls a physician to attend to those in suffering? One answer is the hospital intercom—a physician's life, of course, revolves around being "on call." A more nuanced suggestion comes from the 20th-century philosopher Emmanuel Levinas. Levinas provided a philosophy whereby an individual's primary obligation or calling arises from the encounter with the other—for a physician, the encounter with a patient (Irvine, 2005). The call of the physician, while not necessarily of divine origin, nevertheless requires a kind of faith. As Levinas explained, "Faith is not a question of the existence or non-existence of God. It is believing that love without reward is valuable" (Wright, Hughes, & Ainsley, 1988, p. 176-177.) Thus, the physician responds, not wholly unlike the priest or prophet, to a calling that pulls her toward greater meaning, service, and connection with the other.

The majority of physicians and students of medicine consider their path a calling (Curlin, Dugdale, Lantos, & Chin, 2007; Duffy, Manuel, Borges, & Bott, 2011; Yoon, Shin, Nian, & Curlin, 2015). In a large study of American physicians, nearly three out of four doctors from different specialties felt called to their careers (Curlin et al., 2007). Another study, looking exclusively at primary care doctors, found even higher rates of calling with over 80 percent of generalists endorsing this work orientation (Yoon et al.,

2015). The prevalence of calling seems to emerge in medicine even before beginning clinical training. First and second year medical students regularly reported high incidences of calling long before starting their careers as physicians (Borges, Manuel, & Duffy, 2013; Duffy et al., 2011).

Although callings were historically associated with spiritual or religious vocations, secular occupations are now also framed in terms of calling (Baumeister & Vohs, 2002; Bunderson & Thompson, 2009; Duffy et al., 2011; Wrzesniewski, McCauley, Rozin, Schwartz, 1997). Current psychological literature presents a few distinct definitions of meaningful work (Bunderson & Thompson, 2009; Dik & Duffy, 2009; Wrzesniewski et al., 1997). For the purpose of our discussion, we'll include the definition reported by Dik and Duffy (2009), "a transcendent summons, experienced as originating beyond the self, to approach a particular life role in a manner oriented toward demonstrating or deriving a sense of purpose or meaningfulness and that holds other-oriented values and goals as primary sources of motivation" (p. 427). By reflecting on narratives of physicians and students of medicine who were willing to share their stories, we'll explore how callings manifest in training and practice. Further, we'll discuss the need for further research in how callings can be protected and developed throughout the lives and careers of physicians.

THE CALL OF MEDICINE

Medical practice is changing at a pace that far outstrips traditional medical education. Newly graduated college students who feel "called" to practice are usually unaware of the realities that will confront them both in their training and in their professional lives. Motivators of such students for a medical career can be internal, external, or a combination of the two, and are fairly stereotypical. Sources of motivation are defined in the literature as "intrinsic to the work, such as the opportunity for self-expression and intellectual challenge, and those extrinsic to the work, such as salary and time" (Ratanawongsa, Howell, & Wright, 2006, p. 2010; see also Ryan & Deci, 2000). Sources of intrinsic motivation for medical students include role models (often a pediatrician, family practice physician, or physician parent), a response to the care they or a loved one received during a serious illness, or a religious vocation. For example, athletes may enter medical school with the goal of becoming orthopedists or sports medicine doctors after having experienced multiple musculoskeletal injuries of their own. Others enjoy the study of science, and see medicine as a means of combining this intellectual pursuit with "helping people" (Ratanawongsa et al., 2006). Extrinsic motivators include a response to parental pressure (especially for students entering the accelerated undergraduate/medical school combined programs), a means to achieve upward mobility (important for children of immigrant parents who are members of a culture that places high value on education). In addition, prestige and financial security are powerful external motivators (Ratanawongsa et al., 2006).

Calling may not perfectly fall between the poles of intrinsic and extrinsic motivation. Like intrinsic drives, callings are highly individualized and their meaningfulness suggests authenticity and alignment with a person's values and aspirations. Altruism, a concept related to callings, is often considered intrinsic, and callings similarly are considered a subset of intrinsic motivation in research literature (Curlin et al., 2007). However, callings are also highly informed by the needs and wishes of other people. The external focus and origination of callings (see definition by Dik and Duffy, 2009) could be considered to reflect an extrinsic drive. Thus, callings may present an additional dimension of motivation outside this binary. Although the source of the call can be found in helping other people, callings may acquaint the individual more fully with themselves as well as a meaningful path in life.

In this first narrative, a family medicine physician at Sidney Kimmel Medical College provides her story of calling that developed during residency training.

I knew from the time that I was very young that I wanted to be a physician. When I graduated from medical school, my mother gave me a piece of paper that she had been saving since I wrote it when I was in first grade. Our teacher had asked us to write down what we wanted to be when we grew up, and I wrote "a mommy, a doctor and a Rockette." I've come to terms with the fact that two out of three isn't bad (I still maintain that my destiny to perform on the Radio City stage was limited only by my height).

While I have always wanted to be a physician, it was not until I started practicing medicine as a resident that I became fully aware that medicine really is a calling. We all have an interest in the science behind medicine and this develops for many of us at a very early age. How can one not be fascinated by the intricacies of the human body and wonders of physiology, pathology and anatomy? However, it is the relationships that we, as physicians, develop with our patients and their families that makes medicine a calling. For me, this aspect of this inspiring profession took root while I was a resident. Somewhere amidst the late nights spent wandering the wards fielding pager calls and managing patients, I realized that while I chose medicine, it had also chosen me. As I look back on the past six years since I graduated from residency, I realize that while medicine does not define me as a person, it has become a large part of who I am today. I am privileged to be part of a profession to which one is called and honored that my patients allow me to be part of their celebrations, struggles and transitions. I relish the intimacies of this profession and am inspired by the relationships it has allowed me to foster.

K.T., MD, January, 2015
January, 2015

Several aspects of K.T.'s story are useful for understanding how callings manifest during careers in medicine. For instance, K.T.'s sense of calling didn't necessarily arise before she became a physician. Findings by Borges et al. (2013) demonstrate that K.T. may be in a slight minority when it comes to the timetable of calling development. They analyzed data from over 500 medical students before starting their first year. Just over half of this sample felt that it was mostly or completely true that they were called to a particular kind of work.

SECULAR AND SPIRITUAL SERVICE

Developing a calling can be the result of the life experiences or religious training that influence one's worldview or personal identity. This may be particularly true for those who have served on medical missions and who view the practice of medicine as a ministry. It is useful to consider how spiritual or religious devotion impacts the callings of physicians and the patients they choose to serve in practice.

The following narrative was written by a family medicine doctor who has devoted her career to caring for the disenfranchised population of Philadelphia:

Raised in a traditional Catholic family, I was very familiar with the concept of "vocation" from an early age, most often referring to a calling to religious life. Indeed we were asked to "listen to a call from God" on a very regular basis at St. Katherine of Siena grade school. While still young, the idea that we could be called by God to do a specific kind of work left a strong impression on me, although I remained unsure of what I was "called" to do. Considering myself more of an artist than a scientist, when I was a freshman in high school I created a series of sculptures of the developing fetus for my biology project. While working with the clay, I was overwhelmed with a sense of awe towards the process of human development. Thus started a nascent sense of my "calling." Medicine, I realized, would allow me to become a student in the art and science of the human condition.

I struggled with existential depression on and off through high school and college, and I found that being involved in service activities was one of the few ways I could release myself from the grip of a dark episode. Faced with the potential anomie of the first 2 years of medical school, I knew I would need to get involved in purposeful service as soon as possible. Fortunately, a group of students at my medical school were embarking on a mission to deliver direct medical care to people experiencing homelessness. Being involved in the development and practical implementation of this project over my 4 years at Jefferson Medical College was transformative. Very early in the project, we set up a small clinic at a men's "safe haven", specifically for hard to reach, hard to engage people with severe mental illness and substance use disorders. The relationships I developed with these men would become the model for my approach to patient care for the rest of my career. I specifically recall one night when an elderly gentleman with bipolar disorder was stopped at the door with a half full liquor bottle. He had an appointment at our clinic that night. As he looked with desperation beyond the entryway, his rheumy eyes fixed on me. "You have to tell them to let me stay," he pleaded. In that moment, I felt a profound and clear sense that is was my calling to provide medical care to these alienated and forgotten men and women.

Now, 20 years later, I continue my work with this population as a family doctor and community engaged researcher in an innovative community based healthcare setting. Every day, I am able to answer my "calling." This has been critical for me to avoid burnout from working in the more traditional and dysfunctional system, and I am grateful for my department's help and support in creating this opportunity. Clearly, my experience of medicine as a vocation is a unique and personal one, and there are many different ways to interpret and experience a "calling." As medical educators, I feel it is imperative to share our individual experiences of "calling" with the medical students and residents we work with. Perhaps even more important is giving them support and a safe space to explore and define their own vocation.

L.C.W., MD, MPH
December, 2014

As this narrative illustrates, recent empirical study has confirmed that, indeed, more religious or highly spiritual physicians consider their work in medicine a calling. Yoon and colleagues (2015) found that out of a sample of over 1,000 primary care physicians and psychiatrists, those that reported more spiritual or religious devotion more frequently endorsed the statement, "For me, the practice of medicine is a calling." However, an earlier investigation of physicians from different specialties reveals a more thought-provoking story (Curlin et al., 2007).

Curlin et al. (2007) measured how a physician's religious or spiritual orientation was reflected in his or her sense of calling and commitment to working in medically underserved populations, like the one described in L.C.W.'s narrative. Intuitively, practitioners who endorse religious values may also willingly follow a call to serve communities most in need. While religious physicians felt their work was a calling more frequently than their secular peers, those same religious doctors were no more likely to offer care to the underserved than their secular counterparts (Curlin et al., 2007). The investigators noted an important qualification; physicians who described themselves as highly "spiritual" in contrast to religious did report more frequently working in underserved communities (Curlin et al., 2007).

The distinction between the spiritual and religious callings might reveal an important truth about how modern medical callings relate to sacred life. Perhaps responding to one's calling is unlike following the motions of a sacrament or observing annual holidays within one's community. Callings can demand a deviation from an established path or life script. It could be argued that modern callings, understood as highly individual pathways to service, are more indicative of spiritual as opposed to religious behavior. As Curlin et al. (2007) note, "the term spirituality has come to convey an aspiration toward connection to the sacred and to others" (p. 358). Thus, the finding that spiritual physicians are more likely to practice in underserved communities may reflect their value of connection with struggling populations. This is not to suggest, however, that both religious and spiritual callings do not coexist in many individuals.

BURNOUT AND RESILIENCE

In the above narrative by L.C.W., she briefly discusses the emotional challenges many students face during their first and second year of medical school. L.C.W. explained that her experiences of service as a medical student aided in her recovery from depression and acquainted her with the work that became a life calling. She reflects on how continuing to work in this area has been protective against a potential decline in well-being throughout her career.

While L.C.W. found a life calling during medical school through service, many medical students suffer depression and "burnout" throughout, which peaks during their third year. Isolation, extreme stress, lack of sleep and self-care, "disillusionment with long hours, competition among students and doctors and the lack of time for really caring about, not just caring for, patients," are cited by students (Rosenthal & Okie, 2005, p. 1087). In a seminal study, a "hidden curriculum" was described as prevalent within the learning environment of clinical years (Hafferty, 1998). As opposed to the explicit curriculum in medical school that teaches professionalism, altruism, empathy, and the practice of medicine as a social contract, the "hidden curriculum" may be a source from which students actually learn, particularly in regards to negative practices and behaviors observed in role models.

Physicians are experiencing burnout at rates that far exceed the general population (Shanafelt et al., 2012). The long hours, pressures to perform, and demands of the job contribute to an alarming number of burnout symptoms like depersonalization and emotional exhaustion. In an extensive survey that assessed the psychological health of several thousand American physicians, approximately one out of every two doctors reported symptoms of burnout (Shanafelt et al., 2012). Compounded by the physician shortage in primary care, it is worrisome that the psychological strain of practice often leads physicians to retire early (Dewa, Loong, Bonato, Thanh, & Jacobs, 2014). Although little is known about how to overcome the problem of physician burnout, enhancing the meaningfulness of work or presence of a calling may be a promising start.

Yoon, Daley, and Curlin (2015) support a connection between callings and resilience in primary care physicians. They report that while many doctors who experience burnout regret choosing medicine as a field, those that have a calling are significantly less likely to express the wish that they had chosen a different career. These preliminary results suggest that callings may bolster some physicians amidst the trials of medical practice.

Conversely, in an essay entitled "Disillusioned Doctors," Carl Elliot proposes an unsettling conclusion that the physicians that are most content or happy in practice are the ones who actually view their work as merely a "job". He explains that it is the doctors who see medicine as a calling that struggle within a medical system that does not incentivize or support compassionate care (Elliot, 2006). Although this may be inconsistent with findings presented by Yoon et al. (2015), Elliot (2006) cautions against an assumption that callings are necessarily protective or ensure resilience in medicine.

Negative outcomes associated with burnout in physicians manifest early in medical education. Duffy et al. (2011) followed medical students during their first and second year of preclinical training. They measured how called these students felt to medicine, how far along they were in envisioning and preparing for their eventual careers, and how much meaning they had in life. After two years of medical training, students' feeling of calling had diminished along with their likelihood of reporting that they found their lives were meaningful. These declines were somewhat attenuated in students who entered medical school with a strong sense of calling. These outcomes remain alarming, however, given that vocational training should be a period of building confidence that one's future as a physician will be fulfilling and worthwhile. A former president of the American Association of Medical Colleges wrote in "Our Contract with Medical Students" that "the acculturation process in medical school can often de-humanize students and convert idealistic ones to cynics" (Cohen, 2002).

While Duffy et al. (2011) point out that the decline in personal meaning and calling for students of medicine during their first year of medical school mirrors a decline in empathy, a significant decline in empathy has also been described during the third year of medical school (Hojat et al., 2009). There is preliminary evidence that those students who are most empathetic may also be the most vulnerable to this decline (Rosenthal et al., 2011). Reasons for this may include the influence of the hidden curriculum, overvaluing test scores above interpersonal skills, or an admissions process that highlights academic success above humanistic achievement (Cohen, 2002). These scattered and sometimes contradictory findings related to callings in medicine and medical education paint a complicated picture and require future research to disambiguate these outcomes.

EMPATHY AND COMPASSION IN MEDICINE

While callings manifest in disparate ways between physicians, a common theme in physician stories about their calling is the centrality of caring for patients. Answering the question about whether he viewed medicine as a "calling," a distinguished otolaryngologist on the faculty at SKMC provided this narrative:

Your questions evoke memories of reading Spiderman's origin story in Amazing Fantasy #15 by Stan Lee and Steve Ditko. Spiderman, flush with the smug self-assurance of celebrity, fails to stop a thief running by him on the pretext that "It's not my job." Later, he discovers that the thief went on to kill his beloved Uncle Ben. Spidey's subsequent soul-searching leads to the realization that "With great power comes great responsibility." In another origin tale by Lee and Ditko (Strange Tales #115), Doctor Stephen Strange, a gifted surgeon who cares only for cash and his reputation, injures his hands and loses the ability to operate. Only through a humbling apprenticeship does he come to accept that satisfaction lies in helping others rather than himself. And finally, in an explication of the mighty Thor's origin story (Thor #159), Stan Lee and Jack Kirby reveal that the thunder god was sentenced by Odin to life as the lame mortal Doctor Donald Blake in order that he might learn humility. Only after serving the sick, does he again become worthy to wield the magic hammer, Mjolnir. In moments of self-reflection when I question my work, I recall the heroes of my youth who unknowingly became the architects of my professional life. Like those superheroes, I accept blame and redirect accolades while striving to help others.

Sure, all doctors are famous—famous, at least, to their patients. I remember all my doctors' names well without any prompting. Think about it. As we go through life we meet innumerable people, yet we recall only a score of names easily—family, friends, teachers, colleagues . . . doctors. Through the alchemy of the white coat, a complete and utter stranger becomes your "doctor." And what does doctor mean? Doctor from the Latin word (first transcribed by Cicero) "docere" means to teach. The more we reject the responsibility to learn, to challenge, and to teach, the more we defer to the authority of an accountable care organization; the more we erode the notion of medicine as a calling, the more we forget our doctors' names and replace them with the acronyms of a faceless corporation.

The short view is overwhelming for so many patients—even more so in this world of instant gratification. The notion of a willing ear, a gentle touch on the shoulder and a kind word often gives way to the strident demand for numbers and outcomes. The path to wellness can have as much meaning as the destination. Neither doctors nor hospitals cure—we enable the sick to get well. There are times when all I can offer is a smile of encouragement. Part of medicine is training to know what is needed. Sometimes as doctors we have to keep patients occupied while they get better and there's an art and a gift in this. The sickness—that's our job. The caring—that's our calling.

As reported in the earlier discussion of callings in physicians, empathy seems to be a related phenomenon to calling. Although distinct ideas, having empathy implies understanding the emotions and experiences of others while having a calling suggests responding to the needs of others through a specific path or action (Dik & Duffy, 2009; Hojat, 2007). It is undeniable that significant overlap occurs in practice between feeling empathy and feeling called.

In one study by Rasinski, Lawrence, Yoon, and Curlin (2012) showed that primary care physicians who felt more called to medicine were less likely to blame their patients for addiction-related illnesses. These authors surveyed over 1,000 primary care doctors about their satisfaction in treating diseases of dependence as well as their experience of calling in medicine. Physicians treating alcoholism, obesity, and nicotine addiction who endorsed having a calling were consistently less likely to report dissatisfaction treating these patients. Rasinski et al. (2012) found that physicians' dissatisfaction treating addiction also correlated with their belief that their patients were responsible for developing these illnesses.

Social psychologists studying compassion have noted that a significant barrier to compassion for others is the belief that the recipient of compassion is responsible for his/her suffering (Goetz, Keltner, & Simon-Thomas, 2010). The path to recovery is harrowing for any patient. Receiving treatment from a doctor who lacks compassion presents an additional obstacle to patient health.

PRESERVING THE CALL

Over the past two decades a concerted effort has been made to bring the importance of humanism, compassion, and empathy to the practice of medicine through recognition of exemplars, ceremonies, and support for service activities. Foremost in this area has been the Arnold P. Gold Foundation for Humanism in Medicine ("Humanism in Medicine: FAQ," 2013). This organization, whose mission is the preservation and development of compassionate care by medical students and physicians, introduced the White Coat Ceremony 20 years ago as a ritual at the beginning of medical school ("Humanism in Medicine: White Coat Ceremony," 2013). Prior to the institution of this ceremony, the Hippocratic Oath was recited by medical students at the conclusion of their four-year training. The White Coat Ceremony allowed for an institutional emphasis that entering medical students should be considering their ethical development at the very outset of their medical careers. This ceremony is now an important part of medical school acculturation internationally, where leaders of the medical institution highlight the importance of humanism as well as science in the practice of medicine ("Humanism in Medicine: White Coat Ceremony," 2013). The foundation also established the Gold Humanism Honor Society (GHHS), a service organization with chapters in the majority of U.S. medical schools ("Humanism in Medicine: FAQ," 2013). Students are selected for GHHS membership by their peers on the basis of their outstanding demonstration of the ideals of the organization, including compassionate care, empathy, interpersonal and communication skills, skillful practice of medicine, and service to the community. This designation is included in the students' letter of evaluation for residency programs and sets students apart who are exemplars of humanistic medicine.

The medical humanities and field of narrative medicine present an important route where callings may be developed and nourished by physicians and students. Dr. Rita Charon (2008), who coined the term "Narrative Medicine" and developed its field of study, characterizes the practice as using attention, representation, and affiliation to appreciate narratives of illness. Through narrative practices, physicians and students come to know and share their own stories of illness and calling. The values and events that drew an individual to healthcare are relived and reawakened in the process of creative expression. Dr. Charon (2008, vii) poignantly notes, "By telling stories to ourselves and others—in dreams, in diaries, in friendships, in marriages, in therapy session—we grow slowly not only to know who we are but also to become who we are." Thus, the humanities are an important tool for physicians and students to both express and discover their call to medicine.

A widely incorporated course in medical schools, the Healer's Art elective, gives students and faculty the opportunity to reflect on their calling and commitment to the practice of medicine (Rabow, Wrubel, & Remen, 2009). Developed by Dr. Rachel Naomi Remen over 20 years ago, the course encourages students to explore their personal journey to becoming a physician. The class employs a group format where students share personal experiences in and out of training. In a final class, students offer a personal mission statement for their future practice of medicine that reflects deeply held values (Rabow et al., 2009). In many ways, this exercise prompts students to consider how medicine can be an authentic and meaningful life path and how community and self-reflection can bolster this conviction amidst loss and challenge. In a qualitative analysis of the course, student mission statements were analyzed exposing shared values like courage, love, and calling (Rabow et al., 2009).

This narrative comes from one of the authors (MBS), a current first year medical student at SKMC:

I discovered my calling to medicine in an unlikely setting, I was sitting on the floor, crossed legged, in a conference room learning to teach meditation. Our group of teacher-trainees had assembled from different disciplines to learn Tibetan Buddhist practice, secularized for popular consumption at Stanford University. There were therapists, lawyers, businessmen and women gathered in the room, united by a shared interest in contemplative techniques and the deliberate cultivation of compassion.

At this time, I had just been accepted to medical school and was still unsure if I was cut out for the job. Could I handle the workload, long hours, the awareness of suffering, the proximity of death? Looking down at my yoga pants and informal posture, I found it doubtful. Our teacher, an articulate young woman with red hair and wise eyes, defined compassion for the group as the ability to be moved by suffering and the willingness to act on behalf of alleviating it. As I took notes on the discussion in my red notebook, I doodled the word "medicine?" on my page. I looked up to rejoin the dialogue, when a woman dressed in khakis and a t-shirt asked the group if compassion was meant to be pleasant. She explained that she viewed compassion not as a warm, fuzzy emotion but as a radical act of bravery. Compassion, for her, was understood as a commitment to walk toward suffering, to risk the contagion of pain, line with your highest values of service to others.

On the floor of the sunlit conference room, life seemed to tap me on the shoulder and point me in a direction I may not have otherwise traveled. My eyes resettled on the word medicine and a deep knowing arose within me. This was my moment of calling. I knew medicine wouldn't be an easy route, perhaps callings never are, and yet, I felt myself filled with courage and hope that the journey promised joy even if it portended experiences of challenge and sorrow.

CONCLUSION

In this chapter, we've discussed the prevalence and influence of callings in the lives of physicians. While optimism can seem scarce in a changing medical environment characterized by demanding hours and diminishing rewards, physician callings remain abundant. Doctors in training and practicing physicians consistently frame their service as a calling, and not unlike those called to ministry, doctors often serve as champions of humanity's most noble ideals. Beneficence, compassion, scientific objectivity, and innovation are among the values that are shared and celebrated within this discipline. Returning to the quotation by the great 20th-century physician, William Osler, the practice of medicine gives physicians the privilege of exercising their heart with their mind. Perhaps it is the combination of our highest faculties that births the experience of calling.

ACKNOWLEDGMENTS

Kathryn P. Trayes, MD
Assistant Dean for Student Affairs and Career Counseling
Assistant Professor of Family Medicine Sidney Kimmel Medical School

Lara C. Weinstein MD, MPH
Assistant Professor of Family Medicine, Sidney Kimmel Medical College

Edmund Pribitkin MD
Professor, Academic Vice Chairman
Dept of Otolaryngology, Head and Neck Surgery
Thomas Jefferson University

REFERENCES

Baumeister, R.F., & Vohs, K.D. (2002). The pursuit of meaningfulness in life. In C.R. Snyder & S.J. Lopez (eds.), *The handbook of positive psychology* (pp. 608–618). New York: Oxford University Press.

Borges, N.J., Manuel, R.S., & Duffy, R.D. (2013). Speciality interests and career calling to medicine among first-year medical students. *Perspectives on Medical Education, 2*(1), 14–17.

Bunderson, J.S., & Thompson, J.A. (2009). The call of the wild: Zookeepers, callings, and the double-edged sword of deeply meaningful work. *Administrative Science Quarterly, 54*(1), 32–57.

Charon, R. (2006). *Narrative medicine: Honoring the stories of illness.* Oxford University Press, New York.

Cohen, J.J. (2002). Our compact with tomorrow's doctors. *Academic Medicine, 77*(6), 475–480.

Curlin, F.A., Dugdale, L.S., Lantos, J.D., & Chin, M.H. (2007). Do religious physicians disproportionately care for the underserved?. *The Annals of Family Medicine, 5*(4), 353–360.

Dewa, C.S., Loong, D., Bonato, S., Thanh, N.X., & Jacobs, P. (2014). How does burnout affect physician productivity? A systematic literature review. *BMC Health Services Research, 14*(1), 325.

Dik, B.J., & Duffy, R.D. (2009). Calling and vocation at work definitions and prospects for research and practice. *The Counseling Psychologist, 37*(3), 424–450.

Duffy, R.D., Manuel, R.S., Borges, N.J., & Bott, E.M. (2011). Calling, vocational development, and well being: A longitudinal study of medical students. *Journal of Vocational Behavior, 79*(2), 361–366.

Goetz, J.L., Keltner, D., & Simon-Thomas, E. (2010). Compassion: An evolutionary analysis and empirical review. *Psychological Bulletin, 136*(3), 351.

Hafferty, F.W. (1998). Beyond curriculum reform: Confronting medicine's hidden curriculum. *Academic Medicine, 73*(4), 403–407.

Hojat, M. (2007). *Empathy in patient care: Antecedents, development, measurement, and outcomes.* New York: Springer.

Hojat, M., Vergare, M.J., Maxwell, K., Brainard, G., Herrine, S.K., Isenberg, G.A., . . . & Gonnella, J.S. (2009). The devil is in the third year: A longitudinal study of erosion of empathy in medical school. *Academic Medicine, 84*(9), 1182–1191.

Humanism in medicine: FAQs. (2013). The Arnold P. Gold Foundation. Retrieved from http://humanism-in-medicine.org/about-us/faqs/

Humanism in medicine: White coat ceremony. (2013). The Arnold P. Gold Foundation. Retrieved from http://humanism-in-medicine.org/programs/rituals/white-coat-ceremony/

Irvine, C. (2005). The other side of silence: Levinas, medicine, and literature. *Literature and Medicine, 24*(1), 8–18.

Rabow, M.W., Wrubel, J., & Remen, R.N. (2009). Promise of professionalism: Personal mission statements among a national cohort of medical students. *The Annals of Family Medicine, 7*(4), 336–342.

Rasinski, K. A., Lawrence, R. E., Yoon, J. D., & Curlin, F. A. (2012). A sense of calling and primary care physicians' satisfaction in treating smoking, alcoholism, and obesity. *Archives of Internal Medicine, 172*(18), 1423–1424.

Ratanawongsa, N., Howell, E. E., & Wright, S. M. (2006). What motivates physicians throughout their careers in medicine?. *Comprehensive Therapy, 32*(4), 210–217.

Rosenthal, J. M., & Okie, S. (2005). White coat, mood indigo—depression in medical school. *New England Journal of Medicine, 353*(11), 1085–1088.

Rosenthal, S., Howard, B., Schlussel, Y. R., Herrigel, D., Smolarz, B. G., Gable, B., . . . & Kaufman, M. (2011). Humanism at heart: Preserving empathy in third-year medical students. *Academic Medicine, 86*(3), 350–358.

Ryan, R. M., & Deci, E. L. (2000). Self-determination theory and the facilitation of intrinsic motivation, social development, and well-being. *American Psychologist, 55,* 68–78.

Shanafelt, T. D., Boone, S., Tan, L., Dyrbye, L. N., Sotile, W., Satele, D., . . . & Oreskovich, M. R. (2012). Burnout and satisfaction with work-life balance among US physicians relative to the general US population. *Archives of Internal Medicine, 172*(18), 1377–1385.

Wrzesniewski, A., McCauley, C., Rozin, P., & Schwartz, B. (1997). Jobs, careers, and callings: People's relations to their work. *Journal of Research in Personality, 31*(1), 21–33.

Wright, T., Hughes, P., & Ainley, A. (1988). The paradox of morality: An interview with Emmanuel Levinas. In R. Bernasconi & D. Wood (Eds.), *The provocation of Levinas: Rethinking the Other.* New York: Routledge.

Yoon, J. D., Daley, B., Curlin, F. A. (2015). The association between a sense of calling and physician well-being: A national study of primary care physicians and psychiatrists. Academic Psychiatry [in press].

Yoon, J. D., Shin, J. H., Nian, B. S., & Curlin, F. A. (2015). Religion, sense of calling and the practice of medicine: Findings from a national survey of primary care physicians and psychiatrists. *Southern Medical Journal.*

CHAPTER 9

DISCERNING CALLING: BRIDGING THE NATURAL AND SUPERNATURAL

Bryan J. Dik and Michael F. Steger

For many people, the desire to find or discover a sense of calling—a transcendent, beyond-the-self summons to approach a particular life role with purpose, meaning, and motivation to benefit others (Dik & Duffy, 2009)—is profound. Particularly for those anticipating the outreach of a "caller" from whom a path forward can be discerned, a common default strategy for discovering calling is known as the "pray and wait" approach (e.g., Dik & Duffy, 2012). This strategy involves a prayerful but otherwise passive pleading for the resolution of uncertainty and endowment of a clear sense of purpose, via a discernable inner sense of conviction or, perhaps, an external signal as unmistakable as the burning bush Moses encountered. For some people, these desired-for Moses-in-the-desert experiences—what we will refer to as numinous experiences of calling—do in fact occur. For others, the search for a calling is slower and more effortful, yet still results in the recognition that there is a particular life role that one can serve that provides meaning and benefits entities beyond one's self. The purpose of this chapter is to try to answer two questions related to such varied experiences of a calling. First, we draw from research concerning similar psychological experiences, most notably empathy, to explore the question of what psychological processes might underlie numinous calling experiences. The allure of such spiritually profound experiences is likely compelling for those yearning for a sense of life or career direction, but our assumption (absent of population base rate data) is that their frequency is far exceeded by the demand for them. Hence, the second part of this chapter explores the question of what people searching for a calling should do if numinous calling experiences are not normative. Using a case example as a point of departure, we adopt a levels-of-explanation view to advocate a "pray and be active" approach that leverages career development resources, converges with mainstream theological teaching on callings, and stokes the neuroaffective fires of a sense of calling.

THE CASE OF ROGER VISKER

The most awe-inspiring contemporary example of a numinous calling event we have personally encountered was experienced two decades ago by Roger Visker, at the time a patrol lieutenant in the Kalamazoo (Michigan) Township Police Department. As context, Roger had aspired to do police work from early childhood, plans that were cemented prior to his eighth-grade graduation, the program for which stated, next to Roger's name: "Career goal: I want to be a policeman." Everything about law enforcement appealed to Roger, and he pursued his interests with a laser-like focus, earning a bachelor's degree in law enforcement and eventually accepting an entry-level position with the police force in Kalamazoo. The role fit him perfectly, and by all accounts he performed exceptionally well, earning acclaim from supervisors and peers. He quickly rose up the ranks and ultimately landed the position of patrol lieutenant, second in command and everyone's bet serve as the next chief of police. He was far from seeking a career change, which made what happened next all the more surprising.

A deeply spiritual man, Roger was working through a Bible study one September morning when he felt a strong urge to pray. Immediately upon entering into prayer, Roger heard what he described as the equivalent of an audible voice, experienced as if spoken directly into his ears. The voice—which Roger described as neither booming nor a whisper, but remarkably neutral—very clearly told Roger to leave police work and embark on a career as a pastor. The voice also named for Roger his successor as patrol lieutenant, and then instructed Roger to talk with seven people, listing each one by name. After the message concluded, Roger was understandably shocked by the experience, and described a penetrating feeling of awe. After an intense several days that included what he described as a spiritual battle, Roger began to connect with the seven people who were named during the encounter, all friends and coworkers. Their advice? One urged Roger to read Richard Bolles's (2015) classic career self-help book, *What Color is Your Parachute?* One suggested he take some assessments and enlist the help of a career counselor. Another encouraged him to discuss the matter carefully with his pastor. All seven offered support and affirmation, identifying how Roger's strengths would translate well into a pastor role. Incredibly, all seven had also gone through (or were currently in the process of) a career change, uniquely positioning them to serve as role models. Roger leaned on the seven for support and took their advice, and after a period of exploration and reflection, responded to his calling by making the career change. He has since pastored three churches in three different states, and now serves a large congregation in Illinois.

WHAT PROCESSES MIGHT UNDERLIE THE NUMINOUS EXPERIENCE OF A CALLING?

Roger Visker's extraordinary calling experience offers key insights on how a sense of calling may be experienced and discerned, with or without a palpably numinous calling event. For Roger, the process began with an incredibly clear and directive map to his calling, full of information, procedures, and incentive. If we set aside the factual information that Roger received, what are we left with? Roger describes an initial sense of awe, followed by a spiritual struggle, and then a period of active reflection, at the end of which he successfully made his career change. In this section, it is the resolution of Roger's initial feelings of awe and struggle that we are most interested in, given their role in his response to his calling and impetus to pursue it. What helped Roger resolve his struggle, reflect upon his potential career change, and determine that his new course was a good fit? We suggest that Roger and many others with a calling are able to fully recognize and envision themselves in the role—in this case, career path—to which they are called. That is, prior to *being* the one living the calling, they *empathize* with the person they imagine to be living the calling. Thus, one of the most fundamental aspects of human social life (i.e., empathy) may play a role in experiencing of a calling.

Empathy Defined

In an era when ideas such as "self-compassion" are gaining scientific traction, perhaps it is not so objectionable to suggest that people may use empathy to mentally experiment with their own selves working in a different occupation, or engaging in volunteer activities that are aligned with a possible calling. However, before we can delve into how the brain processes empathy, we need to see whether empathy is a good fit for calling. Succinctly, empathy can be defined as "the ability to share another's internal world of thoughts and feelings" (Walter, 2012, p. 9). More specifically, most empathy scholars state that empathy is marked by people's abilities to infer the cognitive and affective state of others, along with the ability to generate the same affective state in one's self that one infers in others (Engen & Singer, 2013; Walter, 2012). The most common distinction made concerning types of empathy is between affective empathy and cognitive empathy, although the affective form is seen to be more basic and fundamental, and some have argued that the cognitive form often ends up being used to help produce the affective form (Walter, 2012). Empathy can be used in highly sophisticated ways, such as by reinforcing prosocial behaviors, mentalizing the lives of fictitious characters, spurring personal charitable behavior or even national military or humanitarian effort, or reading people well enough to take them in poker or sell them a timeshare in the middle of nowhere. Despite such advanced manifestations, scholars argue that they rest on a common and basic infrastructure that allows us to, essentially, feel what others experience (Decety, Norman, Bertson, & Cacioppo, 2012).

If we accept that this infrastructure just as easily could be used to infer how we might feel and think under different circumstances, then the empathetic infrastructure certainly seems to be a potential candidate for the psychological source of numinous calling phenomena. Would I feel good about myself if I was a teacher, programmer, police officer, or pastor? What would I think about my job duties? Would I perceive an alignment between my occupation and what I know of my values, interests, and meaning in life? What would it be like to be me, doing that job—would it feel like a calling? Perhaps these questions simply seem to reflect self-understanding and deliberative decision-making. As one alternative, we propose that the empathic infrastructure might be useful when people contemplate others who are working. In Roger's case, he spoke with seven people who were similarly changing careers and they offered advice and support. If he had observed other pastors, or imagined himself as pastor of the church he attended, empathy would be quite handy for helping him reflect on what being a pastor would be like for him.

A final alternative is that we may experience a calling via the empathy we feel for the objects of our calling's work. For example, Roger may have felt deep empathy for those who were spiritually unmoored or confused. Any of us might feel empathy for the plight of hungry children, our societal brethren oppressed by discrimination, possibly even animals poached to the cusp of extinction, or ecosystems poisoned, melting, or burning away. Empathy, then, may provide a new lens for studying calling, whether we focus on the empathy we may feel for those our calling might serve, our empathic ability to put ourselves in the shoes of those already working in our possible calling, or the empathy we may use to "try before we buy" our calling.

The Infrastructure of Empathy

Empathy can be thought of as having affective and cognitive components, both conceptually and neurologically (Cox et al., 2012). The affective component has been deemed a bottom-up route to empathy, relying on the *resonance* we feel with others (or with ourselves, if you accept our argument). The cognitive component has been described as a top-down route to empathy, relying on our ability to *mentalize*, or form mental representations of others' experiences (Hétu, Taschereau-Dumouchel, & Jackson, 2012; Zaki & Ochsner, 2012). There is some evidence that the famed "mirror neurons" of the motor areas of the inferior frontal cortex help us to resonate with others' movements. However, a better supported source of resonance may be the way in which we appear to experience the physical pain inflicted upon others (Hétu et al., 2012). For example, if we observe a hand being pricked by a needle, we have a spike in activity within the neurons that enervate the muscles of our own hand. Beyond this kind of embodied resonance, our affective resonance with others has been linked to areas of the brain that process affective stimuli, primarily the insula and the anterior cingulate cortex, especially the area that separates the posterior anterior and anterior medial cingulate cortex (Engen & Singer, 2013; Walter, 2012). The infrastructure for mentalizing appears to be heavily dominated by structures within the brain that are associated with cognitive activity. Brain stimulation as well as imaging research have linked efforts to infer the mental states of others to activity within the posterior cingulate cortex (PCC; Hétu et al., 2012), which is near the temporal parietal junction (TPJ). The TPJ itself helps process cognitive stimuli, and imaging studies have shown it to be active when people are instructed to try to infer others' emotional states, or even just to passively observe others' emotional or sensory experiences (Engen & Singer, 2013). Several other brain structures and regions have been linked to the human ability to mentally create the state of others' minds, including ventromedial prefrontal cortex and superior temporal sulcus (Hétu et al., 2012). The TPJ also has been proposed as one of the structures that helps people differentiate between themselves and others (Hétu et al., 2012). This differentiation might be an important spanner in the works of our argument that empathy underlies some of the numinous experience of calling. So far, it appears as if research has not resolved where this differentiation is made in the brain.

We do not claim to have requisite expertise in neuroscience, yet understanding what happens in the brain when psychological phenomena occur is another tool for understanding the distinctions and similarities among those phenomena. Potentially, neuroscience could lead to interventions that would not arise from more traditional career development strategies (imagine career neurodevelopment!). However, our primary interest in reviewing the infrastructure of empathy is to try to point the way to a new direction in calling research that might leverage the much larger psychological and neuroscience literature that has developed around empathy. Perhaps the numinous experience of calling also uses the separate cognitive and affective apparatuses used by empathy. Knowing this would help clarify some of the conceptual disagreement in calling research, and perhaps help support a variety of approaches to seeking and finding a calling. We suggest that the "eureka" sensation that one has truly found one's calling may arise from the infrastructure that allows us to cognitively and affectively merge with another's experience. The most intriguing possibility is that while contemplating future occupations, people get a sense that one of them "just feels right." When they think about doing that job or claiming that calling, it resonates with them in a deep and profound way. In a sense, we suggest that perhaps the intangible feeling of a calling is empathy—with our future selves, with those we will serve, or with those we will serve alongside.

A Brief Caveat

Some individuals who relish spiritual experience may balk at our suggestion to lean on neuroscience and psychological research as a guide for understanding the discernment process, concerned that this scientific description strips away its spiritual meaning. Conversely, some who prefer positivistic explanatory models may be tempted to infer that the spiritual element of a calling is irrelevant or ineffectual if the process can be explained in neuropsychological terms. Both of these positions are vulnerable to compromising a truly comprehensive view of the phenomenon. Psychological science draws from experience as a way of knowing through the use of the scientific method; this is an extremely important epistemological strategy for understanding human behavior, but it is not the only strategy. Indeed, an explanation of a phenomenon on one level (e.g., neuropsychological) does not necessarily preclude a valid explanation on another (e.g., spiritual). From this levels-of-explanation view, the argument that a description of a calling experience involving activity in the insula and the anterior cingulate cortex "explains away" the spiritual veracity of the experience is a form of unjustified reductionism. Regardless of one's perspective concerning the validity of spiritual experiences and explanations, such experiences at the very least convey data about the phenomenological quality of human behavior—and understanding, predicting, and explaining such behavior is what psychological science ultimately pursues. In our view, a more comprehensive understanding often requires appealing to multiple levels of explanation; in this sense, the supernatural and natural may converge in how one experiences or understands a calling.

WHAT SHOULD PEOPLE DO WHEN THEY ARE SEARCHING FOR A SENSE OF CALLING?

Theologians note that direct divine communication of callings, such as that experienced by Roger, is rare. "Though there are exceptions," offers Douglas Schuurman (2004), "generally God uses mediators to call individuals to particular places of service" (p. 37). By implication, people who are searching for a calling may be wise to focus on the mediators—the seemingly mundane activities and processes that can facilitate the identification of a calling. Schuurman suggests that the New Testament points to gifts, needs, obligations, discussion, and prayer as key mediators often present in the discernment process. (It should be noted that although scholarship on the theology of work has been most vigorous within the Christian tradition, there is remarkable thematic convergence across world religions on the role of work in human life; Dik, Duffy, & Tix, 2012). Psychological science offers additional insights. For example, meta-analytic evidence reveals that career development interventions (e.g., individual or group career counseling and workshops) generally work well in addressing career choice concerns, yielding effect sizes typically in the .40 to .60 range (Whiston, 2002), magnitudes similar to those found in psychological, educational, and behavioral treatment studies (Lipsey & Wilson, 1993).

What activities or behaviors make such interventions effective? Answering this question is an important contribution that vocational psychology can make to the question of what factors may mediate the discernment of a calling. A meta-analysis by Brown and Ryan Krane (2000) investigated this question and found that the most effective career interventions contain some combination of up to five "critical ingredients": written exercises, individualized interpretation and feedback, attention to support building, accurate occupational information, and modeling opportunities. Incredibly, these critical ingredients align perfectly with the directives given to Roger by the seven people with whom he was instructed to talk. That is, *What Color Is Your Parachute?* contains a number of written exercises; individualized interpretation and feedback is precisely what Roger received from his career counselor and the career assessment results; talking with his pastor provided Roger with accurate information about what a career in ministry is like; friends and co-workers provided substantial support and encouragement; and because all of them were highly familiar with career change based on their personal experience, Roger had access to effective models of the target behavior. When we urge replacing a "pray and wait" with a "pray and be active" strategy, these career intervention critical ingredients are the types of behaviors we mean by "be active." Below, we briefly review and provide some context for each within psychological theory and mainstream theological teaching on discerning a calling.

Individualized Interpretive Feedback and Accurate Occupational Information

Individualized interpretation includes interacting with career assessment results and receiving personalized feedback on other self-appraisal information, such as career plans and decision-making strategies. Accurate occupational information consists of up-to-date descriptions of various career paths, including needed training, skills, and other requirements for entry; typical job tasks, roles, and responsibilities; descriptions of the typical psychological profile of happily employed workers within a particular occupation; and prospects for job growth. Taken as a pair, these intervention components reflect a person–environment fit approach that builds on the fact that people differ in important ways that have implications for the types of occupations most likely to lead to success and satisfaction. These individual differences can be described using the catch-all term "gifts" and include things like values, interests, abilities, and personality that are frequently measured by career assessments.

The New Testament contains several passages that articulate a role for gifts within the church (e.g., Romans 12:3–8; Ephesians 4:7–13; I Corinthians 12:4–31). Collectively, they teach that diverse gifts are distributed across people to equip them for serving different functions, and that for the well-being of the whole they must work together in performing these functions like different parts of one body. Reformers applied this basic principle beyond the church to the broader culture, noting that society is bound by common needs and mutual service. Puritans such as Richard Baxter and William Perkins, in richly written treatises on the role of work in human life, used this application of such texts to instruct that attending to one's gifts is a wise strategy for discerning a calling. For example, referring to I Corinthians 12, Perkins (1631) noted that the text shows the diversity of gifts that God bestows on his church, and so proportionally in every society: "And by reason of this distinction of men, partly in respect of gifts, partly in respect of order, come personal callings . . . personal callings arise from that distinction which God makes between man and man in every society" (cited in Placher, 2005, pp. 265–266).

Frank Parsons' (1909) classic person–environment fit model of vocational choice—that understanding one's personal attributes, gathering information about diverse career paths, and making a match between the two—provides an example of this same principle as it applies to career choice. The psychology of individual differences (Dawis, 1992) established a systematic way of measuring "gifts" (e.g., abilities, interests, values, personality) quantitatively, and using scores to predict outcomes in terms of achievement and satisfaction, among other key outcomes. Dominant career choice theories such as John L. Holland's (1959, 1997) theory of vocational types and Dawis and Lofquist's (1984) "Theory of Work Adjustment" extended this framework, laying the groundwork for practical career assessment tools and establishing empirical support for the notion that measuring the person and the environment and striving to optimize "fit" is a useful strategy for career decision-making. These theories are well-supported empirically; a large body of research (including several meta-analyses, e.g., Kristof-Brown, Zimmerman, & Johnson, 2005) points to the predictive validity of fit at multiple levels (e.g., person–job, person–organization, person–team). Therefore, a useful approach for discerning a calling, and part of what helped Roger confirm his, involves identifying one's gifts and exploring promising opportunities for expressing them in the world of work, for the benefit of the greater good.

Modeling and Support Building

Modeling in career development interventions involves learning effective decision-making strategies by interacting with and observing people who already have found success in their own career development process. Attention to support building recognizes that career decisions are best made not in a social vacuum, but in the context of supportive relationships with friends, family, and mentors who can provide advice and encouragement (Dik & Duffy, 2012). Both components appeal to the inherently relational nature of humans, and converge with theological teaching on the role of discipleship in fostering spiritual formation (Andrews, 2010), which draws from an ample supply of biblical examples of mentoring (Moses and Joshua, Naomi and Ruth, Elijah and Elisha, Jesus and his disciples, Paul and Timothy, etc.). Both theological and psychological accounts of modeling and support-building point to their effectiveness in shaping one's development and decision-making, including with respect to discerning a calling.

Social cognitive career theory (SCCT; Lent, Brown, & Hackett, 1994) most clearly posits a role for modeling and support building as it applies to career choice. SCCT, like general social cognitive theory, proposes that career development behavior is driven by self-efficacy (i.e., confidence in one's ability to successfully execute a task) and outcome expectations (i.e., one's belief that accomplishing a task will or will not produce a valued outcome), which influence personal goals (i.e., an individual's intention to engage in a particular activity). Within SCCT, this interplay among self-efficacy, outcome expectations and goals predicts the development of vocational interests, career and educational choices, and job performance. For example, a person may discern a calling to a career in engineering because of a high level of confidence in activities related to science, technology, and math. If these self-efficacy beliefs are accompanied by an expectation that an engineering job will offer an opportunity to use one's talents to make a positive contribution to the world (e.g., through stronger bridges or more efficient water systems), the likelihood of choosing an engineering degree increases. Vicarious learning through observing models, along with social support and encouragement, are some of the most important influences on self-efficacy and outcome expectations, and social support also is one of the contextual factors that moderates the relationship between making plans to enter a career and actually taking steps to make it happen (Lent, 2005). For these reasons, the process of discerning a calling is made smoother when modeling and support building are incorporated.

Written Exercises and Meaning Making

The final ingredient, written exercises, includes activities that invite people to record their thoughts, feelings, and reflections concerning their career development and their work's role within the broader context of their lives. Such exercises assist in the establishment of effective work and life goals. They also provide a means to engage in meaning making, as people strive to make sense of their current experience, reflect on their larger sense of purpose in life, and both envision and create possibilities for translating their sense of purpose into daily activity through work. This process of meaning making is a key component of the calling construct, and the most agreed-upon dimension among diverse definitions of the term (Duffy & Dik, 2013).

Empirical research on meaning usually frames the construct as people's comprehension of their own life experience and their possession of one or more overarching life purposes (Steger, Frazier, Oishi, & Kaler, 2006). There is disagreement about whether additional dimensions beyond these two should be included as part of the construct, and dissatisfaction with how well existing meaning in life measurement illuminates the multidimensional nature of meaning in life (George & Park, 2013; Steger, 2009; Steger et al., 2006). One of the most appealing additional dimensions is the perception of the worth of one's own life (George & Park, 2014). In such a three-part model, a meaningful life would make sense, hold value and importance, and include the pursuit of one's purpose. The application of meaning to work could, by extension, suggest that meaningful work or calling should require that one's job makes sense, is worth doing, and works toward accomplishing some important goal (e.g., Steger, Dik, & Duffy, 2012). As befits the close conceptual alignment of meaning and calling, research has reported fairly close empirical alignment; people who report having a calling in work also report perceiving meaning in their lives (Dik, Sargent & Steger, 2008; Duffy & Sedlacek, 2007; Dik & Steger, 2008;). Calling may itself be an important route to broader meaning in life for some. Among college students who were actively seeking meaning in their lives, having a calling appeared to remedy the reduced life satisfaction that typically accompanies the search for meaning in life (Steger & Dik, 2009). For its part, a sense of meaning in life has consistently been linked to both physical and mental health (for reviews, see Roepke, Jayawickreme, & Riffle, 2014; Steger, 2012).

Christian theologians often interpret the grand narrative of scripture (i.e., creation, fall, redemption, restoration) along with specific teachings (Genesis 1:28; Colossians 1:20; 2 Corinthians 5:18) as charging humans with the responsibility of integrating their religious and spiritual values with their work (Miller, 2009). Often, this integration involves approaching work as a way of cocreating in divine partnership, and/or of serving as a "minister of reconciliation" to restore order and goodness (i.e., *shalom*) in whatever sphere of influence people find themselves in their work, regardless of profession (Plantinga, 2002). Such teachings imply that discerning a calling is not merely a one-time event, but an ongoing process (Dik & Duffy, 2009; Dik, Eldridge, Steger, & Duffy, 2012), for which a wealth of resources is available to assist (e.g., Hammond, Stevens, & Svanoe, 2002). These approaches to faith integration can be interpreted using Park's (2010) meaning-making model. In this model there are two primary levels of meaning. The first is global meaning, encompassing our beliefs about ourselves, life, and the world, as well as the goals that we seek to pursue. Religious worldviews, as understood by those who espouse them, are prototypic examples of global meaning frameworks. The second level is situational meaning, consisting of the interpretations and attributions surrounding events and situations in daily life.

Much of Park's (2010) work has applied her model to the experience of trauma, although she also has explored its linkages to workplace spirituality. With trauma, psychological distress may arise due to discrepancies between global meaning (e.g., the world is a safe place and I am a good person) and situational meaning (e.g., the world is dangerous and I am a victim of malice), stimulating a search for meaning (Steger & Park, 2012). This discrepancy can be resolved through changing one's global meaning to accommodate the trauma, reinterpreting the event's situational meaning to more readily assimilate into one's global meaning, or modifying both levels of meaning to arrive at new meaning systems. In relation to calling, we might imagine that one of the tasks people face is to understand their global meaning in life well enough to be able to recognize the kinds of occupations that would be easily assimilated, or even resonate positively, within their global meaning. If someone is unable to obtain the ideal occupation, then the meaning-making processes may be called upon to either revise global meaning so that it can accommodate the realities of one's occupation (e.g., I don't need to change the world, being a good parent is enough) or to revise the situational meaning of one's occupation (e.g., I can change the world, one person at a time, by supporting my coworkers).

Our meaning-making perspective on calling syncs with the idea of job crafting—"the physical and cognitive changes individuals make in the task or relational boundaries of their work" (Wrzesniewski & Dutton, 2001, p. 179). Job crafting holds a great deal of promise for helping people access greater meaning in their work, and may be an avenue for people to discover a calling within their current occupational confines. A worker might invest more heavily in her relationships with coworkers and use break times or introduce social engagements to support them; she might internally modify her job description to include tending to the positivity of the workplace; or she might take on organizational citizenship behaviors that make the workplace more pleasant. There is more depth to the job-crafting literature than what is presented here, but taken together, meaning-making and job crafting converge with theological teaching to suggest that one way people may find a calling is through changing their interpretations of what it is they are doing within their current occupations or even by doing things differently—more meaningfully—at their workplace and with their coworkers.

CONCLUSION

In this chapter, we sought to appraise the experience of calling from multiple levels and different perspectives, pondering key questions about what calling might feel like for people and how best to pursue one's calling. We suggested that empathy may provide an important new way to understand how people know they have found a calling, and how they may reflect upon and resolve conflict over which of myriad possible pursuits is their true calling. We integrated theological and psychological insights into seeking a calling and raised some alternative procedures people might take if "praying and waiting" is not working for them. Throughout this chapter, we sought to include but look beyond the vocational and organizational literature to help deepen and enrich a field that has been quite good at identifying the presence and potential benefits of a calling, but that has only just begun to flesh out what having a calling is really like. Our conclusion is that there is a wealth of knowledge and perspective that can be plumbed for new hypotheses and practical applications, and that the next decade of calling research will be exciting and invigorating.

REFERENCES

Andrews, A., Ed. (2010). *The kingdom life: A practical theology of discipleship and spiritual formation.* Colorado Springs, CO: NavPress.

Bolles, R.N. (2015). *What color is your parachute? A practical manual for job-hunters and career changers.* Berkeley, CA: Ten Speed Press.

Brown, S.D., & Ryan Krane, N.E. (2000). Four (or five) sessions and a cloud of dust: Old assumptions and new observations about career counseling. In S. Brown & R. Lent (Eds.), *Handbook of counseling psychology* (pp. 740–766). New York: Wiley.

Cox, C.L., Uddin, L.Q., Di Martino, A., Castellanos, F.X., Milham, M.P., & Kelly, C. (2012). The balance between feeling and knowing: Affective and cognitive empathy are reflected in the brain's intrinsic functional dynamics. *Social Cognitive and Affective Neuroscience, 7,* 727–737.

Dawis, R. V. (1992). The individual differences tradition in counseling psychology. *Journal of Counseling Psychology, 39,* 7–19.

Dawis, R. V., & Lofquist, L. H. (1984). *A psychological theory of work adjustment.* Minneapolis: University of Minnesota Press.

Decety, J., Norman, G. J., Berntson, G. G., & Cacioppo, J. T. (2012). A neurobehavioral evolutionary perspective on the mechanisms underlying empathy. *Progress in Neurobiology, 98,* 38–48.

Dik, B. J., & Duffy, R. D. (2009). Calling and vocation at work definitions and prospects for research and practice. *The Counseling Psychologist, 37,* 424–450.

Dik, B. J., & Duffy, R. D. (2012). *Make your job a calling: How the psychology of vocation can change your life at work.* West Conshohocken, PA: Templeton Press.

Dik, B. J., Duffy, R. D., & Tix, A. P. (2012). Religion, spirituality, and a sense of calling in the workplace. In P. Hill & B. Dik (Eds.), *The psychology of religion and workplace spirituality* (pp. 113–134). Charlotte, NC: Information Age Publishing.

Dik, B. J., Eldridge, B. M., Steger, M. F., & Duffy, R. D. (2012). Development and validation of the calling and vocation questionnaire (CVQ) and brief calling scale (BCS). *Journal of Career Assessment, 20,* 242–263.

Dik, B. J., Sargent, A. M., & Steger, M. F. (2008). Career development strivings assessing goals and motivation in career decision-making and planning. *Journal of Career Development, 35,* 23–41.

Dik, B. J., & Steger, M. F. (2008). Randomized trial of a calling-infused career workshop incorporating counselor self-disclosure. *Journal of Vocational Behavior, 73,* 203–211.

Duffy, R. D., & Dik, B. J. (2013). Research on calling: What have we learned and where are we going? *Journal of Vocational Behavior, 83*(3), 428–436.

Duffy, R. D., & Sedlacek, W. E. (2007). The presence of and search for a calling: Connections to career development. *Journal of Vocational Behavior, 70,* 590–601.

Engen, H. G., & Singer, T. (2013). Empathy circuits. *Current Opinion in Neurobiology, 23,* 275–282.

George, L. S., & Park, C. L. (2013). Are meaning and purpose distinct? An examination of correlates and predictors. *The Journal of Positive Psychology, 8,* 365–375.

Hammond, P., Stevens, R. P., & Svanoe, T. (2002). *The marketplace annotated bibliography: A Christian guide to books on work, business and vocation.* Downers Grove, IL: InterVarsity.

Hétu, S., Taschereau-Dumouchel, V., & Jackson, P. L. (2012). Stimulating the brain to study social interactions and empathy. *Brain Stimulation, 5,* 95–102.

Holland, J. L. (1959). A theory of vocational choice. *Journal of Counseling Psychology, 6,* 35–45.

Holland, J. L. (1997). *Making vocational choices: A theory of vocational personalities and work environments* (3rd ed.). Odessa, FL: Psychological Assessment Resources.

Kristof-Brown, A. L., Zimmerman, R. D., & Johnson, E. C. (2005). Consequences of individuals' fit at work: A meta-analysis of person-job, person-organization, person-group, and person-supervisor fit. *Personnel Psychology, 58,* 281–342.

Lent, R. W. (2005). A social cognitive view of career development and counseling. In S. D. Brown & R. W. Lent (Eds.), *Career development and counseling: Putting theory and research to work* (pp. 101–127). New York: Wiley.

Lent, R. W., Brown, S. D., & Hackett, G. (1994). Toward a unifying social cognitive theory of career and academic interest, choice, and performance. *Journal of Vocational Behavior, 45,* 79–122.

Lipsey, M. W., & Wilson, D. B. (1993). The efficacy of psychological, educational, and behavioral treatment: confirmation from meta-analysis. *American Psychologist, 48*(12), 1181.

Miller, D. L. (2009). *LifeWork: A biblical theology for what you do every day.* Seattle, WA: YWAM Publishing.

Park, C. L. (2010). Making sense of the meaning literature: An integrative review of meaning making and its effects on adjustment to stressful life events. *Psychological Bulletin, 136,* 257–301.

Parsons, F. (1909). *Choosing a vocation.* Boston, MA: Houghton Mifflin.

Placher, W. C., Ed. (2005). Callings: Twenty centuries of Christian wisdom on vocation. Grand Rapids, MI: Eerdmans.

Plantinga, C., Jr. (2002). *Engaging God's world: A Christian vision of faith, leaning, and living.* Grand Rapids, MI: Eerdmans.

Roepke, A. M., Jayawickreme, E., & Riffle, O. M. (2014). Meaning and health: A systematic review. *Applied Research in Quality of Life, 9,* 1055–1079.

Schuurman, D. J. (2004). *Vocation: Discerning our callings in life.* Grand Rapids, MI: Eerdmans.

Steger, M. F. (2009). Meaning in life. In S. J. Lopez (Ed.), *Oxford handbook of positive psychology* (2nd ed.) (pp. 679–687). Oxford, UK: Oxford University Press.

Steger, M. F. (2012). Experiencing meaning in life: Optimal functioning at the nexus of spirituality, psychopathology, and well-being. In P. T. P. Wong (Ed.), *The human quest for meaning* (2nd ed.) (pp. 165–184). New York: Routledge.

Steger, M. F., & Dik, B. J. (2009). If one is searching for meaning in life, does meaning in work help? *Applied Psychology: Health and Well-Being, 1,* 303–320.

Steger, M. F., Dik, B. J., & Duffy, R. D. (2012). Measuring meaningful work: The work and meaning inventory (WAMI). *Journal of Career Assessment, 20,* 322–337.

Steger, M. F., Frazier, P., Oishi, S., & Kaler, M. (2006). The meaning in life questionnaire: Assessing the presence of and search for meaning in life. *Journal of Counseling Psychology, 53,* 80–93.

Steger, M. F., & Park, C. L. (2012). The creation of meaning following trauma: Meaning making and trajectories of distress and recovery. In T. Keane, E. Newman, & K. Fogler (Eds.), *Toward an integrated approach to trauma focused therapy* (pp. 171–191). Washington, DC: APA.

Walter, H. (2012). Social cognitive neuroscience of empathy: concepts, circuits, and genes. *Emotion Review, 4,* 9–17.

Whiston, S. C. (2002). Application of the principles: Career counseling and interventions. *The Counseling Psychologist, 30,* 218–237.

Wrzesniewski, A., & Dutton, J. E. (2001). Crafting a job: Revisioning employees as active crafters of their work. *Academy of Management Review, 26,* 179–201.

Zaki, J., & Ochsner, K. N. (2012). The neuroscience of empathy: Progress, pitfalls and promise. *Nature neuroscience, 15,* 675–680.

PART II

SACRED PERSPECTIVES

CHAPTER 10

THE NORMALCY OF THE PARANORMAL: NUMINOUS EXPERIENCES THROUGHOUT THE LIFE SPAN

J. Harold Ellens

Paranormal experiences are common for humans and apparently have always been. Many people have relatively frequent and significant numinous or mystical experiences. These experiences are often referred to as parapsychological events for obvious reasons. They might just as well be called para-spiritual experiences, I suppose. By the term spiritual I mean to refer to the universal irrepressible human hunger for meaning. That hunger reaches out for the transcendent, for connection with God, and we call it spirituality. When it reaches out for connection with others and our world we call it by various terms that imply a humane quest, including science, social relations, and sexuality.

Humans and perhaps other mammals possess an innate drive to make everything about life meaningful and to fit it into a comprehensive picture of reality, as we individually view it. Each human experience has its own implied story, but we unconsciously or consciously weave all our experiences together into what we think of as our master story. In fashioning that master story we feed into it such interpretations as are necessary to make it coherent and meaningful. We edit out or repress material that does not fit in, ring true, or enhance the meaningfulness of the story or the perspective that we wish it to have.

A paranormal, parapsychological, or para-spiritual event is a cognitive or affective human experience that is extraordinary in the sense that it does not seem to fit the pattern of our daily lives. Instead, a paranormal event usually is an experience of special illumination, inadvertent opportunity, compelling guidance, unexplainable help in a time of extremity, or an unexpected intervention into our lives. Such paranormal experiences often have three characteristics. First, they are not sought, longed for, prayed for, or anticipated. They come to us unasked and unexpected. Second, they seem to come from a source other than the empirical or rational world we know. Third, they produce significant constructive life-changing results.

In the ancient and medieval worlds paranormal experiences were understood to be common, meaningful, and trustworthy. People lived by the insight or guidance such experiences offered them and considered them a normal part of life. The ancient Greeks and Romans, Hebrews, Babylonians, and Egyptians, as well as the Europeans of the Middle Ages, generally assumed that their paranormal experiences were important divine interventions into their lives. They saw them as gifts of guidance from God or the gods. They took them seriously and spent considerable energy on trying to discern their meaning.

The Renaissance and Reformation introduced the Aristotelian notion that the material world is tractable, can be studied, and thoroughly understood by means of empirical science. That led to the Age of Enlightenment. From it came the great achievements of the scientific revolution, industrial revolution, technological revolution, atomic revolution, and the current information revolution (IT) with its computerization of our world. A by-product of the Enlightenment was the devaluation of nonempirical human experience. Thus the world of the knowledge quest was shifted from the pursuit of the meaning and purpose issues to preoccupation with cause and effect issues. So psychological and spiritual experiences were sidelined as intractable, unexplorable by empirical science. From that sidetrack the psychospiritual world of reality and experience was relegated to a status of being unreal. Anything said or claimed regarding it was considered speculative, mythic, and untrue.

Thus the spiritual world was left to the priests, who tended toward preoccupation with orthodox traditions, and artists who lost interesting in reality, authenticity. The psychological world was reduced insofar as possible to empirical research. By the 20th century the psychospiritual meaning quest was radically repressed. It was exchanged for the pragmatic satisfactions of learning how the mechanics of this planet work. That, of course, provided some superficial kinds of meaning in itself. However, it failed to fill the human spirit with a comprehensive worldview that was meaningful. This fact of life is certified by the rise in the last half century of a challenge to the Modern Enlightenment worldview in the form of postmodernism.

Postmodernism seems to take many forms, some of which seem to be dreamed up out of thin air. However, one thing is clear about the movement. It is an uncompromising call for the scientific world to take seriously the nonempirical part of human experience It has issued a call to recognize the psychospiritual reality as a source of profound meaning to every person who attends thoughtfully to it. The Postmodern quest is a valuable opportunity to revisit the long-standing premodern record of constructive life-changing numinous experiences. Humans are having such meaning-inducing events regularly everywhere.

During the first eight centuries of our millennium the three major western religions developed standardized rituals, authoritative founding documents, dogmas, organizations, structures, and ethical codes. In the process these movements diverted from the intentions of their initiators by focusing on institutions. This shifted them away from the numinous emphasis of their originators. Each of those progenitors was preoccupied with the inner quality of spirit, vision, and highly personal mystical experiences. Those were visionary experiences of the original impulse that formed their movements. Abraham, Moses, Jesus, and Mohammed took seriously their transcendental illuminations or revelations. It might be said that they urged us to (1) identify such visionary illuminations, (2) name them, (3) keep track of them, and so (4) create a "culture of the divine spirit."

I am a Pan*en*theist. It seems to me that our prevalent human moments of visionary illumination derive from a source that lies beyond each of us. It comes to us unsought and unpursued. It makes us aware of dimensions of reality otherwise not known to us, a dynamic force or energy in us and beyond us. It is my experience that such energy is active in the entire material, moral, and spiritual universes in which we exist. I believe it is related to or identified with the life force in all organisms, perhaps even the energy that keeps electrons in orbit in a rock. That dynamism is, in my view, the phenomenon that may rightly be named, Divine Spirit or God as Holy Spirit.

It is my perception that the Divine Spirit is (1) mindful as we can see in the intricacies, order, and complexity of the evolving creation. (2) That spirit is benevolent as in the way both the pleasure and pain move us to growth. (3) It is motivated by the aesthetic, or sense of beauty, in that evolution and growth move always toward beauty and fruitfulness. (4) It manifests frequently in human experiences that are visionary illuminations leading to life-changing futures. Those events are instances of the energetic presence, persistently relating to us as Spirit. When they occur, these numinous events infuse our psyches, minds, affects, and bodies. They give us a sense of our destiny.

Let me relate a couple personal experiences that illustrate this fact. When I was five years old I was in love with a blond, blue eyed girl of my age named Esther. She lived in a farmhouse across the country road from my home. She was born in April 1932 and I in July of that year. As we played together all summer of 1937 we talked happily of starting school in September. That meant a trek of one mile through the fields and forest to East Side Christian School, a one-room country school with one teacher, eight grades, and 43 students.

On the bright sunny morning of August 3, I stood by the well of our home lost in thought and awaiting Esther's appearance. I heard her screen door slam shut and I remember the lilt of joy in my spirit as I looked up to see her happy face. She stood at the top of the Van Houten drive way, stricken with fear, and completely on fire. I screamed for my mother and we ran to help Esther. Our efforts failed. Esther burned to death right there before my face.

When Esther died something essential in me died as well. A sudden palpable darkness descended upon me like a blanket pulled over my head. It shut down my consciousness and memory. For two years thereafter I can remember nothing. Whoever I was before that is gone. Whatever kind of person I was before Esther died I do not remember. Whoever I would be today if it had not been for that fatal fire, I have no idea. Apparently I carried on at school for those two years, although my brother says I cried all the time. I have no memory of it. I must have been like an automaton.

In the summer of 1939 after feeding the animals and completing the morning chores, I stepped out of the dimness of the horse barn into the bright midday sun. Before I had gone 10 paces I was caught up in a cocoon of brilliance that swirled round me like a pillar of light. It seemed to lift me off the ground and shone right through me. I felt transparent and immediately sensed the intensity of divine presence. I had no particular consciousness of what notion of God I perceived. It was just "godness" that saturated me. Simultaneously I saw a complete vision of my future laid out before me. It was a sensation of joy and relief. I was intensely alive, in touch with the whole universe, with God!

I did not ask for that illumination. I did not seek it. I did not know enough to anticipate it, expect it, or wish for it. It simply came to me unasked. It infused me without any act of response or obedience on my part. It was just there and it radically changed my life. It set me on a course that I have never felt like second guessing or desiring to alter. That profoundly constructive life-changing moment was the first of a number of such numinous events throughout my life, all equally unsought and all equally life changing, illumining, clarifying, healing, and empowering; even though all were not so dramatic.

It was not as though I responded to the event and felt led to the life laid out before me. Spontaneously, and in the same moment that the light embraced me, my life was full of meaning. Its meaning was simply that I was directed to a life of caring for all the needy people around. It was the time of the Great Depression. Our community was beset by poverty, sickness, and death. Twelve children close to me, including my brother and two sisters died during that time. Suddenly I envisioned the pain and loss of humanity and my role in its alleviation. I felt one with all humans, all living things.

I imagine that if we had a highly esteemed and honored physician in our community, well known for his healing powers, I might have imagined him as my model and medicine as my destiny. There was no such person known to us. The one person who seemed to stand above our suffering, with some ability to do something about it, was our pastor. He was an able and learned man who obviously cared for needy humans. I saw my destiny before me in pastoral ministry. My life has been a straight line from that numinous moment to this.

I have had a half dozen numinous experience in my life. They were all unique. Another one that was particularly life changing happened to me at about age 40. I was a minister of a Christian Reformed Church in a new and developing congregation in the Midwest. I was accused of heresy by one of my elders. He brought the charge to the National Synod. They proceeded with a trial in which I was not invited to speak for myself. They condemned me on five counts having to do with my saying that God loves everyone, intends to save everyone, and will do so. They proceeded with the steps to take away my ordination.

I was at the point in my life at which I had five children in college, one in a private Catholic school, and my wife in graduate school at the University of Michigan. To say the least, I could not afford to lose my ordination, my job, my calling. One night after rolling around in bed until midnight, I fell into a profound sleep. I was awakened suddenly at 2:00 o'clock by a sturdy voice in the room which declared, "Trust in the Lord and do good." I sat bolt upright with a sense of God's presence intensely surrounding me. Simultaneous with the voice that awakened me I was completely relieved of all anguish, cleansed of all anxiety. The confusion about the matter was entirely taken away. I had the overwhelming sense of the Spirit, present in the room. I had never memorized that verse but it sounded to me like scripture. I turned to my Bible and discovered it in Psalm 37:3. Not the slightest twinge of anguish about the trial ever returned to me. Fear and threat to my ordination was removed. It was not because I obeyed the voice but because the anguish had been taken away. I was delivered of it. Five weeks later the verdict disappeared on a technicality and at the next Synod the trial was set aside and the charge was removed. The Synod avoided my position of God's radical, unconditional, and universal grace and forgiveness for everybody, for everything, for evermore (Mic 7:18–20).

Apparently we should be far less surprised than we tend to be, by our paranormal epiphanies. Cultivating a culture that is conscious of the pervasive dynamic spirit, present in the world and in our personal lives, means eight things, I think. (1) We can experience that presence in tangible ways. (2) We can profitably *hold ourselves open* to its intimations. (3) We can *notice the presence* in ordinary and extraordinary moments. (4) We may *identify* those experiences as the presence of that spiritual dynamo. (5) It is natural and normal to *name* those events as "moments of the spirit." (6) *Explaining* such events to each other will raise our consciousness level regarding their presence in our lives. (7) We will *recall* that those events continue to happen frequently. (8) We will find it natural to *maintain the awareness that* we live all the time within the force field of that dynamo of spirit. We will *develop a consciousness* of living in the matrix of the active presence of Spirit in us and around us, and we will come naturally to *think of ourselves* as constantly vivified by that life force.

It is interesting that in the present culture of the western world we do not have a greater awareness than we do of the frequency with which humans experience life-changing paranormal events of illumination. There are almost certainly two primary reasons for that. First, within the religious communities of the Western World: Judaism, Christianity, and Islam, the dogmatic and doctrinal standardization of what should be believed as religious truth, and what should be expected as spiritual experience, has been largely prescribed. One would think that religious communities would be particularly interested in the frequency and meaning of paranormal experiences that constructively change people's lives and enhance their understanding of their spirituality. It is the case, however, that the prescribed nature of most religious life squelches openness to the spirit and to the reality and importance of numinous experiences.[1]

Second, paranormal experiences are very difficult to describe, define, and fully comprehend. Since they are mysterious and personal, we are all quite hesitant to report our "otherworldly" experiences. We fear we will be considered strange and pathological. Nonetheless, persons generally have paranormal experiences that are unlikely to be explained except as personalized moments of spiritual illumination, caused by the Spirit or force that pervades all facets of our world. Though such events have recurred frequently in my life, I never shared those with anyone until I discussed them with a physician at age 25 or 30. I began to write about them and mention them in lectures and sermons only *after my 70th year.*

Why did I begin to address this part of my life in my eighth decade? First, I finally had the zeal, time, and energy to attempt to discern what was transpiring in those numinous experiences and why they were so life altering and life giving. Second, I wanted to know why they were so beneficial in the constructive changes they spontaneously brought about without my seeking them. They always came to me. I did not seek them. They just happened to me and gave me a different life and personhood, as a result. Third, I find that with age comes a natural desire to put everything about oneself on the table. Fourth, when I was 71 I was finally discovered by significant publishers who were genuinely interested in getting as much of my work as possible and publishing as much about me as they could get. That finally gave me an adequate pulpit or podium from which to tell my story.

Enriching numinous experiences happen in many people's lives. However, it takes the eyes to see them, the ears to hear them, and openness of spirit to notice them.[2] That is necessary if one is to recognize them for what they are, take them for real, and celebrate them. Otherwise we tend to dismiss them as abnormal moments to be quickly repressed and forgotten.

CREATING A SCIENCE OF THE PARANORMAL

Postmodern science is demanding that the positivism of the Enlightenment recognizes that the human experiences of the psyche, spirit, and transcendent world are crucial arenas for scientific investigation. Moreover, postmodern science is seeking ways to assess the reality, meaning, and value of such numinous experiences. They are uniquely individual but profoundly life changing and constructive. Postmodernism is asking two important questions, among many others. (1) How abnormal is the paranormal? (2) How can we create a science of the paranormal? There was a virtual absence of attention to this in professional and scientific journals before the last decade. To ignore this, however, is to leave at least half of real human experience unaddressed by scientific research or examination.

Of course, the function of peer reviewed journals is to publish replicable research results. A section in each professional journal, however, might be devoted to reporting incidents of the paranormal so that a database might be developed. A universe of discourse and a vehicle for discussion could be then developed for taking such data into consideration. At present no effective instrument is available for collecting and processing the data, assessing the frequency of such events, reporting them clearly, recording them, and then naming, describing, categorizing, and analyzing them.

Undertaking such scientific investigation, of course, will require that we develop a workable state of mind. We must suspend belief and suspend disbelief as I have discussed in the preface of this work.

If we create instruments for raising our consciousness level and increasing our information base, we may discover that there are eight things that strike us with surprising urgency: (1) that the incidents of paranormal events are more frequent—more normal—than we think,[3] (2) that they fit into specific patterns that can be categorized and analyzed more readily than we have imagined, (3) that they may bring to the surface of our thought-processes insights about the nature and sources of paranormal events that are currently ignored because we have not reduced our mystification by steps one and two above, (4) that the paranormal events are more normal in frequency and universality than are the things we call "normal," (5) that we can establish criteria for sorting the real from the unreal in what we are now referring to as paranormal events, (6) that a solicitation of anecdotal reports will produce such a wealth of information as to give rise to an entirely new arena for productive research.

If the dynamo of spirit is communicating with our spirits by way of numinous or visionary experiences, presumably it assumes that we have the capacity to apprehend and interpret the content, if we study it carefully. That would be the same procedure that we have used to study the world that we have mastered by empirical science. (7) We may discover that not all truth is empirical data. A great deal of our understanding of the truth about this world we know from phenomenological investigations and heuristic interpretations. These seem to be trustworthy instruments of research that are particularly suited to investigating paranormal experiences and other psychosocial issues. We should be able by means of them to create useful theories, data collection and data management systems, hypotheses, and laws regarding numinous moments. (8) We name numinous or mystical events as paranormal because we have not yet discovered or created a framework of analysis by which the data can be collected and managed as a normal science.

I have a friend who is a social scientist. He raises the problem that it is difficult to develop a science of numinous experiences because they are so unique and individual in character. In the parlance of empirical research, $n = 1$. That is not a broad base and is not replicable. However, a national or international survey might produce such a wealth of data, in which patterns were readily evident, as in the case of near-death experiences. Then categories, models, and types would show that $n =$ an almost infinite number of characteristic types. Such patterns of data would be amenable to rigorous phenomenological science and at least heuristic conclusion.

Some decades ago, a great deal was made of chaos theory and entropy in interpreting the unknown aspects of the material world, particularly in the field of astrophysics and cosmology. We always think things just beyond our model and grasp are chaotic. That is only because we do not understand them. It is not because they are incoherent, lawless, and unpredictable. We think things just beyond our ken are chaotic because our paradigm is too limited to manage the data out there. Life is always a process of the kind of growth that requires constant expansion of our paradigms. When we cannot expand our paradigm to take in the next larger world we are discovering, whether because of our fear or blockheadedness, we shrink and wither, and our scientific systems go down.[*]

We are at a threshold in scientific research that demands an expansion of our scientific paradigm to take in the data of the paranormal. We must do this in a manner and with a method that can be formed into coherent models of knowledge and understanding. Why would we not hypothesize that what is for us the world of the paranormal is really a very normal world of human process, and that we can find a way to assess it systematically. Doing so was certainly the agenda of our Canterbury Conclave.

Today nearly everyone knows the name and work of Richard Dawkins. He is busy endeavoring to prove that the world of the ethereal, spiritual, and paranormal is not real. We need to take him seriously for four reasons. First, his professional pedigree is impressive. He is a professor of science at Oxford University in the United Kingdom. Second, his work is carefully reasoned and meticulous in attention to detail, so far as it goes. Third, he has published profusely and in a style that engages his readers, laypersons, and professionals. Fourth, his titles are winsome and intriguing and have drawn to his work a worldwide readership, indeed a surprising philosophical and scientific following.[5]

A couple of years ago, *Time Magazine* featured a remarkable article by David Van Biema addressing Dawkins' work.[6] It posed Dawkins in dialogue with Francis Collins. That proved to be a stimulating and in some ways delightful debate about evolution and creation, particularly about the intelligent design (ID) argument. Collins is a genome scientist and pioneer in the field. He perceives that the material outcomes of the genome project, thus far evident, point to a world that is transcendent to space, time, and materiality.[7] The dialogue between Dawkins and Collins took place on September 30, 2006, and the magazine article is a transcript of that exchange.

Dawkins' essential claim is that all the evidence that the empirical sciences can provide regarding the nature of the material world leads inevitably and exclusively to the conclusion that the world that we can study scientifically is a product of natural and empirically evident causes. This conclusion is reinforced, he believes, by the fact that everything in the material world can be explained by processes of cause and effect that we have identified as existing within the material world. We have analyzed them. We have demonstrated that they can be understood without reference to transcendent sources or forces. Collins, however, is sure that the cause and effect dynamics evident throughout this material world are not in tension with, and certainly do not rule out, the presence of an ethereal world of reality that humans experience but that has not been mastered by empirical science. Indeed, he confidently asserts that Dawkins' claim only explains our understanding of the causes and effects by which the material world functions and leaves out any reasonable accounting for meaning, purpose, and the function of the paranormal.

Moreover, Collins makes the telling point that humans experience a great deal of reality that is not material and that cannot be accounted for in terms of what we know about material reality. He is referring to the real world of human experiences that reflects much of the function of the human psyche, spirit, and parapsychological or paranormal ways of knowing: intuition, ESP, prescience, and spontaneous and constructive life-changing illuminations. If we concentrated upon studying these dimensions of human experience more assiduously, we would be able to develop a more complete science of the psyche and the spirit. Such a science is likely to lead us to empirical or phenomenological and heuristic assessments of the world of the paranormal or parapsychological. Surely such a science will lead us, at the very least, to a further understanding of how psychology and biochemistry are at play in our experiences of the world of the numinous.

Since a science of numinous human experiences has not developed we have no language formulated for handling such empirical, phenomenological, and heuristic investigations of that world of the paranormal. No universe of discourse has been developed for discussing it, as we noted above. No categories have been defined for managing the abundant data that seems available for its study. No comprehensive and systematic collection of the data of paranormal human experiences has been undertaken. If such a science were developed, as William James called for a century ago, undoubtedly we would be surprised how much hard data we would have with which to work and what precise categories of evidence we might be able to develop.[8]

The positions taken by Dawkins and Collins constitute the far ends of a continuum of potential notions about the relationship between the truth understood from an exclusively empirical perspective and the truth understood from a phenomenological and heuristic perspective. The late Stephen Jay Gould spent his professional life defending the position that we can explain all that is explainable about life and our world from a strictly empirical perspective. He spent his career as a famous paleontologist on the faculty of Harvard University and published a number of the most interesting books ever written in the field of science. Toward the end of his life, however, he reassessed the situation of his empirical pursuit of knowledge. Gould published his new perspective in a fine little volume entitled *Rocks of Ages*.[9]

In that volume Gould floated the theory that both the claims of empirical science and phenomenology and heuristics, even in the field of religion, can constitute truth. The value and valence of their truth is equal, since all truth, as truth, is equally true. He affirmed the right and truth of each by describing them as existing in *separate, nonoverlapping magisteria*. This was a fascinating and ingenious way of handling the impasse. The difficulty with it was that it leaves one with a haunting sense that a slight of hand has been performed. One would expect that whatever truth we can access as humans, is unified.

QUEST FOR A UNIFIED THEORY

Van Biema tried to push the matter further back to a focal point of unity or integration of all truth, as he teased out the dialogue between Dawkins and Collins. He set the stage with the note that the debate about science *versus* ethereal or transcendent reality has really been double faceted in the last decade or two. On the one hand is the Darwinian suggestion that natural law governs the forces of material development. On the other hand is the question of the apparently mindful design of its structure and function. Collins suggested that the gaps in the evolutionary story "are more meaningful than its very convincing" total model and that the real nature of things cannot be accounted for without a transcendental world of extramaterial reality.[10]

The debate rages and usually takes the form of claims for and against the existence of God rather than simply an address to the issues of the paranormal. Dawkins is riding the crest of a literary wave. Sam Harris's *The End of Faith* sold over half a million copies since 2004.[11] He followed it with the also popular, *Letter to a Christian Nation*,[12] attacking paranormal or psychospiritual experiences in general and the suggestion of an ethereal design in our world of experience, in particular. Tufts University professor, Daniel Dennett, wrote *Breaking the Spell: Religion as a Natural Phenomenon*,[13] which has also appealed to a large audience of readers.

Other prominent contributors to that dialogue are Victor Stenger, an astrophysicist, who wrote *God: The Failed Hypothesis*[14]; and Carl Sagan, whose essays on science and God's absence, were posthumously published as *The Varieties of Scientific Experience*.[15] On the other side of the issue lies the work of Keith Ward of Oxford University, who gave us such recent volumes as *The Big Questions of Science and Religion* and *More than Matter: Is There More to Life Than Molecules?*[16] There is no need to push this dialogue into a debate regarding the existence of God. The real issue at stake is whether human constructive life-changing paranormal experiences are real. It is important to pursue that issue and its implied subordinate questions regarding their source and meaning. Are those experiences, indeed, some kind of miracles or is the universe simply wired as much for producing them as it is for boiling water at 212 degrees Fahrenheit at sea level. Dawkins claims that just the use of the word, miracle, slams the door on scientific investigation. Collins replied that for him it opens the door to a holistic address to all of potential reality.

Collins has been the director of the National Human Genome Research Institute since 1993. He headed a multinational 2,400-scientist team that comapped the three billion biochemical letters of our genetic blueprint, and inspired his institute in studying the genome and mining it for medical breakthroughs. While Dawkins looks at the scientific data and says there is no evidence for the reality of the paranormal, Collins looks at the scientific data and says two things. First, reality is not limited to time, space, or materiality, so scientific exploration of phenomena of time, space, and materiality is not going to be able to describe much of the paranormal. Second, there are numerous *loci* in the scientific database that strongly suggest the presence and probability of an ethereal or transcendental force behind and within the material world.

RULING THE PARANORMAL IN OR
OUT OF THE EQUATION

A number of limitations impose themselves when we try to rule out the reality of the paranormal, ethereal, and spiritual worlds. First, it would be foolishly unscientific to rule out dogmatically the possibility that paranormal experiences indicate a coherent world of reality beyond the tangible and material that effects life-changing actions within the material universe. If science cannot study the paranormal because it is limited to the empirically material, it cannot rule out the reality and meaningfulness of the paranormal. It requires infinite volumes of data to rule it out. It only requires phenomenological evidence and heuristic intimations to rule in its possibility.

Second, it is an imperative of authentic science, therefore, that we take seriously the heuristic and phenomenological data, scientifically available, for the possibility, even the probability of paranormal action within the material universe. Third, positing that assumption of ethereal action within the material world resolves many of those problems which, in a strictly empirical perspective, prove to be large gaps in the scientific model. Fourth, it requires much more comprehensive data to rule out of the equation the reality and significance of the paranormal world of reality than to rule in both its possibility and probability. This is particularly true, in view of the intimations and phenomenological evidence we have, from both the normal and paranormal arenas of identifiable human experience, which suggests the operation of an ethereal and perhaps even a transcendent force or world of reality that impinges upon our material domain.

COMPELLING PHENOMENOLOGICAL DATA

Why should we create a science of the paranormal? The answer seems simple and concrete. There is a great deal of compelling phenomenological data available that requires explaining. John Matzke played football for Dartmouth. He got malignant melanoma in a lump in his armpit at age 30. They said he had 18 months to live. Ten years later it had spread to his lung. They said the inevitable outcome was death within months. John took a month off, decided to delay standard treatment, and began long walks in the mountains. He improved his diet and began to meditate. In his meditation, John visualized himself healthy, with good strong blood cells destroying the cancer.

After his month off, he returned to the Veterans Administration Hospital for further evaluation regarding a treatment regimen. "Dr. O'Donnell repeated the chest X-rays to document the size and location of the tumor before starting treatment. But instead of the large cancerous lesion in Matzke's lung, he saw . . . nothing. O'Donnell recalls, 'When John came back a month later, it was remarkable—the tumor on his chest X-ray was gone. Gone, gone, gone!' . . . Doctors would like to understand cases like Matzke's."[17] So would we all.

> Pinning down spontaneous remissions has been a little like chasing rainbows. It's not even possible to say just how frequently such cases occur—estimates generally range from 1 in 60,000 to 1 in 100,000 patients . . . But genuine miracles do exist, and throughout the history of medicine, physicians have recorded cases of spontaneous remission. . . . not just cancer but conditions like aortic aneurysm, . . . Peyronie's disease, a deformity of the penis; and childhood cataracts.[18]

We may speculate that Matzke's immune system, reinforced by his change in lifestyle and psychospiritual address to his tumors, produced a healing effect. During his month of meditation and healthy living his skin tumors were surrounded by white halo-like rings, indicating that the immune system was attacking the melanocytes, pigmented cells in the skin that give rise to the cancer.[19] Ever since 1700 or so a medical record has been developing indicating that certain serious infections such as erysipelas or those associated with Streptococcus, cure cancer by causing tumor regression. It was by following up on these cures which nature spontaneously induces that physicians were able to develop some of the chemotherapy that is used today.

Lenzer also reports the case of Alice Epstein, a brilliant academic diagnosed with kidney cancer in 1985. A month after the resection of her kidney the cancer showed up in both lungs. Her life estimate at that time was three months.

> Epstein, who says she had a "cancer-prone personality," then turned to psychosynthesis, which she describes as a "combination of psychotherapy and spiritual therapy." It helped her overcome depression, difficulty expressing anger, and suppression of her own needs in order to please others—traits she and some psychologists believe are characteristic of the cancer-prone personality. Although she never received any medical or surgical treatment for the deadly cancer invading her lungs, six weeks after starting psychosynthesis, her tumors began to shrink. Within one year, they had disappeared without a trace. That was 22 years ago.[20]

Epstein lived to 80 years of age and beyond.

The crucial points at stake here are as follows. First, given the right chance, the irrepressible life force in nature is able to induce spontaneous remission of horrible disorder in the physical organism of human beings. Second, the state of psychospirituality of that person seems to have a great deal to do with the onset of illness and the effecting of cure. Third, a decisive shift in orientation in the psychospiritual world of that person seems to be the trigger that induces radical reorientation of the organic forces at play in the physiological organism, the human body.

Focus upon the permission to be well and not sick, and focus upon the will to get well, is a high priority factor in mobilizing the power of our physiological organism to eliminate the deadly forces that work against the well-being of the person. It is clear that this works when the ill person determines to live and be well. One can confidently speculate that a directive to get well, given by an authority whom that sick person respects as a healer, would be enough in some cases to trigger the will to empower the immune system to overcome the pathological and pathogenic condition. It is reported that Jung thought half the healing power of the healer is in the patient's belief that he or she is a effective healer.

Lenzer concludes almost lyrically. "Although medical advances have dramatically improved outcomes in certain cancers . . . modern medicine has yet to come close to nature's handiwork in inexplicably producing spontaneous remission without apparent side effects for people like John Matzke and Alice Epstein, who have experienced the rarest hints of nature's healing mysteries."[21]

Such cures intrigue us all, physicians, research scientists, patients, and friends of the suffering. We want and need to understand what is really going on in those moments when we experience miracles; when ethereal forces, science, and psychology combine in the paranormal and all the rules seem, for a blessed moment, to be set aside or reversed. The scientific research proposed by this article is urgently necessary because of the fact that inadequate cooperation has been achieved so far, between the contribution that the empirical sciences and the psychospiritual analyses can bring to bear upon the study of the paranormal in the ancient world and in our own.

The import of the renovation of my life at age seven is that it grounded the nature of my person and the trajectory of my vocation in a life-changing paranormal event. It marked out in my life a profound and inerasable awareness of an illumining force present to me. I compare that event and the half dozen others in my life, with the host of similar reports of my patients, students, and audiences for 60 years, internationally and cross culturally. This comparison compels me to conclude that the illumining force I experienced is pervasive in the whole world and manifests itself to us naturally. We are forced to see it in what seem to us to be paranormal events that change life. I have never been able to escape that awareness and certitude since I was seven. My life has been regularly marked by such parapsychological events, equally dramatic, equally illumining, and equally life changing for me. Most of those were not experiences of physical healing but of the psychospiritual healing that came from relatively dramatic numinous illuminations. They always seemed to me like interventions from another world. There is much reason to believe that the paranormal is not really abnormal; while our failure so far to attend to it properly is, indeed, abnormal in this wonderfully scientific world.[22]

This question interfaces with our modern perplexity regarding whether the present-day life-changing paranormal experiences operate within the same paradigm as those ancient stories or are of a remarkably different order. It is at present too early to tell, but it is surely the scientific imperative for this century to collect the data of such human experiences that are apparently available, analyze that data, endeavor to discern patterns and paradigms, and carefully categorize and interpret the meaning of it all. Now it looks like chaos, but we must assume, as in all other scientific breakthroughs in the past, that it is only a chaos in our minds, not in the data, and that if we attend properly to the data, we will see its paradigms and the chaos will turn into scientifically describable order.

In 1976 Julian Jaynes published *The Origin of Consciousness in the Breakdown of the Bicameral Mind.*[23] He meant to refer to the fact that our brains are divided into two hemispheres. We have a right brain and a left brain. The left brain is that hemisphere that processes experience mainly in terms of linear logic, problem solving, finely crafted sentences, and bottom-line thinking. It is through these kinds of experiences that people with predominant left brain function get most of their meaning out of life experiences. They tend to be people who like logical arguments, relatively rigid predictability, fixed faucets, solved problems, law and order, and a well-regulated life. The right brain is the hemisphere that generates language resources and processes experience in terms of sensations of color, texture, form, shape, a sense of mass, aesthetic qualities, emotions, and relationships. People who are right-brain-dominant process the meaning of life in terms of those values, expectations, emotions, and hopes.

Seventy percent of the males in the world are left-brain-dominant, and 70 percent of the females in the world are right-brain-dominant. The remaining 30 percent of both genders tend to be high on both scales, a capacity that leads to better and healthier adjustment in life and to less turbulent relationships. This pattern is confirmed by many studies of brain preference, but notably in numerous superb works by Restak, Edwards, and Springer and Deutsch.[24]

Jaynes argues persuasively that human beings have always had surprisingly greater paranormal ways of knowing than people today realize. He raised major concerns about this already decades ago and his argument centers in his claim that the dominant character of the human meaning-quest for most of history was carried out on the psychospiritual plain. His voluminous evidence warrants his conclusion that humans did not depend primarily upon the analytic or logical abilities until a millennium or two before the days of Julius Caesar, Jesus, and Josephus. They did not trust their left brains primarily, as we do today. They trusted their right brains and as a result, lived life listening to and obeying the voices of the gods that they perceived they heard in their affective right brain hemisphere.

This meant that people were primarily interested in the meaning and purpose issues in understanding life, and so they were tuned to the paranormal ways of knowing more than to the empirical ways of knowing, associated with the left brain function. That is, intuition, extrasensory perception (ESP), and prescience, as well as spontaneous healings or deliverances, and moments of unexpected illumination had more value to them and were trusted by them as sources of the knowledge that was valuable and useful. The Bible and ancient Greek legend is full of these reports. Jaynes is sure that it was that orientation that made it possible for the ancient Hebrew prophets, visionaries, and seers to receive ethereal revelations and convey them to the society. They possessed highly functional right brains, which generated the insights of transcendental meaning evident to them in many situations in life. They functioned with high degrees of ESP, intuition, and prescience, and ethereal illuminations or intimations; and they trusted them.

They had no scientific resistance to those ways of knowing, but rather considered them more natural and real than conclusions drawn from empirical assessment or analytical problem solving. They heard the word of the gods in their right brains. Jaynes insists that these same capacities are still as real in humans today, despite the scientific revolution, but we have repressed them in favor of empirical science. Such visionaries as Edgar Cayce,[25] Deepak Chopra,[26] and the subjects in Moody's extensive research on near-death experiences, are tuned to the same wavelengths as such ancients as Abraham, Moses, Micah, Plato, Philo, Paul, Zeno, Jesus, Plotinus, Porphyry, Aurelius Augustine, Theresa of Avila, Thomas Aquinas, Jean d'Ark, and Julian of Norwich.[27] We have allowed our receptors to atrophy and so we are not awake to our paranormal and psychospiritual potentials, as people used to be and we should be. We are afraid of them, downplay them, and do not trust them. We are afraid to share with others the moments when we have experiences that can be accounted for in no other way than as an ethereal illumination.

Consequently, we do not collect the series of memories of such events that have happened to us in our lives. So we lose our cumulative collective awareness of the intensity with which the paranormal is always present to us. Jaynes thought it is imperative that we begin again to value this side of human life, experience, and the meaning quest.

Some of us have some or all of the paranormal ways of knowing to a high degree and some of us to a lower degree. Everyone has had the experience of not having thought of a certain friend for a long time and then out of the blue, so to speak, getting the urge to phone her. Then, just as we are reaching for the telephone to make that call, it rings and it is the person we were intending to call. Some would say that is mere coincidence, however, it occurs so often, consistently in the same way, with nearly every person, cross culturally. So it must be acknowledged that this is a universal human capacity to be aware of the thoughts and intentions of another person over a great distance. It is time that we stop merely repressing the awareness of these kinds of experiences and investigate their nature and function and impact upon our lives.

There is little reason, it seems to me, to reduce the significance of paranormal events or rewrite them differently than they were experienced. Reductionism is often in the direction toward error in a number of ways. It makes our personal or communal biases the determinative principle of interpretation. It erases the relevance of all those parts of the data that do not fit the reductionistic paradigm. So, it assumes that we know more than we know about the phenomena with which we are dealing. With regard to things we do not understand we should always do four things. First, we should watch and listen very carefully to the reports of the data. Second, we should let the phenomena described stand as they are reported. Third, we should attempt insofar as possible to carry out a friendly analysis of possible explanations. Fourth, reductionism of the paranormal generally overlooks the constructive life-changing effect that all these experiences had upon the persons who had them. Such ignoring of data should be assiduously avoided because it is unscientific.

It is a bit astonishing, is it not, that we invest, with absolute veracity, rational thought and empirical experience, as ways of knowing, but thoroughly distrust, repress, and devalue the persistent occurrences of remarkably universal paranormal ways of knowing that prove to be utterly real and factual. The evidence now available for prescience on the part of numerous persons is quite impressive. It is not uncommon for a person to have a clear certainty of a specific event happening in the foreseeable future, and then have that actually happen just as the person had perceived it. Some occurrences of prescience take the form of information perceived in a numinous dream, some as a haunting awareness that draws itself over a person's consciousness, and others as a sudden insight or perception of an event that then transpires, within a time frame that associates it inescapably with that previous moment of prescient knowing.

If such events of intuition, ESP, and prescience took place only in the lives of psychotic patients with confirmed diagnoses, we would very likely accord them little further attention. We would assume that they were manifestations and symptoms of the psychopathology. However, these are not the type of paranormal experiences that occur in psychotic or schizophrenic patients. They occur consistently in stable and healthy persons and in many cases enhance their health and sense of well-being. Whether they are a prescient awareness of a future event, a consciousness of another's thoughts over some distance, an illuminating dream, a voice in the night, a sense of guidance, a helping presence at a time of extreme danger, a miraculous healing, or an illumination accompanied with an ethereal sense of peace or meaning, the numinous event is a constructive life-changing datum. We need to find out how it works and what it means; maybe even from whence it derives.

CONCLUSION

So it is important to create a culture of openness to the investigation of numinous experiences. I have argued herein that we may discover that the incidents of paranormal events are more frequent, should I say more normal, than we think.[28] Collection of already available anecdotal reports will produce more information than will be readily manageable. Let me say again that this process would be a procedure similar to that we have used to study the stuff of this world that we have mastered. A great deal of our understanding of the truth about this world we know from phenomenological investigations and heuristic interpretations. These seem to be trustworthy instruments of research that are particularly suited to investigation of the reported experiences humans have of the paranormal.

As I indicated above, we should be able by means of them to create useful theories, data collection, management systems, hypotheses, and laws that account for the paranormal. Why would we not assume the same lawfulness and coherence to be reigning in the world of the paranormal, if we studied it thoroughly and systematically, as we find in what we call our normal world? We call it paranormal only because we have not yet figured out the paradigm that accounts for and comprehends it. Life's constant change and our widening experience demand an expansion of our paradigms.[29] Failing to expand them obstructs the scientific inquiry into the unknown. Investigation of the paranormal is the threshold waiting for us to cross over, equipped with a new and broader paradigm. Truth is open-ended and requires a courageous open-ended quest.

NOTES

1. Stanislav Grof (2010), Healing Potential of Spiritual Experiences: Observations from Modern Consciousness Research, Vol. 3, *Personal Spirituality*, Ch. 7 in J. Harold Ellens, ed., *The Healing Power of Spirituality, How Faith Helps Humans Thrive*, 3 vols., Santa Barbara, CA: ABC-CLIO Praeger, 131.

2. Cf. J. Harold Ellens (2010), *Light from the other Side, The Paranormal as Friend and Familiar: (Real Life Stories of a Spiritual Pilgrim)*, Westport, CT: Praeger.

3. Ralph W. Hood, Jr. and Greg N. Byrom (2010), Mysticism, Madness, and Mental Health, Vol. 3, Ch 9, in J. Harold Ellens, ed., *The Healing Power of Spirituality, How Faith Helps Humans Thrive*, 3 vols., Santa Barbara, CA: ABC-CLIO Praeger, 173.

4. Robert Fuller (1988), *Religion in the Life Cycle*, Philadelphia, PA: Fortress.

5. Among his works are the following: Richard Dawkins (1976), *The Selfish Gene*, New York: Oxford.; Richard Dawkins (1999), *The Extended Phenotype, the Long Reach of the Gene*, New York: Oxford; Richard Dawkins (1986), *The Blind Watchmaker, Why the Evidence of Evolution Reveals a Universe Without Design*, New York: Norton.

6. David Van Biema (2006), God vs. Science, *Time Magazine*, Nov. 13, 48–55.

7. Francis Collins (2006), *The Language of God: A Scientist Presents Evidence for Belief*, New York: Free Press.

8. William James (1985), *The Varieties of Religious Experience*, Cambridge: Harvard. Previously published in New York, as a Mentor Book of the New American Library (1958), with a famed Foreword by Jacques Barzun. The volume is composed of William James' Gifford Lectures of 1901–1902 at the University of Edinburgh, Scotland.

9. Stephen Jay Gould (1999), *Rocks of Ages, Science and Religion in the Fullness of Life, The Library of Contemporary Thought*, New York: Random House. Also available as a book on tape from Dove Audio of NewStar Media, Inc., Los Angeles: NewStar Publishing.

10. Van Biema, op. cit., 49.

11. Sam Harris (2005), *The End of Faith, Religion, Terror, and the Future of Reason*, New York: Norton.

12. Sam Harris (2008), *Letter to a Christian Nation*, New York: Vintage.

13. Daniel Dennett (2006), *Breaking the Spell, Religion as a Natural Phenomenon*, New York: Viking.

14. Victor J. Stenger (2007), *God, the Failed Hypothesis, How Science Shows That God Does Not Exist*, Amherst, NY: Prometheus.

15. Carl Sagan (2006), *The Varieties of Scientific Experience, A Personal View of the Search for God*, New York: Penguin.

16. Kieth Ward (2008), *The Big Questions of Science and Religion*, New York: Templeton Foundation; Ward (2011), *More Than Matter: Is There More to Life Than Molecules*, London: Lion Press; Ward (1996), *God, Chance, and Necessity*, New York: Oneworld Publications; Ward (2009), *God and the Philosophers*, Minneapolis, MN: Fortress; Ward (2009), *Why There Almost Certainly Is a God: Doubting Dawkins*, London: Lion Press.

17. Jeanne Lenzer (2007), Citizen, Heal Thyself, in *Discover: Science, Technology, and the Future*, Sept., 54–59, 73.

18. Lenzer, 56.

19. Idem.

20. Ibid., 58.

21. Op. cit., 73.

22. Some of the ideas and argumentation of this article appeared in substantially different form in J. Harold Ellens (2008), *Miracles: God, Science, and Psychology in the Paranormal*, Westport, CT: Praeger, Vol. I., and are used with permission.

23. Julian Jaynes (1976), *The Origin of Consciousness in the Breakdown of the Bicameral Mind*, Boston, MA: Houghton Miflin.

24. Richard M. Restak (1979), *The Brain, The last Frontier*, New York: Warner; Restak (1991), *The Brain has a Mind of Its Own, Insights from a Practicing Neurologist*, New York: Harmony; Restak (1984), *The Brain*, New York: Bantam; Restak (1994), *Receptors*, New York: Bantam; Restak (1994), *The Modular Brain*, New York: Scribners; Betty Edwards (1989), *Drawing on the Right Side of the Brain*, Los Angeles, CA: Jeremy P. Tarcher; Sally P. Springer and Georg Deutsch (1981, 1985), *Left Brain, Right Brain*, New York: Freeman.

25. Hugh Lynn Cayce, ed. (1990), *Edgar Cayce, Modern Prophet*, New York: Gramercy.

26. Deepak Chopra (2000), *How to Know God, the Soul's Journey into the Mystery of Mysteries*, New York: Harmony.

27. Ken Wilber (1977), *The Spectrum of Consciousness*, Wheaton, IL: The Theosophical Publishing House; Wilber (1980), *The Atman Project, A Transpersonal View of Human Development*, Wheaton, IL: The Theosophical Publishing House; Wilber (1981), *No Boundaries, Eastern and Western Approaches to Personal Growth*, Boulder, CO: Shambala Press.

28. See Note 3.

29. Robert Fuller (1988), *Religion in the Life Cycle*, Philadelphia, PA: Fortress.

CHAPTER 11

CALLING OF A WOUNDED HEALER: PSYCHOSIS, SPIRITUALITY, AND SHAMANISM

David Lukoff

> Shamanism is a technique of religious ecstasy, an altered state of consciousness frequently accompanied by visions . . . sometimes called enlightenment . . . The future shaman sometimes takes the risk of being mistaken for a "madman" . . . but his "madness" fulfills a mystic function; it reveals certain aspects of reality to him that are inaccessible to other mortals, and it is only after having experienced and entered into these hidden dimensions of reality that the "madman" becomes a shaman. (Eliade, 1951, p. 107)

My calling to become a clinical psychologist began with a psychotic episode when I was 23 years old that provided me with a mental health challenge. I had to figure out how I came to believe that I was a reincarnation of Buddha and Christ tasked with writing a new "holy book." However this episode had also served as a spiritual awakening from being an atheist, totally unconcerned with issues pertaining to religion and spirituality, to becoming a spiritual seeker. Ultimately, this led me to fulfill the archetype of the "wounded healer" by becoming a clinical psychologist with a Calling to integrate spirituality into psychological approaches to psychotic episodes as well into the larger mental health system. With two colleagues, I proposed and helped get a new category accepted into the American Psychiatric Association *Diagnostic and Statistical Manual—IV* (1994 and also in *DSM-5*) for religious and spiritual problems (Lukoff, Lu, and Turner, 1992). In this chapter I recount my journey as a three-stage process: Telling One's Story, Tracing Its Symbolic/Spiritual Heritage, and Finding One's Calling.

My integration of this psychotic episode has been greatly influenced by my perspective on studies of shamanism. Mircea Eliade found that a psychotic episode has served as the initiatory crisis marking for some, a call to become a shaman. For example, the Siberian shaman Kyzaslov entered a state of "madness" lasting for seven years which resulted in his initiation as a shaman. He reported that during those years he had been beaten up several times, taken to many strange places including the top of a sacred mountain, chopped into pieces and boiled in a kettle, met the spirits of sickness, and acquired the drum and garment of a dead shaman. Being "tormented" by spirits, babbling confused words, displaying curious eating habits, singing continuously, and dancing wildly are other common elements in initiatory crises; in our society today these experiences would be considered signs of a psychotic disorder. Yet when Kyzaslov recuperated, he reported that, "the shamans declared, 'You are the sort of man who may become a shaman; you should become a shaman. You must begin to shamanize'" (Halifax, 1979, p. 50).

TREKKING AND TRIPPING TO ENLIGHTENMENT

My psychotic crisis occurred in 1971. After coming to the conclusion that, at 23 years of age, I had lived a very sheltered life and did not know much about the world outside of academia, I precipitously dropped out of the doctoral program in social anthropology at Harvard University, gave away all of my possessions that would not fit into my backpack, from my bed to all my books, and started hitchhiking across the country, up into Canada and down into Mexico. In San Francisco six months later someone offered me a tab of LSD. I took it thinking this was another chance to try another new thing I'd never done. The day went well. I had some wonderful visual effects but I didn't notice anything that seemed transformative or life changing. However, the next day while reading Suzuki's book *Zen Buddhism*, I felt for the first time I had solved the riddle of Zen teachings and understood what it meant to be "enlightened."

I had been "crashing" in an apartment near San Francisco. On my fourth day after the LSD trip, I awoke just after midnight. I walked into the bathroom, stopped in front of the mirror, and gazed at my reflection. Startled, I noticed that my right hand was glowing, giving off a white light. My thumb was touching my forefinger in the ancient mudra of the meditating Buddha. Immediately the meaning of this sign was clear to me: I had been Buddha in a previous life. Then another insight came: I was also a reincarnation of Jesus Christ. Now, in this moment, the luminous image in the mirror was awakening me to my true purpose: to once again bring the human race out of its decline. My new mission was to create a "holy book," which would for the first time unite everyone in the world around the common tenets of a single belief system. Instead of unifying just one social group, as Buddha and Christ had, I was to write a book that would create a new global society free of conflict and full of loving relationships.

I had been trained well for this task. Undergraduate studies in ancient civilizations at the University of Chicago and a master's degree in social anthropology at Harvard had provided me with a comprehensive and scientific understanding of the way societies function and change. This knowledge, added to the wisdom inherited from my previous incarnations, prepared me for my sacred mission. Due to my enlightenment, I was now freed from dependence on society's rigid norms and narrow perceptions of reality. I had acquired the intellectual freedom and creativity of an enlightened being. Furthermore, I had unraveled the mysterious process by which the Zen master creates the enlightenment experience in others. Thus, I deemed myself fully prepared to design a cultural revolution in which everyone would become enlightened.

THE NEW "HOLY BOOK"

My life's mission had been communicated to me during that single glance in the bathroom mirror. I headed for the table where my journal, now to be a "holy book," lay open. Over the next five days and nights, I worked with only short breaks for meals and naps. I found I could contact the "spirits" of eminent thinkers in the social sciences and humanities to help me with the task of writing the new "Bible." As I reflected on their relevance for my work, I would "become" these people of wisdom, actually embody them, and "think their thoughts with them." I had discussions with contemporary people including Ronald Laing, Margaret Mead, and Claude Levi-Straus. To gain insight about taking my work into the popular culture, I sought out the advice of Bob Dylan and Cat Stevens. I also communicated with people who were no longer living: Locke, Hobbes, Rousseau, Voltaire, Adam Smith, Jefferson, Freud, Jung, and, of course, Buddha and Christ. At times during the writing, the clarity of my thoughts and the beauty of my vision for the future brought tears to my eyes. Initially, I assumed "The Scholar" as my penname, alluding to the erudite origins of this project, and I soon realized that "The Scholar" was my new reincarnated identity.

PARABLES AND POEMS TO CREATE THE NEW SOCIETY

After five days of writing, the book was finished. Its 47 pages contained a combination of parables, poems, and instructions on how to organize the new society. I concluded that Berkeley was the New Jerusalem for 1971 and that Cody's bookstore was the center of a communication vortex of hippies and freaks who would be first to herald my new holy book and circulate it to others. So I stood in front of Cody's bookstore in Berkeley, and handed out copies of my new book. I mailed other copies to friends and family, wanting those closest to me to be the first to learn about this new way of living.

Then I awaited the response. To my surprise, none of the people I had mailed it to or given it to made any contact with me. No one reported becoming immediately enlightened; no one expressed a desire to join my mission to change the world. Nevertheless, I remained confident that the revolution I was to lead would materialize. I was so preoccupied with my mission that I didn't work to earn money. I crashed at many friends' homes. They were compassionate and generous in supporting me, both financially and psychologically. None of them ever treated me as though they thought I was crazy. They gave me food and shelter and let me read their books. They listened to my new ideas and talked to me about religion and life.

My sense of being the reincarnations of Buddha and Christ slowly dissipated over the next two months. There was not a specific moment when this belief crumbled or disappeared. I just thought about myself less and less as a new messiah. Although I began to realize that the new holy book was not to be a new "Bible," I still believed that it contained many brilliant and novel ideas and syntheses of previous thought. I was sure it could be published and become a best-selling book.

SOLITUDE, SUFFERING, AND SUICIDAL IDEATION

In early spring of the next year, with my parents support, I went to live by myself in their summer cottage in Cape Cod to continue working on my book; however, my health rapidly deteriorated. It began with headaches and insomnia; my head felt as though it would burst with pain after an hour of reading. Many nights I could not sleep. I felt miserable and depressed. Then I had a recurrence of an illness I had suffered 10 years earlier, Crohn's disease, a serious condition affecting the intestines and producing severe cramping and internal bleeding. Nevertheless I forced myself to keep reading as I was discovering the works of Jung and Joseph Campbell for the first time and they seemed to speak directly to my experiences.

At the same time that it was becoming physically difficult for me to read, it was also becoming more imperative. In giving up my grandiose identity as a messiah, I now turned my attention to becoming a renowned author. However, my research led me to many books on religion and social change that showed me my ideas were not so original. While reading Roszak's *The Making of a Counterculture*, I realized that my "vision for a new society" was a stock "60s" Utopian vision that had led to the founding of numerous communes.

I became embarrassed at the thought of having sent a semi-incoherent "holy book" to all my closest friends and family. Now I questioned whether I had anything worthwhile to say in the book, which had been my *raison d'etre* for the previous several months. I felt totally lost, ashamed, and confused. I was still quite sick physically with Crohn's symptoms, headaches, and insomnia fueled by horrific hypnogogic images of angry faces and the image of my skeleton hovering over me on sleepless nights. I began to seriously consider committing suicide with an overdose of opiate pain medications in my possession.

THE CALLING

Two months after moving to Cape Cod, I was walking on the beach, ruminating about the events of the last several months and feeling depressed. Suddenly I heard a voice speaking to me. I was startled. The voice distinctly said, "Become a healer." At that time, lost in self-recriminations about the past, I did not think of myself as even having a future! However, this voice—the only time I've ever heard a voice emanating from outside of myself—set a whole new train of events in motion and initiated my path toward a new lifestyle and profession.

I decided to leave Cape Cod and go to my parents' home in New Jersey to recuperate. There I took classes in yoga and herbs, and participated in encounter groups. Then I joined a program at a personal growth center and trained in a multitude of healing practices including gestalt therapy, transactional analysis, primal therapy, bioenergetics, massage, and psychodrama. Eventually I became a group facilitator at the Forest Hospital Growth Center outside of Chicago.

After working as an encounter and growth group leader for three years, I realized that being a psychologist was my calling to "become a healer" and entered a doctoral clinical psychology program. In the first year abnormal psychology class I learned that my experience would have been diagnosed as an Acute Schizophrenic Episode. Taking LSD four days before the episode began had probably triggered its onset. In the current diagnostic nomenclature of *DSM-5*, it would be considered a hallucinogen-induced psychotic disorder. The LSD initiated a train of mental events that were amplified over the next days by intensive reading of books on Zen, introverted journal writing, social withdrawal, and little sleep.

My lingering discomfort with its grandiosity and inflated identity initially kept me from delving very deeply into the experience. However, James Hillman (1983) pointed out, "Recovery means recovering the divine from within the disorder, seeing that its contents are authentically religious" (p. 10). In a five-year Jungian analysis, I began my own process of "recovering the divine."

I realized that my book and the events that had surrounded its writing could be analyzed like a dream, examining the personal and universal symbols. True to my "scholar" nature, I began research on psychotic episodes and their parallels to various myths. I turned to writing case studies such as the "Myths in Mental Illness," which was published in *Journal of Transpersonal Psychology* (Lukoff and Everest, 1985). My Jungian analysis and scholarly work provided me with a "dictionary" of symbols for interpreting my own experience. When I reflected on my experiences in therapy, I realized that I had very little knowledge of Christ or Buddha at the time I assumed their identity. These experiences led me to explore Christianity, Buddhism, and other forms of spirituality for the first time in my life. I started a meditation practice and attended retreats with Lamas and Zen masters, took qigong courses, and studied medicine wheel teachings and ceremonies with Wallace Black Elk, a Lakota medicine man.

Perry (1998) noted that after a psychotic episode, "What remains . . . is an ideal model and a sense of direction which one can use to complete the transformation through his own purposeful methods" (p. 34–35). I now view my own experience of having "been" Buddha and Christ as revealing ideal models for my spiritual life. However, the spiritual potential inherent in my experience lay dormant until contact with shamanic teachers enabled me to connect with that dimension. Upon finishing my doctorate in psychology in 1980, I became a faculty member in the Clinical Research Center for Schizophrenia at the UCLA Neuropsychiatric Institute. At the same time, I became a staff member and then program director of The Ojai Foundation, a new educational retreat center north of Los Angeles. In this semiwilderness location, the first structure we erected on the land was a teepee. A sweat lodge was soon added. This hospitable and appropriate setting for training in shamanic practices was created by medical anthropologist Joan Halifax, an author and expert on shamanism (now the Roshi of the Upaya Zen Center). Daily life included chanting; drumming was a frequent activity. Pipe ceremonies marked special events and frequently were held at sunrise. The New Year's celebrations were ceremonies modeled after the peyote ceremony with a water drum and singing stick passed around the circle throughout the night.

The Ojai Foundation was host to many traditional shamans and Native American medicine people who held retreats where they shared ceremonial healing techniques. During the next few years, I attended programs by Wallace Black Elk and Grace Spotted Eagle, Prem Das, Sun Bear and Wabun, Hyemeyohsts Storm, Oh Shinnah, Grandfather Semu Huaute, Rolling Thunder, Harley Swiftdeer, Thomas Banyacya, Evelyn Eaton, Adam Fortunate Eagle, and Elie Hien. Their extended visits after the retreats enabled those of us living on the land to get to know them more intimately and to participate in private ceremonies, prayer sessions, and sweats.

In the altered states of consciousness induced by these shamanistic practices, I re-experienced, for the first time since my psychotic episode, a feeling
of oneness with the universe. Once again, I was communicating with divine
spirits and comprehending the meaning of life itself. Instead of repressing
these ecstatic experiences that were associated with painful memories, I was
now learning to trust them again. Such experiences are a major component
of shamanic life: "Shamans do not differ from other members of the collec-
tivity by their quest for the sacred—which is normal and universal human
behavior—but by their capacity for ecstatic experience" (Eliade, 1951, p. 107).

Shamanistic practices enabled me to reclaim a culturally disapproved and
repressed dimension of my being that psychosis had revealed: my capacity
for ecstasy—the union with higher forces and understanding. However,
these teachers and my daily shamanistic practices taught me how to exercise
voluntary control over entry into and out of ecstatic states, and how to keep
them contained within appropriate social contexts.

During these years, I learned about power animals and discovered some
of my own, including the owl, the coyote, and the lizard. Times of solitude
and spiritual reflection in wilderness settings taught me how to follow my
inner voices. For instance, a dream in which my file cabinets appeared cov-
ered with beads and feathers made me aware that these tools for academic
work are my power objects. One morning bicycling to work, I came across
a dead barn owl. This connection with my first power animal reminded me
of my dream. I spent the next hour intently working to sever its wings and
claws using a sharp stone that was lying nearby. I had the claw beaded and
that beaded owl claw still hangs in my office. These spirit teachers along
with more traditional teachers helped me create a personal mythology based
upon my inner life.

PARALLELS BETWEEN PSYCHOSIS AND SHAMANIC INITIATION

The key themes in shamanic initiation are ascent into the upper world,
descent into the lower world, dismemberment, and rebirth (Eliade, 1951).
These four themes were present in my experience. First, I ascended into a
kind of heavenly abode where I felt myself to be chosen for a mission to change
the world and "became" the gods Christ and Buddha while communicating
with ancient teachers. Then I descended into a hellish realm of suffering
excruciating pain, constant headaches, insomnia, intense abdominal cramps,
and internal bleeding during which I envisioned my death by suicide—which
represented my dismemberment. At the end of my experience, I felt reborn
through an audible call to "become a healer." Thus, the story of my psychotic
experience follows the classic four-part thematic structure characteristic of
shamanic initiatory crises.

Many images that appeared in my experience also parallel the symbolism of shamanic initiations. Shamans frequently have experiences, as I had, of being enveloped in light. Referring to "the disciple's 'lighting' or 'enlightenment,'" Eliade writes: "the experience of inner light that determines the career of the Iglulik shaman is familiar to a number of higher mysticisms" (p. 117). He mentions similar occurrences in the Upanishads, the Tibetan Book of the Dead, and Christian mysticism. Another common initiatory motif that was part of my crisis is discussed at length by Eliade in his book in a section on "Contemplating one's own skeleton." Lastly, the theme of rebirth also occurs in many traditions. Joseph Campbell (1972, p. 237) wrote: "The inward journey of the mythological hero, the shaman, the mystic and the schizophrenic are in principle the same; and when the return or remission occurs, it is experienced as a rebirth."

Of course a key difference between my psychotic episode and the shaman's initiatory crisis is the way it is viewed by our respective societies. From the contemporary Western psychological perspective, it was a psychotic disorder. However, in shamanic societies, such experiences often mark an individual as an ecstatic healer. Another difference relates to the type of divine figures encountered. The shaman encounters animal spirit guides; I met Christ and Buddha. When contacting "spirits of the dead," I did not communicate with dead shamans, but the "spirits" of leading figures from the Western cultural tradition—both dead and alive. My preoccupation with writing a book to change the world is also not a shamanic theme. However, it is somewhat parallel to the shaman's quest to acquire power objects, songs, and drums, which can be used to heal others.

SHAMANIC CRISIS AS A CALLING TO THE MENTAL HEALTH PROFESSION

Psychologist Jeanne Achterberg (1988) pointed out that crises and illnesses bestow upon the shaman the wisdom to serve the community as a healer. She then observed that,

> Such events can occur and have occurred in the lives of health professionals in the modern world and have led to vocational choice. Being disabled, or having a serious disease, or being in recovery from an addiction, or even having a child with a significant handicap has been the wounding or the initiation for many in the health care field. (p. 20)

Etymologically, "vocation" stems from an earlier meaning: the hearing of a divine voice summoning one to a religious career. My vocation as a psychologist followed an audible summoning to the healing profession in the midst of my psychotic episode. During my years of teaching graduate psychology students, giving workshops, and receiving correspondence from readers of my articles starting with *Shaman's Drum* (Lukoff, 1991), many other mental health professionals and people in training have told me about their similar experiences. As in my own case, psychotic, depressive, and other episodes served as "callings" into their vocations as psychologists, psychiatrists, social workers, nurses, and so on. Some people who have had psychotic episodes become visionaries and social leaders as the anthropologist Wallace (1956) has documented in several cultures. Many of the founders of psychology and psychiatry have themselves been "wounded healers" whose "creative illness" involved a crisis including psychotic elements that ultimately were transformative (Goldwert, 1992).

I believe that my crisis awakened certain healing abilities that contribute to my work with patients who have had psychotic episodes. For example, it is relatively easy and personally rewarding for me to empathically enter the delusional reality of patients and to help them find value and meaning in these experiences (Lukoff, 2007). Most mental health professionals seem to find an "abyss of difference" as Jaspers (1963, p. 219), one of the fathers of modern psychopathology, described it between the "normal" and the psychotic mind. I could see that patients have needs beyond pharmacologically based treatments. At Camarillo State Hospital, I developed the first holistic health program for schizophrenic patients (Lukoff, Wallace, Liberman, and Burke, 1986). It incorporated jogging, meditation, stress management, and art therapy along with a weekly "Growth and Schizophrenia" group therapy program. These therapy sessions helped the participants to develop a positive attitude toward their illness and improve their self-esteem by pointing out parallels between their experiences and those of shamans, mystics, and artists. My clinical work has also involved harnessing the creativity of psychotic patients by having them write and draw about their experiences. Several of these writings have been published and the art works displayed. During the past 35 years in my clinical practice as a psychologist at UCLA-NPI, Camarillo State Hospital, the San Francisco VA Medical Center, and private practice, I have often found myself face to face with individuals in the same state of consciousness that I had been in: convinced that they were reincarnations of Buddha and Christ (or other spiritual figures), reporting communication with spiritual figures, believing they had a messianic mission to save the world, and preparing a "holy book" that would form the basis for a new religion.

My ability to work effectively with those individuals has been aided by being given a rare opportunity to journey through the complete cycle and phenomenology of a naturally resolving psychotic episode thanks to the support and mentorship of other healers, shamans, my Jungian analyst, and many others. Thus, beyond serving as a spiritual awakening, my journey held within it the archetypal gift of the wounded healer, providing me with the ability to connect more deeply with persons experiencing psychotic episodes.

Stanislav and Christina Grof coined the term "spiritual emergency" in 1978 to identify a variety of psychological difficulties, particularly those associated with Asian spiritual practices and psychedelic drugs, both of which became popular in the West starting in the 1960s. Grof and Grof (1989) note that, "Episodes of this kind have been described in sacred literature of all ages as a result of meditative practices and as signposts of the mystical path" (p. x). A distinguishing characteristic of spiritual emergencies is that despite the distress, they can have beneficial transformative effects on individuals who experience them. This has been documented in studies on anomalous experiences such as near-death experiences (Cardena, Lynn, and Krippner, 2013).

Had I been diagnosed with a psychotic disorder, hospitalized, and medicated, I'm sure that a positive integration of my experience would have been much more difficult to attain. This experience also launched my concern about others who have similar experiences and end up misdiagnosed and hospitalized. I published an article detailing operational diagnostic criteria for distinguishing mental disorders from spiritual crises, which carry the capacity for self-renewal (Lukoff, 1985). This work to identify potentially positively transformative psychotic episodes led to the proposal for a new diagnostic category for such episodes in the fourth edition of the *Diagnostic and Statistical Manual*. In 1989, along with two psychiatrists (Francis Lu, MD, and Robert Turner, MD, then both on the faculty at University of California, San Francisco Department of Psychiatry), I wrote and submitted a proposal to the task force on *DSM-IV* (Lukoff et al., 1992) for a new diagnosis entitled religious or spiritual problem, defined as follows:

> This category can be used when the focus of clinical attention is a religious or spiritual problem. Examples include distressing experiences that involve loss or questioning of faith, problems associated with conversion to a new faith, or questioning of other spiritual values which may not necessarily be related to an organized church or religious institution.

When the proposal was accepted, articles on this new diagnostic category appeared in *The New York Times, San Francisco Chronicle, Psychiatric News,* and the *APA Monitor* where it was described as indicating an important shift in the mental health profession's stance by including religion and spirituality as an important component of well-being.

SHAMANISTIC PRACTICES AND THE
INTEGRATION OF PSYCHOTIC EPISODES

Psychologist Julian Silverman (1967) noted the similarities between the crises involved in psychosis and those in shamanic initiations. He also lamented the lack of a supportive social milieu in contemporary Western culture as compared with traditional shamanic societies where the social role of the shaman legitimates free access to altered states of consciousness. "For the schizophrenic, the absence of such culturally acceptable and appropriate [access] only has the effect of intensifying his suffering over and above the original anxieties . . . for the crisis solutions of the schizophrenic are totally invalid ones in the eyes of the great majority of his peers" (pp. 28–29).

Becoming a shaman to help integrate psychotic experiences is no longer a viable option for individuals in contemporary Western society. There is little cultural support for a role in which accessing altered states of consciousness is valued or even acceptable. However, in the four decades since Silverman pointed out this lack, the option of utilizing shamanism to integrate psychotic crises has been revived by the neo-shamanic movement. Joan Townsend (1988) points out the practical training that this movement provides: "While one could 'learn' shamanism on one's own by extensive research and experimentation, it is not a very practical alternative. The experience of participating in a shamanic group, even if only for a few days, provides an orientation and a qualitatively different experience so important for a true knowing" (p. 82). In my case, by pursuing shamanistic practices I changed my self-perception about this very significant episode in my life. I like to think that in an earlier era my psychotic episode would have marked me as a shaman-elect and I would have been apprenticed to a master shaman to learn to control these abilities.

While presenting my views in various workshops and classes I have led, I encountered many others who were drawn to shamanistic practices by episodes of mental breakdown/breakthrough. In one workshop, "Psychosis: Mysticism, Shamanism or Pathology?" my co-leader, Joan Halifax, explained how shamanism had provided a map to guide her back from psychosis to wholeness, and led her to create The Ojai Foundation as an educational center where people in such crises would be welcomed into a healing community. During a retreat in Ojai, Lakota shaman Wallace Black Elk shared with me how his initiatory visions in his early twenties not only led to his hospitalization but also to his choosing a path as a medicine man.

In integrating my shamanistic initiatory crisis, I found the literature on shamanism and neo-shamanism both provided archetypal and experiential parallels to those psychotic experiences. Awareness of such correspondences allowed me to translate my culturally discordant psychotic experiences into a personally meaningful mythology. Contact with shamans and shamanistic practices provided training in self-control of ecstatic states and journeying to spirit worlds. Shamanistic practices, pursued with the guidance of knowledgeable therapists and/or trustworthy traditional teachers are an ideal way to extract a symbolically rich personal mythology from a psychotic episode.

Another part of my integration has involved publishing accounts of my own and others transformative psychotic episodes and giving presentations where I shared my experience at professional organization conferences such as the American Psychological Association, American Psychiatric Association, rehabilitation, and recovery associations. These were targeted to increasing the awareness of the important role of spirituality in recovery and in wellness.

Based on what I learned from my own psychotic episode, and through my work with other individuals who had similar episodes, integrating such experiences typically involves three phases:

Phase 1: Telling one's story
Phase 2: Tracing its symbolic/spiritual heritage
Phase 3: Finding one's calling

Phase 1: Telling One's Story

In several published case studies I found that people in recovery from psychotic disorders are usually not asked to recount in detail or reflect on their experiences. Yet based on my case studies and contact with people in recovery, telling one's story is the first step in integration. At Camarillo State Hospital, UCLA Neuropsychiatric Institute, and the San Francisco VA Day Treatment Program, I asked patients to talk about and write out a full account of all they had experienced. Some clinicians have expressed the concern that having patients discuss their delusional experiences could exacerbate their symptoms by reinforcing them. In my study of a holistic health program conducted at a state psychiatric hospital, the patients were encouraged to actively explore their psychotic symptoms in group therapy sessions entitled "Schizophrenia and Growth" which encouraged them to compare their experiences to those of mystics, Native American vision quests, and shamanic initiatory crises. Telling their stories did not result in exacerbation of symptoms (Lukoff et al., 1986).

Phase 2: Tracing Its Symbolic/Spiritual Heritage

During psychosis, the mind is driven to reveal its deepest, most intimate workings, images, and structures. Whereas the myths are *metaphors* for journeys into the psyche, psychosis *is* a journey into the psyche. Jungian analyst John Bebee (1982) has noted that,

> Minimally, the experience of psychotic illness is a call to the Symbolic Quest. Psychotic illness introduces the individual to themes, conflicts, and resolutions that may be pursued through the entire religious, spiritual, philosophical and artistic history of humanity. (p. 252)

Pursuing the elements in my "holy book" through both reading about religion and shamanism and through direct experience played an important role in integrating my experience.

Phase 3: Finding One's Calling

Experiences of altered states of consciousness, such as dreams and the non-ordinary experiences from a psychotic episode can play a significant role in finding one's calling by enabling the person to transcend ordinary life concerns and experience a "higher" or "deeper" reality. Campbell identified three stages in the hero's journey. First the Call, which triggers the change, then Initiation, which includes battles and contests, and finally the Return stage, which

> requires that the Hero shall now begin the labor of bringing the runes of wisdom, the Golden Fleece, or his sleeping princess, back into the kingdom of humanity, where the boon may redound to the renewing of the community, the nation, the planet, or the ten thousand words. (Campbell, 1949, p. 193)

My personal boon has involved working to get a new diagnostic category into the DSM for spiritual crises, as well as publications and presentations aimed at increasing the awareness of mental health professionals regarding the important role spirituality plays for many in recovery and in wellness. Another area my commitment to spirituality as a resource has led is to promote assessment of spiritual strengths, beliefs, practices, and problems. I helped design and conduct surveys of mental health service recipients in California (Lukoff, Mancuso, Yamada, & Lim, submitted for publication) that have triggered public policy initiatives to mandate spiritual assessment as a routine part of clinical care in several California counties (Lukoff, 2014).

Awareness of spirituality is increasing throughout the global culture (Miller, 2012). Psychology is increasingly embracing spirituality as a core component of multicultural diversity. I feel blessed to have been witness to a major transformation of the mental health field, and to have contributed in a small way to its acceptance of spirituality. Being a psychologist is my Calling.

It was initiated by a shamanic crisis that had been triggered by a psychotic episode. Psychotic disorders have been associated with leading to a sense of Calling (Perry, 1974). Depression has its own literature on "wounded healers" (Rippere and Williams, 1987) and there are parallels in substance abuse (Ruiz and Strain, 2011) and posttraumatic stress disorder (e.g., the online *Wounded Healer Journal* for psychotherapists who have experienced trauma including child abuse: www.twhj.com).

QUEST FOR A CALLING

In today's culture it is common for individuals to contemplate life through characters and events in the media. Television, books, internet, video games, sports, films, and music express themes that parallel the shaman's journey where the hero/heroine may experience time travel, alternate realities, challenges, and metamorphoses. Many individuals feel an inner longing, perhaps a Calling, to find a sense of direction, for renewal after a crisis, or to discover their true life path. Dreams, synchronistic and anomalous experiences (Cardena et al., 2013), as well as experiences during episodes of crisis or dysfunction can be part of finding a Calling. Meditation, journaling, bibliotherapy, expressive arts, shamanic practices, and psychotherapy can clarify their value and relevance to one's life. They can facilitate significant life changes as in my journey experienced within a state of psychosis as described in this chapter on Calling.

REFERENCES

Achterberg, J. (1988). The wounded healer. *Shaman's Drum, 11*, 18–24.

American Psychiatric Association. (1994). *Diagnostic and statistical manual, fourth edition*. Washington, DC: American Psychiatric Association.

Bebee, D. (1982). Notes on psychosis. *Spring, 9*, 233–252.

Campbell, J. (1949). *The hero with a thousand faces*. Princeton, NJ: Princeton University Press.

Campbell, J. (1972). *Myths to live by*. New York: Bantam Books.

Cardena, E., Lynn, S., & Krippner, S. (Eds.) (2013). *Varieties of anomalous experience: Examining the scientific evidence*. Washington, DC: American Psychological Association Press.

Eliade, M. (1951). *Shamanism: Archaic techniques of ecstasy*. Princeton, NJ: Princeton University Press.

Goldwert, M. (1992). *The wounded healers: Creative illness in the pioneers of depth psychology*. Lanham, MD: University Press of America.

Grof, S., & Grof, C. (Eds.). (1989). *Spiritual emergency: When personal transformation becomes a crisis*. Los Angeles, CA: Tarcher.

Halifax, J. (1979). *Shamanic voices*. New York: Dutton.

Hillman, J. (1983). *Healing fiction*. New York: Station Hill Press.

Jaspers, K. (1963). *General psychopathology.* Manchester: Manchester University Press.

Lukoff, D. (1985). The diagnosis of mystical experiences with psychotic features. *Journal of Transpersonal Psychology, 17*(2), 155–181.

Lukoff, D. (1991). Divine madness. *Shaman's Drum, 22,* 24–29.

Lukoff, D. (2007). Visionary spiritual experiences. *Southern Medical Journal, 100*(6), 635–641.

Lukoff, D. (2014). From personal experience to clinical practice to research: A career path leading to public policy changes in integrating spirituality into mental health *Spirituality in Clinical Practice, 1*(2), 145–152.

Lukoff, D., & Everest, H. C. (1985). The myths in mental illness. *Journal of Transpersonal Psychology, 17*(2), 123–153.

Lukoff, D., Wallace, C. J., Liberman, R. P., & Burke, K. (1986). A holistic health program for chronic schizophrenic patients. *Schizophrenia Bulletin, 12*(2), 274–282.

Lukoff, D., Lu, F., & Turner, R. (1992). Toward a more culturally sensitive DSM-IV: Psychoreligious and psychospiritual problems. *Journal of Nervous and Mental Disease, 180*(11), 673–682.

Lukoff, D., Mancuso, L., Yamada, A., & Lim, C. Integrating spirituality and mental health: Perspectives of individuals receiving public mental health services in California, submitted for publication.

Miller, L. (2012). Introduction. In L. Miller (Ed.), *The Oxford handbook of psychology and spirituality* (pp. 1–4). New York: Oxford University Press.

Perry, J. (1974). *The far side of madness.* Englewood Cliffs, NJ: Prentice Hall.

Perry, J. (1998). *Trials of the visionary mind: Spiritual emergency and the renewal process.* Albany: State University of New York Press.

Rippere, V., & Williams, R. (1987). *Wounded healers: Mental health workers' experiences of depression.* Hoboken, NJ: Wiley.

Ruiz, P., & Strain, S. (2011). *Substance abuse: A comprehensive textbook.* Philadelphia, PA: Lippincott Williams & Wilkins.

Silverman, J. (1967). Shamans and acute schizophrenia. *American Anthropologist, 69*(1), 21–31.

Townsend, J. (1988). *Neo-shamanism and the modern mystical movement in shaman's path* (Doore, G. Ed.) Boston, MA: Shambhala Publications.

Wallace, A. (1956). Stress and rapid personality changes. *International Record of Medicine, 169*(12), 761–774.

Chapter 12

The Circus Snake: A Numinous, Initiatory Calling from Below

Thomas Singer

Vocation acts like a law of God from which there is no escape. The fact that many a man who goes his own way ends in ruins means nothing to one who has a vocation. He *must* obey his own law, as if it were a daemon whispering to him of new and wonderful paths. Anyone with a vocation hears the voice of the inner man: he is *called.* (Jung, 1954, pp. 175–176)

INTRODUCTION

In this chapter, I explore the relationships between three deeply interconnected phenomena: initiation, the numinous, and a calling. It is my conviction that some experiences of the basic elements of this triad are among the most precious things one can have in life. Such experiences are not often singled out in studies of human development as essential gifts for navigating the more important thresholds of life. But in today's world, where people seem to slip from job to job and relationship to relationship without anchors, experiences of initiation, the numinous, and a calling may make the difference between a life of meaning and purpose as opposed to a life of aimless, rootless wandering. Without an inner, orienting focus that allows an individual to tap into non-ego sources of meaning and purpose, there is little access to the necessary psychic energy that allows one to endure ordeals, hardships, and suffering.

It is important to note that there are different kinds of initiations, numinous experiences, and callings, as the following quote from a Turkish ISIS recruit in Syria reveals: "When you fight over there, it's like being in a trance.

Everyone shouts, 'God is the greatest,' which gives you divine strength to kill the enemy without being fazed by blood or plastered guts" (Yeginsu, 2014, p. 1). Many people do experience a calling to communal struggles, whether religious, political, or social. Such callings are increasingly prominent in fundamentalist faiths around the world—from Christian to Islamic to Buddhist. This calling is not the kind I am writing about here, although such a calling can well be viewed as a first or second cousin of the sort that is my current focus of attention.

This leads to the first distinction to be drawn in this chapter—the difference between the *calling* an individual experiences and those more communal callings that have promised so much while at the same time wrecking such havoc in the modern world. Both individual and communal callings can be thought of as originating in the need to find one's bearings in a disorienting, fragmenting, and often meaningless world. In addition to the distinction between individual and group callings, there are also what might be thought of as callings from "above" and callings from "below." The callings from "above" often have a transcendent quality, or "voice" of a spiritual nature. The callings from "below" may be thought of as originating in an instinctual connection to nature (inner and outer) that can be as compelling and transforming as a call from a god on high.

INITIATION, THE NUMINOUS, AND A CALLING: A BACKGROUND

This triad of phenomena—initiation, the numinous, and a calling—have circled around one another in the psyches of individuals and groups from every era. As a focus of scholarly interest as well as fulfilling a deep human need, however, I am drawn back to the end of the 19th and beginning of the 20th centuries with their explosion of interest in anthropology, archaeology, sociology, psychology, and related studies. Van Gennep's seminal study (1961) on *The Rites of Passage*, first published in 1906, marked a landmark of classifying and understanding the role of initiatory ceremonies that have helped generations after generations of cultures usher their individual members and their entire communities through every major life threshold—from birth, through puberty, marriage, and ultimately death. It seems clear from these rites of passage that some initiatory experiences result in a calling, and sometimes a calling leads to an initiatory experience. Van Gennep delineates three basic phases through which almost all types of initiatory ceremonies pass: separation, transition, and incorporation. The more shamanistic experiences of seeking an individual calling are not necessarily contained in such initiatory rituals, but they are certainly part of that same deep human urge to find meaning and purpose in life.

No one more fully explored the notion of a "numinous calling" that could grow out of an initiatory experience than Rudolf Otto (1958), in his classic, *The Idea of the Holy*, first published in 1917. His wonderfully florid Latin definition of the numinous became the calling card of a young men's club that spontaneously formed during one summer of my youth: we loved Otto's description of the *mysterium tremendum*. The *mysterium* refers to the fact that the numinous is something totally different than and truly mysterious from anything we experience in ordinary life. Its otherness strikes us as amazing and fascinates (*fascinans*) us, even enrapturing us in its numinosity. The *tremendum* refers to the hugeness of the experience, of feeling overwhelmed with awe, terror, and enormous energy in encountering the *mysterium*.[1] Otto's goal in coining the phrase *mysterium tremendum* to describe the numinous creates a vocabulary of the most fundamental emotions that are common to all deeply religious experiences.

To pull the various strands of Van Gennep and Otto together, as I circle around initiation, the numinous, and a calling, think of a calling as an encounter with a non-ego "other" that emerges either from inside or outside of oneself. This "other" presents a numinous reality, energy, and orientating principle to the ego based on which the possibility of a new adaptation to life can emerge. And this "other" can come not only from within or without but also from "above" or "below." Such an encounter leads from one stage or adaptation in life to another.

EARLY JUNGIAN INTEREST IN INITIATION, THE NUMINOUS, AND A CALLING

The Jungian tradition to which I belong has long emphasized the importance of initiation, the numinous, and a calling because that triad of interrelated phenomena is deeply rooted in Jung's own personal journey, which has been further revealed in the recent publication of his early diaries entitled *The Red Book* (2009). Filled with Jung's own numinous drawings, the book can almost flood the reader as Jung was flooded by his encounter with the unconscious, an encounter that totally reoriented his life in a prolonged initiatory journey.

Indeed, many of the early groups that surrounded Jung were in search of their own initiatory experiences and a calling to a more meaningful, purposeful life. The notions of Van Gennep and Otto, neither of whom were members of the early Jungian circle, were in the "air" of those who were attracted to Jung. One of those who traveled from America to see Jung in Zurich in the late 1920s was a young Joseph Henderson.

As a result of his time with Jung, Henderson took as his life's work the theme of initiation in the psychospiritual development of men and women.

In a dream seminar in 1929, Jung broke his students into two groups to study the symbolism of the moon and the crescent in the dreams of a Swiss businessman. Henderson joined Esther Harding, another student of Jung's, in the "moon" group. Out of those studies, Henderson (2005/2011) went on to develop his ideas about the archetype of initiation that eventually took shape in his 1967 *Thresholds of Initiation*, and Harding (2001) did the same with women's dreams of initiation in her 1955 *Women's Mysteries*. Henderson's book on initiation became a guiding beacon for the C. G. Jung Institute of San Francisco, of which Henderson was a founding member.

Initiation has become a core notion in the training of analysts, a process that is, in fact, viewed as an initiatory experience. This tradition has been recorded in *Initiation: The Living Reality of an Archetype*, written by those trained by Henderson (Kirsch, Rutter, & Singer, 2007). A core part of the Jungian-transmitted teachings focuses on the threads of initiation, the numinous, and a calling as they express themselves in the dreams, psyches, and lives of modern men and women. These experiences become the core building blocks of what Jung called *individuation*, a lifelong journey toward wholeness and the realization of individual selfhood. Central to this Jungian vision is an emphasis on the emergence of symbolic material from the depths of the psyche and its indwelling archetypal patterning of basic human themes around such universal experiences as life and death, death and rebirth, heroic quests and shadowy forces.

This focus did not emerge in a cultural or historical vacuum. When Henderson traveled to Switzerland in the late 1920s he felt a profound inner and outer disorientation in a world that seemed to have lost its moorings after the Industrial Revolution, World War I, the Roaring Twenties, and the beginning of the Great Depression. The interest in initiation and a numinous calling to a life of meaning and purpose grew out of the deepest need for grounding in depth in a world in which the traditional structures of meaning, which had originated in religious and other traditions, seemed of little value or relevance. These early Jungians felt that the inner world would have to become a primary source of any solid, new orientation to the psyche and the world if one was to emerge at all.

THE CIRCUS SNAKE: A PERSONAL ACCOUNT OF A NUMINOUS, INITIATORY CALLING

I offer these background notes about Van Gennep, Otto, Henderson, and Jung as an introduction to some personal material that I will now present to let the reader see how these various threads may come together in an individual's life journey. I will write about a dream I had as a young man and how it became an essential building block of meaning and purpose that came to my life. Whenever one writes about personal experience, it gives an illusion of distance and objectivity to say that it occurred decades ago—in this case, almost 50 years ago. That is true, but as with any enduring initiatory calling with a numinous charge, the experience is both old and new at the same time, just as the needs for initiatory experiences in general are both ancient and absolutely new in the modern moment. As Henderson (2005/2011) noted, "Each generation needs to discover the archetype of initiation for itself. Although the archetype of initiation is as old as human experience, it is always experienced as something new" (p. xv).

The material I will write about is initiatory; it is numinous; it contains a "calling"—and it comes from "below" rather than "above," that is, from the instinctual layer of the human psyche rather than the overtly transcendent or spiritual. Jung believed the human psyche and its archetypal underpinnings moved on a spectrum between the instinctual and the spiritual. In this model, one can have deeply moving experiences that can occur anywhere on this spectrum—from "below" where an initiatory call can come from an animal such as the snake or wolf, or from "above" where the initiatory call can come from an angel or God. Therefore, the circus snake call came to me from the earth or even from beneath the earth, from "below," from the instinctual pole of the psyche rather than the spiritual pole, where many believe such callings originate. And finally, my call came to me as an individual rather than as a member of a group—although, in a sense, it was a significant part of my being initiated into the group of the medical profession.

Let's start with what surely must appear to the reader as a strange, primitive drawing (Figure 12.1). It forms the centerpiece of this narrative. I drew this image from a dream that I had during medical school. It occurred in the midst of a time of great personal crisis and was the kind of event that Van Gennep (1961) had labeled a "life crisis ceremony" some 50 years previous to my 1969 experience (p. vii). I hope that during the course of this narrative, you will come to see what is initiatory, what is numinous, and what is a calling about this drawing and the experience it portrays.

The drawing shows a large, red snake looming above a young boy running away from it. The snake radiates energy. Behind the boy, a feminine figure hovers slightly off the ground, seemingly encouraging the boy to hold his ground. A green tree grows to the left and, along with the hovering female figure to the right, provides a container to the central action between the boy and the serpent.

The drawing is based on the following dream:

I stand face to face with a large "circus" snake. I don't know how I know it is a "circus" snake or even what a "circus" snake is. The name simply announces itself to me in the dream. I know that I want to flee from the snake. My mother

Figure 12.1   The circus snake. (Courtesy of Thomas Singer)

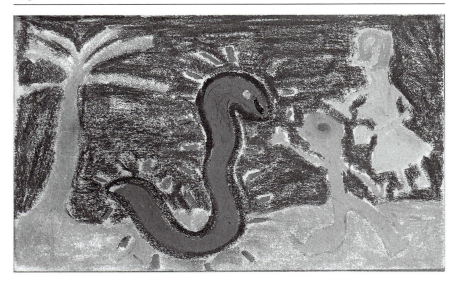

stands behind me and insists that I stand my ground. The snake stands as tall or even taller than I am and is glowing and radiating energy. We look one another straight in the eye, and I sense that its intentions toward me are not malevolent. They might even be good.

Around this time, I was a third-year medical student at Yale Medical School, one of the most compassionate and liberal medical institutions in the country. I was a quite mediocre medical student who had arrived at Yale after teaching English in Greece for a year upon graduating from college. I hadn't had a science course in three years and was barely able to stay afloat, even though Yale did not examine its students for the first two years of medical school. I felt woefully unprepared in every way. My science background met the most basic premed requirements, but otherwise I was emotionally and psychologically unprepared for the rigors of medical school and for facing illness, suffering, and death. One of the hallmarks of the initiation archetype that Joseph Henderson describes is the *ordeal*, which Henderson adds as an equal partner to Van Gennep's phases of separation, transition, and incorporation. By my third year, I was fully launched in the ordeal part of the archetype of initiation—which, by the way, does not necessarily take place within the constructs of a well-ordered ceremony. Among the most overwhelming moments of that time was my first physical and history exam with a patient as a third-year student on the internal medicine wards.

I walked into the hospital room to face a very old man lying motionless on the bed. He was uncommunicative, unresponsive, and hardly breathing. His family surrounded him and seemed totally devastated. I had no idea how to proceed in terms of taking a history and physical given that he was unresponsive in every way, although I managed barely to bluff my way through it. I then joined the rounds with the other medical students, interns, residents, and attending physician—all in their white coats parading from room to room. After visiting my patient's room, we stepped outside, and I was asked how to tell the difference between a midbrain preparation and a stroke at a higher level of the brain. I did learn that the midbrain can keep vegetative functions such as heart rate and breathing going, even as all higher cortical functions had failed. After the rounds, I literally fled the ward, retreated to my dormitory room, and refused to emerge for a few days. Eventually I ended up in the psychological services of the medical school and so began my very long initiatory journey to finding my way as a physician. Although I had said I wanted to be a doctor since the age of eight or nine and had fulfilled all the premed requirements, those turned out to be the merest preliminaries to the real experience of initiation, of the numinous, of a calling. After fleeing the wards, it was a few months before I actually got back to the medical wards and restarted the slow, tough work of becoming a doctor.

What does this skeletal narrative of a difficult moment in my life and a peculiar dream and its drawing have to do with initiation, the numinous, and a calling? I had the dream in the midst of a crisis, just months after fleeing the medical wards. In its own strange, symbolic way, the dream pointed to moments from the past and a tough passage in the present, and it would become an unexpected guide to the future. The past personal associations to this dream (not the past impersonal, archetypal amplifications of the dream—more about this later) were enlightening in terms of the relevance of its content. Not long before this experience on the medical wards, I had returned to my native home in the Midwest to visit my parents before leaving on a trip in which I would be studying medical practice in the remote, third-world country of Bolivia. My father was about to have a complicated neurosurgical procedure on his spine, and I was anxious about going away a few days before he faced his own ordeal. Nevertheless, on the appointed day I went to the airport, got on the plane, and proceeded to watch the man in the seat next to me drop dead of a heart attack before the plane took off. I had to fight my way off the plane as the airline officials wanted to take the body off but nothing else. I arrived back at my parents' house and told my mother what happened, and she announced I could stay for 24 hours and then I would have to leave. Her order seemed cold and brutal, but I later learned she was afraid I would get trapped into staying at home to protect both my parents as they had done with their parents. She wanted me to be free to live my own life. So I left the home of my mother and father, who, in fact, survived my departure. Over the years, I carried on with developing my own life while also being able to maintain close relationships with both my parents. I was fortunate to be at each of their bedsides when they died many years later—all in the same home where they had lived for 70 years.

But the episode of being told by my mother that I had to leave home on the occasion of my father's surgery and my departure for Bolivia joined together with the experience of fleeing the medical wards just a few months later, and both came to mind when I had the snake dream. My mother forced me to get on with my life's journey, just as the mother in the dream several months later helped lead me back to the medical wards to face the realities of life and death head on.

That is a bit of the personal background to the dream. What of the dream itself? What did it come to mean to me over time in terms of initiation, the numinous, and a calling? A good place to start is Otto's description of the numinous as *mysterium tremendum*. I am face to face with a large, even towering "circus" snake. I never really figured out what calling it a circus snake meant, or even how I came to know it was a circus snake. It seemed simply to announce itself to me. Maybe that is just the point. It is mysterious. It is not known. It is not clear. It simply is—looming there in its own reality. That reality is a *mysterium*—something completely other, nonhuman, that is confronting me with its own being and its own totally unfamiliar reality. One thing I do know is that the circus snake is terrifying, and the terror it induces is the emotion of the *tremendum* that Otto (1958) described. Not only is it tremendous in size, it is overpowering in its sense of strength and its dreadful focus on me. I wanted to get away from the snake as quickly as possible, just as I wanted to run from the wards as fast as I could and just as I was instinctually driven to flee from the dead man on the plane. The most natural thing to do when faced with terror—including the terror of death—is to flee. We, as humans, do that all the time when faced with mysterious dangers, the ravages of disease, and the inevitability of death (consider our response to first case of Ebola in the United States).

As to the *fascinans* part of Otto's equation of *mysterium tremendum*, my emotional reaction at the end of the dream is most suggestive. There is direct, eye-to-eye contact between the snake and my dream ego—as if it were possible to meet or look directly in the eye of this other, seemingly threatening reality. In that eye contact, I sense the snake's intentions are not malevolent and are perhaps even good. We all know that most snakes do not inspire trust, either in dreams or in reality. But this seems to be a different order of serpent with whom some sort of nonverbal communication is possible. This makes the snake fascinating, suggesting the possibility of some kind of connecting help—what Otto refers to as the "mercy" or "grace" that can come from a most unexpected source. The quality of a compelling presence that brings something totally unexpected, new, and potentially beneficent to the dramatic situation makes the snake a *fascinans*. Its indwelling dynamism is enhanced in the drawing by the lines of energy that radiate from the snake, suggesting a supercharged or even supernatural energy. The highly charged energy gives the scene a kind of electricity and, along with the bright colors of the drawing, lends the drawing its numinous quality—a "glowing" life and vitality that is beyond the every day. The word *numinous* denotes something of a divine presence or a force that arouses spiritual or religious emotions. It is awe inspiring.

So what is this awe-inspiring dream experience pointing to? Why do I think of it as initiatory and describe it as a "calling" dream?

It is at this juncture of the narrative that we enter what, in my Jungian tradition, we refer to as the *symbolic* or *archetypal* realm. The snake presents me with a symbolic reality that is no less real or powerful than everyday reality. The snake demands I pay attention to it. Of course, this leads to the next obvious question: What does the snake symbolize? What reality does it speak to? In the course of human history, the snake has taken on many different meanings across cultures. The meaning and culture that spoke most directly to me about the snake is my own Western tradition and particularly the ancient, prepatriarchal, matriarchal level of the Greek psyche. You might wonder how that would occur to me. Isn't this getting too academic or intellectual?

Symbolic reality demands that we use all of our faculties to comprehend it as best we can. This certainly includes the intellect, but it also includes the deeper emotional realities. For such symbolic levels of experience to have convincing authenticity, they must be completely grounded in the immediate, experiential, and existential being of one's unique life. On the one hand, subsequent to this "big dream," I have spent decades learning about the multiple symbolic meanings of the snake and what I have to say now is informed by that study. On the other hand, and much more immediate to the actual occurrence of the dream and my "calling" in medical school, is the fact that I had spent a year in Greece before going to medical school and had steeped myself in its history, legends, and myths. Although I knew virtually nothing of snake symbolism when I had the dream, I had developed a bit of an inner cultural container about the ancient Greek psyche that at least allowed me to want to take in the dream, to become curious about it, and to be shaped by it. This is another way of saying that the message of a dream and its calling is not necessarily immediately clear or transparent. One needs to work at its meaning to get a "feel" for it. I quickly learned that in the early Greek tradition, the snake is associated with medicine (the *caduceus*), with death and rebirth, and with healing. It is also associated with the initiation of young men into the mysteries of the ancient Greek world.

Put most simply, this dream became my own inner, non-ego calling to be a doctor. In it, I was called to face and learn what I could about the mysteries of life and death, of renewal and healing. I wanted to run from it, but the "mother of the dream" made me turn and face the snake. Let me show you an image from ancient Greece that I came across decades after this dream (Figure 12.2). The image shows a young man being initiated into the mysteries of life and death and of death and rebirth by a "great mother" behind whom stands the serpent symbolizing those underground, hidden, and mysterious realities.

This image comes from an early strata of Greek culture in which the great mother, Demeter, was the goddess and source of agriculture and, by extension, all the natural forces that are part of living and dying and regenerating. And her consort, her underground companion in these mysteries, was the serpent who was viewed as a most creative and essential force in the eternal round of nature.

Speaking even more directly to the inner calling to become a doctor is another image from the same early Greek canon (Figure 12.3). The god of healing in ancient Greece was known as Asclepius. Citizens in need of healing would go to Asclepeions to participate in sacred rituals, including dream incubations, where they hoped to have healing dreams. Asclepius had both a human form and an animal form as a snake. In the following image, one sees Asclepius

Figure 12.2   The great mother, the youth as initiate, and the snake as *mysterium tremendum*. (Harrison, J. E. *Themis: A Study of the Social Origins of Greek Religion*. Figure 76. Cambridge: Cambridge University Press, 1974, 286)

Figure 12.3 *Asclepius in Human and Snake Form Healing a Young Man.* (Photo by Universal History Archive/UIG via Getty Images)

standing in his human form ministering to the arm of a standing patient. And, to the right, the same patient is sleeping on a bed as Asclepius comes in a dream in his snake form to minister a healing bite on the same right arm. God appearing in both human and animal form is not uncommon to the psyche of both ancient and modern men and women. For that reason, as I have already indicated, a calling can come from "above"—the transcendent realm—or from "below"—the instinctual realm—both of which have spiritual qualities.

CONCLUSION: TIME AND INITIATION, THE NUMINOUS, AND A CALLING

By now, it should be clear to the reader that I have taken great liberties with the time factor in exploring the triad of initiation, the numinous, and a calling. This is by no means an accident because all three of these phenomena have unique relationships to time, to an individual's cycle of life, and to a culture's cycle of life. There are three interrelated elements to the experience of time in relationship to these phenomena.

The first element of time is the *once and for all event* quality of a numinous, initiatory calling. Such events are singular; they occur at a very specific time and place in the unfolding of an individual life. Their specificity with regard to context and content make them unique and unforgettable. Certainly, my snake dream had this quality, and one reason I took the time to give some details about context is that this specificity gives such events their authenticity and transformative urgency.

The second element of time in a calling is the growing knowledge that it is *not a singular event*. It takes time for a calling to get a real "body." Another way of saying this is that it takes time for a calling to incarnate itself, and this can become an initiatory journey. Callings are both once and for all events and gradually unfolding incarnated realities over time. In this sense, the calling leads one into the future by revealing an unknown potential for growth and development. For example, the snake dream helped me to see that I had a calling to be a doctor and that I could in time become one. It gave me faith to persevere. Over time, a calling deepens and gains in experience, just as the symbolic meaning of a snake grows over time, sheds its skin, and renews itself. To grow and deepen, callings have to renew themselves over the course of an individual's life. For example, many people have had hallucinogenic experiences that are revelatory and potentially transformative; however, the potential does not manifest itself in lived experience.

The third element of time in a calling might best be described as *archetypal* or even *eternal*, that is, not bound by a once and for all event or by the gradual unfolding of that event over time. It is as if there is a structure or ontogeny to a calling that has a recurring pattern or form over time, which is both absolutely unique to each individual who has it and universal in the sense that many people throughout human history have had identical or similar callings. This archetypal pattern or eternal quality gives one the feeling that a calling is both brand new and, at the same time, of and from all time. So the very experience of time itself can be altered by a calling in that it is both highly specific in terms of time and can feel timeless or even eternal in its giving one a glimpse into an essential, enduring quality of being that offers the energy and vision to live a life of meaning and purpose. The archetypal timelessness of a calling is part of what gives it the power to move one into the future.

The calling to become a healer through initiation into the mysteries of death and rebirth symbolized and embodied by the snake did not immunize me from the fear of death, or give me any special mastery over the mysteries of life and death. It might be better to say that it sensitized me to the mysteries of life and death and, through an experience of the numinous, allowed me to access sources of energy that are not available to the everyday ego, that it has given me the ability to tolerate ordeals and suffering while sustaining a commitment over time.

NOTE

1. I can't help but wonder if those responsible for naming the bombing attacks on Baghdad in March 2003 as "shock and awe" were familiar with Otto's definition of the numinous.

REFERENCES

Harding, E. (2001). *Women's mysteries: Ancient and modern.* Boston, MA: Shambhala.

Harrison, J. E. (1974). *Themis: A study of the social origins of Greek religion.* Gloucester, MA: Peter Smith.

Henderson, J. L. (2005/2011). *Thresholds of initiation.* Wilmette, IL: Chiron Publications.

Jung, C. G. (1954). The development of personality. In G. Adler & R. F. C. Hull (Eds.), *The collected works of C. G. Jung* (Vol. 17). Princeton, NJ: Princeton University Press.

Jung, C. G. (2009). *The red book: Liber novus* (S. Shamdasani, Ed.). New York: W. W. Norton and Company.

Kirsch, T., Rutter, V. B., & Singer, T. (2007). *Initiation: The living reality of an archetype.* London: Routledge.

Otto, R. (1958). *The idea of the holy* (J. Harvey, Trans.). London: Oxford University Press.

Van Gennep, A. (1961). *The rites of passage.* Chicago, IL: University of Chicago Press.

Yeginsu, C. (2014, September 16). ISIS draws a steady stream of recruits from Turkey. *The New York Times*, p. 1.

CHAPTER 13

HOPE AND ETERNITY: GOD AS TRANSCENDENT PRESENCE IN THE ORDINARY

Theo D. McCall

Sometimes in the middle of a moment of total ordinariness, something extraordinary and transcendent can be glimpsed, if we have the eyes to see it. If we are alert to such things, these moments can draw us into the future, in spirit if not literally in time, and inspire us to embrace a process of self-transcendence. Whether such experiences are understood to be the work of God, my own tradition, or arising from within the self—not that these two ideas are necessarily mutually exclusive—the hope remains that within our ordinary, daily lives, we can be drawn into the extraordinary.

My own experience of such moments was shaped from an early age by the richness of what is sometimes termed "High Church Anglicanism", a part of the Anglican tradition, which embraces sacramental liturgy in all its glory. There is something about the use of physical symbols, which still resonates deeply within my soul to this day. Every Easter Eve, for example, my parish priest (for many years my actual father) would light a new fire in the church grounds and then, in the darkness, light the Paschal Candle and carry the candle in procession with the whole congregation into the church. The light of the candle was small, even pathetic in the darkness of the surrounding night, and yet it became for many of us a profound symbol of hope and transcendence.

The lighting of the new fire on Easter Eve, symbolizing the hope of the resurrection and the light of Christ shining in the darkness, still motivates me to strive to spread the light of hope in the world. There is something incredibly earthy and ancient about the use of fire, yet in the context of the Easter Liturgy it also points to something greater. In the dark night we are called to a greater glory, called to become something more. The German catholic theologian Karl Rahner (1978) describes this process as "self-transcendence," a journey in which we are drawn to the divine from the ordinary.

My own sense of vocation to the Anglican priesthood, and to systematic theology, reflects this notion of self-transcendence arising from the ordinary. The sense of vocation occurred almost by accident: a chance word said on the soccer field, which recalled an earlier statement by a parishioner in my local church.

My first sense of vocation to the priesthood, which over the years has become inextricably entwined with a sense of being called to study and write systematic theology, came when an elderly parishioner made a comment to me at our weekly church choir rehearsal. She had witnessed me serving at the altar during one of our church's significant festivals (probably during Holy Week, but my memory of the actual occasion has long since faded). She commented at our following choir rehearsal in the Rectory that she felt, very strongly, that I would make a good priest. My memory is that she was quietly insistent, though not inappropriately so. I suppose I must have been about 14 or 15 at the time. Intriguingly my memory of where I was sitting at the time in the large lounge room in the Rectory is crystal clear, as is my memory of my subsequent experience.

My next sense of vocation came at the age of 16 and from the most unlikely of sources: a fellow schoolboy soccer player, and not a particularly religious one at that. Again I remember exactly where I was on the soccer pitch at the school where I am now chaplain. I interpret this experience as both utterly coincidental and banal, and yet at the same time providential and transcendent. The experience itself could have occurred on any soccer pitch at any school around the world: a chance comment, a mere observation, made to an ordinary student, "You're going to become a priest, aren't you?" My response was equally ordinary, "Yes, probably." Yet, even as I recall those words, I realize there was nothing ordinary about them. That conversation led not only to my recalling the earlier encounter with the parishioner from the church choir, but also to a profound sense of vocation and inevitability. It may be expressed, "I'm going to end up a priest, and I'll be fine." This sense of, "This is what is going to happen and it will be okay," gave me great comfort and purpose as I struggled through the remainder of my teenage years with many of the same anxieties that most teenagers experience.

At my diaconal Ordination Retreat, held for a few days before I was made a deacon, the Archbishop who ordained me, Bishop Ian George, described this feeling (that things would work out in the end, even if we struggled in the meantime) as being like one of Bach's great pieces of music. There may be great suffering and pathos conveyed in the music, yet there is equally a great sense of the music driving forward to its climatic and triumphant conclusion.

My experience as the father of a beautiful daughter who lives with a significant disability brings this same feeling. My laughing, guileless daughter Miriam, who brings so much joy into the world, has Angelman's Syndrome, a rare, genetic condition, which means she doesn't speak and will never live independently. In the difficult times, the days when she is sheer hard work for my wife and me, I experience a tiny share of Christ's suffering. There are moments, the times when we've cleaned feces off the carpet in her bedroom spring immediately to mind, when I have cried out in frustration and anger to God. Yet, in the midst of that pain, I have also experienced a sense that everything will work out in the end. Somehow, even in the midst of the anger and the sense of futility, there is a deeper song, which calls me to a brighter future.

The hope for some kind of eternity, some kind of ultimate transcendence, is similar; we receive hints of this promise in the most ordinary events of life. Each year in the season of Advent, when people around the world look forward to Christmas and the celebration of the coming of the light of Christ into the world, my thoughts often turn to what it means to hope. One significant part of Christian hope, shared in various forms by other traditions, is that, despite the reality of death, there is an eternal future, which awaits us.

This hope may be expressed as the hope in God as the "Absolute Future," as Rahner believed, and the hope that an eternity of joy awaits us. What Rahner meant was that the future is God, and God is the future: that through the uncertainty of life, God is drawing us toward that future, drawing us to "active self-transcendence" (see Denis Edwards, 2004, p. 138 for an excellent summary of Rahner's theology of God as the Absolute Future), but that process is not limited or subjective. God as the Absolute Future is drawing us to the divine, to the transcendent. We receive glimpses of this future, visions if you like, when the beauty of a moment catches our breath and we glimpse the eternal.

These future visions often occur in the most ordinary of settings, so that what are otherwise common events in life can become times and places when we experience visions of transcendent hope. My experiences of being called to a future, which was different from what I might have otherwise imagined, occurred in the most ordinary of settings. This is, I suspect, a common experience. Most church traditions have formalized this, in one way or another, the most common of which is the celebration of the sacraments. In the Catholic, Orthodox, Lutheran, and Anglican traditions, among others, the sacraments are one place where we experience this foretaste of an eternal future.

My understanding of sacraments, shaped by my tradition, is that they are outward, physical signs of God's grace, which is inward and spiritual. They are also by their very nature participatory. For all of the disagreements at the time of the Reformation over the theology of the sacraments, a great gift to

Western Christianity at least was a restoration of the participatory nature of the celebration of the sacraments. The sacraments were restored as rites celebrated by the whole people of God. Of course, in many traditions the main celebrant remained a priest or a bishop, set apart for particular work, including the celebration of the sacraments. Yet the Reformation restored that sense of the priest or the bishop celebrating the sacraments surrounded by the people of God. As an Anglican priest, whenever I celebrate the Eucharist, it is in the context of a gathered community of faith, even if that gathered community is only one other person.

Perhaps more significantly for the purposes of reflecting on transcendent visions, which come to us in the everyday moments of life, sacraments also have their roots in, and are grounded in, the most ordinary of events of life:

- the sharing of a meal together in the case of the Eucharist, with its origins in the Jewish celebration of the Passover meal;
- the blessing of a person in the waters of baptism, with water signifying life and the possibility of new life. We Australians are not alone in knowing the value of water, but we certainly *do* know it;
- the hands of blessing extended over those to be confirmed, reminding us of the blessings bestowed by a father on the first-born in the Hebrew Scriptures;
- the hands of blessing extended over those to be ordained, also reminding us of the fatherly blessings, but in addition of the importance of choosing leaders and setting them apart for particular work;
- the joining of a couple's hands in marriage: an ancient rite, which blesses the most natural and wonderful of unions;
- the active listening and gentle counsel of a friend in the healing sacrament of reconciliation;
- and, finally, the anointing with oil for the sick and the dying: the healing balm given to those who are suffering.

The sacraments are ordinary events, or have their roots in ordinary events, which then become extraordinary events, because they give us a glimpse of the divine. They point to the divine, and a glorious future, yet they are grounded in the reality of our present life.

In recent years this has found particular expression for me in the sacrament of baptism. One of my joys is baptizing the children of old scholars of my school. Young men return to the school to have their children baptized, supported, and usually very actively encouraged by their wives! At one level, these occasions are incredibly ordinary. Though perhaps not as common as they were in Australia 50 years ago, baptisms still occur with remarkable regularity, as parents come to ask for a blessing on their children.

Yet, despite, or perhaps exactly because of, the ordinariness of these events, when I gaze down at the little person and pour the water of baptism over his or her forehead, I have a remarkable sense of transcendent hope. Often my internal prayer as I speak to the gathered family and friends, and as I baptize the child at the school chapel's font, is something like, "May God richly bless this child. May she live a wonderful life of service and grace."

Theologically much of the tradition of baptism has been caught up with notions of original sin and the need to wash this sin away, before the person can be admitted as a full member of the Christian Church. Influenced as it was by the Reformation, my own Church's rite has a significant emphasis on this in its older, yet still revered liturgies, as the introduction to "The Ministration of Publik Baptism of Infants" in the 1662 Book of Common Prayer makes crystal clear:

> Dearly beloved, forasmuch as all men are conceived and born in sin; and that our Saviour Christ saith, None can enter into the kingdom of God, except he be regenerate and born anew of water and of the Holy Ghost; I beseech you to call upon God the Father, through our Lord Jesus Christ, that of his bounteous mercy he will grant to *this child* that thing which by nature *he* cannot have; that *he* may be baptized with Water and the Holy Ghost, and received into Christ's holy Church, and be made *a lively member* of the same.

Later liturgies have toned down the language, as it were, without dispensing with the theology behind it.

Yet, there is another theological tradition, which is equally significant and may assist in describing the concept of ordinary events giving, at the same time, glimpses of a transcendent hope. My own theology has been significantly shaped by my reading of Orthodox theologians, especially the work of Alexander Schmemann. Schmemann focused in much of his liturgical theology on reminding his readers that the world was essentially sacramental. According to Schmemann, the world has a "natural sacramentality," by which he meant that it reveals something of God. His argument was that the world itself is "an essential means both of knowledge of God and communion with Him" (Schmemann, 1973, p. 120).

In the Christian tradition, to continue using Schmemann's ideas, Christ is the fulfilment of God's manifestation to the world. Christ is the completion of the world's sacramentality (McCall, 2010, p. 236). The natural sacramentality of the world finds human expression in worship. In the worship of God, we offer our prayers for the world up to God. Indeed, in the Orthodox tradition, we offer up the world itself, by which is meant the whole of creation, the entire cosmos, to God. Our participation in such worship serves to remind us, at the very least, of the possibility of experiencing God's presence in the sacrament of creation.

Schmemann also strove against what he perceived as a rise in secularism. His definition of secularism is important to understand, because he wasn't making a simple distinction between the secular and the sacred (McCall, 2010, p. 233). Rather, his definition of secularism was that it denied the possibility of the sacramentality of the world. A person who completely accepts a purely secular view of the world cannot allow for the possibility of the transcendent being made manifest in the ordinary stuff of life. The notion of the world as a sacrament, and the ordinary things of life such as water being a means of the communication of the divine, is rejected by the secularist.

Schmemann's work reveals a terrible irony in post-Reformation society: a religious person may in fact be quite secular. Schmemann is quick to point out that secularism is not actually the same as atheism (Schmemann, 1973, p. 124). Atheism is essentially the rejection of the possibility of the existence of God (McCall, 2010, p. 238). Secularism, on the other hand, does not *necessarily* deny the possibility of the physical things of life having their cause of existence elsewhere, but does deny the possibility of physical things being the "manifestation and presence of that *elsewhere*" (Schmemann, 1973, p. 124). Atheists may well also be secularists, but so too may some Christians. For example, puritans, arguably, are secularists according to Schmemann's definition. At its logical extreme Puritanism is a form of dualism, "a separation of the cerebral and the spiritual from the bodily and material" (Porter, 2006, p. 21).

My personal experience, shaped at least partly by my reading of Schmemann, is that ordinary events can and do reveal the extraordinary, if we have eyes to see the extraordinary. Pouring the water of baptism over the foreheads of little children is one such event for me. Through the waters of baptism the child is blessed by God. The water becomes "holy," not in the sense that it is suddenly radically different from "secular" water—that would be to create a false distinction between the "holy" and the "profane," something Schmemann vehemently opposed—rather the water reveals something of the divine. The water makes manifest the blessing of God. The ordinary event becomes an extraordinary one: a little miracle of daily life. These little sacraments of daily life point to a greater vision: a vision of a transcendent future in God's presence. The Christian tradition uses various words to describe this: the "Beatific Vision," the "Eschaton," the "Parousia," each with different meanings and emphases, yet linked by the hope that one day we will experience the divine more fully and completely in a transcendent, eternal future.

But, much like Bach's extraordinary music or my experience of life with a disabled daughter, a hope for a transcendent future cannot negate the reality of suffering in our present world. The problem of theodicy does not disappear. "How can a loving, all-powerful God, permit suffering in the world he has created?" This question has had personal and powerful meaning for me on many occasions, usually in the form, "How can you, O God, allow me, your gift to the world of theology, to be forced to scrape poo off my daughter's bedroom walls?"

Even, or perhaps I should say, *especially* theologians as hopeful in the transcendent future as Karl Rahner and Jürgen Moltmann stressed the reality both of suffering and randomness and change. So a significant issue is raised, which is, if we hope for some kind of transcendent future, an objective future as distinct from the subjective memory of our descendants for example—not that I would want to deny the importance of memory, far from it—but if there is this hope for a transcendent future, then inevitably we must examine what kind of God we believe in.

For there to be hope in an eternal future, a future that writers such as Walter Benjamin (discussed in Katerberg, 2004, p. 67) and Jürgen Moltmann, in developing some of Benjamin's ideas (Moltmann, 2004, p. 17), believe will break into time, or perhaps more precisely transform time and space, then we have to have some notion of the transcendent. Moltmann understands eschatology principally using the framework of *adventus*, and understands God as "the Coming God" (Moltmann, 1995, p. 22). The key principle from which Moltmann works is that the eschaton is neither the future of time, in the sense of *futurum*, nor is it a concept of timeless eternity. Rather God comes from the future, bringing conversion, that is, new life, with him. Moltmann understands this conversion as being more than a mere interruption of time, in the sense that a prophet might interrupt the ordinary flow of events. Rather "the future made present creates new conditions for possibilities in history" (Moltmann, 1995, p. 22). God's coming toward us means that he brings eternal life and eternal time. The coming of God means a fundamental change in the conditions of time. Moltmann understands the "transcendental future of time" as surpassing the present and the past. Consequently, when God comes from this future, he will gather up all of time and transform it.

Whether the understanding of God here is a traditional notion of God as a transcendent being, or something quite different, there is a sense in which Rahner's concept of God as the Absolute Future is necessary if we are to conceptualize this eternal hope.

Yet the reality of suffering, evolutionary change, and decay, is with us. In the 20th-century notions of a progressive, linear time, were challenged by the horror of war. No concept of the transcendent can fail to talk about this, nor can the integrity of creation itself be compromised. In other words, the knowledge of the way evolution works from a scientific perspective has changed our understanding of God. However we might imagine God interacting with creation, there has to be a consideration that creation has the freedom to evolve and change, and there is an evolutionary cost along the way: the cost of suffering and extinction. But also, putting it more positively, creatures are free to realize their own potentialities.

God as the Transcendent Future is not present *in the all-powerful sense* in the ordinary parts of life now, otherwise suffering and injustice are theologically intolerable. So we have to imagine God calling us to the future in a different way. Some ideas and thoughts:

1. It is as if God has restricted himself, put limits on what he will do in this life (that this world may have its freedom and its integrity). God therefore is not present as the omnipotent Being in the reality of this world, otherwise suffering in a good world, which God has created, becomes intolerable. The notion of "self-emptying," which St Paul (Philippians 2: 7) uses to refer to Christ "who did not think of equality with God something to be exploited, but emptied himself, taking the form of a slave," can equally be applied to the divine presence in creation: vulnerable, self-limited love (Edwards, 2004, p. 109). In this understanding, God has created this world, made room for it to come into being and evolve (there are some lovely images of making room in the womb that theologians have used as a symbol of this), and then cannot interfere, without breaking his creation. To change the metaphor slightly, the Universe we know is a fragile sphere, and if God breaks into that sphere in time and space, he breaks it. Ironically that image is probably not far from the apocalyptic concept of the end of the world. Significantly transcendence or omnipotence is redefined as "the free unlimited capacity to make room within the self for the other" (Dunn, 1998, p. 14).

2. God may be thought of as being present as Spirit, influencing, shaping, drawing us forward to the future. Perhaps God may be conceived as "wholly other" and "radically interior" to creatures. So the Spirit draws us to a transcendent future, but does so from within, subtly, gently. This need not be seen as a diminishment of the Spirit's transcendence, but rather the real expression of it.

3. Notions of the eternity of God challenge our concepts of time. Is there any way we can talk, as the Celts do, about "thin places," places where the eternal breaks into time and space, giving us a glimpse of a transcendent future? This would allow the possibility of the transcendent to be imagined, without the loss of the integrity of this world.

4. What about something completely radical, a notion of God in which God sees the big picture, the Absolute Future, but in the meantime blots out the "white noise" the background noise?

5. The apophatic tradition is instructive here. It literally means "flight from speech," in other words, that any notions of God we might utter must be set against the background of human ignorance of the nature of God. In one sense that is obvious, but it's important to acknowledge. We rightly put limits, or perhaps provisions, on our knowledge and our words, our expressing of any ideas. Eschatology has to learn to "speak of

hope without over-determination, to navigate between the presumption of claiming to know too much and the emptiness of knowing nothing at all." "Both eschatological continuity and change are affirmed, but only in apophatic paradox" (Hughes, 2004, pp. 103, 115).

6. Ironically, acknowledging the limits of our knowledge, or acknowledging that statements about God are inevitably and fundamentally provisional, then frees us to imagine and describe God as radically different. So, in that vein, perhaps the concept of a transcendent Being is beyond what we can say, so we simply talk about the future Spirit, or even more simply, "Eternal Hope."

"The challenge of eschatology is to articulate a hope that is neither presumptuous nor empty" (Hughes, 2004, p. 105). There are clear links with the mystical tradition here. The mystic might *experience* the future "proleptically" whereas in the eschatological tradition the future is *anticipated* and *imagined*. In the sacramental tradition the distinction between experiencing the future proleptically and anticipating it is less clear—both are integral. The call to self-transcendence is both an experience and a promise. Precisely because we have the hope, or the anticipation, of transcendence in an ultimate sense, it is possible to experience something of that transcendence while we are on the journey toward it. The promise of transcendence is at the same time both a distant mystery and a familiar face. As Rahner (1978, p. 131) puts it, a person

> experiences rather that this mystery is also a hidden closeness, a forgiving intimacy, his [*sic*] real home, that is it a love which shares itself, something familiar which he can approach and turn to from the estrangement of his own perilous and empty life.

For me, this mystery is experienced in the midst of suffering and pain. It is this experience of God reaching into the ordinary events or life, even the painful and frustrating events of life, and revealing something precious, that causes me to imagine and fleetingly experience a transcendent future.

When we finally pass from this life, the gray curtain of this world will pass away and the glory of the transcendent will be revealed. I hope with every fiber of my being that this is indeed true. Though St Paul (1 Corinthians 13) names love as the greatest of all the gifts, I nevertheless have some sympathy with the character "Andy" from the wonderful film *Shawshank Redemption*. One of my colleagues at St Peter's College, Ciaran Geraghty, reminded me of this quote:

> *Andy Dufresne: [in letter to Red]* Remember Red, hope is a good thing, maybe the best of things, and no good thing ever dies.

REFERENCES

The Church of England. (1662, 1953). The ministration of publik baptism of infants. *Book of Common Prayer*. London: Oxford University Press.

Dunn, J. (1998). *The Christ and the spirit*, volume 2, *Pneumatology*. Grand Rapids: Eerdmans.

Edwards, D. (2004). *Breath of life: A theology of the Creator Spirit*. Maryknoll, NY: Orbis Books.

Hughes, K. (2004). The crossing of hope, or apophatic eschatology. In Volf, M. & Katerberg, W. (Eds.), *The future of hope* (pp. 101–124). Grand Rapids: Eerdmans.

Jackson, P. et al. (2003). *The lord of the rings: The return of the king*. WingNut Films: The Saul Zaentz Company, distributed by New Line Cinema.

Katerberg, W. (2004). History, hope and the redemption of time. In Volf, M. & Katerberg, W. (Eds.), *The future of hope* (pp. 49–73). Grand Rapids: Eerdmans.

McCall, T. (2010). *The Greenie's guide to the end of the world: Ecology and eschatology*. Adelaide, ATF.

Moltmann, J. (2004). Progress and abyss: Remembrances of the future of the modern world. In Volf, M. & Katerberg, W. (Eds.), *The future of hope* (pp. 3–26). Grand Rapids: Eerdmans.

Moltmann, J. (1995). *The coming of god: Christian eschatology*. Minneapolis: Fortress Press.

Porter, M. (2006). *The new puritans: The rise of fundamentalism in the Anglican Church*. Melbourne: Melbourne University Press.

Rahner, K. (1978). *Foundations of Christian faith: An introduction to the idea of Christianity*. New York: Crossroad.

Schmemann, A. (1973). Worship in a Secular Age. *For the life of the world: Sacraments and orthodoxy* (pp. 117–134). Crestwood, NY: St Vladimir's Seminary Press.

Chapter 14

Called to Shape the Future

Stephen Lewis

INTRODUCTION

Why are you here? What is your life's purpose? These are questions for
which many people would like to know the answers concerning their lives.
Some pursue lifelong quests in search of the answers to these questions.
Others reflect on their own family and personal stories for clues. Acclaimed
psychologist, Carl Jung said:

> I feel very strongly that I am under the influence of questions that were left
> incomplete and unanswered by my parents and grandparents, and more
> distant ancestors. It has always seemed to me that I had to answer ques-
> tions fate had posed to my fore-parents or that I had to finish or continue
> things which previous ages left unfinished.[1]

Whether you are excavating deeper insights from your own story or on a
lifelong hunt for answers, Jung's statement implies that these questions are
historical, perhaps ancestral, but more importantly, are present and call us in
ways that shape the future.

In this chapter, we will explore the idea that Christians are called to
shape the future. We consciously and unconsciously participate in shaping
it through our calling. However, when we become more conscious of our
own callings and the unfolding answers to these deep questions of our lives,
we can become more proactive co-creators with God in creating the future
before us.

DEFINING CALLING AND WHO HAS ONE

Historically, calling typically has been associated with a religious occupation. The origin of the word can be traced to its Latin root *vocatio*, which means a call or summon. It was commonly understood that God was the caller of one who responded to a life of faith in Jesus Christ and called some people to be preachers or the Lord's servant. The Hebrew Bible or Christian's Old Testament notes that the prophets were among those who prominently spoke for and were called by God. The New Testament carries this tradition forward with Jesus calling followers into discipleship. Early Christians debated about how to qualify the parameters of a calling. Theologian Martin Luther was the first person to redefine the term to include religious and nonreligious occupations. This broadening of the definition suggests that God is interested in the larger concerns of society and communal life, and has endowed each person with particular gifts and a purpose in service to the common welfare of a larger community.

The term *calling* has evolved over time to have a more social role in society. It has become synonymous with the word purpose. Less concerned with origins or sources of calling, purpose is concerned with one's unique role in life. In the words of the poet Mary Oliver, "What will you do with your one wild precious life?"[2] Purpose, however, is not confined to an individual's self-serving desires. Instead, it is concerned with the meaning and impact of an individual's life. William Damon, one of the leading authors on the topic of purpose, defines it as an individual's intention to accomplish something meaningful that has consequences on the world beyond oneself.[3] With this understanding, everyone can pursue a purpose and have an impact on their families, communities, organizations, and the broader society.

Damon's definition is a helpful contribution, builds on Martin Luther's work, and broadens the understanding of calling that makes it more accessible to a pluralistic society and individuals seeking to understand their life in meaningful but nontheistic ways. However, we lose something when we fail to wrestle with the subject of a call—who is doing the calling.

David Cunningham offers an expanded definition of call that teases out this important nuance and suggests that a call acknowledges something beyond us that calls us beyond ourselves for others.[4] While Cunningham understands that "something" to be God, his definition suggests that the caller in our lives could appear to be nontheistic and take on various forms—individuals, communities, social ills, or cries of the marginalized. As an example, the recent protests we have witnessed across the country of instances where police officers killed unarmed African American boys and men have called, if not compelled, many people to work toward solutions that will improve the distrust between the African American community and law enforcement. While many people will not consider that call to be religious, Cunningham and other theologians would offer an interpretation that suggests through other people and circumstances, God calls us to get involved in human affairs beyond those of our own. Therefore, the word calling is inherently a theological term that is concerned with individuals' relationship to God, humanity, and the earth. A purposeful life is not limited to our own intentions, physical abilities, and ambitions. Rather, it is a life that calls us to religion—which means to reconnect—whether it's organized, disorganized, or organic, to the profound unity of life that is deep within us, between us, transcends us, and that guides us, if not conspires with us, to work on behalf of shaping a more hopeful future.

This future assumes that all of us have a calling and that we are called to participate in shaping the world beyond ourselves in impactful ways. Whether we are in search of a purposeful life or sensing and responding to the world that calls us to act, the future requires our leadership.

CALLING AND LEADERSHIP

Too often people think leadership is limited to the practice of a few people endowed with innate leadership qualities. If this is true, what does leadership mean for the majority of us? What does calling have to do with leadership? These are questions that my colleagues and I at the Forum for Theological Exploration (FTE) have been wrestling with in our work with young adult leaders exploring their purpose, passion, and potential callings to ministry. We challenge traditional understandings of leadership that suggest it is the practice of a few people in key positions in a church, an organization, a community, or the broader society. I would like to define leadership as the practice of inspiring and cultivating individuals to enact God's vision for themselves and their communities. This definition offers an understanding of leadership as a practice that can be exercised by everyone. Leadership is concerned with developing the capacity in oneself and others to act. It assumes that there is a more hopeful vision for each of us and the larger community, and that this vision inspires and invites us to participate in making it a reality.

The assumption is that a calling stands in the gap between what is—reality as we know it—and what could be—a vision of what reality could become in the future. Leadership is the practice between these two domains. Calling, therefore, is a dance with change or a two-step between the present and future. Those pursuing purposeful lives are committed to leading profound change within and beyond themselves.

Leading change within oneself is an invitation to a deeper exploration of the self. Vocation—one's purpose or call—is the foundation of leadership because it asks us to examine questions about our identity, gifts, experiences, values, and passions in relationship to God, others, and the world. The quality of our leadership is inextricably tied to the degree we are willing to examine the vocational themes of our lives. Because we are shaped and formed by multiple communities and experiences, self-examination is best accomplished in relationship to a community or people who are willing to hold us accountable for own actions. Otherwise, there is potential for self-deception and uninformed or destructive leadership practices. People pursuing a calling become aware of a greater interdependency between their inner and external lives. They recognize that their engagement in the world is connected to the degree they are aware of the light and shadow sides of their own practice of leadership. They become more aware of their leadership, values, and needs when they are engaged in the world. Therefore, our commitment to change within and beyond ourselves is an invitation to lead and to shape the broader world in the midst of our own lives in response to an envisioned future we are all called to help create.

CALLED TO SHAPE THE FUTURE

What future does God envision for us? What future do we long to see? What are we willing to do to help give shape to it? These are the types of questions that call us to discern and enact a faithful response. In every generation, Christians have been exploring answers to these questions as more people are called and inspired to follow in the way of Jesus. It's a call to those who partner with God to make the world anew.

Callings are an invitation to take our next most faithful step from the present into a future that is dynamic and responsive versus linear and fixed. What the future will become is shaped by our collective efforts of sensing and responding to the world that is evolving or devolving around us. A dynamic future holds many possibilities. Some scenarios of the future are more probable than others and depend on the degree to which we are willing to work together to create a shared vision of what lies ahead. It is an invitation to co-create, with the Spirit and others, and work toward God's dream for the world that we all long to see, and where the least among us achieve their greatest potential and pursue a purposeful life.

Purposeful people tend to be inspired and compelled to use their gifts and influence to help create a more hopeful future. While some people recognize their purpose as an opportunity to help make the world better without any overt religious convictions, Christians understand purpose in terms of a calling. We understand that our purpose means that we have a role in making the world better and that the future God envisions is dependent on our faithful response to God's calling in our lives. Teresa of Avila reminds us of this fact when she writes:

Christ has no body now but yours. No hands, no feet on earth, but yours. Yours are the eyes through which Christ's compassion looks out on the world. Yours are the feet with which God walks to do good. Yours are the hands with which God is to bless us now.

This is a call to those who are foolish, idealistic, and courageous enough to believe they can help shape the future and ultimately transform the world on behalf of God's peace and love for all.

CARE FOR THE FUTURE

In my work at FTE with young adults, my colleagues and I have discovered that young people want to know what they do with their lives matter. Young adults as well as those not so young want to know that they can make a difference in the world and how to lead change effectively and serve their communities well. These leaders are in search of practices that will help build their capacity to hear and respond to God's calling in their lives and make an impact in the world. We have distilled four communal practices that aid young adults in the exploration of their purpose, passion, and calling, and help catalyze faithful action. Observed and cultivated in faith communities and organizations that notice, name, and nurture people's sense of calling, these practices are:

1. Create space to explore
2. Ask self-awakening questions
3. Reflect theologically about self and community
4. Enact the next faithful step

They grow out of three disciplines—learning, discerning, and acting together—that are essential for creating a rich environment for self-discovery and collective action. When faith communities and organizations continuously engage in these CARE practices over time, they develop their capacity and commitment to care for and attend to people's callings.

The CARE practices are more than an individual and group process for discerning a call. Instead, the practices offer a framework for a faith-based change process for individuals, organizations, and communities, grounded in vocational discernment.[5] It is a process for those who want to lead change out of their own sense of call and desire to partner with what the Holy is doing anew in each of us and for the larger world on behalf of God's care for the earth; compassion for the least of those in our midst; and abiding love for all of humanity. This is a process for those who are looking for a resource to discover their call and what they care deeply about. The CARE process is also for those called to care for the future.

The future that God envisions for us is woven into our own sense of call. The CARE process offers us a way to discern and shape our own future as well as the future of organizations and communities around the world. Recalling that the process is grounded in vocational discernment, the four practices invite us to explore our experiences and our relationship to God, others, and the world. These practices then invite us to take some initial action on what we have discerned in response to the ways we might be called to move from a current reality toward an envisioned future. Throughout the process, we are sensing, responding, and shaping the future as it emerges. There is no one or right way to enact this process because the ways for doing so vary with context and practice over time. Let's explore the four CARE practices.

Create Space to Explore

Legendary educator and theologian Howard Thurman says:

There is something in you that waits and listens for the sound of the genuine in yourself—and if you can not hear it, you will never find whatever it is for which you are searching and if you hear it and then do not follow it, it was better that you had never been born.[6]

This "something" is known by many names—God, spirit, inner voice or knowing, intuition or gut instinct—and seeks to reveal what is authentic or rings true within us. Thurman suggests that this something is our only true guide in life. Creating space is about establishing an environment to listen and explore the guiding force that animates our lives and discloses what is true or genuine in our lives, others, and the broader world. Given our busy, frenetic lives, we need breathing space to think and listen to our lives into fuller expression. Thurman offers a description of the busyness we experience too often particularly within ourselves. He writes:

There are so many noises going on inside of you, so many echoes of all sorts, so many internalizing of the rumble and the traffic, the confusions, the disorders by which your environment is peopled that I wonder if you can get still enough—not quiet enough—still enough to hear rumbling up from your unique and essential idiom the sound of the genuine in you.[7]

Thurman's point about stillness suggests another important character in creating space to explore. It is about establishing moments of stillness in order to explore the depths of our lives. Stillness can disrupt patterns of busyness in order for us to be present in the moment and to facilitate meaningful conversations and reflections between ourselves and others.

Spaces of stillness require that we slow down and will improve the quality of our awareness and exploration. For example, the posted interstate speed limit where I live typically is 65 miles per hour. Drivers, however, travel at a speed of 75–80 miles per hour. What I have observed is moving at a faster pace or in a hurry requires more intense focus than traveling at a slower pace and limits our ability to appreciate the people, places, and things we pass by quickly. The interstate is a metaphor for our lives. The quality of our experiences and exploration are diminished when we move quickly through life. Establishing explorative spaces coupled with stillness enable us to slow down and become more aware and present to our experiences and questions.

Another quality about creating explorative space has to do with place. In some instances, space is a created place where we go to retreat from the monotony of routine. Aesthetically appealing places play an important role in establishing a rich environment for exploration. We are able to connect on a deeper level and explore possibilities more fully in places aided by nature, beauty, and the arts. In other instances, these types of places are not always available and we create space by the way we are present with each other.

Agreements with regard to talking, exploring, and reflecting together are another important way to create space necessary to explore questions of meaning and purpose. These agreements represent how we covet to be present with one another, which may be different from normative ways we interact with others. I use the following covenants when creating space:[8]

- Be fully present, extend welcome, and presume we are welcomed.
- Acknowledge one another as equals.
- Stay curious about each other.
- Recognize that we need each other's help to become better listeners.
- Slow down so we have time to think and reflect.
- Expect our conversations to be messy at times.
- Know that it is possible for us to emerge from our time together refreshed, surprised, and less burdened than when we came.

The agreements you may use will vary depending on the context and space that you are trying to create with the people with whom you are working.

Spaces that incorporate stillness, slowing down, place, and agreements create environments for deep exploration and help us shift the way we see, think and act together. People called to shape the future create these types of spaces for themselves and others to listen and to investigate the deep callings in their lives.

Ask Self-Awakening Questions

When we create safe environments for exploration, we offer each other opportunities to search the deeper meaning of our lives and hear one another into deeper expression. Self-awakening questions have the capacity to open us to a lifelong journey of discernment and self-excavation. They "offer you a lifetime of pondering, that will lead you toward what you need to know for your integrity, draw to you what you need for your journey, and . . . lead you to others whose lives are propelled by the same questions."[9]

People who explore these types of questions discover a sacred invitation to listen for the deep yearnings in their lives. Callings are often hidden in these yearnings—what moves us and makes us come alive. This was the case for Romal Tune. Several years ago, he attended an event I was hosting and began exploring self-awakening questions. Tune's reflections on his experience demonstrate the power of these questions and the hidden callings waiting to be discovered in our lives. One of the self-awakening questions Tune was prompted to explore was: Why do you do what you do, love what you love, or care about what you care about? He writes[10]:

> The reflections, group discussions and questions raised and spending time with people courageous enough to help each other pursue deeper meaning and purpose, changed my life. It gave me the courage to try. With the help of friends I started writing the plan for a new organization that would seek to connect churches across the country to implement strategies that will improve the academic performance of under-performing students living in poverty and attending high needs schools. With the help of friends courageous enough to try something new, we created Faith for Change.

While we may not initially know what moves us, self-awakening questions start us on quests in search for the elusive clues disclosed in the synchronicity of our hopes and dreams, gifts and passions, choices we are deliberating, what breaks and breaks open our hearts, what we are motivated by, what we value, and what matters to us. Our personal encounters and relationships with the world around us will help us to become more aware of the clues that help us excavate our life's callings.

Self-awakening questions also provide an opportunity to listen intently to one another into fuller expression. The gift of listening is probably one of the best gifts we can offer to each other. In Tune's reflection, he attributes this kind of listening to be an act of courage—from the Latin root word *cor*, which means heart. When we listen courageously, we listen with our hearts to the hearts of others. Self-awakening questions are in many ways an expression of love and remind me of Rainer Maria Rilke's wisdom about questions: "Be patient toward all that is unsolved in your heart and try to love the questions themselves . . . Live the questions now. Perhaps you will then gradually, without noticing it, live along some distant day into the answer."

Reflect Theologically about Self and Community

How do we make sense of the clues that emerge from our responses to self-awakening questions? What do our answers reveal in us, to us, and to others? Theological reflection helps us to address these questions and provides an opportunity to reflect differently on our stories and circumstances that typically are explored within the domains of business, economics, health, science, psychology, the environment, politics, and so on. Reflecting theologically encourages us to explore these domains in relationship to God, self, others and the world, and to discern what actions to take.

When we reflect theologically we ask questions like: Where do we see God engaged in the world? What aspect of the future will mourn if we don't discover and pursue our calling? What scriptures, traditions, stories, or artifacts offer insights into our circumstances? This practice enables us to pay attention to the deeper patterns and connections in our lives. We connect the dots between our stories and longings with God's story and yearnings for humanity and the world. We become aware of our feelings in response to the circumstances of life because what moves us moves God.

When practiced in community, theological reflection will help us become more aware of the needs of others, our communities, and the world and, in turn, discover how God calls us to develop purposeful solutions to address these needs. Let's return to Tune's reflections to illustrate this point. He says[11]:

> I have a passion for reaching out to poor and at-risk youth, which seems simple enough, but this time I was asked to explain why through my personal story. After reflecting on my life experiences, I told a story about when I was 11 years old. It was a cold, foggy morning in San Francisco. My mother had given me bus fare to get to school and home at the end of the day. When she handed me my bus fare, she looked at me with sadness in her eyes and said, "We don't have enough for you to eat lunch today." I got to school and went through the routine of the day, attending classes but was somewhat distracted by the fact that I was getting hungry and concerned that if other kids saw that I didn't get in the lunch line, they would know I didn't have money and make fun of me. When lunchtime came I had to make a hard choice: use my bus fare to buy lunch, eat and avoid potential embarrassment but then have to figure out how I was going to get home, or go hungry but get home without a problem. On that day I chose lunch.
>
> At the end of the school day I walked as far as I could so that the other kids could not see me. I started looking for strangers that I could ask for bus fare. There were those who cut their eyes at me as if I should be ashamed of myself for asking if they had any change to help me get home. There were those who avoided making eye contact with me so that I wouldn't ask. But

then there was that one woman who looked me in the eyes, smiled and said, "What do you need to get home?" It was a dollar and 25 cents.

It wasn't until I attended this retreat, I recognized that day in my life as an encounter with God, an experience of grace. I learned that my story and experiences are what God has used to guide my vocation and passion for helping poor and at-risk youth.

Tune's story is a wonderful theological reflection and example of how he became more aware of why he cares about at-risk youth. He is shaping the future of at-risk youth around the country as a result of discovering what he cares about. His story shows us that reflecting theologically can be a meaningful exercise of making sense of the dots that connect our lives and lead us toward how we are called to act.

Enact the Next Faithful Step

Caring for the future is an act of responsibility. Theologian Dietrich Bonhoeffer says, "Action springs from a readiness for responsibility." Enacting our next faithful step assumes a readiness to act responsibly on what we have been discerning. It is an invitation to dream and envision what is possible—what the world could become if we acted boldly and lived faithfully into our callings. This type of enactment is a call to change the things we can no longer live with in the world. It offers us an opportunity to try something small, experiment with an idea, learn from it and see what may bloom in the days and years to come. Enactment is a movement toward a future distinct from the present but informed by the wisdom of the past. We do not know what our faithful acts will yield but we step forward on the substance of hope and the evidence of what is possible.

When we begin to enact our next faithful step, we first envision what is now possible given what we have explored and discerned. We then explore how we might enact what resonates with us by asking questions. How might I shape the future of my city through my interests in politics and religion? How might we make a difference in the community through Christian ministry? The key is to dream and ask questions in close proximity to your gifts and talents, what you care about, constituents you seek to work with or communities you want to serve.

These questions then spark our own imagination and invite us to brainstorm the number of ways we can address them. Brainstorming is a participatory process that takes advantage of multiple people's perspectives in hopes of surfacing a viable idea that people have some level of investment in or care enough to try something. Last year, I hosted a consultation with congregational leaders because FTE was interested in discerning how it might best support congregations working with young adults in vocational exploration. On the last day of the event, I invited participants to brainstorm the best ways we might resource congregations in vocational discernment efforts with young adults. We explored the following question: How might FTE best utilize grants over two years to seed or strengthen congregations' efforts to assist young adults in exploring vocation and Christian ministry? Participants divided into two teams and began exploring a number of possibilities. In 30 minutes, they generated more than three dozen ideas. We then looked for common themes between the ideas, what resonated with FTE, and what was complimentary to the organization's own sense of call. Recalling Tune's story, he explored: How might I shape the future of at-risk youth as a result of my own experiences? In his reflection, Tune noted that with the help of friends he came up with a solution aligned with his emerging sense of call.

The next step is to step out on faith and try something. It is an invitation to take small, bold steps of enactment in order to learn and discover new insights into the ways we might be called. Trying something new involves acting quickly and prototyping vocational inclinations in order to discern, test, and affirm our purpose. It often does not come without some kind of change or sacrifice. Tune tried something new and started the organization Faith for Change, authored and published *God's Graffiti: Inspiring Stories for Teen*, and began traveling across the country and internationally, working with at-risk youth. Faithful steps toward opportunities that disclose deeper meaning and purpose bring with each step changes in our lives. Taking small but bold, faithful steps is about experimenting with incremental change necessary to shape the future. While change is hard for most, people pursuing their calling cannot avoid it.

What we are called to care deeply for in the world demands nothing less of us because callings change us. The future that calls us to shape it on behalf of God and our deep yearnings is possible when we are committed to taking the next faithful steps toward pursuing our calling. These four practices can help catalyze the faithful action of all of us who feel called to shape the future.

CONCLUSION

How are you called to shape the future? This is a self-awakening question for all of us who sense a call to live a life of meaning and purpose. What other reason could there be for our existence? If we never develop the capacity to listen to the truth of our lives and discover the ways we are called to care for ourselves, others, and the world, it's better if we had never existed at all. The faithful, wise, and courageous young leaders I have the pleasure of working with feel the fierce urgency of now that calls them to care and shape a world that is more just, equitable, green, bountiful, and more filled with peace and goodwill toward all. Motivated by faith, these leaders search for what all citizens of the world seek: a more hopeful and promising future for themselves and those they love. Will you join them and help shape the future of our communities, religious institutions, schools, businesses, and economic systems around the world? When you embark upon this journey, you will begin to build a bridge that generations to come will cross over into a future we all helped to shape.

NOTES

1. Jung, C.G. (1961). *Memories, dreams, reflections* (pp. 233–234). New York: Random House.

2. Oliver, M. (2008). Summer days. In *Truro bear and other adventures: Poems and essays* (p. 65) Boston, MA: Beacon Press.

3. Damon, W., Menon, J., & Bronk, K.C. (2003). The development of purpose during adolescence, *Applied Developmental Science, 7,* 121.

4. From a Conversation I had with David Cunningham, Professor of Religion at Hope College in Holland, MI, August 28, 2013.

5. Baker D, Lewis S, & Williams M. (Forthcoming, 2016). *The Care Effect: Living and Leading Change for Good.* St. Louis: Chalice Press.

6. Thurman, H. (1980, May 4). *Sound of the genuine.* In the Spelman Messenger. Moore, Jo. (Ed.). Baccalaureate Address at Spelman College, Atlanta, GA, *96,* 14–15.

7. Ibid.

8. Adapted from the Center for Courage and Renewal. (2010). *Circles of trust.* Seattle, WA and Wheatley, M. (2002). *Turning to one another: Simple conversations to restore hope to the future* (pp. 335–336). San Francisco, CA: Berrett-Koehler, Kindle Loc.

9. Levoy, G. (2008). *Callings: Finding and following an authentic life* (p. 7). New York: Three Rivers Press.

10. Tune, R. (2011, September 2). Finding purpose in the field [Web log post]. Retrieved from: http://fteleaders.org/blog/finding-purpose-in-the-field.

11. Tune, R. (2010, September 27). Finding grace at a bus stop: Why I owe my vocation to a childhood encounter with God [Web log post]. Retrieved from: http://www.huffingtonpost.com/rev-romal-j-tune/finding-vocation-at-a-bus_b_740093.html.

CHAPTER 15

SACRIFICE: THE SHADOW
IN THE CALLING

Gregg Levoy

Sacrifice is rightly considered the shadow in the calling, the price we pay for following it. But the aim of sacrifice—true to its definition, "to make sacred"—is to forge a link with whatever is greater than ourselves, whether that is God, community, nature, the future, the greater good, or even our own potential.

This chapter explores the nature of sacrifice as it relates to callings, and to the work of unfolding and evolving that we deem essential to us both individually and collectively. Weighing historical, psychospiritual, anecdotal as well as personal evidence, it examines the various forms that sacrifice can take, the role it plays in the fruition of callings, and the ways in which it is a demand of the soul against the ego, a surrender that may feel like defeat but is liberation.

In his book *Care of the Soul,* psychotherapist and former monk Thomas Moore refers to sacrifice as "the shadow in the calling"—the price we pay for following it.

We may be called upon to relinquish the precious commodities of time and energy, securities of one kind or another, a regular paycheck, other people's approval. Or we may have to cede self-limiting beliefs, the internal resistance that stands in our way, and the false composure—the bliss of ignorance—bred by living safely and avoiding risk.

Faith will eventually ask of the faithful, "What are you willing to give up to follow your callings?"

My aim in this chapter is to explore the role that sacrifice plays in callings, in the work of unfolding and evolving that we deem essential to us both individually and collectively. I'll examine the various forms that sacrifice can take, why people tend to avoid it (and thus often the fruition of their callings), and the ways in which it is a demand of the soul against the ego, a surrender of the bounded for the boundless, the profane for the sacred, which may feel like defeat but is liberation. I'll also examine the ways in which sacrifice is a *skill*, a muscle that can be strengthened.

As a writer and reporter, I've investigated the topic of callings for several decades, written about it for numerous publications, and dialogued with hundreds of people about their callings, culminating in my book *Callings: Finding and Following an Authentic Life* (Random House). My approach is less from a traditionally scientific or theological vantage point than from an applied and intuitive perspective, geared more toward the lay person.

I've come to see that the future isn't just a place where we'll be spending a great deal of our time; it's also the abode of the life we want, the place where word becomes flesh, and the visions we have for ourselves solidify. And callings are like homing pigeons for these visions, showing us not so much the way back to ourselves, as forward.

But they also invariably come bundled with the call to surrender the past, and even the present, in order to move forward and respond to what our lives are calling-for from us, and this requires reckoning with what these calls will demand of us.

Sacrifice is part of the ferocity of faith, the unspoken demand that in order to maintain that faith, we have to part ways with the familiar and comfortable, perhaps even dismantle what may seem like the very girders of our lives, in the process of which we're likely to suffer a kind of sticker shock.

But the act of turning away from the familiar is central to a calling. The Islamic call to prayer, for example, sounds from the minarets five times a day, as it has for 15 centuries, calling the faithful to turn from their daily chores, toward worship. But the anxiety people feel around the notion of sacrifice is evident in the visceral associations we have with it—loss, deprivation, punishment, suffering, slaughter, virgins into volcanos.

Callings may point us in the direction of the transcendent, but that's not all we contemplate when considering whether to follow them, even when they arrive on the wings of the numinous. After the initial epiphany subsides, we're faced with very human anxieties: am I going to succeed or fail, am I going to be able pay the bills with it, what will others think, what will I sacrifice if I say yes, what will I sacrifice if I say no? After all, in order to quit a job and become self-employed, one has to let go of a regular paycheck. To write a memoir, one has to yield privacy. To collaborate with others, power and control need to be shared.

This undoubtedly explains, as the mythologist Joseph Campbell has shown in *The Hero With a Thousand Faces* (1949), why phase-one of responding to a call is typically avoiding it, backing away lobster-like into safe recesses. Campbell named this stage of the hero's journey "the refusal of the call."

It explains, too, why at the edges of ancient maps, the old cartographers depicted terra incognito—what lay beyond the known world—as a place populated with dragons, ogres, sea serpents, and ships being pulled under by the tentacles of giant squid, all of which was sufficient to keep most folks within the confines of the village. The philosopher Friedrich Nietzsche was fond of encouraging people to "live dangerously. Build your cities on the slopes of Vesuvius! Send your ships into uncharted seas!" (1882, p. 106) But it's a sentiment that sounds inspiring on a poster, and is another matter entirely in the lives of ordinary people.

Sacrifice is also a sensitive subject for recovering Catholics, adult children of martyrs, and anyone who has spent substantial portions of life sacrificing their own needs for those of others. To them, sacrifice comes freighted with an emotional charge that repels them.

TRADING THE TEMPORAL FOR THE TRANSCENDENT

Sacrifice, in a Jungian context, may feel like a renunciation the ego makes in deference to the soul or spirit, to more transcendent yearnings, a surrender that may be liberation but often feels like defeat, like a demotion from being the Mover to being the Moved. But it's also a swapping of something temporal for something transcendent. In fact, the aim of sacrifice is to forge a link with what's greater than ourselves, whether that's God, community, nature, the future, the greater good, or even our own potential.

The original Hebrew word for sacrifice meant to bring nearer (Jewish Virtual Library.org), and, like gift-giving, it creates a bond. It's the signature of a contract, a covenant between two parties who need each other for some larger purpose, and a mutually beneficial one.

It could be said that Thy Will Be Done merges with My Will Be Done to create Our Will Be Done, and this may be the only way anything *gets* done.

Anyone who's experienced a long-term relationship probably knows intuitively that healthy mutuality is very much a function of the small sacrifices of self—if not ego—that the individual partners make over time. To the degree that both communal life and callings involve us in service, in something greater than ourselves, they require a decentralizing of self, an extending of awareness beyond our own borders, which is often felt as relinquishment.

A rabbi of my acquaintance once counseled me that I should write despite all obstacles and resistances from within and without, because writing is ultimately a labor of love, like service, and he said, "it's not about you. It's not about whether you're comfortable, or whether you can measure the effect of your good deeds, or whether anybody even says thank you. It's about something you need to say that you believe the world needs to hear, and you should say it as much because the world needs to hear it as because you need to say it."

Another aid to reframing sacrifice from deprivation to liberation, if not sublimity, is this historical footnote: whatever (or whoever) was sacrificed was first often placed on an altar—a Hebrew word that literally means a place of slaughter or sacrifice. In other words, elevated, revered, made sacred. Not just done away with. By making a sacrifice, we honor not just what dies, but the *act* of death, the skill of dying.

Whatever we have to relinquish to follow a calling is, in a sense, giving its life for our benefit and unfoldment, and we sanctify it by recognizing that we wouldn't be able to liberate ourselves to follow that calling without its sacrifice. This is no more defeat than a flower suffers defeat by going to seed. And as theologian Frederich Buechner has said, "What's lost is nothing to what's found, and all the death that ever was, set next to life, would scarcely fill a cup."

In the religions, mythologies, and psychologies of the world, as Joseph Campbell (1949/2008) reveals in his treatises on the "hero's journey," surrender is seldom envisioned as defeat, but liberation, and sacrifice typically precedes a resurrection. This explains why God proved merciful once Jonah finally took the plunge. It explains why the "birthdays" of the Christian martyrs—those extremists for liberation—are celebrated on their death days, because that's when they were considered to have been truly "born." Like evaporating water, we give up an earthly bond in order to rise.

And whether we sacrificed a fatted calf or our precious time and money, in the spirit of healthy denial we sacrificed something we wanted for something we wanted even more, which was typically the good graces of the gods and goddesses; to literally draw the divine down into human affairs. And ideally what we gained by our veneration was more valuable than what we lost.

To insure fertility, farmers and shepherds thus yielded up their first fruits to the gods. To help educate people about wildlife, zookeepers cage a certain number of animals in hopes of saving the bulk of them. In helping children build self-esteem, parents and teachers encourage them to weigh their *own* voices along with those of their elders.

If we didn't devoutly believe that a greater good would be served by our sacrifices, we probably wouldn't make them. Forward momentum requires that the prospect of what might be gained in pursuing a call needs to outweigh the loss sustained in attempting it, and if we can convince ourselves that though our loss may be significant, it's still a small price to pay for the possible benedictions, we've cleared a high hurdle in following a call.

Even when leaving a job or a home, relinquishing security or status, can be seen as worth the chance at a more authentic life, a clearer conscience, and a deeper connection with whatever is greater than ourselves. The scale can tip in favor of sacrifice, and the odds tip in favor of a payoff.

WIRED FOR CAUTIOUSNESS

Humans, however, tend to avoid sacrifice, and the risk-taking inherent in it, in part because it's human nature to worry about the future. The brain that helped get us through the evolutionary maze comes equipped with a worry meter set somewhere near the middle of the spectrum. Too much of it would have been constraining, too little would have incited foolhardiness, but either way we're wired to be cautious, our brains having clocked quite a bit more time focusing on danger than delight, on negative than positive stimuli.

For example, brain imaging studies conducted at the University of Iowa, cited in Kay Redfield Jamison's book *Exuberance* (2004, p. 95) have demonstrated that when people are shown pictures that are either pleasant (an ice cream sundae, puppies, mountain scenery, a couple on the beach at sunset), unpleasant (a garbage pile, a rotting dog carcass, a dead soldier with part of his face missing, an unflushed toilet, a sink full of dirty dishes), or neutral (a fire hydrant, an umbrella, a dustpan, a blow-dryer), the unpleasant pictures activated ancient subcortical parts of the brain that scientists call the danger-recognition system, while the pleasant pictures lit up a much younger part of the brain, the prefrontal cortex.

This may help explain why it's easier to focus on the negative than the positive in challenging situations, on what could go wrong rather than what could go right—what we might sacrifice rather than what we might gain. It may explain, too, as Harvard psychiatrist George Vaillant has shown in the journal *Mental Health, Spirituality, Mind* (2008, pp. 48–62) why psychology textbooks have traditionally devoted far more space to negative emotions like depression and phobia than positive ones like joy and happiness, and why, as Robert Schrauf (2009, pp. 266–284) wrote in an article in *Journal of Multilingual and Multicultural Development* cross-cultural language studies have found that nearly every society has a great deal more words and concepts for negative than positive emotional states.

Furthermore, at any stage of the game, from infancy on, if someone has a choice between satisfying the need for security and the need for growth, security will generally win out. For example, when toddlers venture beyond the protected harbor of their mothers in order to explore their surroundings, even just an unfamiliar room, that odyssey is dependent on their mothers being there when they look back over their shoulders. If she suddenly disappears, the urge to explore is short-circuited and the toddler returns to port, and might even regress to crawling back rather than walking.

Anxiety makes evolutionary sense, of course, prompting us to consider the consequences of our actions, concern ourselves with the fate of our offspring, and anticipate what dangers might lie around the next bend. But when it comes to that equally human need for what is commonly called "self-actualization"—in which callings play a prominent role—the worry-meter may need to be gently reset toward exhibition rather than inhibition, toward risk and growth rather than security and comfort, and a vigilant eye may need to be kept on the modern brain's tendency to grind us to a halt sweating the small stuff and spinning out fearful scenarios.

That is, we worry not just because we come from a long line of worriers, and been tutored in the arts of worry since childhood—and certainly not because we always have good *reason* to worry—but because that's what happens when you mix fear with abstract thinking, fear with the question "What if?"

The future, of course, is squarely in the realm of "What if?" And sacrifices are bets with the future, wagers that the investments we make now will pay off then. They're also prime examples of anxiety meeting courage. This is because the future is like fog. It can't be seen into it and can't be controlled, and that worries us. We can plant seeds, or bury them for later, but there's no guarantee they won't get dug up before then, or germinate and bear fruit. The arts of prophesying and prognostication are little more than blowing on dice and rubbing magic lamps. Even weather forecasting and medical prognosis—attempts to bridle nature with science—are riddled with uncertainties.

Similarly, we probably intuit that following calls is no guarantee of success or security or happiness. The shadow in the calling sees to that. There are sacrifices, surrenders, renunciations, and suffering involved in any call, in addition to successes and self-actualization.

Our forebears who first devised rites of passage, says Campbell (initiations from childhood to adulthood, single to married, or ignorance to wisdom), understood that one must be tested, that death must precede resurrection into a new way of being, that even ritual or symbolic death is frightening, and that the entree into enlightenment comes with a side-order of holy terror ("Let this cup pass from me"), and that one must have the appetite for it.

Callings, too—in any arena, whether vocational, relational, spiritual, or creative—come bundled with not only a measure of sacred anxiety, but the passion to help fuel them, and passion comes from a word meaning to suffer. In other words, it's inherent in whatever future we're called toward that there's going to be some suffering, and as software designers say about glitches in their programs, it's a feature and not a bug.

In fact, if sacrifice doesn't involve some suffering, doesn't put us out, it might be insufficient to bring on the changes we're after in following calls. If one's marriage is crying out for attention, giving up the occasional golf game probably won't suffice to call it back from the brink. If we're called to share our art or writing with the world, showing it only to friends and family isn't stepping all the way up to the plate.

One of the common misconceptions about callings—and the heroes' journeys they propel us into—is that if we just say yes, the universe will fall in line behind us and the supernal gates will swing open before us; that if we bear the cross, we'll automatically get to wear the crown.

Maybe, maybe not.

Nor are great struggles inevitably followed by great triumphs. Sometimes great struggles are followed by more great struggles.

To say yes to a calling is to move toward it, and to move toward it is to confront the paradoxical universe. We may move toward light and be beset by shadows, move toward wholeness and be pried apart, reach for a dream and be rudely awakened.

Just as in monastic life, in which there are periods of candidacy and novitiate before the taking of vows, so callings are tested. We're tempted and distracted, suffer laziness, amnesia, and the siren song of old habits, and must continually answer the question of whether our commitments are real or imagined. We're also tested on our ability to prevail over setbacks—in mythic parlance, to transmute their flax into gold.

THE ADVENT OF SACRIFICE

The ability to navigate this transmutation—to see setbacks and surrenders as act one of a two-act play, the second of which is breakthrough and liberation—is key to strengthening the muscles of risk-taking, and the skill of sacrifice.

The original definition of adventure, after all, was that of "something about to happen," as in Advent celebrating the coming of Christ. So a sense of adventure is related to a sense of *anticipation* about life, the prospect of new growth. This is helped along if we always give ourselves something to look forward to, and if we understand that though we have anxiety about the future, we also have *hope*, and it's this adventurous hope—perhaps even the blind spiritual instinct that tells us our lives have purpose and meaning—that propels us to make sacrifices on behalf of calls.

But hope is not just the conviction that things will turn out well. It's the intuition that things make *sense*, regardless of how they turn out. So even if callings don't unfold according to hope and expectation, there's still adventure to be had even in disappointment and suffering. There's discovery in it, and fascination, and growth, should we choose to investigate. Dark nights of the soul and trials by fire are every bit as rich in these things as days of wine and roses. The poet E. E. Cummings wrote a book called *The Enormous Room* while in *jail*. And Wendell Berry once remarked that "The mind that is not baffled is not employed. The impeded stream is the one that sings."

Abraham Maslow, who popularized the term self-actualization, didn't generally believe in a big-bang theory of it, in which peak experiences suddenly bring us into being as the people we've always imagined ourselves to be, or deliver us to transcendence on the back of a great white stallion of revelation. Toward the end of his life, he talked about a kind of time-release version of the peak experience that he called the *plateau* experience (1964).

It's a sort of an ongoing peak experience that is more calm and less climactic, more a discipline than an event, and which we only slowly and painstakingly teach ourselves to experience by choosing to *sacrilize* life. To witness it in the deepest and most mindful ways by paying exquisite attention to it, exposing ourselves to inspiring people, great music and art, the raptures of nature, and living in a more or less permanent state of being turned on to the *full* spectrum of experiences, from the joyous to the jarring. Maslow called it "holding classes in miraculousness," the word miracle coming from a Latin root meaning to wonder at.

Thus, looked at rightly—that is, turning them into objects of contemplation—sacrifice and suffering, or for that matter any item from our daily litany of complaints, can potentially become a portal back, or perhaps forward, to a sense of wonder and sacredness, and reconnect us to the primary calling of *all* creatures: maximum aliveness. As the author and psychotherapist Mark Epstein says in *Open to Desire*, "Practitioners of the yoga of desire have discovered that the disappointment inherent in desire can be *interesting.*"

Malsow also believed that self-actualizing types are "those who make the growth choice instead of the fear choice—a dozen times a day." And herein may lie one of the keys to strengthening the skill of sacrifice and pushing ourselves beyond the limits we perceive and set for ourselves, into the uncertain future: the regular taking of manageable risks, stepping from the sidelines onto the playing field, and identifying those moments of choice that take us either toward or away from our calls, and the authenticity they lead us toward.

A useful analogy might be that in the natural world the edge is where the action is. The zone between two ecosystems—water and land, or field and forest—is where the greatest diversity and productivity are found, as well as the most predation. This is fitting, as the Greek word for this region, an ecotone, means tension. But it's characterized by a fertility that biologists call the edge effect.

In human affairs, the ecotone between the life we have and the life we want, between our present condition and our potential, is equally fruitful if not fitful, full of productivity and predation, passion and suffering. The exercise of pushing beyond our assumed limits into this zone of intensity and virility, in search of fulfillment or new possibilities, is rightly referred to by sociologists as edgework, which is a kind of personal anarchy, an affirmative revolt against stuckness, as well as the entrapments and over-determined nature of everyday life.

But it's not a loss or even surrender of control so much as an acute sort of self-control, argues Texas Christian University sociologist Jeff Ferrell in *Making Trouble*. It's self-control in place of control by others, whether church and state or job and gender, and it's based on the understanding that if you don't control yourself, somebody else will. "It's self-control for the sake of self-determination," Ferrell says. "Self-control in the interest of holding on to your life while letting go of it."

When facing into the headwinds of a calling, which challenges us to let go of the familiar and turn our sights toward the future, to forgo who we are for who we must become, another skill that we can bring to bear is what Winifred Gallagher, the former psychology editor of *American Health* magazine and author of the book *New*, refers to as "neophilia"—the enthusiasm for novelty that's at the heart of the exploratory urge.

She considers it the quintessential human survival skill, whether we're adapting to climate change on the primordial African savannah, sending our ships into uncharted seas, or coping with the computerization of modern life and what she calls our desk-tethered world. And researchers studying the traits that characterize people who tend to flourish over the years, Gallagher claims, have found that such people tend to score high in novelty-seeking.

Some of us are neophiliacs and some neophobes—people who shy away from novelty and adventure, and the sacrifices they entail—and most of us fall on the broad spectrum between. But neophilia's grand design, Gallagher says, is to help us learn and create, as well as adapt to the moving target that is the world, both then and now. "It's all about anticipation, desire, *wanting*."

So is a calling. It may come unbidden, but it requires human desire to come to life, to bring flesh to word and form to faith. We have to *want* to follow it. In other words, a calling is negotiable. It's not a divine subpoena, irrespective of free will and desire. We have a vote, a voice. We get to decide when and how and how much.

But a call also has the effect of setting a weight down on one side of a scale, and equilibrium isn't restored until we set an equal weight on the other side—a response. And that response is a coming back to the center of gravity, an almost physical sense of relief. And as we become practiced at following calls—the big ones as well as the small daily risks that are the fire-drills for the bigger ones—even our most spontaneous responses to life begin to take on the quality of well-considered decisions. Reason and instinct become nearly indistinguishable.

Furthermore, the physics of inspiration being what they are, our individual work serves the work of the world, the work of evolving. And then, as the psychologist Rollo May put it in *Freedom and Destiny*, "We don't just dream. We dream in a socially useful way."

And when we look to the future with anticipation, with a sense of adventure—and see ourselves as passionate and resilient—we make ourselves a gift to the life of the spirit. And that life reciprocates. Our lives then become a seamless broadloom of call-and-response, and an endless exchange of gifts.

REFERENCES

Berry, W. (2011). *Standing by words*. New York: Counterpoint.

Buechner, F. (1999). *Godric*. New York: HarperCollins.

Campbell, J. (1949/2008). *Hero with a thousand faces*. Novato, CA: New World Library.

Epstein, M. (2006). *Open to desire*. New York: Gotham Books.

Ferrell, J. (1999). *Making trouble*. Piscataway, NJ: Aldine Transaction.

Gallagher, W. (2011). *New*. New York: Penguin Books.

Jamison, K., R. (2004). *Exuberance*. New York: Alfred A. Knopf.

Maslow, A. (1964). *Religions values and peak experiences*. New York: Penguin.

May, R. (2012). *Freedom and destiny*. New York: W.W. Norton & Co.

Moore, T. (1994). *Care of the soul*. New York: Harper Perennial.

Nietzsche, F. (2009). *The gay science (The joyful wisdom)*. New York: Digreads.com.

Schrauf, R. (2009). *Journal of Multilingual and Multicultural Development*, 25(2–3), 266–84.

Vaillant, G. (2008). *Mental Health, Spirituality, Mind*, 6(1), 48–62.

CHAPTER 16

"I HAVE BEEN ANOINTED AND I HAVE FLEECED THE LORD": THE CONTEMPORARY SERPENT HANDLERS OF APPALACHIA AND THEIR EXPERIENCE OF BEING CALLED BY GOD

Ralph W. Hood Jr.

Based upon over 20 years of ethnographic research on a marginal religious sect located primarily in the Southern Appalachian Mountains, this chapter aims to explore believers who feel called by God to be obedient to what they take as the plain meaning of the Gospel of Mark 16:17–18. In the words of the only Bible acceptable to serpent handlers, the King James Bible, Mark 16:17 states: "And these signs shall follow them that believe; In my name shall they cast out devils; they shall speak with new tongues; They shall take up serpents; and if they drink any deadly thing, it shall not hurt them; they shall lay hands on the sick, and they shall recover" (Mark 16:17–18).

The meaning of this Gospel was debated among Primitive Pentecostals as they moved toward denominational status in America. The handling of serpents and drinking of poison specified in this passage in Mark was strongly supported by the Church of God and its splinter offshoot, the Church of God of Prophecy. However, as maiming and death became more common, these denominations backed off from supporting serpent handling and it remained for the renegade Churches of God to continue the practice (Williamson & Hood, 1994).

This study uses the in-depth interviews with three serpent handling families by Brown and McDonald (2000). They were edited and approved by those interviewed. It places the words of these families within the data base of the Hood-Williamson Research Archives for the Holiness Serpent Handling Sects of Appalachia. The archive is housed in the Lupton Library of the University of Tennessee at Chattanooga that contains over digitized video material that has followed these families for over 20 years. In their own words, this study explores how handlers called to obedience in their understanding of Mark 16:17–18 narrate why they handle serpents and drink poison. Whether by faith alone in the anointing, or by fleecing their Lord, these handlers describe what is like to be called by God to snake handling, in a tradition that we argue is more maligned than understood.

Concerns regarding the persistence of faith in modern secular countries continue to raise serious questions for contemporary psychology. One position with a long history is the adoption of Flournoy's (1907) demand that the then emerging scientific psychology of religion adhere to the methodical principle of the exclusion of the transcendent in any psychological explanation of religion. While such a principle has appealed to many contemporary psychologists, its limits are now recognized to be far from neutral. The debate that has emerged in psychology is mirrored in Porpora's (2006) critical analysis of the sociology of religion whose overarching assumption is the methodological atheism most forcefully championed by Peter Berger (1967, p. 100) and best summarized by the claim that "every inquiry that limits itself to the empirically available must necessarily be based upon 'methodological atheism.'" However, Berger (himself a believer) has noted that to adopt a position of methodological exclusion of the transcendent is to provide not a neutral objective explanation of religion, but rather amounts to a "quasi-scientific legitimation of a secularized worldly view" (Berger, 1974, p. 128). Recently, we have argued that the methodological principle appropriate to the psychology of religion is a methodological agnosticism that cannot argue that individuals who experience God must in some sense be deluded (Hood, 2012). To suggest that is but an act of hubris. Porpora has argued the same for the sociology of religion. This methodological agnosticism leaves open important ontological issues such as the existence of God. That is all the more relevant to a psychology or sociology of religion that would expand our understanding of religion rather than explain it away.

In a volume devoted to those who feel called, it is appropriate that data derived from ethnographic research, more common in anthropology than psychology, be addressed. For instance, in her own research about modern American Evangelicals who talk to God, Luhrman 2012) as a psychological anthropologist, documents the ways Evangelicals learn to identify and respond to their God, who in fact is perceived to talk back to believers. Wisely, she brackets any claims to delusion that have troubled psychologists whose commitment to Flournoy's principle. Their commitment would diminish the data and insights Luhrman provides. Flourney's principle brings to bear discussions of hallucination or delusion that have haunted mainstream psychologists. They are always baffled by religious experiences whose occurrence psychologists cannot attribute to the reality. Many simply do not believe what other actually experience as God (See Hood, Hill, & Spilka, 1999, pp. 293–294).

Thus, Luhrman wisely titled her book, *When God Talks Back*. Luhrman neither denies nor affirms the ontological claims explicit or implicit in the testimony by Evangelicals who talk to God and to whom God respond. Nor does Lurhman cross the line that would permit an honest dialogue between religious (or theological) assertions and more social scientific claims. This is one reasonable tactic, but not one that should necessarily be taken as a model. In this chapter we will approach the issue of anointing and fleecing among contemporary serpent handlers of Appalachia. In a book devoted to callings, serpent handlers provide a litmus test on being called within a faith tradition, marginalized especially by social scientists distant from the beliefs and practices of those handlers (Hood, Hill & Williamson, 2005; Hood & Williamson, 2008a, 2008b). Thus, to place our analysis of being called by God among these people, a brief account of the data base used in this chapter is relevant here.

DATABASE FOR THE CONTEMPORARY SERPENT HANDLING TRADITION

The database for this chapter comes from two related sources. First, we shall use as a primary source *The Serpent Handlers: Three Families and Their Faith* (2000), which contains in-depth interviews with three powerful serpent handling families, focused upon how they live and experience their faith. We wrote the introduction to this book by a reporter sympathetic to the serpent-handling tradition (Fred Brown) and his wife, an accomplished writer (Jeanne McDonald). What makes this text unique is that the written summary of interviews with handlers was submitted to them to be edited and corrected. Thus for each handler the section devoted to them "In Their Own Words" (hereafter ITOWs) is in fact handlers describing their calling, faith, and practice in their own words, carefully edited by them to be as they intended.[1]

The second source contextualizes these interviews with the data base of the *Hood-Williamson Research Archives for the Holiness Serpent Handling Sects of Appalachia*, housed in the Lupton Library of the University of Tennessee at Chattanooga.[2] That archive currently consists of over 400 hours of digital documentation of the contemporary serpent handlers of Appalachia. It contains extensive interviews with contemporary handlers, focusing upon what it is like to be anointed, to fleece the Lord, and to handle serpents. Other interviews focus upon near-death experiences of bitten handlers who anticipated their own death. They including some who subsequently actually died from bites latter received. There are DVDs of lethal bites during services and rare VHS footage (converted to DVD) of services in private homes. Funerals, both with and without the handling of serpents, are documented.

However, perhaps most important is the unedited footage is of entire services of some of the major serpent handling churches in Appalachia. These recordings are of probably the most photographed serpent handling churches, the Church of the Lord Jesus in Jolo, West Virginia. It is now struggling to survive but was long headed by the now deceased (from natural deaths) Bob and Barbara Elkins. Members of the Elkins family are interviewed in the Brown and McDonald book. The Elkin family, especially Barbara, gained fame in defending the right to handle serpents after the West Virginia legislature planned to ban the practice when Columbia Hagerman, Barbara's daughter from a first marriage, received a fatal bite in 1961. Our archive has extensive footage of this church, of interviews with its members, and of the funeral of Barbara Elkins where serpents were handled.

The archive also has extensive recordings of the Rock House Holiness Church in Macedonia, Alabama, a vibrant and thriving serpent handling church that continues a tradition many have thought to be incapable of surviving into the 21st century. It is the church within which John "Punkin" Brown Jr. received a fatal bite in 1998. The Brown family is one of the three families interviewed by Brown and McDonald, and the largest. Finally, we focused upon Jamie Coots' church, The Full Gospel Tabernacle in Jesus Name church in Middlesboro, Kentucky. There Melinda Brown, wife of Punkin, received a fatal bite in 1995, leading to a court custody fight for her five surviving children. This is the church where Jamie also received a fatal bite in 2012.

Much of our footage covers these families and churches, and several others not discussed here, for over two decades, allowing longitudinal documentation of handlers, their calling, and the churches they attend. All of our documentation is "unedited" in the sense that, except for the focus of the camera that necessarily excludes what is not in the field of view, every effort was made to simply document entire services. In some cases the camera was simply set in the rear of the church to document the entire service. In other cases the camera was focused on the variety of activities that endow serpent handling services with such intensity and passion. Something rarely documented are entire sermons and testimonies of believers. All of these allow us to contextualize the handlers own words in the Brown and McDonald text by archival data that both preceded and followed these interviews.

This is the database from which we develop our own understanding of this tradition; and an appreciation for the depth of its faith and the sincerity of belief. It now has been preserved and practiced into a fourth generation of believers. Most importantly for this chapter, is the fact that we can document how it is that ITOWs serpent handlers feel called by God to what matters most in their lives, being obedient to God in all things. This includes especially the handling of deadly serpents that we have documented do actually maim and kill the believers. To understand this tradition through the words of the three families interviewed by Brown and McDonald, and extensively filmed by us, will hopefully allow an understanding of a faith and a tradition in which being called is taken seriously, even when that calling is to death. To contextualize this calling, we first need to trace a brief historical account of this tradition.

HISTORY OF THE SERPENT HANDLING TRADITION: PRIMITIVE VS. PROGRESSIVE PENTECOSTALS

Serpent handlers are best contextualized within the history of American Pentecostalism. While Pentecostalism has emerged in the 21st century to be one of the most successful expressions of Christian faith, its roots remain firmly localized in the Appalachian Mountains where they form permeable boundaries with both the holiness traditions and fundamentalism (Hood, 2000). The exponential growth of Pentecostalism outside Appalachia is a global phenomenon with current success measured by the most rapidly increasing growth rates in the Southern Hemisphere, such as Asia, Africa, and Latin America (Pew Forum 2006). Given such global success it is not surprising that the differences among persons identified as Pentecostals often can be greater than those between Pentecostals and other self-identified Christian groups. This is perhaps best illustrated by the contrast between what we shall refer to as Primitive and Progressive Pentecostals and their difference of appeal to the signs specified in Mark 16:17–18.

Progressive Pentecostals is a term coined by Miller and Yamamori (2007) to refer to Pentecostals who are involved in social ministries focused upon education, health care, and economic development. Progressive Pentecostals are by no means the majority of Pentecostals in any nation. Miller (2009, 280) suggests they are less than 5 percent of all Pentecostal churches worldwide. Miller's choice of "progressive" reveals his sympathy for Pentecostals that promise to challenge liberation theology whose Marxism focuses more upon direct challenges to political power than upon "life-transforming worship" (Miller 2009, 286).

If Progressive Pentecostals suggests a positive evaluation, our concern with what we call Primitive Pentecostals does as well. We use the term, "primitive," in the sense that Freud used the term in *Totem and Taboo*: "There are men still living who, as we believe, stand very near to primitive man, far nearer than we do, and whom we therefore regard as his direct heirs and representations" (Freud 1913, 1). Wacker (2003) sees the tension between primitiveness and pragmatism as the genius of the early Pentecostal movement. However, by emphasizing the primitivism of the earliest Pentecostals we wish to focus upon a small group, located largely within the Appalachian Mountains, who continue to preserve and practice what is best defined as a sectarian form of Pentecostalism. They endorse practices that stand in opposition to the larger host culture, so much so that one of its central rituals, the handling of poisonous serpents, has been banned in every state where it emerged, except for West Virginia (Hood & Williamson 2008b, Ch. 12; Williamson & Hood 2004). The signs of glossolalia, serpent handling, and healing continue to be practiced by primitives, while only healing, and glossolalia to a lesser extent, are championed by progressives. The central issue for primitives is being called to experience godly obedience. To understand this we must understand the central role the Gospel of Mark plays in the serpent handling tradition.

THE GOSPEL OF MARK 16:17–18

Those who have traced the history of serpent handling have generally credited one man with originating this ritual practice. However, it is unlikely that serpent handling has a single origin nor can be linked to a single person (Hood, 2005; Hood & Williamson, 2008b). Only a few emerging Pentecostal groups considered that the biblical justification for tongues speaking, in Mark 16:17–18 was also linked with a call to handle serpents (McVicar, 2013; Hood & Williamson, 2014). While some Pentecostal groups such as the Assemblies of God and the Pentecostal Holiness Church rejected serpent handling as a legitimate religious ritual (Crews, 1990; McVicar, 2013), they did interpret Mark 16:17–18 to mean that if believers accidentally handled serpents they would not be harmed. This interpretation alludes to the story of Paul in Acts 28: 3–6. While laying sticks he had gathered upon a fire, a viper came out and fastened onto Paul's hand. Onlookers are said to believe that Paul was a murderer that "vengeance suffereth not to live" (Acts 28: 4). Paul shook the viper off and "felt no harm" (Acts 28: 5). The onlookers anticipated swelling or sudden death, however, seeing neither, they changed their minds about Paul and "said that he was a god" (Acts 28: 7).

The Pentecostal groups who affirm that Mark 16:17–18 refers to protection from accidental bites salvaged a meaning that is too distant from the meaning of the text. The plain meaning of the text was interpreted by other Pentecostal groups as an imperative, "they *shall*." Recall that Mark 16:17 states: "And these signs shall follow them that believe; In my name shall they cast out devils; they shall speak with new tongues; They shall take up serpents; and if they drink any deadly thing, it shall not hurt them; they shall lay hands on the sick, and they shall recover." (Mark 16:17–18).

The conditional meaning applies only to poisons ("*if* they drink") and would more appropriately allow for the accidental interpretation that the Assemblies of God and the Pentecostal Holiness Church tried to apply to serpent handling. Interestingly, the same imperative applied to tongues-speaking in Mark 16:17 is also applied to serpent handling in Mark 16:18. Thus the early

Church of God and Church of God of Prophecy endorsed the more consistent position as reflected in the stand taken by their very first General Overseer, A. J. Tomlinson (1930): "The Church stands for the whole Bible rightly divided, and it is wrongly dividing to cut out the tongues and serpents" (p. 1).

GEORGE WENT HENSLEY

While serpent handling likely had independent origins, its origin is often linked to one man, George Went Hensley. Hensley was said to have climbed atop nearby White Oak Mountain to seek God in prayer and face his own spiritual struggle (Collins, 1947). His insight was that the signs in Mark 16 were in fact a calling for believers to obey. He felt his eternal security rested upon obedience to these mandates—and specifically, at the present moment for him, the taking up of serpents. Collins (1947) reported:

> His decision was to risk his life in order to have rest from his spiritual burden. Thus it was that he set out on probably the first religious snake hunt in modern civilized history.
>
> In a great rocky gap in the mountainside he found what he sought, a large rattlesnake. He approached the reptile, and, disreguarding [*sic*] its buzzing, blood-chilling warning, knelt a few feet away from it and prayed loudly into the sky for God to remove his fear and to anoint him with "the power". Then suddenly with a shout he leaped forward and grasped the reptile and held it in trembling hands. (1–2)

It was from this life-changing experience that an inspired Hensley descended the mountain, with rattlesnake in hand, and launched only a few days later his first evangelistic effort in his own community of Grasshopper Valley, with a challenge that believers should practice *all* that Jesus had commanded—including that of taking up serpents (Collins, 1947). Hensley traveled widely throughout the southern Appalachian Mountains, preaching and modeling the call to take up serpents. His appeal was persuasive for Primitive Pentecostals, especially those affiliated with the Church of God and its sister offshoot, The Church of God of Prophecy (Hood & Williamson, 2008a,b; McVicar, 20013). Burton (1993) noted that Hensley asserted that Mark 16 demonstrated a modern day example of God's deliverance for his children. According to Hensley, serpent handling was

> a modern manifestation of Old Testament deliverance by the Lord, such as Daniel from the lion's den, the three Hebrew children from the fiery furnace, and Jonah from the belly of the whale: "But you don't know that," he said. "That was before your time. I'll show you something in your time.

I'll show you how to handle a rattlesnake, and you all know the result of rattlesnakes." (Burton, 1993, pp. 45–46).

Hensley's serpent handling practice influenced and inspired unknown numbers in the Church of God to follow his lead, as the serpent handlers of Appalachia became part of an American indigenous faith tradition that McCauley (19 95) has identified as Appalachian Mountain religion. What unites these different groups is not dogma but the focus upon experiences of the Holy Spirit mediated by grace in opposition to any imposed regulations or authority typically associated with mainstream denominational forms of Protestantism or Progressive Pentecostalism. It is a faith tradition based simply upon being called to obedience to God. While often characterized as a religion of deprivation and even desperation associated with "yesterday's people" (Wheeler, 1965) but rather in the fullness of the certainty of their own salvation rooted in their own authoritative religious experience by which they feel called.

The Church of God and the Church of God of Prophecy were among the strongest Pentecostal groups that early on supported serpent handling. They became identified as sign following believers based upon their commitment to the signs specified in Mark 16:17–18. Until as late as 1943 articles in support of serpent handling appeared in the *Evangel,* an official publication of the Church of God. However, as the practice increased, believers began to get bit. Eventually there were documented cases of maiming and death. Jamie Coots is the last documented death in February 2014 and he is one of at least 94 documented deaths from serpent bite and at least nine from poison drinking (Hood & Williamson, 2008b, pp. 239–246). George Hensley himself died from a serpent bite in Athena, Florida, in 1955. In the face of maiming and death from serpent bites the emerging Pentecostal denominations that had supported the practice reversed course and gradually began to denounce the practice. Beginning with Kentucky in 1940 gradually all Appalachian states in which serpent handling was practiced made it illegal. West Virginia is the sole exception due to efforts of the Elkin family, noted in the following.

In the early 21st century, serpent handling continues in what we call renegade churches of God. These churches are generally small, often with only 15 to 25 members. They typically have some version of Church of God in their name, such as the pastor Jimmy Morrow's Edwina Church of God in Jesus' Name (Hood, 2005). The renegade Churches of God are scattered primarily across Appalachia with no formal accounting as to their exact number or membership totals. Today, there are likely less than a hundred churches in all of Appalachia. However, serpent handling churches have been identified as far north as Canada and on both coasts of the United States. Many churches are hard to locate as they protect themselves from laws that ban the practice in most of the states where handlers have been active. However, we have a strong data base in which to contextualize our understanding of these believers of ITOWs. How is it that they see themselves called to handle serpents as a sign rather than a test of belief?

THREE FAMILIES: THE ELKINS, THE BROWNS, AND THE COOTS

The Elkins Family

Bob Elkins was the pastor of Jolo Church in West Virginia for many years. However, he was overshadowed by his wife Barbara who had handled serpents with Hensley and was widely recognized as the matriarch of the Elkins family and the Jolo church. Like all handlers, Barbara and Bob feel called to obedience that includes handling serpents. Once this is accepted their beliefs center on the likely consequences of handling. As we have documented elsewhere (Hood, 1998) poisonous serpents can be handled with success ("victory") but from a purely secular perspective the probability of a bite is largely a function of the frequency of handling. Thus, as handling became more frequent, and deaths and maiming relatively common, the renegade Churches of God who feel called to handle needed to confront the simple fact that handlers often were maimed and sometimes died. Barbara lived to an old age and died a natural death on February 5, 1999, at 83. She witnessed many bites, maiming, and deaths. At her funeral, many of her family members with maimed bodies handled serpents in obedience to Mark 16:17–18 and the faith their shared with Barbara. However, the crucial role that the Jolo church played occurred in 1961 when Columbia Hagerman, Barbara's daughter from a first marriage, was handling in the Jolo church and received a bite that proved fatal. Recalling this event, Barbara noted: "We had never worried about Columbia handling serpents. No. Never did. She lived four days after she was bitten. We was praying for her. Every one of the children was praying and stood right by us. She was sitting up in bed, talking in tongues with the Holy Ghost. I knew it was the Holy Ghost talking to her. I'm sure it was" (ITOWs, 249).

Lydia Elkins, the daughter of Columbia later adopted by Barbara and Bob Elkins, recalls her mother's death matter of factly. "I knew my mother was serpent-bit, but that was nothing uncommon to me. It was just something I knew. We handle serpents. We get bit" (ITOWs, 297). Lucille Chafin Church, Columbia's sister, was only a few years younger than her sister when Columbia died. She gained national notoriety when the *Saturday Evening Post* published a picture of her handling a serpent in the late stages of her pregnancy. However, like most handlers she understands the depth of what it means to be called to handle serpents: "This is our point. You could be harmed by driving too fast or drinking too much. But people say we bring it on ourselves. We go out, we catch the serpents, [and] we handle serpents. Others think we say, 'Well, bite me and kill me,' but that's not the intent. It's the verse, 'Thou shalt take up serpents.' That's the intent.'" (ITOWs, 333).

Like many handlers, she dislikes being called a snake handler: "And don't call me a snake handler. I'm a child of God. Serpent handling is a Sign of the Lord's Gospel, not a person. It is a small part of my religious belief, not who I am." (337). And although never bitten, Lucille ponders on being called to be obedient in terms of scripture: "I think sometimes when the Lord tells you to pick up a serpent and you know you will be bitten, it's a test, like when God told Abraham to take his son Isaac out, and offer him up as a burnt sacrifice. God meant to see how much faith Abraham had." (ITOWs, 338). The distinction between handling by faith or by anointing is a constant discussion among handlers (see Hood & Williamson, 2008b) but ought not to be only contrasted with one another. Both are responses to a calling integral to the serpent handling tradition, acceptance of Mark 16:17–18. Bob Elkins, who died from natural causes only a few years after Barbara noted, "When you are handling them by faith, you are waiting on the anointing . . . If you move by faith you are moving out on the promise of God. And if you get bit while handling on faith, you are just bit. We are just bit, and we have to trust God to heal us . . . It is not more dangerous to take up serpents on faith alone and not waiting on the anointing. The anointing is faith in action. And I can't explain the feeling of the anointing (ITOWs, 262).

Dewey Chafin, Barbara's son and perhaps the most photographed of all handlers and the one who has suffered the most serious with numerous bites, explains being obedient under the anointing as follows: "I let God guide me. I hear His voice in my own sense. . . . I hear it in my mind and head. You hear a voice that's not like me talking to you. I hear it in my mind, and head. You hear a voice that's not a reach-out voice like a deep voice. It is like ringing in your head, except it is a voice. Nobody can hear it but you. God tells me it is okay to handle serpents. Now, I have had Him say, *'Don't do it.'* And I won't do it. [And sometimes,] He just says, 'You are going to get bit.' He doesn't say not to do it. He just says, 'You are going to get bit.'" (ITOWs, 293).

It is the Jolo Church and largely the Elkins family that persuaded West Virginia to support their right to handle serpents as a simple act of obedience. It is the only state wholly within the Appalachia Mountain region, and has successfully asserted its right to religious freedom. In the words of Bob Elkins, "People think we are crazy, but it is a wise man who fears the Lord and keeps His Commandments" (ITOWs, 265).

The Brown Family

The Brown family is perhaps the most well known of the serpent handling families due largely to the notoriety of John "Punkin" Brown Jr. an Evangelist who devoted his life to preaching throughout the Southern Appalachian Mountains and was a major figure maligned in the popular *Salvation on Sand Mountain* (1995) by Denis Covington. While Covington's talent as a writer is superb his book is less an ethnographic study of handlers than a fictionalized attempt to stereotype a tradition and to make Punkin into an almost demonic figure (Hood, 1995).

John Brown, Punkin's father, is the pastor of The House of Prayer in the Name of Jesus Christ, but Punkin preached widely, often teamed with Jamie Coots who pastored the The Full Gospel Tabernacle in Jesus Name in Middlesboro, Kentucky, a church now pastored by his son, Cody, after Jamie's death by a serpent bite. Punkin's death by a serpent bite, preceded Jamie's by 16 years. While preaching a revival in Alabama on Sand Mountain at the Old Rock Holiness Church, a church well noted for its support of serpent handling, Punkin was bit and died within 15 minutes. His death (caught on film and in our archive) was foretold by a handler, Cameron Short: "He never knew it in the beginning, but I told my wife he wouldn't live very long . . . He just had this look in his eyes that he wasn't sent in this world to stay here long. I've seen that look in people's eyes before. I think that every man is sent here for one specific purpose or another; and when that purpose is fulfilled I think he or she dies" (ITOWs, 110).

Punkin was aware his death was imminent. Immediately after being bit he said to the church, "No matter what comes, God's still God" (ITOWs, 14). Punkin's father is not convinced that his son's death was directly caused by the serpent bite—handlers typically take several days to die from bites they have suffered and chosen not to treat. John senior believes God revealed the true cause of Punkin's death to him in a dream: "I was praying about why Punkin died, what caused his death. I dreamed I was talking to Punkin, and he had a sand rattler. . . . I asked him, 'Is that a bad serpent?' And he said, 'No, this seems to be all right, Daddy.' In the dream he took and put it to his ear three times. And then the third time, they was a little serpent crawled out of his ear. I believe the Lord was showing me that it wasn't the one he had on the *outside*, it was something on the *inside* [some internal problem] that caused his death" (ITOWs, 70).

Rachelle Brown, a handler married to Mark Brown, Punkin's surviving brother who also handles, echoes the sentiment of most handlers regarding what puzzles outsiders who cannot understand a ritual that can maim and kill. For her, as for John senior, is does not ultimately matter if Punkin died from a serpent bite or not. "When they're in the church service and God's

moving. That does not scare me. Because if they die, it's their time to go"
(ITOWs, 82).

What can be viewed narrowly as a form of fatalism is simply the acceptance of the reality of death and the focus upon salvation achieved by being
obedient to God. The Brown family is the only on record to have suffered
two deaths from serpent bites. Punkin's wife, Melinda, was bitten at a home-
coming in Jamie Coots church in 1995. The mother of five children, she was
handed a large rattlesnake by her husband, Punkin, was bitten and refused
medical treatment. Taken to Jamie's apartment, she suffered for three days,
succumbing to the bite. Asked if she wanted medical treatment, her words
were simple, to those who tried to persuade her to seek medical aid: "Have
you lost your faith" (ITOWs, 20). We were beside Melinda when she was bit
and served as an expert witness (pro bono) at a custody trial when Melinda's
parents tried to take the children away from Punkin. At the trial for custody
in Tennessee (where the Brown's reside) the juvenile court judge Phil Owens
initially awarded joint custody to Melinda's parents and Punkin with the
condition that Punkin could not take any of his children (then aged from 4 to
12) to any church that handled serpents. Punkin reacted to the verdict with
defiance about how he would raise his children: "I'll teach them what the
Bible says . . . I don't care what nobody else says. . . . My wife died for what
she believed in. *She believed it.* Whatever Phil Owens does, he cannot change
the Bible. You turn to Mark 16 and it still reads, *They shall take up serpents . . .*
They can change their laws, make the law, but they can't change the Word of
God" (ITOWs, 31–32)."

Our archive not only documents Melinda's death, but documents the
Brown children at services where handling occurred. John Brown, Sr. echoes
the moral imperative subscribed to by most handlers, "God say to submit
yourself unto every ordinance of man which is pleasing to God. Where that
crosses His law, then we ought to obey God rather than man" (67). Today,
three of the Brown children handle serpents, despite the death of both their
mother and father from serpent bites.

Understanding handling is more than simply understanding how anointed
believers, sometimes only by faith, answer what they perceive is God's call to
obedience. Fleecing is a common means by which handlers seek God's will
for them. John Brown, Sr. tells how he became a handler at a once famous
church in Carson Spring, Tennessee. Jimmy William, Sr. was pastor of the
church and later to die the same night Buford Pack also died, both from
drinking strychnine (Buford was also bitten by a rattlesnake in the same
service). However, Jimmy Williams had long preached March 16:17–18, but
had never actually handled serpents. John Brown tells the story of Gideon
in the book of Judges (6: 14–16) where Gideon placed a fleece before the
lord. Brown tells how he was praying with Burford Pack who like John had

not yet handled serpents. Then, John notes that: "God spoke to Brother Pack and said, 'There will be a sign, and a round where the sign's at, there will be oil.' About a week or two after that, we went to church on Saturday night, and Brother Jimmy Ray Williams—the one that [later] died with strychnine—his daughter was going out the church door, and there was a copperhead crawling in the door. That snake just came in by itself. It happened like God said it was to beforehand, and it came to pass. It crawled back into the yard and where the serpent was at, there was oil all the way around it. This was no car oil. It was just oil. I don't know how it got there. It was fresh oil. Sure was. Brother Jimmy took and put [the snake] in a paper bag, took it into church, and handled it. So that is why we say a *fleece*. We put it before the Lord, and if that comes to pass, we go ahead and mind the Lord. So that copperhead was a fleece" (ITOWs, 61).

Fleecing is a common practice among handlers seeking to understand God's calling in a particular situation. Both John, Sr. and Mark Brown tell how they fleeced the lord to see if they should challenge the court again when Punkin Brown died and another custody battle for the Brown children was launched. As Mark tells it, "After the court ruling father put fleece before Lord. Asked Lord to provide funds within three days if he was to fight the decision." John notes he didn't put out word or tell anyone. Envelopes came in unsolicited: "There were envelopes that come in here with twelve hundred dollars, one hundred dollars. One time two thousand dollars. Sure did. That's why we went ahead with it" (ITOWs, 41–42). At the initial ruling against the Brown family, John Brown, Sr. challenged the negative ruling in an emotional outburst: "My son gave his life for what he believed. Is this the freedom we are guaranteed by the constitution" (ITOWs, p, 39). Today the Browns are secure in recognizing that their fleece was eventually rewarded with a legal victory that gave them full custody of the Brown children.

Fleecing is used in most instances as a means of receiving guidance for a particular situation. For instance, Mark Brown notes that Cameron Short taught him that even when anointed to handle, one can fleece God for guidance with respect to a particular serpent. "Cameron, he taught me this—he used to lay a box out, and if it had two or three, he'd lay them out there, and he'd tell the Lord, whichever He wanted him to take, let them crawl in the box . . . And he'd say, the one the Lord wanted him to take would crawl into the box. It might be two of them, or whatever. It is just different ways" (ITOWs, 98–99). The Brown family are exemplars relative to a practice that baffles those that cannot accept the death that many see as courted by a ritual that maims and kills. However, in the words of Jimmy Morrow, that pastored the Edwina Church in Jesus Name in Tennessee commenting on Punkin's death, "This wasn't a test of faith. This is our faith" (ITOWs, 20).

The Coots Family

Cody Coots now pastors the Full Gospel Tabernacle in Jesus Name in Middlesboro, Kentucky. It is the church where Melinda received her fatal bite and where (as we write this) Jamie Coots was the last handler to die from a fatal bite at a service in February 2014. After his dad's funeral, Cody and some believers went to the church and handled the serpent that killed his father. The puzzle for outsiders is always why this ritual, given the possibility of death. While the simple fact of obedience to Mark 16:17–18 is not an explanation that satisfies outsiders, for believers it is all the explanation needed. Jamie had been bitten several times before, including the loss of a finger to a copperhead bite. Jamie notes that he had always affirmed, "Lord, if I ever go to the hospital, I'll quit handling (ITOWs, 153). It took Jamie some time after that bite to handle again.

As he tells it, at one service, "Finally, the Lord moved on me real strong, and I reached and took it. Well, when I did and handled it, then the Lord let me know it was all right to get the one out that bit me. I had a copperhead in there with him. I got the one out that bit me and handled it. The Lord gave me real good victory. So from then on, I began to get over it, a little bit at a time. But I had to get over the fear of that one snake. He had me in such a shape, and the Lord let me know that I had to handle him first. I had to get over that." (ITOWs, 155).

Jamie handled his first serpent after fleecing the Lord. "I had wanted to handle one for a long time. I went to church that night and prayed—prayed the whole night. And I fleeced the Lord for Bruce Helton to bring it to me. During the entire service no fleece. But after service Bruce was switching out two big copperheads—I was standing there all this time meditating, [telling] the Lord I'd like to handle one . . . Well, it got all the way up to the end of the meeting, and I hadn't got to handle one. So I was real discouraged. . . . Well, somebody had brought Bruce two big Southern copperheads, and after church, he was switching 'em out. He reached and got the first one with a hook and got it out of the box and put it in the other one, and then he laid his hook down. I was standing alone all this time meditating [telling] the Lord I'd like to handle one. That is all I had on my mind. I wanted to handle one. Bruce reached down and got it out of the box and handled it. He just turned around and offered it to me. I handled it" (ITOWs, 162–163). Bruce Helton preached Jamie's funeral and praised him for standing firm in his faith and for obeying the call for believers to take up serpents.

While as noted above, Jamie was eventually to die from a lethal bite for which he refused medical care, his wife, Linda Coots, had to overcome her own fear of handling. She tells of a time when she fleeced the lord to allow her to handle, but in a rare occurrence she did not accept the fleece. When she was pregnant with Cody, she fleeced the Lord: "'Now Lord, it's you, and it's all right for me to handle a serpent. You let Brother Sherman look back here at me.' He went one further than that. Brother Sherman looked right at me and *handed* it to me. And he prophesized. He said, 'The Lord says, "Tonight I lock their jaws. There'll be no harm." All kinds of people were going up there that night and taking serpents up and when he looked at me, he said, "This is for you." I dropped down on my knees. I didn't have the courage to do it. And I said, "Lord if I go handle that serpent and me pregnant, it'd kill my baby if I was to get bit. I just can't do it. I'm afraid to do it.' So I didn't do it. And needless to say, I desired it, but I was scared to do it" (ITOWs, 183).

However, Linda did not lose her desire to handle. After the birth of Cody she fleeced the Lord again at Jamie's church: "'Now, Lord, if this is You let Jamie turn around and look at me.' So he turned around and looked right at me. And then mocked [motioned] it to me. And I was still scared. I was right there in front. And I stepped out. And when I took hold of it, I'll never forget the first time I handled one. It was like silk. I expected it to be rough and real nasty feeling. It was like cold silk. All that could go through my mind was how smooth and silky it was. It was a rattlesnake, a big one. Anyways, I handled the serpent and handed it back to Jamie" (ITOWs, 185).

Rattlesnake bites are the most frequent that prove fatal to handlers. So it was with Jamie. His children that now both handle witnessed his death. At the time of her interview with Brown and McDonanld, Jamie's wife admitted to being terrified, thinking about her own children handling serpents. However, we have documentation of her handling serpents with her children after the death of Jamie. She recalls how she overcame her own fear of Jamie handling after he had a near death experience from his first bite.

"I would go to bathroom or leave church when Jamie handled. One day as I was leaving church I said, 'Lord God, I don't know. I just don't know if I can handle it, him handling snakes.'" And right at that minute, Jamie, in a strong, loud, authoritative voice, started prophesying, speaking in tongues, and that's what made me turn around. He said, 'Yes, my child, I say this is for you, and have no fear that I am in this.' And honey, I turned around and shouted all the way up to the front of the church and took the serpent. When he prophesized this to me, Lord, the anointing just fell all over me, and I went up to the front of the church, and I knew it was God. I *knew* it was God" (ITOWs, 196). As noted above, Cody leads his deceased father's church where both he and his mother continue to be obedient to what they understand as God's calling for those that believe.

We can close this look at three families whose faith is marked by the assurance that obedience trumps any fear of mere mortal death. This belief is not to be taken to mean that as humans, handlers' do not battle with fear. This is best exemplified by mothers who anticipate the time when their children will practice what they are taught to believe. Melissa Evans notes that her mother Lidia who handles and whose own mother Columbia died from a serpent bite as noted above, nevertheless cautioned Melissa: "Mama did not like for me to handle serpents. She said, "You have two kids. You do not need to handle. There are other things you can do to follow the Signs. Oh, she worried about me. But the Lord is going to take care of me. If I die, then He's going to take care of my kids. He's going to see that they're raised right" (ITOWs, 308).

Expressing similar concerns, Barbara Church, a handler whose mother was sister to Columbia notes: "When my kids are old enough to handle serpents, I will probably be terrified. As a mother, I don't want them to. You look at your kids and you think, 'What if something were to happen to them?' You think, 'How would they grow up without me?' When the anointing comes you don't think about it. With the flesh, though, it's always there. You think, 'If I get bit, how would I cook for my kids? How would I clean for my kids?' You always think about them, whether it is thinking about yourself or protecting them. A daddy is good, but a daddy is not a mommy. Nobody can replace a mother. You can't. That's when you have to trust the Lord. Sometimes that does get hard" (ITOWs, 272). Peggy Brown, Punkin's mother, notes that she was never scared when Punkin handled serpents or drank poison while in church. However, she recalls a time when Punkin drank strychnine and his legs buckled, "We got home, *he* was fine. I got home, I went all to pieces. Because what it was, it was the spirit of the Lord was gone, the peace in me was gone, and I was the mother again" (ITOWs, 44–45).

CONCLUSION

Our focus upon three families interviewed by Brown and McDonald is primarily to place an admittedly marginal faith tradition in a larger context in which those who feel called can be understood by others who are unlikely to be persuaded of the meaningfulness of their faith. We have followed these families (and many others) for over 20 years and we have seen children raised in the faith continue the tradition while others have left. We have witnessed handlers get bit. Some without harm, others with permanent maiming, and some died from their bites. However, the focus upon deaths in this chapter ought not to mask the fact that most handlers have victory over their serpents, and die from natural causes. For those who use the fact that this tradition has a ritual that can maim and kill as a rejection of the legitimacy of their faith is something we hope to persuade the reader is unwarranted. The issue is less the focus upon risk than upon believers who actually are called to obedience in terms of their understanding of Mark 16:17–18. As more than one handler has urged, if you do not believe in handling, simply pray for those who do.

NOTES

1. The expressions and grammar are as spoken by handlers and since these are all in their own words, edited and corrected by the handlers, we make no "corrections." Occasional inserted clarifications in quotes used are those of Brown and McDonald.

2. The digital collection contains 400 hours of church services and interviews, documenting contemporary serpent handlers of Southern Appalachia, from 1975 to 2004. Besides extensive footage of the three families, numerous other families and churches are documented. In addition, several documentary films are soon to be archived with hundreds of hours of original footage not used in the documentaries. The Coots family was a focus of the documentary "Snake Salvation," produced and shown by National Geographic Television (2014), which also produced a memorial to Jamie after his death in February 2014.

REFERENCES

Berger, P. (1967). *The sacred canopy: Elements of a sociological theory of religion.* Garden City, NY: Doubleday.

Berger, P. (1974). Some second thoughts on substantive versus functional view of religion. *Journal for the Scientific Study of Religion, 13,* 126–133.

Brown, F. & McDonald, J. (2000). *The serpent handlers: Three families and their faith.* Winston-Salem: John F. Blaire.

Burton, T. (1993). Serpent handling believers. Knoxville: University of Tennessee Press.

Collins, J.B. (1947). *Tennessee snake handlers.* Chattanooga: Chattanooga News and Free Press.

Covington, D. (1995). *Salvation on Sand Mountain: Snake handling and redemption in Southern Appalachia.* Reading, MA: Addison-Wesley.

Crews, M. (1990). *The church of God: A social history.* Knoxville: University of Tennessee Press.

Freud, S. (1913). *Totem and taboo. Standard edition.* James Strachey (Ed.), vol. 13 (pp. xiii—162). London: Hogarth Press.

Flournoy, T. (1903). Les principles de la psychologie religieuse. *Archives de Psychologie, 2,* 33–57.

Hood, R. W. Jr. (1995). (Review) *Salvation on Sand Mountain: Snake handling and redemption in Southern Appalachia.* Reading, MA: Addison-Wesley, in *Appalachian Heritage,* 1991, Summer, 54–56.

Hood, R. W. Jr. (1998). When the spirit maims and kills: Social psychological considerations of the history of serpent handling and the narrative of handlers. Invited paper. *The International Journal for the Psychology of Religion, 8,* 71–96.

Hood, R. W. Jr. (2000). Introduction. In F. Brown & J. McDonald (Eds.), *The serpent handles: Three families and their faith* (pp. ix–xii). Winston-Salem: John F. Blaire.

Hood, R. W. Jr. (Ed.) (2005). *Handling serpents: Pastor Jimmy Morrow's narrative history of his Appalachian Jesus' name tradition.* Mercer, GA: Mercer University Press.

Hood, R. W. Jr. (2012). Methodological agnosticism for the socials sciences? Lessons from Sorokin's and James's allusions to psychoanalysis, mysticism, and Godly love. In Matthew T. Lee & Amos Yong (Eds.), *The science and theology of Godly love* (pp. 121–140). DeKalb: Northern Indiana University Press.

Hood, R. W. Jr. & Williamson, W. Paul (2008a). Contemporary Christian serpent handlers and the new paradigm for the psychology of religion. *Research in the Social Scientific Study of Religion, 19,* 59–89.

Hood, R. W. Jr. & Williamson, W. P. (2008b). *Them that believe: The power and meaning of the Christian serpent-handling tradition.* Berkeley: University of California Press.

Hood, R. W. Jr. & Williamson, W. P. (2014). Case study of the intratextual model of fundamentalism: Serpent handlers and Mark 16:17–18. *Journal of Psychology and Christianity, 33,* 58–69.

Hood, R. W. Jr., Hill, P. C. & Williamson, W. P. (2005). *The psychology of religious fundamentalism.* New York: Guilford.

Hood, R., W. Jr., Hill, P. C., & Spilka, B. (2009). *The psychology of religion: An empirical approach* (4th edition). New York: Guilford.

Luhrmann, T. M. (2012). *When God talks back.* New York: Vintage.

McCauley, D. V. (1995). *Appalachian Mountain religion: A history.* Urbana and Chicago: Illinois University Press.

McVicar, M. J. (2013). Take away the serpents from us: The sign of serpent handling and the development of Southern Pentecostalism, *Journal of Southern Religion 15.* http://jsr.fsu.edu/issues/vol15/mcvicar.html

Miller, D. E. (2009). Progressive Pentecostalism: An emergent trend in global Christianity. *Journal of Beliefs and Values 30,* 275–287.

Miller, D. E. & Yamamori, T. (2007). *Global Pentecostalism: The New Face of Christian Engagement.* Berkeley: University of California Press.

Pew Forum. (2006). *Spirit and power: A ten country survey of Pentecostals 2006.* Accessed April 14, 2011. www.pewforum.org/2006/10/05/spirit-and-power

Popora, D. V. (2006). Methodological atheism, methodological agnosticism, and religious experience. *Journal for the Theory of Social Behavior, 36,* 57–75.Tomlinson, A. J. (1930). Editorial. *White Wing Messenger,* 7(21), 1.

Wacke, G. (2003). *Heaven below: Early Pentecostals and American culture.* Cambridge, MA: Harvard University Press.

Wheeler, J. (1965). *Yesterday's people: Life in contemporary Appalachia.* Lexington: University of Kentucky Press.

Williamson, W. P. & Hood, R. W., Jr. (2004). Differential maintenance and growth of religious organizations based upon high cost behaviors. *Review of Religious Research, 46,* 250–268.

Chapter 17

Already but Not Yet: Calling and Called in Religious Time

Gordon Bermant

This chapter continues a conversation I have carried on for decades with my first Buddhist teacher, Kenryu T. Tsuji (1914–2004). What it is about, really, is one four-line verse of a poem that Reverend Tsuji wrote for children. I met Reverend Tsuji in 1986, when I was almost 50 years old and not easily moved by poems for children. He captured my mind and heart at our first meeting, as I have explained elsewhere (Bermant, 2005). The effect of the poem came a little later. I continue to work out my debt of gratitude to him.

Here is the verse from his poem *Gassho to Amida. Gassho* is Japanese for the gesture of putting your palms together close to your chest, signifying respect or reverence. Who Amida is, and what Amida means, comes later in the chapter.

> When I call Amida's name
> It's Amida calling me.
> His voice and my voice are one.
> I gassho to Amida.

A contemplative response to this verse concludes the chapter. Between here and there I attempt to create a context in which the deep meaning of the verse can emerge clearly. The key terms in the context are *religions, religious experience,* and *calling.*

By *religions* I mean religious doctrines and narratives as generally identified. I will not attempt a formal definition, because I agree with Doug Oman (2013) that "religion" is a prototype or family resemblance concept that is not well-served by definitions aiming for precision. What I mean by *religious experience* will emerge throughout the chapter, but William James' definition of religion itself is a good placed to begin: ". . . the feelings, acts, and experiences of individual men in their solitude so far as they apprehend themselves to stand in relation to whatever they may consider the divine" (James, 1902, p. 42). James was decidedly skeptical about organized religion, so his definition of religion excludes it in favor of personal experience (Taylor, 2003). James also added that some "godless or quasi-godless creeds," including Buddhism as one example, should be included as religions. In what follows I use examples from Buddhist and Biblical traditions.

Five sections follow. The first introduces a framework with five partially overlapping scales of religious time. The second focuses on an important temporal condition in religion and religious experience: *already but not yet.* Section three introduces an argument made by John Dewey that criticizes the already-but-not-yet nature of many religious claims because, in his view, accepting them thwarts social progress by creating complacency among believers (Dewey, 1933/2013). The fourth section establishes what I mean by *calling* and *called,* distinguishing them in religious context as oral and aural responsiveness. Bringing the materials on time and calling/called together, the final section draws from the Japanese Shin Buddhist tradition to amend Dewey's argument. I conclude that the experience of responding to an already-but-not-yet religious promise has consequences that are personally wholesome and can be socially more valuable than Dewey had allowed.

SCALES OF RELIGIOUS TIME

Religious doctrines and narratives have vexed relationships with time, particularly when they aim to affect religious experience. Here I consider five scales of religious time:

- Cosmic duration
- Memorial/historical past
- Immemorial/mythical past
- The future (my lifetime, the hereafter, the impersonal future)
- The present

Cosmic duration. *Cosmic duration* may be continuous or discontinuous, arise from a creation story, and be punctuated by one or many cosmic catastrophes. In the biblical tradition, God, as uncaused cause, creates the material world and all that is in it beginning from nothing (Genesis 1). The ultimate state of the world can bring either complete chaos and destruction or perfect peace and harmony, on a timetable that is God's alone to determine (e.g., Isaiah 65; Matthew 24; 2 Peter 3; Revelation 21). There is uncertainty and dispute among Jewish and Christian theologians about when the end times will happen, and what will happen to those living and those already dead when they do happen (Raphael, 2009; Smith, 2011). Biblical prophecies of the end of days have been followed by many more in the ensuing centuries (Browne & Harrison, 2008). To date, it seems, all have failed. The psychological consequences of failure became famous in psychology as the theory of cognitive dissonance (Festinger, Riecken, & Schachter, 1956).

In a very different cosmology, the Buddhist tradition portrays a *psychophysical* universe, some of which is subject to cyclical destruction and re-creation, as a natural process, with cycle periods equivalent to many billions of years. Comprehending the psychophysical nature of the world is important for understanding Buddhist teachings, especially Mahayana Buddhism. As one scholar puts it, "The key to understanding the Buddhist cosmological scheme lies in the principle of *"the equivalence of cosmology and psychology* . . . The various realms of existence relate rather closely to . . . experienced states of mind" (Gethin, 1998, pp. 119–120; emphasis in original). For example, one can ascend to various levels of "heaven" through meditative practice alone. Psychologists, cognitive scientists, and philosophers have made important contributions to clarifying this difficult topic. For example, Varela, Thompson, and Rosch (1991) introduced a spectrum of Buddhist teachings, European phenomenology, and neuroscience to argue for a middle way between materialism and idealism, toward an experientially grounded, embodied mind. See also Thompson (2007, 2014). The core principle is that consciousness is the context of all knowledge. Though consciousness is thoroughly dependent on our biological nature, it is not reducible to it.

The duration of a Buddhist cosmic cycle is vast. The cosmological unit of time, the *kalpa*, is defined as "incalculably long." Metaphorically, it was sometimes described as the amount of time required to remove all the mustard seeds from a space of 7.4 cubic kilometers (1 *yojana*) when one seed is removed every 100 years. The Hindu tradition also measures cosmology in *kalpas*, for them 1 *kalpa* = 4.32 billion years (Hindupedia, 2014). A single cosmic cycle lasts for many *kalpas*, and successive cycles vary in their durations (Cheatham, 1994).

The complexity of the cosmological future also has a moral dimension: as time has progressed since the death of Gautama (Sakyamuni) Buddha a few centuries before Jesus, the ability to comprehend the Buddha's teachings has weakened irreparably. In one form of this doctrine we are now living in the age of the degenerate dharma (*mappo*), when the teachings remain but humans are incapable of comprehending them—without assistance from another source, at least. As will be elaborated later, this teaching is involved in connections between calling and called, self and other, and salvation in the hereafter, preceded by awakening in the present, based on an event in the mythical past.

Also important for our themes of time and calling, Mahayana cosmology went further to emphasize the existence of many Buddhas: as many Buddhas as "grains of sand in the river Ganges" (e.g., Régamy, 1938/1990), each with a "Buddha land" in the psychophysical universe. If this is evaluated as a claim about the physical universe as we understand it from big bang or biblical cosmologies, the Buddhist world picture seems fanciful and factually ludicrous. But if it is evaluated as an exhortation to locate the warrants for the Buddha's teachings throughout the world, it speaks directly to religious/spiritual aspirations: it is a shift in emphasis from what the Buddha taught to what taught the Buddha.

The memorial/historical past. An important partition of cosmic duration is *duration from the beginning of time to the present moment.* This is the past in which are anchored, more or less firmly, the subject matter of a religion's chronicles.

Precise anchoring of persons and events in time and space can be of great importance. For example, establishing an objectively verifiable life of Jesus became a large undertaking for religious historians (Evans, 2008). Accompanying the "quest for the historical Jesus" is a controversial theological issue, viz., the relationship between the historical Jesus and Jesus, Son of God. Many doctrinal viewpoints have been expressed (Burkett, 1999; Casey, 2007; Ehrman, 2013; 2014; Schweitzer, 1911), but the broad consensus among experts is that Jesus "walked among us" and was executed by crucifixion in Jerusalem sometime in the third decade of the first century (Montreuil, 2003).

Theologically and psychologically, establishing the lifetime of Jesus is so important because his crucifixion and afterlife are so important: his sacrifice offered salvation from original sin (Augsburg Confession, 1530; Catechism of the Catholic Church, 2003; Westminster Confession, 1646). Locating the life, death, and resurrection of Jesus on an ordinary calendar establishes a key religious claim: these events *really happened.* If one accepts this as a matter of historical fact as well founded as any other ancient fact, the relationship between oneself and what transcends self becomes real. It is different from accepting the life, crucifixion, and resurrection of Jesus as a myth or a semi-fictional account of a supremely virtuous life. Most simply, on this view the resurrection miracle *actually* happened; that the work of salvation is *already done.* Such literal acceptance of the past grounds the anticipation of a particular future. For example, approximately half of American Christians polled by the Pew Research Center reported that Jesus is likely to return to earth within 40 years (U.S. Christians' Views on the Return of Christ, 2013).

There are other well-known examples of controversial dating of biblical events on the secular calendar, including the ages of the world and the earth, the duration of the world's creation, and the historical duration of our species' development (Ferngren, 2002). All exemplify the effort on the religious-theological side of the matter to establish the factual reality of the theological historical account. From this perspective, the historical past provides proof of religious claims about the nature of the present and the future. Arguably, the obvious trends in the United States away from traditional religious affiliations and toward unchurched spirituality are due in large part to the inability or unwillingness, or both, of many young people to accept the validity of such claims grounded in traditional histories (Fuller, 2001).

Buddhism's relationship to the past is different from the biblical tradition. It is uncontroversial that the founder, Siddhartha Gautama, lived for 80 years on the Gangetic plain a few centuries before the Common Era. But there is no consensus about the exact dates of his lifetime. Ranges from 563. to 483 BCE and 466. to 386 BCE have been offered based on different sources and inferences (Bechert, 1982). There are also uncertainties about the spread of the teachings and organizations in the first few centuries after the Buddha's death, but none of these appear to rise to the level of religious controversies as opposed to scholarly debates (Hirakawa, 1993).

The immemorial/mythical past. Not all accounts of religious origins are anchored completely in the historical past. For example, the extraordinary time scales of Buddhist cosmology and the proliferation of Mahayana Buddhas located in a psychophysical universe are not commensurate with the facts of western cosmology. But if they are used as concepts and images in contemplation, they can bring the mythical past into sharp focus as an experienced fact in the present moment. This is a move from a religious teaching to a religious experience. A strong intention arises in the practitioner to relocate religious truth from the mythical past to immediate present moment. On occasion, the intention leads to a sudden opening of awareness, of warmth like a fond parental embrace, of satisfaction beyond all doubt. In Shin Buddhism, the word *shinjin* is used. This awareness dissolves concerns about conflict between ancient doctrinal metaphysical claims and modern world views of time, space, and place. But the experience is brief. Quotidian concerns return. This sort of religious experience is well known in the contemplative tradition, epitomized in Jack Kornfield's wonderful phrase: after the ecstasy, the laundry (Kornfield, 2001).

Buddhist writings and artifacts frequently point back to events in a mythical past time. For example, biographies of Gautama Buddha in his most recent life and six earlier lives were inscribed on buildings going back to the second and third centuries BCE (Hirakawa, 1993). Tales of Gautama's earlier lives were also collected as the *Jātakas*; different early schools in India had different collections, some with as many as 550 narratives (Strong, 2007).

The past-times during which the Buddha's earlier lives played out in various identities are not clearly connected to the past-times described by the Mahayana sutras in which Bodhisattvas and Buddhas accomplish(ed) their acts of salvation. The futures are also different: Gautama Buddha's predecessors in the *Jātakas* died and ceded their places to their successors, just as Gautama Buddha died to be succeeded eventually by Maitreya, who awaits his turn on earth in one of the heavens of the Buddhist cosmos. But the Buddhas of the Mahayana sutras, who evolved in the past beyond reckoning, still reside influentially in their Buddha lands, doing their salvational work. We know this because Gautama Buddha told us so in the canonical scriptural collections. The sutras begin with the traditional phrase "Thus have I heard," a device that places the sutra's author as an amanuensis of Gautama Buddha's sermon on a particular location to a particular assemblage.

Putting Buddhist teachings onto a single calendar can be a daunting task. Consider the very important Larger Pure Land Sutra (Jp: Daimuryojukyo, Sk: Sukhavativyuha Sutra), which is the foundational text for Pure Land Buddhism, the most popular Buddhist tradition in China and Japan (Bowker, 1997). Here an anonymous first-century author relates a long sermon that Gautama Buddha (five or six centuries earlier) delivered to 12,000 monks who had developed supernatural powers. The sermon tells of a king whose own Buddha, in the immemorial past, sent the king on a mission to all the Buddha lands of the universe (a very large number) in order to learn what the king must do to become a Buddha himself. Approximately five billion years later the king returned to his Buddha with his solutions and announced them in the form of 48 vows to prepare all sentient beings for a single rebirth into a glorious place, the Pure Land, followed without doubt by nirvana. He fulfilled these vows, so the erstwhile king became the Buddha of Infinite Light and Life, Wisdom, and Compassion (Inagaki, 1994). As *Amida Buddha* in Japan, this Buddha of the western paradise is the accomplished guarantor of enlightenment for all who are genuinely open to him. True Pure Land Buddhism (Jodo Shinshu, Shin Buddhism), following the teaching of Shinran Shonin (1163–1272/3), became enormously influential in the ensuing centuries, in part because it reached out to individuals in all the strata of Japanese society with a remarkably simple and universal message of salvation (Foard, Solomon, & Payne, 1996).

In this and other Mahayana sutras, the immemorial past becomes connected to a perpetual future through an account of an event (Buddha's sermon) with an oral history beginning some centuries before the Common Era but not written until one or more centuries after the era had begun.

This is a chronology that might promote skepticism regarding the true location in time and place of the religiously crucial events, even for a life domain in which miracles are often part of the story. Religious seekers are likely to be disappointed if they seek security for their soteriology in chronology supported by the physical and life sciences. The religious truth lies elsewhere, as will be described below.

The future. The future got a renewed lease on life in psychology when Seligman, Railton, Baumeister, and Sripada (2013) encouraged psychologists to leave "psychological Laplacianism" (p. 136) behind in favor of a paradigm that emphasizes the central role of internal individual guidance arising from "present, evaluative representations of future states" (p.119). Of course such evaluations are extraordinarily important in religious life. The details of the religious future need to be carefully parsed. What follows is a mere sketch.

There is a reasonably clear distinction between personal and impersonal futures. One's personal future comprises the rest of one's lifetime plus the *hereafter*, if any. The details of the hereafter, as a continuation of persons or minds after death, vary widely across religious traditions (Raphael, 2009; Walker, 2000). The Western ethos since the Enlightenment has challenged the reality of a continuation of souls after death. Biological and psychological perspectives on death have become prominent.

From the psychodynamic perspective, one's awareness of death is a singularly important fact. Ernest Becker (1973), expanding on Kierkegaard, Freud, and Rank, elaborated a theory of heroic effort as a form of denying the terror of death. His account is placed in a cultural context in which the afterlife contains no traditional heaven. "Modern man" has lost God and seeks a form of immortality through a form of heroism: "If you don't have a God in heaven, an invisible dimension that justifies the visible one, then you take what is nearest at hand and work out your problems on that" (p. 162). The aspiration, seldom brought to full awareness, is to defeat the annihilation of death by living heroically in the present moment. Becker's work became the foundation of terror management theory, which remains an area of active research (e.g. Vail et al., 2012).

The future in Buddhism, as an afterlife, is highly conditioned by the doctrine of nirvana. It must suffice here to refer briefly to two 20th-century texts that exemplify distinct approaches to communicating what nirvana means. In his text *What the Buddha Taught* (1974), the Sri Lankan monk and political activist Walpola Rahula, after devoting almost 10 pages of talking about what nirvana is *not*, concluded that nirvana is ineffable:

Nirvana is beyond logic and reasoning. However much we may engage, often as a vain intellectual pastime, in highly speculative discussions regarding Nirvana or Ultimate Truth or Reality, we shall never understand it that way. A child in the kindergarten should not quarrel about the theory of relativity. Instead, if he follows his studies patiently and diligently, one day he may understand it. . . . [we] may one day realize it within ourselves—without taxing ourselves with puzzling and high-sounding words. (pp. 43–44)

About a century later, the American Buddhist practitioner and psychiatrist Mark Epstein was more definitive:

> While nirvana once connoted "freedom from rebirth" in South Indian cultures . . ., the freedom that the Buddha taught might be more accurately described as the ability to maintain one's composure in the face of an impermanent, always changing, and apparently imperfect, world. . . . The freedom of nirvana is the freedom that emerges when self-centeredness is no longer organizing reality.(Epstein, 2007, pp. 9–10).

So in Epstein's view, the freedom of nirvana is a psychological reality in the present rather than an ontological potentiality in the hereafter. Rahula's caveat is best understood as insisting that locating nirvana is a consequence of completing a task rather than discussing an idea. Thus, both authors emphasize the importance of attending properly to the present moment.

The present. Initially, there seems to be nothing simpler than the present: it is just right now. But several apparently simple questions quickly throw the present into conceptual obscurity. For example, how long does the present last; can we measure its duration? Does the present emerge from the past and move into the future? If so, how? If not, what does "right now" mean relative to the past and the future? After all, the heart of religion beats from ancient past to promised future, yet we are always stuck in the right now.

Saint Augustine, for example, said "What, then, is time? If no one asks of me, I know; if I wish to explain to him who asks, I know not." Despite the disclaimer, he proceeded over Book 11 of his *Confessions* to present accounts of past, present, future, eternity, what it means to measure time as long and short, distinctions between time and motion, and between human and divine knowledge. (Augustine, ca. 397/2007) In one sense and perhaps more, Augustine set the agenda for religious and scientific inquiries for all time.

The difficulties and conjectures that Augustine expressed in understanding time are just those that have since been addressed by both scientists and philosophers, especially phenomenologists (Callender & Edney, 2001; Gallagher & Zahavi, 2012; Unger & Smolin, 2015).

One of Augustine's conclusions is especially significant for our concern here about the "now" in religions and religious experience. Augustine was troubled about claims for the reality of past and future, because the past has gone and the future is not yet; neither can exist in the present. He concluded that the times of past and future are in fact forms of present time: "The time present of things past is memory; the time present of things present is direct experience; the time present of things future is expectation" (Augustine, 11.20.26). In this way Augustine identified times of future and past with *psychological faculties* of memory and expectation, which are always experienced in the present. Modern accounts compatible with this view engage with cognitive science (e.g., Prinz, 2012, pp. 243–272) and phenomenology (e.g. Noë, 2012, pp. 74–81).

There are also resonances of Augustine in the descriptions of time by Paul Tillich in his sermon "The Eternal Now" (Tillich, 1963):

> The riddle of the present is the deepest of all the riddles of time. Again, there is no answer except from that which comprises all time and lies beyond it—the eternal. . . . Not everybody, and nobody all the time, is aware of this "eternal now" in the "temporal now" . . . People who are never aware of this dimension lose the possibility of resting in the present. . . . They are held by the past and cannot separate themselves from it, or they escape towards the future, unable to rest in the present. (pp. 130–131)

"Resting in the present" also characterizes Buddhist contemplative practice and its secular forms in modern mindfulness protocols (Analayo, 2004; Kabat-Zinn, 2009). The "resting" may be in the form of highly focused concentration, or in a more open noticing of the passing contents of consciousness without attaching to them. Finally, many will recall that Ram Dass, writing from the Hindu/yogic tradition, famously urged attention to the present moment in *Be Here Now* (Ram Dass, 1971), a book which had sold more than two million copies by 2009 (Hanuman Foundation, 2009).

Old and new, East and West, religions celebrate the profound importance of the present moment. It is always in the present that one prays and calls out, and always in the present that one hears the response and call of the divine.

ALREADY BUT NOT YET

In the first section I introduced the idea of "already but not yet" using a Pure Land Buddhist example, which I return to here. The idea is by no means unique to Buddhism, however. It also evident in Christianity, when evangelical theologians distinguish messianic *fulfillment*, identified as the presence of Jesus Christ in history, from messianic *consummation*, which awaits the Second Coming of Christ (Ladd, 1996). The phrase "already but not yet" is used to tag this distinction (e.g., Storms, 2014). Divergences in the details of doctrine, under different categories of *preterism*, have long histories and still generate vigorous disputes (e.g., Sullivan, 2012).

The Buddhist example of already-but-not-yet teaching in Pure Land Buddhism differs from its Christian counterpart in several important ways. King Dharmakara's traverse of the myriad Buddha lands over the duration of billions of years, which culminated in his making 48 pledges for universal salvation in front of Lokesvararaja Buddha, cannot be placed on any historic calendar. It is mythical, and thus radically different from the Christian account of the life, death, and resurrection of Jesus in Palestine in the first century. To gesture at a point made explicit below, we can understand that the Buddhist account *is not in the past at all.*

The not-yet futures of the two traditions share similarities and retain profound differences. They are similar in that the doctrinal details of what is entailed by salvation, and what is required to be assured of it, have been changed by numerous councils, fiats, and influential writings over the centuries. They are also similar in that the hereafter is an important future in both traditions. In Christianity, the hereafter is tied in various ways to works, morality, and faith in this lifetime. The Christian's aspiration is to end up in heaven. In Pure Land Buddhism, the hereafter is tied to religious practice, particularly practice regarding the image and/or name of the Buddha of Wisdom and Compassion, Amida Buddha. The Pure Land Buddhist's aspiration is to end up in the Pure Land, with nirvana yet ahead. (There is much more to say about this, for example regarding the status of the Bodhisattva, but that is beyond our scope here.)

The religions diverge in respect to the religious significance of the impersonal future. In the future of the Christian account is the end time; whatever is to happen then, it will be the same "then" for everyone who has ever lived. And this will be a singular time of judgment. The end of a world cycle in the Pure Land Buddhist account, by contrast, does not loom as a significant threat or promise. Of far greater value is awakening to the reality of Amida Buddha's vows of salvation for all sentient beings. By some accounts this awakening can arise in this lifetime, and by other accounts it occurs just at the moment of death (Inagaki, 1994). (Note that Pure Land teachings on this topic are just one set of strands in Buddhist tradition, though a major one.)

To summarize: already but not yet describes the status in time of an act of salvation accomplished in the (historical or mythical) past, which has yet to be realized (sincerely recognized or actualized) by a religious seeker. If the seeker should at some point realize the true nature of the act, he or she will have seen and heard what is already there. "If I am in the mountains and someone tells me there is a beautiful view of a waterfall, I may walk for a distance to see that view. I do not cause the waterfall by my walking" (Bermant, 2005). But my joy in experiencing the beauty can overflow into beneficence for all and everyone that surround me.

JOHN DEWEY'S CRITIQUE OF THE ALREADY BUT NOT YET

In *A Common Faith* (1934), John Dewey tried to save the benefits of a religious attitude from the wasted effort and factual error of supernatural belief:

". . . I shall develop another conception of the nature of the religious phase of experience, one that separates from the supernatural and the things that have grown up around it" (p. 2). Dewey had a particular definition of God: ". . . the unity of all ideal ends arousing us to desire and actions" (p. 39), which he elaborated later by emphasizing the here-and-now nature of ideal ends: "For there are forces in nature and society that generate and support the ideals. They are further unified by the action that gives them coherence and solidity. It is this *active* relation between ideal and actual to which I would give the name 'God'" (p. 47).,

What Dewey condemned were already-but-not-yet religious promises. "It is argued [by religions] that the ideal is already the final reality at the heart of things that exist, and that only our senses or the corruption of our natures prevent us from apprehending its prior existential being" (pp. 19–20). Dewey found only negative consequences arising from this claim by religions. And in his concluding statements he urged that we disentangle our aspirations for an ideal with "the proposition that the ideal is already embodied in some supernatural or metaphysical sense in the very framework of existence" (p. 78).

Dewey was talking about already-but-not-yet promises. In his view, teaching that all the work required for salvation (or any other ideal outcome) has been already accomplished inevitably saps individual and social energy toward the actual human achievement of ideal ends.

In the next two sections, using concepts of *calling* and *called* in connection with the phenomenology of time in religious experience, I will propose that the experience of the Pure Land already-but-not-yet promise is compatible with Dewey's views of religiousness and is contrary to his social critique of such promises.

CALLING AND CALLED

Vocal and auditory terms are extraordinarily important in Pure Land Buddhism, including Shin Buddhism. Shin writers often use vocal and aural terms. (e.g., Akegerasu, 1977; Fukuma, 1983; Kakehashi, 2012; Ohtani, 2012; Seki, 1989). So central are the vocal act and aural response that one author identified Shin Buddhism as "the religion of hearing" (Yokagawa, 1939/2011).

One can trace the importance of vocalizing and hearing back to the Larger Pure Land Sutra. Dharmakara's transit of the Buddha lands led him to announce 48 vows, which are all conditionals: for Dharmakara to accept Buddhahood, 48 consequences must follow. If any consequence is not realized, Dharmakara will reject perfected enlightenment for himself. In Shin Buddhism the 18th vow is taken to be the primary, primal, or central vow. It reads "If, when I attain Buddhahood, sentient beings in the lands of the ten directions who sincerely and joyfully entrust themselves to me, desire to be born in my land, *and call my name even ten times*, desire to be born in my land, should not be born there, may I not attain perfect Enlightenment. Excluded, however are those who commit the five gravest offenses and abuse the right Dharma" (Inagaki, 1994, p. 243; italics added).

I must mention one other part of the sutra's story. Recall that it is being told by Gautama Buddha in front of a large crowd, and occasionally during the narrative, the Buddha's attendant Ananda interjects an important question. For our purposes, Ananda's supremely important question comes up soon after the Buddha has finished his account of Dharmakara's vows. Ananda asks if Dharmakara has actually attained Buddhahood or is still awaiting it. The Buddha answers plainly: "The Bodhisattva Dharmakara has already attained Buddhahood and is now dwelling in a western Buddha-Land, called 'Peace and Bliss', a hundred thousand kotis of lands away from here." Ananda then asks how long the transformed one has been in his new abode. The Buddha responds "about ten kalpas have passed" (Inagaki, 1994, p. 253). Using traditional conversion factors, the sutra thus informs us that there are 10 billion lands between North India and the Pure Land, and that the transformed Dharmakara, now Amida Buddha, has been there between 1 and 43 billion years. Moreover, these cosmological facts prove that every sentient being who has met or will meet a few simple requirements, is assured of rebirth in that Pure Land, and thence realize nirvana.

For modern Americans who would like to be faithful practitioners of Shin Buddhism, the literal narrative of the Larger Pure Land Sutra creates a conflict with common sense. How can one gain solace or spiritual guidance from such a fanciful story? One response is to set oneself into the context identified in Japanese Buddhism centuries ago. It is *mappo*, a condition of spiritual and religious degeneracy measured in historical time beginning with the death of Gautama Buddha. Shinran accepted it as reality in the 13th century (Marra, 1988). He acknowledged and contemplated his own condition as a flawed human being incapable of spiritual progress through his own effort—yet he had been flooded with the sure sense that he was the beneficiary of Amida's saving grace. He had practiced as a monk for more than 20 years when he experienced the certainty that he had received the gift of understanding the depth of wisdom and compassion, Amida Buddha, in his life. The meaning and truth of the Pure Land had opened to him. Yet he yet took no personal credit for religious or spiritual attainment. His response was humble gratitude for the great undeserved gift. In this condition of awareness, calling the Buddha's name, the *nembutsu*, became a spontaneous act of gratitude rather than a petition for merit or prayer for help. Very late in his life, in conversation with a member of his circle, he said this: "The saying of nembutsu is neither a religious practice nor a good act. Since it is practiced without my calculation, it is 'non-practice.' Since it is not a good created by my calculation, it is a 'non-good.' Since it is nothing but Other Power, completely separated from self-power, it is neither a religious practice nor a good act on the part of the practicer" (Unno, 1984, p. 13). Shinran felt within himself the working of that which had been beyond him but now worked through him spontaneously and naturally.

PUTTING CALLING AND CALLED TOGETHER IN TIME

We end where we began. Kenryu T. Tsuji (1914–2004) was a modern Shin teacher and leader who founded Shin temples in Canada and the United States following the dispersal of interned Japanese North Americans at the end of World War II; he was also Bishop of the Buddhist Churches of America during the 1970s. I became his student and a Shin Buddhist in 1986 and with his encouragement became the president (lay leader) of the Buddhist Churches of America (Nishi Hongwanji) for a two-year term in 2006. Sadly for me, this was two years after he died.

Reverend Tsuji wrote a children's poem, *Gassho to Amida*, which is well known among North American Shin Buddhists though it has not been formally published. Here again is the verse that motivated the chapter:

> When I call Amida's name
> It's Amida calling me.
> His voice and my voice are one.
> I gassho to Amida.

Contemplating the identification of calling and being called is a powerful trope that opens a pathway to the significance of the Larger Pure Land Sutra and Shinran's radical interpretation of it. I conclude by drawing a sketch of the path.

Consider the problem of the sutra in place and time. From right here and now, we cannot apprehend with certainty either the "there" or the "then" to which the sutra points. Is it the first-century place of the sutra's anonymous author? Or is it, as the author says, several centuries earlier on the Vulture Peak at Rajagriha, in the midst of 12,000 supernaturally accomplished monks gathered to hear the Buddha? Or is it the time recounted by the Buddha of countless *kalpa*s earlier when Dharmakara encountered the Buddha Lokesvararaja and begged to become a Buddha? Or five billion years later when he returned to Lokesvararaja and made his vows, which were then fulfilled? Or is it none of the above? When and where are the significant time and place of the sutra?

Sooner or later, I experience a growing sense of embarrassment. Why should it have taken me so long to understand that the only time and place for the truth to emerge are exactly here and now? *Where else, when else, could it possibly be?*

When my voice and the voice of Amida are the same voice, then my small self and weak voice transform to the selfless lion's roar of Amida, wisdom, and compassion. Amida's voice emerges from the voice and work of ordinary persons, enmeshed in the hindrances and defilements of *mappo*, who have discovered that the power beyond them is within them. The person whose voice unfailingly projects compassion is a Bodhisattva: one who lives for the benefit of others. Such a person enacts the fulfillment of the sutra's ancient promise. The gap between already but not yet disappears.

Two questions remain: What ends and means are worthy to be worked through the other power of Amida Buddha, wisdom, and compassion? There are many answers, because there are so many needs to fill, so many tasks to complete. Using Dewey's language, there are many worthy ideals to be actualized. The person who has accepted the power of wisdom and compassion will find ways to actualize her aspiration toward the ideal she has identified, as a physician, a parent, a philanthropist, a teacher, a pastor; the list of worthy callings is very long.

Finally, people who share ideal ends can recognize each other and band together in their common interest. Their personal aspirations become constructive social action. They fulfill Dewey's hopes for religion. They also show that sincere engagement with an already-but-not-yet promise can lead to constructive social action rather than to the apathy that Dewey criticized.

REFERENCES

Akegerasu, Haya (1977). *Shout of Buddha: Writings of Haya Akegerasu* (G. Saito & J. Sweany, Trans.) Chicago: Orchid Press.

Analayo (2003). *Satipatthana: The direct path to realization.* Birmingham, UK: Windhorse Publications.

Appold, Kenneth G. (1998). *Abraham Cavlov's doctrine of vocatio in its systematic context.* Tübingen: Mohr Siebeck.

Augustine of Hippo (ca. 397/2007). *Confessions* (Outler/Vessey, Trans.). New York: Barnes & Noble Classics.

Augsburg Confession (1530). http://carm.org/augsburg-confession. Accessed January 7, 2015.

Barbour, Ian G. (1997). *Religion and science: Historical and contemporary issues.* New York: HarperCollins.

Bechert, Heinz (1982). The date of the Buddha reconsidered. *Indologica, 10,* 29–36.

Becker, Ernest (1973). *The denial of death.* New York: Free Pess.

Bellah, Robert N., Madsen, Richard, Sullivan, William M., Swidler, Ann, & Titpon, Steven M. (1985). *Habits of the heart.* Berkeley: University of California Press.

Bermant, Gordon (2005). *Seeing what is already there.* New York: American Buddhist Study Center.

Bowker, John (Ed.). (1997). *The Oxford dictionary of world religions.* Oxford: Oxford University Press.

Browne, Sylvia, with Harrison, Linda (2008). *End of days*. New York: Dutton.

Burkett, Delbert (1999). *The son of man debate: A history and evaluation*. Cambridge, UK: Cambridge University Press.

Callender, Craig, & Edney, Ralph (2001). *Introducing time*. London: Icon Books.

Casey, Maurice (2007). *The solution to the "son of man" problem*. London: T & T Clark International.

Catechism of the Catholic Church (2003). http://www.vatican.va/archive/eng0015/_index.htm. Accessed May 4, 2015.

Cheatham, Eric (1994). *Fundamentals of mainstream Buddhism*. Boston: Charles E. Tuttle.

Dewey, John (1933–34/1991). *A common faith*. New Haven: Yale University Press.

Ehrman, Bart D. (2013). *Did Jesus exist?* New York: HarperOne.

Ehrman, Bart D. (2014). *How Jesus became God*. New York: HarperOne.

Epstein, Mark (2007). *Psychotherapy without the self*. New Haven, CT: Yale University Press.

Evans, Craig A. (2008). *The Routledge encyclopedia of the historical Jesus*. New York: Routledge.

Evershed, Liz (2001). Introductory study guide for *mere Christianity*. http://www.cslewis.org/resources/studyguides/Study%20Guide%20-%20Mere%20Christianity.pdf

Ferngren, Gary B. (Ed.). (2002). *Science & religion: A historical introduction*. Baltimore, MD: Johns Hopkins University Press.

Festinger, Leon, Riecken, Henry W., & Schachter, S. (1956). *When prophecy fails: A social and psychological study of a modern group that predicted the destruction of the world*. New York: Harper-Torchbooks.

Foard, James, Solomon, Michael, & Payne, Richard K. (Eds.). (1996). *The Pure Land tradition: History and development*. Berkeley: Berkeley Buddhist Study Series.

Fox, Douglas A. (1968).Soteriology in Jodo Shin and Christianity. *Contemporary Religions in Japan*, *9*, 30–51.

Fukuma, Seikan (1983). *Monshin: Hearing/faith*. Los Angeles: Nembutsu Press.

Fuller, Robert C. (2001). *Spiritual but not religious: Understanding unchurched America*. New York: Oxford University Press.

Gallagher, Shaun & Zahavi, Dan (2012). *The phenomenological mind* (2nd ed.). New York: Routledge.

Gethin, Rupert (1998). *The foundations of Buddhism*. Oxford: Oxford University Press.

Hamlin, Edward (1988). Magical *Upāya* in the *Vimalakīrtinirdeśa-sūtra*. *The Journal of the International Association of Buddhist Studies*, *11*, 89–122.

Hanuman Foundation (2009). History. http://www.hanuman-foundation.org/history.html. Accessed January 2, 2015.

Hindupedia (2014). Kalpa. http://www.hindupedia.com/en/Kalpa. Accessed December 8, 2014.

Hirakawa, Akira (1993). *A history of Indian Buddhism: From Śākyamuni to early Mahāyāna* (Paul Groner, Trans.). Delhi: Motilal Banarsidass.

Hood, Ralph W. & Chen, Zhuo (2013). Mystical, spiritual, and religious experiences. In Paloutzian, Raymond F. & Park, Crystal L. (Eds.), *Handbook of the psychology of religion and spirituality* (2nd ed.). New York: The Guilford Press.

Inagaki, Hsiao (1994). *The three Pure Land sutras: A study and translation from Chinese*. Kyoto: Nagata Bunshodo.

James, William (1902). *The varieties of religious experience*. New York: Longmans, Green.

Kabat-Zinn, Jon (2009). *Full catastrophe living*. Fifteenth Anniversary Edition. New York: Bantam Dell.

Kakehashi, Jistuen (2012). *Hearing the Buddha's Call: The life, works, and words of Shinran* (T. Arai, Trans.). Honolulu: Buddhist Study Center.

Kornfield, Jack (2001). *After the ecstasy, the laundry*. New York: Bantam.

Ladd, George Eldon (1996). *The presence of the future: The eschatology of biblical realism* (rev. ed.). Grand Rapids: Wm B, Eerdmans.

Marra, Michele (1988). The development of *mappo* thought in Japan (II). *Japanese Journal of Religious Studies, 4*, 287–305.

Montreuil, Margaret (2003). *God in sandals: When Jesus walked among us*. Maitland, FL.: Xulon Press.

Noë, Alva (2012). *Varieties of presence*. Cambridge MA: Harvard University Press.

Oman, Doug (2013). Defining religion and spirituality. In Paloutzian, Raymond F., & Park, Crystal L. (Eds.), *Handbook of the psychology of religion and spirituality* (pp. 23–47). New York: The Guilford Press.

Ohtani, Koshin (2012). *The Buddha's call to awaken*. New York: The American Buddhist Study Center.

Prinz, Jesse J. (2012). *The conscious brain: How attention engenders experience*. New York: Oxford University Press.

Pye, Michael (2011). *Beyond meditation: Expressions of Japanese Shin Buddhist spirituality*. London: Equinox.

Rahula, Walpola (1974). *What the Buddha taught*. New York: Grove Press (revised edition).

Ram Dass (1971). *Be here now*. Cristobal, NM: Lama Foundation.

Raphael, Simcha P. (2009). *Jewish views of the afterlife*. Lanham, MD. Rowman & Littlefield Publishers.

Régamy, Konstanty (1938/1990). *The Bhadramāyākāravyākaraṇa*. New Delhi: Molital Banarsidass Publishers.

Sadakata, Akira (1997). *Buddhist cosmology*. Tokyo: Kōsei Publishing.

Schweitzer, Albert (1911). *The quest of the historical Jesus: A critical study of its progress from Reimarus to Wrede*. London: Adam and Charles Black.

Seki, Hozen (1989). *The great sound of enlightenment*. New York: The American Buddhist Academy.

Seligman, Martin E.P., Railton, Peter, Baumeister, Roy F., & Sripada, Chandra (2013). Navigating into the future or driven by the past. *Perspectives on Psychological Science, 8*, 119–141.

Smith, Gary S. (2011). *Heaven in the American imagination*. New York: Oxford University Press.

Smolin, Lee (2013). *Time beborn*. Boston: Houghton Mifflin Harcourt.

Steele, Albert T. (1918). Jesus' attitude toward his miracles. *The Biblical World, 51*, 195–203.

Storms, Sam (2007). The kingdom of God: Already but not yet—Part I. http://www .samstorms.com/all-articles/post/the-kingdom-of-god:-already-but-not-yet--- part-i/. Accessed May 4, 2015.

Strong, John S. (2007). *Relics of the Buddha*. Delhi: Motilal Banarsidass.

Sullivan, Mike (2012). . . . Sovereign grace Preterism. http://preterism.ning.com/ page/foundational-beliefs. Accessed May 4, 2015.

Sullivan, Patricia (2004). Kenryu T. Tsuji dies at 84; Buddhist bishop. *The Washington Post*, March 10, 2004. http://www.highbeam.com/doc/1P2-153585.html. Accessed January 4, 2015.

Taylor, Charles (2003). *Varieties of religion today: William James revisited.* Cambridge, MA: Harvard University Press.

Thompson, Evan (2007). *Mind in life.* Cambridge: Belknap Press.

Thompson, Evan (2014). *Waking, dreaming, being: Self and consciousness in neuroscience, meditation, and philosophy.* New York: Columbia University Press.

Tillich, Paul (1963). *The eternal now.* New York: Scribners.

Unger, Roberto Mangabeira & Smolin, Lee (2015). *The singular universe and the reality of time.* Cambridge, UK: Cambridge University Press.

Unno, Taitetsu (1984). *Tannisho: A Shin Buddhist classic.* Honolulu: Buddhist Study Center Press.

U.S. Christians' Views on the Return of Christ (2013). Pew Research Religion & Public Life Project. http://www.pewforum.org/topics/religious-beliefs-and-practices/ pages/3/. Accessed December 16, 2014.

Vail, Kenneth E., Juhl, Jacob, Arndt, Jamie, Vess, Matthew, Routledge, Clay, & Rutjens, Bastiaan T. (2012). When death is good for life: Considering the positive trajectories of terror management. *Personality and Social Psychological Review, 20,* 1–27.

Varela, Francisco, Thompson, Evan, & Rosch, Eleanor (1991). *The embodied mind.* Cambridge, MA: MIT Press.

Walker, Gail C. (2000).Secular eschatology: Beliefs about afterlife. *Omega, 41,* 5–22.

Walshe, Maurice (1995). *The long discourses of the Buddha: A translation of the Digha Nikaya.* Sommerville, MA: Wisdom Publications.

Westminster Confession (1646). http://www.reformed.org/documents/index .html?mainframe=http://www.reformed.org/documents/westminster_conf_of_ faith.html. Accessed January 7, 2014.

Wrzesniewski, Amy, McCauley, Clark, Rozin, Paul, & Schwartz, Barry (1997). Jobs, careers, and callings: People's relations to their work. *Journal of Research in Personality, 31,* 21–33.

Yokagawa, Kensho (1939/2011). Shin Buddhism as the religion of hearing. *The Eastern Buddhist* (1939), 7, 296–341. Reprinted in Pye (2011), 177–184, cited above.

Chapter 18

"Be Thou my Vision": Mystical
Experience and Religious Calling

J. Hugh Kempster

Be Thou my Vision, O Lord of my heart;
Naught be all else to me, save that Thou art.
Thou my best Thought, by day or by night,
Waking or sleeping, Thy presence my light.

Eochaid "Dallán" Forgaill (ca. 600)
translated by Mary Byrne (1880–1931)

There is a New Zealand Maori saying "ka mura, ka muri," which may be paraphrased as "walking backwards into the future." Ordinarily we see only the past, it directs and drives us; the future is unseen territory. But the phenomenon of mystical experience can be an exception to this rule. Mystical experiences, such as visions or dreams, often give the recipient a perceived glimpse of the future. They draw us toward possibilities that do not yet exist. Scriptural and historical narratives are full of stories of such experiences, and most religious practitioners today would attest to a contemporary reality in the lives of those they work with. Mystical experience is more often than not a healing experience, a powerful motivating force that drives a person toward future flourishing. In the Western post-Enlightenment world, however, it has slowly but surely become taboo to take seriously such phenomena. Many people who experience the numinous in this way today suppress the memory for fear of being judged as irrational. Recently I was flying to London, and by coincidence was seated next to an old acquaintance I had not seen for a long time. We started talking and I mentioned the paper I was writing on mysticism. This spurred my friend to recount a particularly vivid dream he had around the time of his father's death. "I've never told this to anyone before, outside my immediate family" he said. A sense of the numinous became palpable as we spoke, and for several hours between Melbourne and Dubai we exchanged story after story, in hushed tones, of our spiritual experiences. Time flew; it was a sacred and I suspect a healing conversation.

Talking about religious experience is not common today because the mystical has largely been excised from our secular society. Important as this corrective may have been for the development of science and technology, there is undoubtedly a baby that has been thrown out with the bathwater. It is not only theologians who have observed this absence and the need for a corrective. Marty Seligman (2011, pp. 261, 75) writes, "After a half century of neglect, psychologists are again studying spirituality and religiosity in earnest, no longer able to ignore their importance to people of faith" and considering his own life journey he notes, "I did not choose positive psychology. It called me. It was what I wanted from the very first, but experimental psychology and then clinical psychology were the only games in town that were even close to what was calling me. I have no less mystical way to put it." William James, in his seminal work on religious experience, holds mysticism in the highest regard (James, p. 428):

> Mystical states indeed wield no authority due to them being mystical states. But the higher ones among them point in directions to which the religious sentiments even of non-mystical [people] incline. They tell of the supremacy of the ideal, of vastness, of union, of safety, and of rest. They offer us hypotheses, hypotheses which we may voluntarily ignore, but which as thinkers we cannot possibly upset. The supernaturalism and optimism to which they would persuade us may, interpreted in one way or another, be after all the truest of insights into the meaning of this life.

I am an Anglican parish priest. Soon after I moved to my present incumbency in Melbourne, Australia, a woman asked to see me about a profound mystical experience that had recently overwhelmed her. She had heard that I was interested in mysticism. What did her experience mean? Was she going mad? Could I help her make sense of it all? Then a week later a young man turned up to church with a similar story. I asked if they would like to meet together with me to talk about these experiences, and before long a third person joined us. We decided to call the group (slightly tongue-in-cheek) Mystics Anonymous. Word soon spread that this was a safe place to talk about spiritual experience and the group grew. Nearly three years later Mystics Anonymous is a part of the furniture of our church. One of the first things I did with the group was to suggest that we read a mystical text together. "Your experience may be overwhelming, but it is not unique; many others have traversed this terrain before you and have left us some pretty amazing road maps." We use the Benedictine monastic method of reading, known in Latin as *Lectio divina* or "spiritual reading." It is a mindful way of approaching a text, slowing down the reading process, chewing over each word, and using each word as a springboard into silence and meditation. Week by week we imbibe the wisdom of the world's great mystics: the 20th-century contemplative Thomas Merton, the anonymous author of the medieval classic *The Cloud of Unknowing*, or the contemporary mystical writer Esther de Waal. These authors have become our spiritual guides as we met each week to break the taboo and talk freely about our spiritual experiences, both great and small. There is a lot of laughter in the group, some tears, a little healing, and perhaps even a glimpse of something that draws us into the future.

My first encounter with the mystical took place more than three decades ago. While playing in a rock band (and studying electronic engineering at university on the side) I had the first of three deeply formative religious experiences. It was a waking vision that overwhelmed me when I was visiting my parents' church in the north of England. To this day I can picture the bright red flames that engulfed two lions standing at the entrance to a large house. As quickly as the vision came it was gone, but the impact of what I saw has stayed with me to this day. It was a spiritual awakening that left me with a piercing sense of the reality of God's presence. Several years later, after a brief post-university sojourn in Israel and India, I arrived in New Zealand, commenced an engineering job, and had the privilege of sharing in the last year of my maternal grandmother's life. She is the great-granddaughter of one of the pioneering Anglican bishops of New Zealand, and it was when I was living with her for a few months that I had a second intense religious experience. It occurred while I was exploring the possibility of becoming an Anglican priest. My grandmother's Vicar had popped the question, "Hugh, have you ever considered ordination?" I responded with a tentative "yes," and decided to make my first career change, working as a youth leader in the church and taking up a study of theology. The second mystical experience came in the wake of this decision. It was soon after my grandmother had died. I was in my room, praying, when an overwhelming awareness of God's presence passed through me. The air was electric. It was dark outside, but I had a growing desire to climb a nearby hill that I had walked up many times. It felt as if God was speaking to me, telling me to climb the hill. This made no sense, and was even rather unwise given that it was night, but I felt the urge so strongly that I jumped on my bike, cycled with heart pumping past the graveyard to the start of the track, and then with a torch in hand set off up the hill. When I reached the top, I wrapped my blanket around me and sat praying until dawn. It was beautiful; a mountain-top experience quite literally. As I sat there in contemplative prayer I had a moment of profound clarity: I was being called by God to be a priest.

From that time the core strands of my adult life wove surprisingly quickly together: I met my wife, became a stepfather, continued my study of theology, and took up holy orders. I then was called to serve in a number of New Zealand parishes, became a father, dabbled with social rights activism, built a labyrinth, undertook a doctoral study of the medieval English mystics, and moved to Australia to take up the position of Senior Chaplain at Geelong Grammar School. By this time the heady days of mystical experience and intense religious calling had slipped into fond but distant memory. I worked hard at maintaining the spiritual disciplines of prayer and virtue, but my inner life often became quite dry. Then some three years ago another significant milestone of my faith journey took place; I had a third mystical experience of calling. My bishop had invited me to take up the incumbency of the historic Anglo-Catholic parish of St. Peter's Eastern Hill, Melbourne. It was a hard decision to make, because I was thoroughly enjoying life as a school chaplain, but when I agreed to respond to this call my inner life unexpectedly burst into flame once more, echoing my earlier mystical experiences. I was driving on the motorway after a successful final interview with my bishop and the St. Peter's incumbency committee. I started to pray, giving thanks for the new ministry opportunity that was opening up. Then, totally unexpectedly, I was overcome by a powerful sense of God's presence, such as I had not experienced for many years. I began to cry. The tears began gently, but gradually intensified until they began to pour out from deep within me. It felt like a mix of grief and joy. I had to pull to the side of the road and could not start driving again for nearly half an hour. Something new was stirring in my spirit. Then a few weeks later I was walking through Melbourne's Chinatown, when I came across two carved stone lions in a memorial garden. The hairs stood up on the back of my neck when I realized the scene that was laid out before me. I had an overwhelming sense of déjà vu. Up ahead, framed by these two heraldic beasts, was the large Victorian Vicarage of my new parish. All around me were the flame-like colors of Chinatown. This was a picture-perfect enactment of my first visionary experience all those years ago. I shuddered. Could it really be that the past 28 years had been leading to this particular point in time? I have never had, and expect never again to have, such a profound sense of being called into the future.

Telling one another our stories of mystical experience is unusual today, even for a priest who runs a group called Mystics Anonymous. I have to confess that I am much more comfortable writing a sermon, or an historical essay, than I am putting into print the deeply personal mystical experiences I have outlined above. Such stories are so subjective. Are they all in my mind? How will people judge me? Were these actually periods of insanity rather than revelation? Then I turn to the stories of my Christian tradition. There are numerous ancient tales of mystical experience. They were deemed important enough to tell and retell over thousands of years, and in the telling they somehow validate our present-day mystical experiences. The story of Moses at the burning bush, for example, is an archetypal tale of spiritual awakening. A displaced person, a Jewish refugee spared from execution as a child, rises to great power and wealth. But then Moses's fall from grace is equally great when he awakens to the injustice of the power structures of his culture, and impulsively murders an Egyptian oppressor. He flees the wrath of his adopted grandfather, the Pharaoh, and takes up the simple life of a shepherd. One day, after many years in self-imposed rural exile, he and his flock come to Horeb "the mountain of God" (NRSV, Exodus 3:1). An angel of God appears to him in a vision; a bush is ablaze but not consumed. Verse 4 notes an interesting detail: "When the Lord saw that he had turned aside to see, God called to him out of the bush." God's prerequisite is an openness on the part of Moses to the angelic vision, and into that openness God is able to speak: "Moses, Moses! Come no closer! Remove the sandals from your feet, for the place on which you are standing is holy ground . . . . The cry of the Israelites has now come to me; I have also seen how the Egyptians oppress them. So come, I will send you to Pharaoh to bring my people, the Israelites, out of Egypt." Somewhat reluctantly Moses responds to this mystical vision, this divine call into the future, and through God's miraculous grace and Moses's inspired leadership the people of Israel are liberated.

It is also on Mount Horeb, in another age, that a second great biblical prophet receives a supernatural revelation. This too is a beautifully crafted story of divine sustenance and ongoing call into an uncertain future, in the midst of horrific political violence. The prophet Elijah has been involved in a bloody power struggle with King Ahab, his wife Jezebel, and the false prophets of Baal. Elijah flees for his life, seemingly having failed his God, and in a state of deep depression he walks alone out into the wilderness. There is nothing to live for. He comes to a solitary broom tree and sits under it (NRSV, 1 Kings 19:4): "It is enough; now, O Lord, take away my life, for I am no better than my ancestors." As with Moses, there is an angelic vision that paves the way for a mystical intervention from God. The angel touches the sleeping prophet and says to him: "Get up and eat." Elijah looks up to see cake and water laid out for him. He eats and drinks and goes back to sleep but the angel wakes him and feeds him a second time. Strengthened by the angel's mystical fare, Elijah's trek into the wilderness to die is transformed into a spiritual pilgrimage, and after the requisite 40 days and 40 nights the prophet arrives at Mount Horeb, the site of Moses's spiritual awakening and call into leadership. Exhausted, he goes to sleep in the shelter of a cave. "What are you doing here?" God asks. He is on sacred ground. Elijah is afraid and explains that he has been very zealous for the Lord, in spite of his own people forsaking the covenant, throwing down the altars, and killing

the prophets. "I alone am left, and they are seeking my life, to take it away"
(v. 10). God instructs Elijah to go and stand on the mountain "for the Lord
is about to pass by." What happens next is worth quoting in full (NRSV,
1 Kings 19:11–14):

> Now there was a great wind, so strong that it was splitting mountains
> and breaking rocks in pieces before the Lord, but the Lord was not in the
> wind; and after the wind an earthquake, but the Lord was not in the earth-
> quake; and after the earthquake a fire, but the Lord was not in the fire; and
> after the fire a sound of sheer silence. When Elijah heard it, he wrapped
> his face in his mantle and went out and stood at the entrance of the cave.
> There came a voice to him that said, "What are you doing here, Elijah?"
> He answered, "I have been very zealous for the Lord, the God of hosts; for
> the Israelites have forsaken your covenant, thrown down your altars, and
> killed your prophets with the sword. I alone am left, and they are seeking
> my life, to take it away."

God is not revealed in the powerful tornado, the earthquake or the fire, but
in the gentleness of "a sound of sheer silence"; and into that silence God
repeats the question from verse 9 "What are you doing here?" Elijah again
affirms his righteousness and the great danger to which he is exposed. God
finally speaks into the prophet's spiritual and physical crisis; he is fed by
the divine—body, mind, and soul—and empowered for the next leg of the
journey.

In the Christian scriptures there is a third story, a carefully crafted addition that is presented as a crown to the mystic trilogy. Probably drawn from
one of the very early Christian texts, the story is preserved in all three of
the synoptic gospels: the Transfiguration (Matthew 17:1–13; Mark 9:2–8;
Luke 9:28–36). Jesus and his disciples have been proclaiming the good news,
healing the sick, and miraculously feeding the great crowds that have been
following them. The rabbi is exhausted and takes three of his closest com-
panions, Peter, James, and John, "up a high mountain apart, by themselves."
Parallels with the Moses and Elijah narratives are unmistakable (NRSV,
Mark 9:2b-8):

> [Jesus] was transfigured before them, and his clothes became dazzling
> white, such as no one on earth could bleach them. And there appeared
> to them Elijah with Moses, who were talking with Jesus. Then Peter said
> to Jesus, "Rabbi, it is good for us to be here; let us make three dwellings,
> one for you, one for Moses, and one for Elijah." He did not know what to
> say for they were terrified. Then a cloud overshadowed them, and from
> the cloud there came a voice, "This is my Son, the Beloved; listen to him!"

Suddenly when they looked around, they saw no one with them any more, but only Jesus.

This mountain-top experience is both spiritual awakening and ongoing revelation for the three disciples. They see their rabbi as the Messiah for the first time. And as they come down the mountain and back to normality, nothing will ever be the same; their shared mystical experience has changed everything and powerfully reaffirmed their call.

The telling of mystical experience is by no means restricted to scripture. In 14th- and 15th-century England there was a particular flourishing of Christian mysticism, and a number of mystics wrote of their experience. The vast network of monasteries that existed at that time was a highly sophisticated spiritual environment where the faithful who gave their lives to God, and took up a professional life of prayer, were initiated into the mysteries and complexities of divine encounter. Such a contemplative life was considered the highest Christian calling, as Augustine of Hippo writes (*On the Trinity*, i, 20): "Our Lord Jesus Christ . . . shall bring believers to the contemplation of God, wherein is the end of all good actions, and everlasting rest, and joy which never will be taken from us." But it was a life and an intimacy with God that was highly structured and had generally become reserved for those who took monastic life-vows. In late-medieval England, however, as on the Continent, change was afoot. Spiritual writings, even the Bible, were being translated from Latin and made available in the everyday language of the people. The Lady of the manor, and lay people of the new merchant class with a little discretionary income, were able to own and in some cases read manuscripts that had previously been restricted to the monastic cloister. A few of the laity, such as Margery Kempe, even reported having mystical encounters themselves (Windeatt, 1985, p. 75): "sometimes the Father of Heaven conversed with her soul as plainly and as certainly as one friend speaks to another through bodily speech."

One of the fathers of this medieval democratization and flourishing of mystical experience was Richard Rolle, who was born around the turn of the 14th century at Thornton, near Pickering, in Yorkshire, and died in 1349 at Hampole probably from the plague. Most of what we know of his biography comes from his own writings, and also from the *Legenda* found in the *Office of Saint Richard*, a collection of lections, antiphons, and a table of miracles drawn up in the 1380s in an unsuccessful attempt to effect his canonization (Comper, 1914, pp. xlv–lxii). The young Rolle must have shown considerable promise, because at the age of 13 or 14 he received a scholarship to study at Oxford University. In his 19th year, however, he became disenchanted with his studies and dropped out. There is a delightful story in Lection I of the *Legenda* where Rolle arranges a secret meeting with his favorite sister in the woods near their home, no doubt afraid of what his parents' reaction would be. Rolle asks her to bring two dresses, one gray and one white, and their father's rain-hood. He then proceeds to rip the sleeves off the gray tunic and the buttons off the white one. He slips into the white dress, and puts the now sleeveless gray one on top. Finally he dons his father's rain-hood, and stands before his bemused sister. She is not impressed: *Frater meus insanit,* she says, "my brother has gone mad!" The scene marks the launch of Rolle's life as a self-styled hermit, embarking on a faith journey outside the more established monastic and priestly pathways.

Rolle was a mystic with evangelistic zeal, who wrote prolifically about his experiences of God. His earlier writings are full of allusions to these mystical encounters, and the remarkable contemplative theology he develops is clearly shaped by them. For example, in *The Fire of Love* he tells of a spiritual awakening, with echoes perhaps of the biblical story of Moses (Wolters, 1972, p. 45):

> I cannot tell you how surprised I was the first time I felt my heart begin to warm. It was real warmth too, not imaginary, and it felt as if it was actually on fire, I was astonished at the way the heat surged up, and how this new sensation brought great and unexpected comfort. I had to keep feeling my breast to make sure there was no reason for it. . . . Before the infusion of this comfort I had never thought that we exiles could possibly have known such warmth, so sweet was the devotion it kindled. It set my soul aglow as if a real fire was burning there.

Arguably Rolle's greatest work is *Mending of Life.* Written near the end of his life, it is a 12-step programme detailing how ordinary Christians might flourish and mend their lives by progressing from conversion to the mystical heights of contemplation. Previously such a text might have been written for a novice nun or monk, but Rolle's audience was probably secular priests and through them the ordinary women and men of the parish. Although originally written in Latin, by the end of the 15th century there were no less than seven independent Middle English translations. It had become a veritable best-seller, especially popular among the new class of spiritually aware lay people with an interest in the contemplative life. So well known was Rolle's *Mending of Life* that the 12 chapter headings (or "twelve degrees") of this medieval spiritual classic found their way into the popular poetry of the day (McGovern-Mouron, 1996, p. 156):

Of perfect living twelve degrees
Grows in the tree that you here sees:

Conversion is the first that is heard,
The second is despising of the world,
The third is poverty of man and wife,
The fourth is the setting out of a good life;
Tribulation the fifth is then,
The sixth is patience of man,
The seventh is prayer, as it says in the text,
Meditation, the eighth is next;
The ninth is reading wisely sought,
The tenth is cleanness of deed and thought,
The eleventh is the love of God's Son,
The twelfth is contemplation.

Rolle's *Mending of Life* offers spiritual mending, or healing, to its readers. It plots a course for all would-be mystics and contemplatives in four parts, each made up of three chapters: from conversion and the related processes of detachment from the world, through pursuit of the good life and the spiritual battle that is required to maintain it, to the exercise of traditional monastic spiritual disciplines (prayer, meditation, and reading) and finally by God's grace to an earthly taste of the mystical through contemplation. Although an informed work, drawing from the scriptures and the great medieval theologians, *Mending of Life* has an attractive simplicity to it, which may have been the secret to its popularity. It is a work of affective rather than scholastic piety, urging the reader to delight in meditation "so that you may in time come to the inward feeling of love." Chapter 11, for example, opens with one such meditation designed to draw the reader into an experience of the mystical love of God (my own translation, from Kempster, 2007, p. 35):

. . . O Love, enflame my heart to love God,
So that nothing but the sweet embraces of God may burn in me.
O good Jesus, who could give to me the grace of feeling you,
The one who may not be seen or felt in this body?
Enter the very depths of my soul,
Come into my heart and fill it with your full bright sweetness.
Make my soul drunk with the fervent wine of your sweetest love.
. . . Come, I beg you, soft and true joy;
Come, O sweetness most desired;
Come, my beloved, my comfort, have pity on my languishing soul.
Sear into my heart with your sweet burning;
Enflame the innermost parts of my being;
And with your inward light enlighten me.
Feed my body and my soul with such great joy of love, that it may not be told.

The final chapter of *Mending of Life* lays out Rolle's goal for his readers: that they might remain in God's love and ultimately be gifted with the mystical heights of contemplation. "What is contemplation?" Rolle asks. "Contemplation is a wonderful joy of God's love conceived in the soul with the sweetness of angels praise. This wonderful joy is the goal of perfect prayer and of highest devotion." Where biblical narratives lay out in broad brushstrokes the possibility of mystical encounters with God, Rolle puts forward a detailed program of how to attain it, or at least how to cultivate an inner life whereby such encounters become possible. His work was in one sense nothing new; contemplative theologians and monastic spiritual directors had been doing such work for centuries. What was ground breaking, however, was his intended audience. Rolle's writing demystified the mystical. The pathway to the ancient monastic reality of revelation, and intimacy with God, was laid out for anyone who had the will to walk it.

Julian of Norwich is a prime example of one such medieval layperson who did indeed have the will, and through her writings we have remarkable insight into her own mystical experience. We know very little about Julian's biography, even her name is not her own, she is called after the church in which she lived as an anchoress for more than 20 years, St Julian's church in Norwich. Most of what we do know comes from a book she penned in two versions called *A Revelation of Love*. The book is based around a complex mystical vision in sixteen "showings" that she had of the crucifixion in 1373, 24 years after Richard Rolle's death, when she herself was "thirty and a half years old." Julian's intense spiritual awakening, experienced while suffering a serious illness, was so profound that it spurred her into the austere life of an anchoress. She was called into a rather extreme life of prayer, where she chose to die to the world quite literally and be walled into a tiny cell, or anchorhold, appended to the church. There she would remain for the rest of her life.

An anchoress' cell had three windows: one for her maid to pass through food and care for her physical needs; one through to the church next door, which catered for her spiritual needs; and a third window out onto a porch on the street. Here people would come for counsel from the wise woman of prayer. In this tiny cell Julian had plenty of time to reflect on her visionary experience, and following in the pioneering footsteps of Richard Rolle she wrote her theology in the vernacular. Julian was, in fact, as much a pioneer of mysticism for the ordinary person as Rolle. She was the first woman in late-medieval England to write anything in the common tongue, let alone a profound work of mystical theology. Julian's starting point for theology was her visionary experience, which she was convinced God had given her to pass on to others. It not only called her into the future, but gave profound meaning to a life that many might view as incredibly restrictive, but which for her opened up great richness and meaning.

In chapter five of the Longer Version of *A Revelation of Love* (Colledge and Walsh, 1978, p. 183) for example, Julian comes to an understanding that her Lord "is to us everything which is good and comforting." She does not then head off into the realms of Thomistic theology: How did Plato define "the Good"? What are the differences between the corporeal and theological virtues? Rather, she earths her mystical theology in metaphors that will speak to her intended lay audience, her "even Christians." This crucified Christ is mysteriously present for us all, not just the religious professionals. Divine revelation is all around you. Wake up! Christ's mystical presence is like the clothes you are wearing—can you feel them? Can you feel him? He is enfolding you, close to you, embracing you, surrounding you with love and warmth. Or let me put it another way (perhaps she has a spiritual directee in mind who came to the window yesterday to seek counsel) did you notice the hazelnuts that have fallen from the tree over there? You might not have seen them as you walked past. Pick one up on the way home. Hold it in your hand. Look at it, I mean really look at it. It is so small, so inconsequential. It could so easily become nothing, be crushed underfoot, decay and disappear. And yet it exists. Why? Because God loves it. It is no different from you and me and all creation. We exist because of the love of God, nothing more, nothing less.

Despite being walled into a tiny cell for the remainder of her life, Julian's theology is remarkably down to earth. This may have been because the role of anchoress was so integral to medieval life. The three windows of her anchorhold connected Julian with domestic reality and gossip, church politics and liturgy, as well as the hustle and bustle (and dangers) of life on the streets of Norwich, England's second largest city. It was a time of war, the hundred-year war between England and France. Those the church deemed heretics were being burnt to death in Lollard Pits, within smelling distance of her anchorhold. Julian lived through the bubonic plague, which killed one third of England's population, and by the 1380s the sociopolitical effects of this crisis were manifesting in riots and assassinations. Institutions that had held strong for centuries were crumbling, and a world-changing technological revolution was dawning with the explosion of lay literacy and the soon to be invented printing press. In all of this complexity and threat Julian was gifted with a profound optimism through her mystical experience, and by putting this in writing her *Revelation of Love* has been a gift to numerous others over the centuries. Thomas Merton, one of the 12th-century's greatest mystical theologians and contemplatives, judged Julian as one of England's greatest theologians (Merton, 1964, p. 275):

Julian is without doubt one of the most wonderful of all Christian voices. She gets greater and greater in my eyes as I grow older, and whereas in the old days I used to be crazy for St John of the Cross, I would not exchange him now for Julian if you gave me the world and the Indies and all the

Spanish mystics rolled up in one bundle. I think that Julian of Norwich is with Newman the greatest English theologian. She is really that. For she reasons from her experience of the substantial centre of the great Christian mystery of Redemption. She gives her experience and her deductions, clearly, separating the two. And the experience is of course nothing merely subjective. It is the objective mystery of Christ as apprehended by her, with the mind and formation of a fourteenth-century English woman. And that fourteenth-century England is to me and always has been a world of light.

Religious experience is by definition subjective, and impossible to define concretely, but it is also as real and as widely encountered as almost any other human experience. Tertullian, one of the early Christian theologians, takes as normative the experience of the mystical (Inge, 1899, p. 16) "The majority, almost, of [people] learn God from visions." We now live in a very different age but to ignore such experience, whether one perceives it from a faith perspective or not, is to neglect something foundational to who we are as human beings. Dreams, visions, numinous encounters, and other mystical phenomena have long been a source of well-being and inspiration. Until relatively recently in the West they have been a valued and well-documented component of human understanding and wellbeing. In a world where the common perception of "religion" is now almost synonymous with terror or abuse, it is high time that the mystical riches of the human condition are one again taken seriously. These realities of human existence have the capacity to heal and to call us as individuals and as communities into a flourishing future.

REFERENCES

Augustine, *On the Trinity*, i, 20, online edition, http://www.newadvent.org/fathers/130101.htm. Accessed September 26, 2013.

Colledge, Edmund and Walsh, James (Trans.). (1978). *Julian of Norwich. Showings.* New York: Paulist Press.

Comper, Frances (Trans.). (1914). *The fire of love or melody of love and the mending of life or rule of living.* London: Methuen.

Inge, William Ralph (1899). *Christian mysticism: Considered in eight lectures delivered before the University of Oxford.* London: Methuen.

James, William (1902; repr. 1985). *The varieties of religious experience: A study in human nature.* London: Penguin.

Kempster, Hugh, ed. (2007). "Richard Rolle, *Emendatio vitae: Amendinge of lyf,*" unpublished doctoral thesis. University of Waikato. http://researchcommons.waikato.ac.nz/handle/10289/2578. Accessed September 26, 2013.

McGovern-Mouron, Anne (1996). "The *Desert of Religion.*" *Analecta Carthusiana, 130* (9), 149–162.

Merton, Thomas (1964). *Seeds of destruction*. New York: Farrar, Straus and Giroux.

Seligman, Martin E. P. (2011). *Flourish: A visionary new understanding of happiness and well-being*. New York: Free Press.

Windeatt, Barry A. (Trans.) (1985). *The book of Margery Kempe*. London: Penguin.

Wolters, Clifton (Trans.). (1972). *The fire of love: Richard Rolle*. London: Penguin.

CONCLUSION

Answering the Call

David Bryce Yaden

In light of the time-bending ideas that open this book, the story of its beginning makes for a fitting ending.

FROM UNDER THE CATHEDRAL

"Being Called Into the Future" was a meeting held in the fall of 2013 on the grounds of the Canterbury Cathedral, England. A group of scholars and scientists representing vastly different beliefs hoped to gain clarity on the role that being called into the future plays in spiritual traditions.

Invitations to the event read:

> Prospection, the internal representation of possible futures, is a ubiquitous feature of the human mind, with roots going back into our animal ancestry. Most of social science, however, understands human action as determined by the past, and views any sort of teleology as mysterious and metaphysical. Understood as prospection, teleology is neither mysterious nor metaphysical - it simply is guidance by one's internal, evaluative representations of possible future states. We call this being drawn into the future.
>
> You will be participating in a gathering of eminent religious and secular scholars with the purpose of pre-scientific discussion of prospection in religion and spirituality. The presence of numinous dreams and hallucinations, the sense of fulfilling one's potential for oneself, and seeing the future so vividly that it shapes one's sense of the present are all views of

how one may be drawn into the future. From this pioneering meeting, Dr. Seligman and his research team hopes to gain clarity on the role of being drawn or called into the future in religion and spirituality.

This book arose out of these extraordinary conversations.

Ecumenical meetings of this kind are rare in the contemporary climate of mutual distrust between science and religion. This is especially so in the case of monotheistic religions. Whereas Buddhism has embraced psychology and neuroscience—largely due to the efforts of the Tenzin Gyatso, The 14th Dalai Lama (Kabat-Zinn & Davidson, 2012) —Western religions have been generally slower to openly engage with empirical scientists. The Canterbury meeting was conceived as an opportunity to foster the cross-fertilization of ideas across these traditional barriers.

The customary divide between religious and scientific worldviews was on display at the first dinner. At one end of the Canterbury Cathedral Lodge's long table sat men and women from various religious traditions, including some wearing dark robes and clerical collars. These were "the supernaturalists," according to the parlance adopted for the occasion. Chief Rabbi of the UK Lord Jonathan Sacks, Australian Vicar Hugh Kempster, and Union Seminary president Serena Jones were among those in attendance. The senior editors of this book were also present, chaplain and author Theo McCall and theologian, minister, and clinical psychologist J. Harold Ellens.

Martin Seligman, the mind behind the meeting, sat at the other end of the table with his wife and two youngest daughters as well as other psychologists and researchers—"the naturalists." They included psychiatrists George Vaillant and Diane Highum, psychologist Amy Wrzesniewski, and, as luck would have it, me, a junior research fellow. Between these two groups sat a distinguished and varied group of believers and skeptics. They included world-renowned authors, business leaders, and politicians, such as best-selling author Robert Wright, John Templeton Foundation representative Chris Stawski, international employment CEO Therese Rein, and Australian prime minister Kevin Rudd. Over the course of the meeting, these divides would fall away as discussions and debates revealed more and more overlap on underlying values.

For the dialogue to get off the ground, participants were encouraged to "suspend belief" and "suspend disbelief" both by Martin Seligman, a scientist, and J. Harold Ellens, a theologian. The resulting open-mindedness toward the ultimate source of calling experiences allowed a creative and free-wheeling discussion to emerge. Personal experiences anchored the conversations and speculation centered on how callings influence the lives of those who have them, rather than fixating on their oft-contested origins. The supernaturalists imagined how empirically guided recommendations could help make well-being part of their teaching and ministries. The naturalists identified research questions and generated hypotheses worthy of further empirical testing in their laboratories.

Experiences of calling became the centerpiece of the retreat and a point of connection among all the guests. At one point, the guests were asked who among them felt a sense of calling in their lives. Everyone in the room raised a hand. Despite this unanimously affirmative response, each guest likely had a different meaning of the word "calling" in mind. They may have meant, for example, particularly meaningful work, an intuitive feeling of being drawn in a particular direction, a revelatory experience, or a sense of destiny.

This book is a continuation of the Canterbury conversation. It explores how scientists and scholars can have very different backgrounds and belief systems and yet, can converge in their conception of *being called*.

THE MEANING OF WORK

Meaningful work emerged as a major theme during the Canterbury conversations. Historically, the capacity for work has held a valued position within psychology. Freud (1909/1960) elevated the capacity for work alongside love as the two primary signs of mental health. In popular imagination, the inability to work is an index of psychological difficulties and a return to work a benchmark of therapeutic success. Career counselors and vocational psychologists have since contributed to a rich empirical literature on how to play matchmaker between an individual and a career, while organizational psychologists and human resource professionals explore productivity and health in the workplace (Cameron, Dutton, & Quinn, 2003). The research presented in this book demonstrates that work and love, well-being, productivity, and an authentic person-career fit can come together in the form of a calling.

Psychological perspectives on callings as meaningful, prosocial work are developed throughout this book. Amy Wrzesniewski describes different orientations to work. Given this framework, "jobs" are undertaken only for the paycheck, "careers" are a path of professional advancement, and "callings" are personally fulfilling, socially useful work that would be done with no pay and with no promotions (Wrzesniewski, McCauley, Rozin, & Schwartz, 1997). The distinctions between jobs and careers and callings are measurable, and they predict important job and life outcomes. The field of Positive Organizational Scholarship works to clarify and leverage callings and other work-related concepts that bring about well-being. According to this view, someone with a calling would likely find statements like these true:

- My work makes the world a better place.
- My work is one of the most important things in my life.

- If I was financially secure, I would continue with my current line of work even if I was no longer paid (Wrzesniewski, McCauley, Rozin, & Schwartz, 1997).

A number of chapters in this book chart new ways forward for research on callings. Susanna Wu-Pong's calling curriculum for biomedical students provides a starting place to help students find or integrate their calling. Susan Rosenthal and Mary "Bit" Smith's chapter provides physicians' perspectives on callings and suggests including the concept in medical education. Scholarship by Chinese psychologists Kaiping Peng and Yukun Zhao suggests that callings can benefit the working lives of individuals in diverse, cross-cultural populations. Psychologists Bryan Dik and Michael Steger focus on the "transcendent summons" found in callings as a framework to bridge the divide between secular and sacred perspectives.

Many major religions valued and sanctified meaningful work long before the birth of psychology. Calls to the ministry or the monastery are the classic cases, illustrated in this volume by Chaplain Theo McCall's story of his own religious calling. In Christianity, Martin Luther expanded the concept of a calling to any work, sacred or secular, that serves a greater good (Weber, 1930). Stephen Lewis's chapter describes modern faith-based programs designed to inspire adolescents from diverse backgrounds to adopt purpose-driven work in fields beyond religious domains.

While callings have benefits, they also incur significant costs. Two chapters emphasize the disadvantages of callings. Ryan Duffy, Richard Douglass, and Kelsey Autin present research on how people with callings can be exploited to work more hours for less pay and are at greater risk for workaholism and burnout. Gregg Levoy illustrates how a spiritual perspective of callings views these sacrifices as an inevitable part of the path to a calling. Even those willing to brave the sacrifices may never get the opportunity to answer a calling. The risk of losing a reliable paycheck in the pursuit of more risky but rewarding work underscores how callings are, unfortunately, still more accessible to the privileged than the disadvantaged. And of course, many people never find their calling at all. Callings are not for everyone, nor is everyone called.

ILLUMINATING THE NUMINOUS

One afternoon during the Canterbury meetings, guests sat in the Cathedral's garden for a session of "Mystics Anonymous" (see Appendix for more information on Mystics Anonymous) led by Vicar Hugh Kempster. Kempster created this group format for clergy to share their personal encounters with extraordinary experiences. Our session of Mystics Anonymous demonstrated to all present that callings also come as revelatory experiences. Rudolph Otto (1958) called these "numinous experiences," encounters with a sense of otherworldy presence that fill us with awe, fear, and inspiration. William James (1902/1985) also described these experiences in his classic *The Varieties of Religious Experience.*

In this book, we use "calling experiences" to denote profoundly meaningful, temporary mental states that contain a revelation or directive that seems to come from beyond the self. The prototypical case is Saint Paul's road to Damascus moment, when a beatific vision and commanding voice transformed Saul the violent persecutor into Paul the saint (Longenecker, 1997). Some interpret Paul's experience and similar cases as nothing more than a seizure, while others view them as revelations from God; this book provides a spectrum of perspectives between these two views.

J. Harold Ellens (2011), who has led much of his life based on the guidance of his own numinous experiences, describes the *ordinariness* of these extraordinary events in his chapter. Nevertheless, for many people who have such experiences—about 30–40 percent of the population—they are unforgettable and profound sources of meaning and purpose. People who have had a calling experience would likely agree with the following:

- I have had a profound religious experience or awakening that changed the direction of my life (Gallup, 2003).
- Have you ever been aware of, or influenced by, a presence or a power—whether you call it God or not—which is different from your everyday self? (Hay & Morisy, 1978).
- I was drawn by something beyond myself to pursue my current line of work (Dik, Eldridge, Steger & Duffy, 2012).

Many people who have these experiences are reluctant to talk about them. In Mystics Anonymous, stories often begin with "I've never told anyone about this, but . . . " A number of chapters in this book break the cultural silence surrounding calling experiences. Psychologist Martin Seligman and psychiatrist Thomas Singer both describe numinous dreams that called them to their present work. David Lukoff relates the calling experience that inspired him to successfully argue for including explicit mention of the positive potential of these experiences in the *DSM-IV*, the diagnostic "bible" used by psychotherapists around the world.

While all major religions are mentioned in this book, callings are most commonly discussed within Christian traditions. Ralph Hood describes some Christian conceptions of callings and how they typically involve the discomfort and sacrifice that come with serving God and other people. He contrasts these mainstream views with the extreme case of "snake handling" in

Appalachian churches. This death-defying practice demonstrates both the awe-inspiring courage that calling experiences make possible as well as the questionable ends people can feel called to pursue. The personal and ethical analysis that all callings require before accepting them is a perennial caution in religious traditions and a warning reiterated in nearly every chapter in this book.

This book also looks beyond monotheistic contexts to Hindu and Buddhist traditions. These traditions stress unity. Psychologists Zoran Josipovic and Judith Blackstone describe feeling called to a nondual understanding of reality, the awareness that everything is simultaneously different yet unified. Feeling at one with other people provides a powerful motivation to reach out to reduce suffering in others. In states of unity, the suffering of others becomes one's own and the impulse to relieve it immediate.

Psychologist and Buddhist lay leader Gordon Bermant articulates a Buddhist account that is aptly captured by the phrase "already, but not yet." This koan-like phrase emphasizes how religious understandings of the past can inspire benevolent action by individuals and organizations in the present and future.

Scientists are beginning to discover the neurocognitive grammar that underpins calling experiences. In their chapter, neuroscientists Cristiano Crescentini, Cosimo Urgesi, and Franco Fabbro provide a review of changes in brain activity that tend to occur during different religious and spiritual experiences. This research helps to explain how the body and brain mediate the feelings of transcendence, communion, and union that are commonly reported during calling experiences. Building on this research, neuroscientist Andrew Newberg and I suggest that the content—the voices, visions, and intuitions—that accompany calling experiences may come to consciousness in a way similar to creative epiphanies.

Like a compass finding true north, calling experiences can align us with what is most authentic in our own lives and point us towards what the world needs most. Whether one interprets callings through scientific, secular, or sacred perspectives, they are often counted among life's most meaningful moments and they can orient people towards the work of their lives. Thus, a calling can refer to the initial inspiration, the journey, or the destination. That is, callings are alternately defined as specific experiences, intuitions that continue to draw one forward, or an ongoing commitment to meaningful, prosocial work.

WE WOULD BE BUILDING TEMPLES STILL UNDONE

The Canterbury meeting was about more than callings and so is this book. We hoped then—as we do now—to find new modes of sacred and secular collaboration. During the Canterbury proceedings, Martin Seligman remembered a hymn from his school days that speaks to this hope, "We Would be Building Temples Still Undone." The hymn became a theme for the meeting, demonstrating how originally religious concepts can strike universal chords:

We would be building; temples still undone
O'er crumbling walls their crosses scarcely lift,
Waiting till love can raise the broken stone,
And hearts creative bridge the human rift.

As this book demonstrates, being beckoned to the work of building a better future is a conception of calling shared by sacred and secular traditions. But the shape of these temples to come is unknown, and there are plenty of obstacles for sacred and secular cooperation. Fundamentalists of both groups seek hegemony and balk at cooperation. No doubt some religious individuals will object to subjecting so sacred and personal an experience as a calling to the cold eye of science. In the same way, some secular individuals will undoubtedly feel scandalized that scientists opened their minds to topics traditionally supernatural. So polemics go.

But let us imagine that we may be witness to the dawning of a new era of unprecedented cooperation between sacred and secular perspectives.

In such a future, religious and spiritual traditions might further incorporate scientific discoveries, as Pope Francis has just done by acknowledging the evidence supporting Darwin and the big bang (Neuman, 2014). We might see empirically guided recommendations for more effective religious and spiritual practices, charitable giving, and counseling to help people understand their calling. Religious and spiritual beliefs that provide examples of mental processes, such as feeling deeply connected to the world, might receive further psychological study. Perhaps the emphasis on the big questions found in religious and spiritual traditions will inspire society to support more scientific inquiry into the nature of consciousness, our place in the universe, and the future of our species. Perhaps psychology and secular society will learn from and use some of the concepts, rituals, and practices that religious and spiritual traditions offer. The list of worthy causes that could be enhanced by cooperation goes on and on.

For now, however, beginning to find common ground over shared values and working together to build new forms for human flourishing is a call that we all can answer.

REFERENCES

Cameron, K., Dutton, J., & Quinn, R. E. (Eds.). (2003). *Positive organizational scholarship: Foundations of a new discipline*. San Francisco: Berrett-Koehler Publishers.

Dik, B. J., Eldridge, B. M., Steger, M. F., & Duffy, R. D. (2012). Development and validation of the Calling and Vocation Questionnaire (CVQ) and Brief Calling Scale (BCS). *Journal of Career Assessment, 20,* 242–263.

Duffy, R. D., Dik, B. J., & Steger, M. F. (2011). Calling and work-related outcomes: Career commitment as a mediator. *Journal of Vocational Behavior, 78*(2), 210–218.

Ellens, J. Harold (2011), *Light from the Other Side, The Paranormal as Friend and Familiar (Real Life Experiences of a Spiritual Pilgrim)*, Eugene, OR: Wipf and Stock.

Freud, S. (1909/1960). *Letters of Sigmund Freud* (E. L. Freud, Ed.). New York: Basic Books.

Gallup Organization. (2003, January 14). *Religious awakenings bolster Americans' faith.* Available from http://www.gallup.com

Hay, D., & Morisy, A. (1978). Reports of ecstatic, paranormal, or religious experience in Great Britain and the United States: A comparison of trends. *Journal for the Scientific Study of Religion,* 255–268.

James, W. (1902/1985). *The varieties of religious experience,* Vol. 13. Cambridge, MA: Harvard University Press.

Kabat-Zinn, J., & Davidson, R. (Eds.). (2012). *The mind's own physician: A scientific dialogue with the Dalai Lama on the healing power of meditation.* Oakland, CA: New Harbinger Publications.

Longenecker, R. N. (Ed.). (1997). *The Road from Damascus: The Impact of Paul's Conversion on His Life, Thought, and Ministry.* Grand Rapids. MI: William B. Eerdmans Publishing.

Neuman, S. (2014, October 28). Pope Says God Not 'A Magician, With A Magic Wand.' *National Public Radio.* Retrieved from http://www.npr.org/blogs/thetwo-way/2014/10/28/359564982/pope-says-god-not-a-magician-with-a-magic-wand

Otto, R. (1958). *The idea of the holy.* New York: Oxford University Press.

Weber, M. (1930). *The Protestant Ethic and the Spirit of Capitalism.* T. Parsons, trans. New York: Routledge Classics.

Wrzesniewski, A., McCauley, C., Rozin, P., & Schwartz, B. (1997). Jobs, careers, and callings: People's relations to their work. *Journal of Research in Personality, 31*(1), 21–33.

Appendix

Mystics Anonymous: An Introduction

J. Hugh Kempster and David Bryce Yaden

Can you tell the story of how Mystics Anonymous first came into being?

Mystics Anonymous was conceived in a car in 2008. The Archbishop of Melbourne, Dr. Philip Freier, had invited Professor Marty Seligman to discuss the implications of positive psychology for the Church. I was Marty's driver that evening. We struck up a conversation on the way home and Marty asked me about my calling to be a priest. I told him about an intense spiritual experience I had as a young man. Marty listened attentively and then replied with his own story of a formative dream he had experienced. It was a sacred moment, a simple exchange of stories about our respective calls into the future, but in that conversation something new came into existence.

Four years later, soon after being appointed the Vicar of an inner-city Anglican parish in Melbourne, I was having coffee with a new parishioner. "I hope you don't think I'm crazy, but I've been having some very intense religious experiences. Can I talk to you about them?" After listening to her story I assured her that she was not losing her mind, and shared my own story of spiritual awakening as a young adult. We then touched on the work of some of the great Christian mystics, such as Julian of Norwich and Thomas Merton; an hour disappeared in a moment. "This has been so helpful Fr Hugh. I've been carrying this for months and I didn't know who to turn to. Can we talk again soon?" I assured her that we could and made another appointment.

Just three days later, over refreshments after church, a young man confided in me with a remarkably similar story. He had been sitting alone in our church the previous week and had an overwhelming sense of peace and the presence of God. When he asked if I had time for a coffee to unpack this further, and I looked at a rather full diary, a thought occurred to me. "Just this week I was talking to another parishioner who I think you'd have a lot in common with. Perhaps the three of us could meet together." They did indeed have a lot in common, and soon afterward a woman I was preparing for marriage joined the group. She had expressed a desire to deepen her spiritual life, and reconnect with her Christian roots, and the others were more than happy to welcome her on board. The meeting format seemed to work well and over the coming months the group grew. After a while we decided to call ourselves (a little tongue-in-cheek) Mystics Anonymous.

As well as this core group, I also run occasional one-off Mystics Anonymous sessions. The first of these was at a small gathering of theologians and positive psychologists at Canterbury Cathedral in England. Marty Seligman and the John Templeton Foundation had brought us together around the theme of "Being Called into the Future." When it was time for me to present, I made a spontaneous decision to abandon my paper and conduct a Mystics Anonymous session in the garden. We sat in a circle, with the ancient Cathedral as a backdrop, and I asked the group to share their stories of mystical experience. Initially there was a long silence and I wondered how wise my decision to abandon the paper had been. What if no one engaged with the idea? After all we were essentially a group of strangers from a wide variety of religious and nonreligious backgrounds. But over the course of that afternoon every member of the group volunteered a story. There was a tale of nature mysticism on a Buddhist retreat, two stories of numinous experiences in the Holy City of Jerusalem, accounts of formative calls and spiritual awakenings, and several stories of encounters with death. It was a deeply moving and memorable afternoon.

What was your intention or hope behind creating Mystics Anonymous?

Mystics Anonymous is a little subversive. People open up and tell their stories because there are not many places in the modern world where one can talk freely about religious experience; even in many faith communities I might add. Research suggests that a significant percentage of people have had such experiences, and yet talking about the numinous has almost become taboo. People often begin their stories with "you'll probably think I'm mad" or "I've not told anyone this before." So from the very beginning the intent of Mystics Anonymous has been to provide a safe place where such stories can be shared and treasured.

That being said, the overall aim of Mystics Anonymous is not to encourage people to seek out or generate exotic mystical experiences. Mystics Anonymous is not a show-and-tell: my religious experience is bigger and better than yours! There is a long history of spiritual direction that strongly advocates against this thrill-seeking tendency. Open and honest talk about mystical experience is really just a means to an end. And the end is silence.

The great mystics of history, across faith traditions, all led lives seeped in silence. It was the air that they breathed. Silence is fast becoming a lost art in contemporary Western culture, and yet it is foundational to our health and flourishing as human beings. We aim to conclude each Mystics Anonymous meeting with a period of 15 or 20 minutes of communal silence or contemplative prayer. Fostering a contemplative spirit in an increasingly frenetic and angst-filled world is the primary intent of Mystics Anonymous.

Is there historical precedent for such groups that you are aware of?

Yes, numerous. There is something ancient, even primal in what we do. Most of the world's sacred texts were born out of oral tradition, faith stories both past and present, were told seated around a campfire or dining table or altar. In a small way, this is what Mystics Anonymous does. We meet in a home, share hospitality, sit in a circle, delve into the spiritual stories of our ancestors, and tell our own stories in response bringing the ancient stories to life. The silence aids our listening and reminds us of the richness and truth that dwells beneath and beyond our words.

Tell me about the group format. How should a Mystics Anonymous session begin?

The first meeting of a new group and a one-off session of Mystics Anonymous are very similar in format. The leader gives a brief introduction, perhaps sharing a story of her or his own, inviting people to listen attentively and respectfully in silence to the stories of others. Analysis or even a short response to each story by the leader or other group members should be avoided. Let the story sit in silence once told. It needs to be emphasized that the story does not have to be miraculous or supernatural. The medieval visionary Julian of Norwich, for example, writes about the mystical experience of meditating on a hazelnut in her hand.

I usually talk in my introduction about "big-M" and "little-m" mystics. Our libraries are replete with accounts and writings of big-M Mystics: Moses, Jesus, Buddha, Mohammed, Anselm, Hildegaard, Rumi, Moses de León, Mother Teresa, Thomas Merton to name but a few. These figures are inspiring, but the vast majority of us will never attain such heights of mysticism. Most of us are little-m mystics. We will never be the founder of a religious order, or be called into the eremitic life, but we are still mystics. My experience of simply receiving the holy sacrament and being brought to tears, or the strong sense of connection with nature that overwhelmed you on the wilderness retreat, are valid mystical experiences. It is important that the group is aware of this.

After this brief introduction the leader's work is largely done until the end of the session. Silence between stories does not need to be filled; in fact should not be filled by the leader or other members of the group. And it is fine if a member of the group does not feel ready to share a story. That person can wait until the end of the session, or share the experience at another meeting.

All Mystics Anonymous sessions end in silence. Ideally at the start of the session, or beforehand, the leader will have ascertained if group members are used to practicing mindfulness or meditation for prolonged periods, or whether some teaching will be required in this area. At least 20 minutes before the end of the session the leader needs to sensitively draw the sharing to a close. The leader then takes the group through a short centering prayer or mindfulness exercise. There are numerous resources in this area. One I often use is a Christian classic, Anthony de Mello *Sadhana, a Way to God: Christian Exercises in Eastern Form* (1978; repr. Melbourne: HarperCollins, 1998). Recorded meditations are also widely available by mindfulness practitioners such as Jon Kabat-Zinn. With a faith-based group this time of guided meditation can take the form of spoken prayer. The leader may prepare such a prayer beforehand, or group members could be encouraged to offer a short extemporary prayer themselves. Ideally there is then at least 10—15 minutes of intentional silence. The leader is responsible for gently bringing the silence to an end, and then making any final announcements before the close of the session.

What about an ongoing Mystics Anonymous group? How does that meeting format differ from a one-off session?

After the opening session, the weekly Mystics Anonymous meetings need to subtly move away from a primary focus on individual stories of mystical experience, and into the facilitation of discussion on a classic mystical text. Personal stories will still naturally emerge in the discussion, and this is good, but it is important that there is no perceived pressure for group members to generate tales of their mystical prowess (or to fear the lack thereof).

The sustainable ongoing weekly pattern is a mix of modern and ancient formats. In order to provide a safe space for members to freely discuss mystical experiences, as and when they arise, we have chosen a format similar to the tried-and-true book club. The books we select are classic mystical texts, and in our case are from the Christian faith tradition, texts such as the medieval treatise *The Cloud of Unknowing* or St Teresa of Avila's *Interior Castle*. A Google search around the word "mysticism" generates numerous possible texts that groups from other faith traditions could choose. Over the weeks these authors of mystical theology become our spiritual guides as we slowly work our way through the book.

Mystics Anonymous also draws on a much older model of communal reading, attributed to St Benedict of Nursia (ca. 480–547 AD) and later expounded by the Carthusian monk Guigo II (ca. 1115–ca. 1198 AD) in his treatise *Scala Claustralium* or "The Ladder of Monks." The model is known as *lectio divina* or "spiritual reading." It is a four-step method of communally reading sacred texts in such a way that they become a springboard into silence. Although Christian in origin, it can easily be adapted by groups from other faith traditions.

The *lectio divina* framework has four parts to it. Our weekly group moves through these in about an hour, but in a conference, workshop, or retreat setting, this can easily expand to several hours. Firstly the group reads a portion of the chosen text, out loud, slowly mulling over each word. This is Guigo's first rung of the ladder, in Latin *lectio*. The ideas and thoughts the words evoke are then drawn out and mulled over by the group, which is the second rung of the ladder *meditatio*. This group meditation on the text should be inductive rather than didactic or analytic, a reader response that comes out of group discussion, rather an over dependence on the specialized knowledge of the leader. What is this passage saying to you? How do you resonate with the ideas presented here? Or with a faith-based group: what is God saying to you through these words? Verbal prayer may then be used to provoke an affective response and draw the group discussion into sharp focus. This is the third rung of Guigo's ladder *oratio*. Nonfaith groups could easily replace such prayer with an invitation to verbalize focus words from the preceding discussion. The group finally alights the fourth rung of the ladder, *contemplatio* or contemplative silence. The leader may assist the group to enter into this space by offering a short centering prayer or mindfulness exercise, and then the group sits in intentional silence for around 15 minutes.

What is an appropriate mindset to take in participating in or leading a Mystics Anonymous session?

I think listening is paramount. Listening respectfully to others. Listening honestly to one's self. Listening to the subtle stirrings of the human spirit within. And for those of us from faith traditions, listening to God. It is as simple and as complex and challenging as that.

What are, if any, the rules of Mystics Anonymous?

We don't have a rulebook, but the usual rules of small group membership and requisites of leadership certainly apply. What is said in the group is confidential. There may be pastoral or counseling work to be done outside of the group, especially if deep hurts are brought to the surface through the stories or discussion, and in the silence. Also, it is vitally important not to pass judgment on anyone's story. That is why the best response from both the leader and group members is generally silence, especially in a one-off session or during the earlier sessions of an ongoing group when trust is being built.

Timing can be an issue. Once an ongoing group forms it is often a challenge to keep to time and preserve the 10—15 minutes of complete silence at the end of the meeting. The group discussion around a mystical text, in this context, can be deeply engaging. After running out of time on numerous occasions, my core group finally decided to appoint a timekeeper who rings a quaint antique bell 20 minutes before the end of the session. It seems to work most weeks.

How should very emotional stories be received?

There have been many tears shed in Mystics Anonymous meetings over the years. We can visit some deep places in our storytelling and discussion. In the group context the best response to a very emotional story is silence. These are not therapy sessions, and it is important that the leader or group members do not jump in and attempt to rescue someone who is simply telling their story. The tears or strong emotions are a part of this person's mystical narrative. One of my favorite mystics from the middle ages is Margery Kempe. She was renowned for her tears, although many found her emotional exuberance an annoying distraction. They were an element of her devotion.

While the group session is probably not the best place to respond to any deep emotions that may come to the surface, the leader does have a duty of care once the session has finished. This might involve a chat at the door on the way out, a cup of coffee later in the week, a phone call, or if appropriate an eventual referral to a counselor or psychologist. As a priest I have been asked to hear the formal confession of a number of group members. It should be stressed, however, that the group session itself is not really the best place to address these individual needs.

What about your future vision for the group? Do you see Mystics Anonymous as a group format that could potentially help other people?

I understand that at least one interfaith/secular Mystics Anonymous group has begun meeting at the University of Pennsylvania with David Yaden. When I told this news to our little group in Melbourne there was much laughter. "Mystics anonymous has gone global" one member announced with glee. All I know is that it works really well for us here in our parish setting, and that it has proven to be a useful tool for one-off sessions at conferences, workshops, and retreats that I have been involved with. Beyond that I guess it is up to others to give it a go and see if it works for them.

One thing that the Mystics Anonymous format has going for it, is its adaptability. I am an Anglican priest, and our group here is a Christian group. What I discovered at Marty Seligman's Canterbury Cathedral colloquium, however, was that the format also works in a multifaith or secular context. If people find the Mystics Anonymous format to be a useful tool, then I hope they will feel free to use it and adapt it to their needs.

How do you recommend individuals who are interested in forming a group in their community to get started?

The first step is probably to develop your own mystical narrative. Talk to people in your community about mysticism and religious experience. If you are a priest or pastor, preach about it or bring it up in your pastoral visits. If you are in a university, weave it into a lecture or a tutorial. Or you may prefer a less public platform: over lunch, or on a plane trip, or with a close friend or partner. Just try it out. Tell your story. And read the stories of others, books about mysticism and the classics of your faith tradition.

You might want to journal your personal stories too, reflecting back on significant moments of call or numinous encounter in your life. Then tell one of those stories to someone and see what happens. My experience is that the telling of your narrative will unlock mystical stories that the other person has been carrying around unspoken for years. I have no evidence, other than anecdotal, but I suspect that this simple activity of spiritual storytelling is good for your well-being and for the well-being of communities that you belong to.

I am happy to give advice or encouragement to anyone interested in starting up a Mystics Anonymous group. People are welcome to contact me through my church's website: www.stpeters.org.au

A brief guide to hosting a Mystics Anonymous session:

Participants should know that stories shared by others must remain confidential and stories should not be met with analysis or judgment. A session of Mystics Anonymous should always include:

1) A short introduction by the leader of the session that may include a poem or reading
2) Sharing stories about religious, spiritual, or mystical experiences without comment or analysis from other participants
3) Time for contemplative, meditative silence

The following elaborates on these three steps with general advice and guidelines:

Announce & Gather: The first step is to announce that you plan to hold a session of Mystics Anonymous at your regular book club, faith community, yoga/meditation group. Or, you could start an ongoing Mystics Anonymous group. In either case, ensure that participants know that they will be encouraged to share a personal, religious, spiritual, or mystical experience in a group format.

Mindset & Setting: Hold the group in a quiet, private, and peaceful place with seating arranged in a circle. Participants should be encouraged to open themselves to the stories of others without judgment. The group should feel like a safe place to explore deeply meaningful and sometimes emotional personal experiences.

Listen & Share: Active listening should encourage the courageous act of sharing. Stories should not be interrupted by comments, side conversations, or lack of attention from other participants. Sharing should be completely voluntary. Participants should be encouraged to keep the content of their stories as close as possible to the experience itself, rather than their beliefs or interpretations of the event.

Integrate & Prospect: Silent contemplation or meditation should begin 15–20 minutes before the end of the session. This time of personal reflection allows each participant time to integrate their own act of sharing as well as the other stories told throughout the session. The group can then turn its attention to the future. On the group level, the session can end with plans to either meet again or at least exchange contact information. On the individual level, each participant should think about how the session influenced his or her own spiritual or existential journey. Ideally, Mystics Anonymous sessions refresh participants by putting them back in touch with their most meaningful experiences.

ABOUT THE EDITORS

DAVID BRYCE YADEN is a research fellow and assistant instructor at The University of Pennsylvania in the Positive Psychology Center, under the direction of Dr. Martin Seligman. He works in collaboration with neuroscientist Dr. Andrew Newberg of Thomas Jefferson University and The Center for Cognitive Neuroscience at The University of Pennsylvania. He provides public health education and consulting with a focus on end-of-life care and stress management techniques at Our Lady of Lourdes Medical Center and serves as a Humanist Chaplain for Rutgers University. David's research focus is the psychology and cognitive -neuroscience of the varieties of self-transcendent and spiritual experiences.

THEO D. MCCALL, PhD, is the Chaplain at St. Peter's College, an Anglican School for boys in Adelaide, Australia. He has a passion for the links between ecology and eschatology. He is also exploring the connections between positive Psychology and Christianity, from a systematic theology perspective, but with a keen interest in interfaith dialogue. This has led to a keen interest in "'hope'" and the future, which in the Christian tradition finds one expression in eschatology. How this links to different faith traditions is one of his ongoing interests.

J. HAROLD ELLENS, PhD, has held 15 pastorates, military and civilian, and taught at Oakland University full time, and as adjunct at Calvin Theological Seminary, Princeton Theological Seminary, Oakland Community College,

Wayne County Community College, Wayne State University, and the Ecumenical Theological Seminary. He is series editor for the Praeger series of books, Psychology, Religion, and Spirituality. For 15 years, Ellens was the executive director of the Christian Association for Psychological Studies and founding editor and editor in chief of the esteemed *Journal of Psychology and Christianity*. He is author, coauthor, or editor of 285 books and 178 professional journal articles.

About the Contributors

MARTIN SELIGMAN is a best-selling author, having written 25 books, which have been translated into more than 40 languages. His bestsellers include *Learned Optimism* (1991), *The Optimistic Child* (1995), and *Authentic Happiness* (2002). His latest is *Flourish* (2011). He was elected president of the American Psychological Association in 1996 by the largest vote in history. He graduated summa cum laude from Princeton in 1964 and received his PhD in psychology from the University of Pennsylvania in 1967. He is currently the Zellerbach Family Professor of Psychology and director of the Positive Psychology Center at the University of Pennsylvania. Dr. Seligman works on learned helplessness, depression, optimism, positive psychology, and comprehensive soldier fitness. His research has been supported by the National Institutes of Health, the National Science Foundation, the John Templeton Foundation, the MacArthur Foundation, the Guggenheim Foundation, the Annenberg Foundation, and the Robert Wood Johnson Foundation. Seligman is the recipient of three Distinguished Scientific Contribution awards from the American Psychological Association, the Laurel Award of the American Association for Applied Psychology and Prevention, and the Lifetime Achievement Award of the Society for Research in Psychopathology. Seligman received both American Psychological Society's Williams James Fellow Award (for contribution to basic science) and the James McKeen Cattell Fellow Award (for the application of psychological knowledge). He received the inaugural Wiley Psychology Lifetime Award of the British Academy for lifetime contributions to psychology in 2009 and the Tang Prize for his life's work in 2014. He holds five honorary doctorates, including the University of Uppsala, Sweden, and Complutense University, Spain.

KELSEY L. AUTIN, M.S., received her undergraduate degree from the University of Florida in 2012. She continued her academic career at UF and is currently a doctoral student in the Counseling Psychology program. She is interested in researching the relationship between culture and career calling as well as work volition in marginalized populations.

GORDON BERMANT is a psychologist (PhD from Harvard University, 1961) and an attorney (J.D. George Mason, 1991) who began his professional career in comparative and physiological psychology and went through several transformations before being invited to teach psychology and religion, psychology and law, and the embodied mind at the University of Pennsylvania in 2008. He has been a Jodo Shinshu Buddhist since 1986, and in 2006 he served as president of the Buddhist Churches of America (BCA), the first person not of Japanese descent to hold that position. In addition to his teaching duties at Penn, he lectures on Buddhist psychology at the Institute of Buddhist Studies, Graduate Theological Union, in Berkeley.

JUDITH BLACKSTONE, PhD, developed the Realization Process, a method of embodied nondual realization. She is the author of *Belonging Here, The Enlightenment Process, The Empathic Ground, The Intimate Life,* and *The Subtle Self.* She is a founding director of Nonduality Institute.

CRISTIANO CRESCENTINI, PhD, obtained a degree in experimental and general psychology at the University of Florence (Italy) in 2004. In 2009 he got a PhD in neuroscience at the International School for Advanced Studies (SISSA) in Trieste (Italy). Since January 2012, Dr. Crescentini is a research fellow and adjunct professor in psychobiology and developmental psychology at the University of Udine. His studies relate to frontal lobe functions and the neuropsychology of meditation and human spirituality. Dr. Crescentini is author of more than 30 scientific publications.

BRYAN J. DIK is associate professor of psychology at Colorado State University and cofounder and chief science officer of jobZology. Bryan earned his BA in psychology from Calvin College and his PhD from the University of Minnesota. His research explores perceptions of work as a calling; meaning, purpose, religion, and spirituality in career decision-making and planning; measurement of vocational interests; and career development interventions. He has served on editorial boards for six research journals, and regularly consults with colleges affiliated with the Network for Vocation in Undergraduate Education (NetVUE). Bryan is coauthor of *Make Your Job a Calling: How the Psychology of Vocation Can Change Your Life at Work*, and coeditor of two other books: *Psychology of Religion and Workplace Spirituality* and *Purpose and Meaning in the Workplace*. He also led development of the Calling and Vocation Questionnaire (CVQ) and Brief Calling Scales (BCS), and collaborated on development of the Work as Meaning Inventory (WAMI). Bryan is an APA Fellow and received the 2010 Early Career Professional Award from the Society for Vocational Psychology. He lives with his wife Amy and their four sons in Fort Collins, Colorado.

RICHARD P. DOUGLASS (B.S., 2013) is a graduate of the University of Florida's psychology program and is currently a doctoral student in the counseling psychology program at the University of Florida. Richard works under the mentorship of Dr. Ryan Duffy and anticipates to graduate in the summer of 2019. His research interests are broadly in the areas of positive and vocational psychology, and he specifically focuses on the study of character strengths and career calling. Outside of work Richard enjoys running, cycling, and hiking.

RYAN D. DUFFY, PhD, is assistant professor of psychology at the University of Florida. Ryan's research is primarily in the areas of vocational psychology and positive psychology. Topics he has studied include calling, job satisfaction, well-being, work volition, work values, and the interface of spirituality and work. He serves on the editorial boards of the *Journal of Career Assessment* and *Journal of Counseling Psychology*.

FRANCO FABBRO, MD, obtained a degree in medicine and surgery at the University of Padua in 1982 and then a master's in neurology at the University of Verona in 1986. From 1985 to 1991 he worked as researcher in neuropsychology and neuropsychiatry and as child neurologist in Trieste. From 1991 to 1999 he worked as assistant professor of linguistics, neurolinguistics, and neurophysiology at the Faculty of Medicine in Trieste and as visiting researcher for three years at the Department of Linguistics of the McGill University in Montreal, Canada, and at the Department of Neurolinguistics of the Vrije Universiteit in Brussels, Belgium. From 2001 to 2005 he was full professor of neurosciences (Department of Philosophy) and from 2006 full professor of developmental neuropsychiatry at the University of Udine. Prof. Fabbro is author of more than 200 scientific publications (international articles and books) on the neurolinguistics of bilingualism, neuropsychology of altered states of consciousness, and neuropsychology of religious and spiritual experience and meditation.

RALPH W. HOOD JR. is professor of psychology at the University of Tennessee at Chattanooga. He is a former editor of the *Journal for the Scientific Study of Religion* and a former member of the executive council of SSSR. He is former coeditor of the *Archive for the Psychology of Religion* and *The International Journal for the Psychology of Religion*. He is a past president of division 36 (psychology of religion) of the American Psychological Association and a recipient of its William James, Mentor, and Distinguished Service awards. He has published over 250 articles in the psychology of religion and has authored, coauthored, or edited numerous book chapters and 15 books, all dealing with the psychology of religion. His ethnographic research on the serpent handlers of Appalachia is archived in The Hood-Williamson Research Archives for the Serpent Handling Holiness Sects, Lupton Library, at The University of Tennessee at Chattanooga.

ZORAN JOSIPOVIC, PhD, is a research scientist at the Cognitive Neurophysiology Laboratory, NYU School of Medicine, and an adjunct faculty at the Psychology Department, New York University. He is interested in the effects of contemplative practice on the brain organization, and how these can inform about the nature of consciousness and self. With his wife Judith Blackstone, he is also a founding director of Nonduality Institute, a center for theory and practice of nonduality.

J. HUGH KEMPSTER, PhD, is the vicar of St Peter's Eastern Hill, an historic Anglo-Catholic parish in Melbourne, Australia. Hugh also is a director of the Brotherhood of St Laurence, an Anglican not-for-profit organisation that works toward the vision of an Australia free of poverty. He has a doctorate in Mediaeval Studies, through the University of Waikato in New Zealand, and is an adjunct lecturer at Trinity College School of Theology, Melbourne. His research interests include the Middle English Mystics and the interface between theology and positive psychology.

GREGG LEVOY is the author of *Callings: Finding and Following An Authentic Life* (Random House)——rated among the "Top 20 Career Publications" by the Workforce Information Group and a text in various graduate programs in Management and Organizational Leadership—and the forthcoming *Vital Signs: The Nature and Nurture of Passion* (Penguin). A former adjunct professor of journalism at the University of New Mexico, former columnist and reporter for *USA Today* and the *Cincinnati Enquirer*, he has written about the subject of callings for the *New York Times Magazine, Washington Post, Omni, Psychology Today*, and many others, as well as for corporate, promotional, and television projects.

STEPHEN LEWIS is the president of the Forum for Theological Exploration (FTE), which focuses on cultivating a new generation of Christian leaders. He has more than 15 years of experience in corporate and nonprofit leadership, strategic planning, program development, and group facilitation. Stephen's interest lies at the intersection between leadership development, vocation, and leading change, and he is passionate about inspiring the next generation of leaders to make a difference in the world through Christian communities.

DAVID LUKOFF, PhD, is a professor of psychology at Sofia University in Palo Alto, California, and a licensed psychologist in California. He is author of 80 articles and chapters on spirituality and mental health and coauthor of the *DSM-IV/DSM-5* category Religious or Spiritual Problem. He presents internationally on spirituality in grief, death, and illness, and on spiritual problems and emergencies. He has been actively involved with the mental health consumer movement for 25 years.

ANDREW B. NEWBERG, MD, is currently the director of research at the Myrna Brind Center of Integrative Medicine at Thomas Jefferson University and Hospital in Philadelphia. He is also a professor in the Departments of Emergency Medicine and Radiology at Thomas Jefferson University. He is the coauthor of the books titled, *Words Can Change Your Brain, How God Changes Your Brain*, and *Why God Won't Go Away: Brain Science and the Biology of Belief.* He is also the author of the books, *The Metaphysical Mind: Probing the Biology of Philosophical Thought* and *Principles of Neurotheology.*

KAIPING PENG, PhD, is a tenured faculty member at the Psychology Department of the University of California at Berkeley. He received his PhD in social psychology from the University of Michigan, Ann Arbor in 1997. Before coming to the United States in 1989, he served as a faculty member at the Psychology Department of Peking University of China for five years. In addition to directing the Culture and Cognition lab at UC-Berkeley, he has published six books and over 100 articles on culture and cognition, and the psychology of Chinese people.

Dr. SUSAN ROSENTHAL is the dean of Student Affairs at Sidney Kimmel Medical College at Thomas Jefferson University. A Harvard-trained pediatric gastroenterologist, Dr. Rosenthal practices and advises medical students within the Jefferson community. Her research interests include the preservation of empathy throughout training and the cultivation of authentic career trajectories for student doctors.

THOMAS SINGER, MD, is a Jungian analyst and psychiatrist. After studying religion and European literature at Princeton University, he graduated from Yale Medical School and later trained at Dartmouth Medical Center and the C. G. Jung Institute of San Francisco. He is a member of the board of ARAS (The Archive for Research into Archetypal Symbolism). His writing includes articles on Jungian theory, politics, and psychology, and he has written and/or edited the following books: *Who's the Patient Here? Portraits of the Young Psychotherapist* (Oxford University Press, 1978, with Stuart Copans); *A Fan's Guide to Baseball Fever: The Official Medical Reference* (Elijim Publications, 1991, with Stuart Copans and Mitchell Rose); *The Vision Thing: Myth, Politics and Psyche in the World* (Routledge, 2000); *The Cultural Complex: Contemporary Jungian Perspectives on Psyche and Society* (Routledge, 2004, with Samuel L. Kimbles); *Initiation: The Living Reality of an Archetype* (Routledge, 2007, with Thomas Kirsch and Virginia Beane Rutter); *Psyche and the City: A Soul's Guide to the Modern Metropolis* (Spring, 2010); *Ancient Greece, Modern Psyche: Archetypes in the Making, Volume I* (Spring, 2011, with Virginia Beane Rutter), *Placing Psyche: Exploring Cultural Complexes in Australia* (Spring, 2011); *Listening to Latin America: Exploring Cultural Complexes in Brazil, Chili, Columbia, Mexico, Uruguay, and, Venezuela* (Spring, 2012); *Ancient Greece, Modern Psyche: Archetypes Evolving* (Rutledge, 2015); and *Europe's Many Souls: Exploring Culture Complexes and Identities* (forthcoming, Spring, 2016, with Joerg Rasche).

MARY "BIT" SMITH is a medical student at Sidney Kimmel Medical College. She has a master's degree from the University of Pennsylvania in applied positive psychology and a degree from Columbia University in narrative medicine. While still in training, Bit hopes to research the neurobiology of spiritual and prosocial states within clinical settings as well as the professional self-care of physicians.

MICHAEL F. STEGER, PhD, is an associate professor of counseling psychology and applied social psychology at Colorado State University and at North-West University, Vanderbijlpark, South Africa. Dr. Steger received his PhD with a dual specialization in counseling and personality psychology from the University of Minnesota in 2005. His research interests concern better understanding the factors that promote human flourishing and ameliorate psychological suffering. In particular, he has focused on researching how people generate the sense that their lives are meaningful, as well as investigating the benefits of living a meaningful life. He has published numerous peer-reviewed journal articles, book chapters, and scholarly publications. He has served as an associate editor for *Journal of Personality*, and on the editorial board of several additional journals. His published works include two books, *Designing Positive Psychology, Purpose and Meaning in the Workplace*, and the forthcoming *Handbook of Positivity and Strengths Based Approaches at Work*. He also developed the Meaning in Life Questionnaire, which has become the most widely used measure of meaning and purpose in the world.

COSIMO URGESI, PhD, obtained a degree in experimental psychology at the University of Rome "La Sapienza" (Italy) in 2003. In 2006 he got a PhD in neuroscience at the University of Verona (Italy) conducting research on body and action representation. Since 2008, Urgesi is assistant professor at the University of Udine (Italy) where he carries out behavioural, neuropsychological, and transcranial magnetic stimulation studies on body representation, eating disorders, and human self-transcendence. Urgesi is author of 50 international research articles.

AMY WRZESNIEWSKI is associate professor of organizational behavior at Yale University's School of Management. She earned her B.A. from the University of Pennsylvania, where she graduated magna cum laude with an honors degree in psychology. She received her PhD and MS degrees in organizational psychology from the University of Michigan. She has won the IBM Faculty Award for her research, and has won awards for her undergraduate, graduate, and executive teaching. Her research on the meaning of work has been published in a wide range of top academic journals and highlighted in several best-selling books and popular press outlets, including *Time, BusinessWeek, Harvard Business Review, U.S. News and World Report*, and *The Economist*, as well as best-selling books such as *Drive* by Daniel Pink, *The Happiness Advantage* by Shawn Achor, *Authentic Happiness* by Martin Seligman, *Give and Take* by Adam Grant, and *The Art of Happiness* by the Dalai Lama and Howard Cutler. Her current research involves understanding the experience of work as a job, career, or calling and studying how employees shape their tasks, interactions, and relationships with others in the workplace to change the meaning of the job.

SUSANNA WU-PONG is the director of the Pharmaceutical Sciences Graduate Program and associate professor at the Virginia Commonwealth University School of Pharmacy. She has been teaching at VCU for 20 years and has a PhD in pharmaceutical sciences. Her passion is personal, career, and professional development using positive psychology and strengths. Susanna channels her passion to others via her blog, her student and faculty development activities at VCU, and through pharmaceutical sciences graduate program development nationwide.

YUKUN ZHAO is the founder and president of Huaren Applied Positive Psychology Institute (HAPPI), which is dedicated to promoting positive psychology and its applications in Chinese communities. He cofounded the Global Chinese Positive Psychology Association. He is also an acclaimed author of two books published in China.

Index